DIVERSE VOICES
IN FAMILY LAW

Diverse Voices

Series Editors: **Se-shauna Wheatle**, Durham University and **Jonathan Herring**, University of Oxford

Diverse Voices presents a ground-breaking platform for critiquing the law from the perspective of minoritized and marginalized groups and debating and understanding the impact of the law on these different groups. Each book brings together an inclusive group of authors to explore a range of underexplored perspectives on the law and amplify voices that remain underrepresented in the field.

Also available in the series:

Diverse Voices in Health Law and Ethics
edited by **Elizabeth Chloe Romanis, Sabrina Germain** and **Jonathan Herring**

Diverse Voices in Tort Law
edited by **Kirsty Horsey**

Diverse Voices in Public Law
edited by **Se-shauna Wheatle** and **Elizabeth O'Loughlin**

Find out more at
bristoluniversitypress.co.uk/diverse-voices

DIVERSE VOICES IN FAMILY LAW

Edited by
Rajnaara C. Akhtar

BRISTOL
UNIVERSITY
PRESS

First published in Great Britain in 2026 by

Bristol University Press
University of Bristol
1–9 Old Park Hill
Bristol
BS2 8BB
UK
t: +44 (0)117 374 6645
e: bup-info@bristol.ac.uk

Details of international sales and distribution partners are available at bristoluniversitypress.co.uk

© Bristol University Press 2026

DOI: 10.51952/9781529245349

British Library Cataloguing in Publication Data
A catalogue record for this book is available from the British Library

ISBN 978-1-5292-4531-8 hardcover
ISBN 978-1-5292-4532-5 paperback
ISBN 978-1-5292-4533-2 ePub
ISBN 978-1-5292-4534-9 ePdf

The right of Rajnaara C. Akhtar to be identified as editor of this work has been asserted by her in accordance with the Copyright, Designs and Patents Act 1988.

Cover design: Nicky Borowiec
Front cover image: iStock/ivetavaicule

Contents

Series Editors' Preface

Law is dominated by a select range of actors: the wealthy, the White, the male, and the enabled. Their prevalence among those who appear before the courts, whether as litigants or legal representatives; and those who judge the cases, is inescapable.

This is true in much academic discourse too. The privileged dominate the practice of law; the law reports; and the professorati. *Diverse Voices* is an attempt to engage with a wider range of voices and perspectives than are typically encountered within the legal academy and legal studies. What are the stories which are not told in traditional law courses? Whose values are permitted and who is ignored? Who is rendered visible and who subjected to the legal gaze? Who is controlled and who is empowered by the law?

Inevitably this series will not capture all the voices that need to be heard. It cannot capture the depth of nuance that a deep intersectional analysis requires. What the series does do is to disrupt the dominant discourse, to highlight those marginalised, silenced, or misrepresented by the law. It seeks to start a listening process and begin a journey. It is certainly not the last word or the final destination. It is a beginning.

List of Figures

Table of Statutes, Regulations, and Cases

Statutes

Marriage Act 1949
Marriage and Civil Partnership (Minimum Age) Act 2022
Marriage (Same Sex Couples) Act 2013
Married Women's Property Act 1882
Matrimonial and Family Proceedings Act 1984
Matrimonial Causes Act 1973
National Assistance Act 1948
Offences Against the Person Act 1861
Parliament (Criminal Justice and Court Services Act) 2000
Perjury Act 2011
Private International Law (Miscellaneous Provisions Act) 1995
Serious Crime Act 2015
Sexual Offences Act 1967
Surrogacy Arrangements Act 1985
United Nations Convention on the Rights of the Child (Incorporation)(Scotland)
    Act 2024
Youth Justice and Criminal Evidence Act 1999

Regulations

Civil Legal Aid (Procedure) Regulations 2012
Civil Partnership (Opposite-Sex Couples) Regulations 2019

Cases

A City Council v T, J and K [2011, EWHC] Fam 1082
A Local Authority v N, Y, K (by Her Children's Guardian) [2007] 1 FLR 399
A v B and C (Lesbian Co-Parents: Role of Father) [2012] EWCA Civ 285
A-M v A-M (Divorce: Jurisdiction: Validity of Marriage) [2001] 2 FLR 6
Akhter v Khan [2018] EWFC 54
Ali v Ali [1966] 2 WLR 620
AM v SSHD [2022] EWHC 2591
Ampthill Peerage [1988] AC 547
AR v RWB and SWB [2011] EWHC 3431 (Fam)
AS v (1) BT, (2) CT, (3) S, A Child by His Guardian [2016] EWFC B112
Attorney General v Akhter and Khan [2020] EWCA Civ 122
Bibi v Chief Adjudication Officer [1998] 1 FLR 375
Bull v Hall [2013] UKSC 73
C v C (A Minor) (Custody: Appeal) [1991] 1 FLR 223
Charman v Charman (No 4) [2007] EWCA Civ 503
Chaudhry v Chaudhry [1975] 3 WLR 559
Cheang Thye Phin and Others v Tan Ah Loy (since Deceased) [1920] AC 369
Cheni v Cheni [1965] P.85
Churchill v. Merthyr Tydfil County Borough Council and Ors [2023] EWCA Civ 1416

Notes on Contributors

Rajnaara C. Akhtar is Associate Professor of Family Law at the University of Warwick and an Editor of *Child and Family Law Quarterly*. Rajnaara has led several grant-funded empirical family law projects and has conducted research in the UK, Australia, Qatar, and South Africa. With Professor Rebecca Probert and Sharon Blake, she published *Belief in Marriage: The Evidence for Reforming Weddings Law* (Bristol University Press 2023), and with Dr Conrad Nyamutata *International Child Law* (4th edn, Routledge 2020). Rajnaara was primary investigator (PI) on the Nuffield Foundation-funded study 'When Is a Wedding Not a Marriage? Exploring Non-Legally Binding Ceremonies', which culminated in a briefing paper to the Law Commission, influencing its recommendations to government on the reform of weddings law (2022). She is PI on a collaborative Nuffield Foundation funded study 'Exploring the Child Arrangements of Separated Families' (2026–28).

Sundari Anitha is Professor in Sociological Studies at the University of Sheffield. She has published widely across the two areas of violence against women and girls (VAWG) and intersections of gender, race, and ethnicity in employment relations. She previously worked as a domestic violence caseworker and managed a Women's Aid refuge, and has been engaged in activism and policy making to tackle VAWG for over 25 years. She is a co-editor of *Families, Relationships and Societies* and a member of the Editorial Board of Women's Studies International Forum. She was a member of the Research Excellence Framework 2021 Sociology sub-panel.

Elizabeth Bates is Associate Professor in Family Violence and Abuse, and Principal Lecturer in Psychology and Psychological Therapies, at the University of Cumbria.

Rachael Blakey is Associate Professor at the University of Warwick School of Law. She completed her PhD at Cardiff University, focusing on the purpose of, and perceptions around, family mediation. Her research primarily considers the purpose of family mediation in today's family justice system, leading to further work on the meaning of family justice itself. She is also interested in the regulation of family law professionals and how they are accessed by disputants. Rachael is currently a director of the Family Mediation Council.

Caroline Bryson works within an independent research partnership, Bryson Purdon Social Research LLP. She is a quantitative social scientist specialising in the experiences and outcomes of separating and separated families. She was a co-investigator on the Fair Shares project: sorting out property and finances on divorce study, from which the outputs included a full report as well as papers focusing on divorcees who had experienced domestic abuse; divorcee parents with dependent children; regional disparities in spousal maintenance arrangements; and public understanding of the laws around financial remedies.

Mandy Burton is Professor of Law at the University of Loughborough. She has been researching legal responses to domestic abuse for two decades. She is author of *Domestic Abuse, Victims and the Law* (Routledge 2022) and co-editor of the *Research Handbook on Domestic Violence and Abuse* (Edward Elgar 2024).

Gillian Douglas, FBA, FAcSS, FLSW, is Professor Emerita at The Dickson Poon School of Law, King's College London. Her research has covered a wide range of issues in family law, with a particular focus on the working of the law following relationship breakdown. Her recent publications include *Access to Justice for Separating Families* (JUSTICE, Chair of Working Party, 2022) and *Fair Shares? Sorting Out Money and Property on Divorce* (with E Hitchings, C Bryson, and J Birchall, Bristol University Press 2023).

Aisha K. Gill, CBE, is Professor of Criminology and Head of Centre for Gender and Violence Research, University of Bristol. Her main areas of interest and research are health and criminal justice responses to violence against Black, minority ethnic, and refugee women in the UK, Afghanistan, Georgia, Jordan, Libya, Iraqi Kurdistan, India, Pakistan, Romania, Syria, and Yemen. She has been involved in addressing the problem of VAWG, 'honour' crimes and forced marriage at the grassroots level for the past 20+ years. Her recent publications include articles on crimes related to the murder of women/femicide, 'honour' killings, coercion and forced marriage, child sexual exploitation and sexual abuse in Black and minoritised communities, female genital mutilation, sex selective abortions, intersectionality, and women who kill.

Andy Hayward is Professor of Family Law at Durham Law School, Durham University. His research focuses on domestic and comparative family law, especially the legal regulation of adult interpersonal relationships. With Professor Jens Scherpe, he published *The Future of Registered Partnerships: Family Recognition beyond Marriage?* (Intersentia 2017) and with Professor Margaret Briggs, the *Research Handbook on Family Property and the Law* (Edward Elgar 2024). In 2021 Andy acted as Special Advisor to the UK Parliament's Women and Equalities Committee for their Rights of Cohabiting Partners Inquiry and in 2024 was appointed to the Family Justice Council.

Connie Healy is Lecturer in Law, University of Galway, Ireland. A qualified solicitor, she practised for several years before undertaking her doctoral thesis entitled 'Resolution of Conflict in Family Law Matters: An Alternative and Child-Inclusive Approach' (2014), funded by the Irish Research Council. She is an accredited mediator (Centre for Effective Dispute Resolution: CEDR) and collaborative law practitioner (Irish Association for Counselling and Psychotherapy: IACP). Her monograph *Collaborative Practice: An International Perspective* was published by Routledge in 2017. Connie is currently the lead PI in a Research Ireland-funded project 'Voice of the Child in Family Law Mediation: Overcoming Barriers to Ensure Participation as a Right, Not a Privilege (VOCAL)'.

Ben Hine is Professor of Applied Psychology at the School of Human and Social Sciences, University of West London, and is an expert on parental alienation.

Emma Hitchings is Professor of Family Law at the University of Bristol Law School. She is an expert on financial remedies on divorce and family justice issues and has been involved with a range of empirical studies in family law. A key theme underpinning her research has been exploring how family law works in practice and its impact on individuals, professionals, and the family justice system. She has written widely on issues in family law and her recent publications include five research reports from the Fair Shares study (https://www.bristol.ac.uk/law/fair-shares-project/).

Mohammad Mazher Idriss is Senior Lecturer in Law at Manchester Metropolitan University, Manchester Law School. He specialises in honour-based abuse and forced marriages among female and male victims.

Maria Federica Moscati is Reader in Law and Society at the University of Sussex. She is a lawyer and trained mediator. Her main research interests lie in issues relating to dispute resolution, comparative legal studies (focus on kinship, family relations, dispute resolution), children's rights, queer people and the law, and their intersection. New areas of research that she is exploring concern dance and the law and hormones and the law. Recent publications include a chapter in the co-edited *Queer Judgments*: 'Diversity, Inclusion and Equality in Mediation for Family Relations' (Counterpress 2025).

Zainab Batul Naqvi is Reader in Critical Feminist Legal Studies at Manchester Metropolitan University. Her research focuses on legal and judicial responses to racially minoritised communities and practices and she is a leading critical race and postcolonial family law scholar in the UK. She has published widely in these areas; among such works is her book *Polygamy, Policy and Postcolonialism in English Marriage Law* (Bristol University Press 2023). Zainab is also an experienced academic journal editor who sits on the board of *Feminist Legal Studies* and has led the board's activities to address marginalisation and inequalities in academic publishing.

Rehana Parveen is a former family law solicitor and is currently Associate Professor at Birmingham Law School. Rehana teaches a wide range of modules including Family Law, Decolonising Legal Concepts, Legal Skills & Methods, and Equity & Trusts. Rehana's research interests are in investigating the developing relationships between English family law and Islamic family law and how women navigate these interacting frameworks, including their use of sharia councils. More recently, Rehana has been exploring how legal concepts and structures may be decolonised to place them within their social, historical, political, and postcolonial contexts.

Rachel Pimm-Smith is Associate Professor of Law at the University of Warwick Law School. Her work is principally interested in the intersection of public law interference within private life, particularly in the context of parent–child relationships. She has written widely on this topic and has contributed to another family law textbook for the undergraduate curriculum: *Cretney and Probert's Family Law* (Sweet & Maxwell 2023). Another recent publication is the article 'Adoption of Children Act 1926: Another Punishment for Being Poor' (2025) in *Law and History Review*.

Brian Sloan is Assistant Professor in Law at the University of Cambridge and a Fellow of Robinson College. Brian has published widely on family and property law, covering England and Wales and several other areas. Brian writes on topics including child law (particularly parenthood and adoption), succession, the regulation of adult relationships, and gender recognition. His work on adoption was cited by the Supreme Court in *Re B* [2013] UKSC 33. His publications include *Parental Guidance, State Responsibility and Evolving Capacities: Article 5 of the United Nations Convention on the Rights of the Child* (co-edited with Josh Fenton-Glynn, Brill 2021).

Introduction

Rajnaara C. Akhtar

As the first quarter of the 21st century passes, the historical frameworks underpinning family law and family life are undergoing rapid transformations. Modern family life in England and Wales bears little resemblance to its historical norms. The concept of 'diversity' now encompasses a broad range of meanings for families, influencing both the composition of family units and the way they are understood in law. Historically a normatively 'Christian country', we have developed into a diverse society characterised by multi-faith, multi-belief, multi-ethnic, and multi-cultural identities. Despite this shift, 'The law regulating marriage is a historical relic which reflects a bygone age of a Judaeo-Christian society.'[1] With no single faith community comprising a majority of the population,[2] there is no longer a clear dominant influence shaping family law. Family values, once the hallmark of religious traditions, are now shaped by debates about the *how* we believe rather than *what* we believe, with the law slow to accommodate change.[3]

In this increasingly diverse society, family law in England and Wales stands at a critical juncture. Historically framed within narrow normative paradigms, this area of law has often failed to reflect the nuanced and complex realities of the families it governs, marginalising many voices or excluding them altogether from mainstream legal discourse.[4] *Diverse Voices in Family Law* challenges these

---

[1] R Sandberg, 'Introduction: Marital Problems' in *Religion and Marriage Law: The Need for Reform* (Bristol University Press 2021) 2.

[2] Office for National Statistics (ONS), 'Religion, England and Wales: Census 2021' (29 November 2022) https://www.ons.gov.uk/peoplepopulationandcommunity/culturalidentity/religion/bulletins/religionenglandandwales/census2021, accessed 9 December 2024.

[3] For example, the Law Commission of England and Wales has reviewed multiple areas of law, many of which have not led to government implementation or legislative reform, including weddings law, prenuptial agreements, financial resolution on divorce, and pensions orders.

[4] See for example: ZB Naqvi, *Polygamy, Policy and Postcolonialism in English Marriage Law: A Critical Feminist Analysis* (Law, Society, Policy Series, Bristol University Press 2023); R Sandberg and S Thompson, 'The Sharia Law Debate: The Missing Family Law Context' (2016) 177 Law and

shortcomings by engaging with a broad spectrum of perspectives that critically interrogate the foundations of family law, as well as the intersections of socio-economic status, gender, race, religion, belief, and sexuality in shaping how individuals and families are treated within the law. In doing so, it interrogates the evolving definitions of family in contemporary society. Inevitably, not all voices will be represented, even within the diverse perspectives included in this volume; such limitations reflecting the availability of scholars and relevant scholarship.

Through these diverse insights, this volume seeks not only to broaden the scope of academic and legal conversation but also to contribute to the development of a family law framework that is inclusive, equitable, and reflective of the complex and multifaceted nature of modern life. *Diverse Voices in Family Law* prepares students for the realities of family law – whether in legal practice or the myriad of institutional, social, and cultural contexts where families are formed and navigated. Reflecting our diversity of belief systems, racial identities, socio-economic statuses, and ways of living, this collection aims to bridge the gap between theory and practice, offering a dynamic and comprehensive understanding of family law.

A critical mind-set

For students reading this volume, in whole or in part, we begin by outlining the parameters of engagement and pedagogic style, drawing inspiration from the pioneering work of Folúké Adébísí.[5] Our approach aligns with critical legal studies, which seeks to disrupt and challenge the perceived neutrality and objectivity of legal knowledge.[6] Far from being impartial, family law is deeply influenced and shaped by the social, cultural, political, and economic history of the state. As such, intersectionality is central to understanding how family law affects individuals differently, depending on their identity and circumstances.[7]

In *Decolonisation and Legal Knowledge*, Adébísí critiques how law schools claim to teach students 'about *the* world' while often remaining disconnected from the realities of '*their* world' – the lived experiences of the students themselves.[8]

Justice: The Christian Law Review 181; R Akhtar, P Nash, and R Probert (eds), *Cohabitation and Religious Marriage: Status, Similarities and Solutions* (Bristol University Press 2020).

[5] F Adébísí, *Decolonisation and Legal Knowledge: Reflections on Power and Possibility* (Bristol University Press 2023).

[6] A Bianchi, 'Critical Legal Studies and the New Stream' in *International Law Theories: An Inquiry into Different Ways of Thinking* (Oxford 2016; online edn, Oxford Academic, 19 January 2017) https://doi.org/10.1093/acprof:oso/9780198725114.003.0007, accessed 9 December 2024.

[7] K Crenshaw, 'Demarginalizing the Intersection of Race and Sex: A Black Feminist Critique of Antidiscrimination Doctrine, Feminist Theory and Antiracist Politics' (1989) University of Chicago Legal Forum, 139.

[8] Adébísí (n5), 2.

> Disrupting the production of global and local social injustices and inequalities, means reconsidering the supposed neutrality of our knowledge processes – both in teaching and research.[9]

This observation underscores the need for a pedagogical approach that is reflexive, inclusive, and critically attuned to the diverse perspectives and realities that students bring to their legal education.[10] *Diverse Voices in Family Law* aims to disrupt, critique, and disenfranchise 'traditional' family law knowledge. It challenges students to reconsider their vision of family justice and critically interrogate the dominant narratives that underpin the discipline. This volume seeks to expand narrowly defined family law curriculums by reconnecting theory with genuine critique, encouraging students to question established norms and practices.

Furthermore, it invites student to critically reflect on their institutional environments – to 'look up and around' – to question the extent to which the diverse voices and issues raised in this volume are represented, acknowledged, and engaged within their own law schools. Where law schools continue to 'look and feel' elite, this lack of intersectional representation will inevitably perpetuate systematic inequalities in the family justice system (FJS). Where there may be adequate representation among the undergraduate student body, to what extent is this visible in the postgraduate cohorts and among academic staff? Without multilayered diversity across all levels, the issues preventing representation and inclusion will persist into the profession.

Described by Adébísí as 'colonial ground zero',[11] law schools can often reflect and reinforce Eurocentric frameworks, which shape family law and perpetuate hierarchies around how different family forms and behaviours are treated. These hierarchies sustain inequalities for diverse families, while defining legal subjects in a way that marginalises and excludes. This volume encourages students to engage critically with these structures, recognising that law is power and that law students can wield that power to challenge inequities and advocate for change.

Modern families, modernising family justice

Families have long been the subject of legal regulation, with marriage regarded as the cornerstone of family formation, establishing defined rights and responsibilities for each party. These inevitably include a 'legally binding tie with specific legal consequences'.[12] Historically, family laws have been shaped by the prevailing religious, cultural, and social norms within communities, as well as other values

---

9   Ibid.
10 M Iszatt-White, S Kempster, and B Carroll, 'An Educator's Perspective on Reflexive Pedagogy: Identity Undoing and the Issues of Power' (2017) 48(5) Management Learning 582.
11 Adébísí (n5).
12 Law Commission, 'Getting Married: A Scoping Paper' (Law Com No 396, 2015) 1.

linked to group dominance, such as 'wealth, status, age and gender'.[13] In relatively stable societies, these regulations often remained unchallenged over extended periods. However, contemporary dynamics – such as global migration, religious and cultural diversity and pluralism, shifting relationship norms, and the rapid mobility of populations – pose significant challenges for states in adapting family law to the complexities of modern society.

The historically static nature of communities stands in stark contrast to the fluid and dynamic realities of contemporary times. Family laws in many jurisdictions have remained largely unchanged for decades if not centuries, despite facing challenges worldwide driven by ease of travel and patterns of migration, diversity of faiths and beliefs, evolving relationship norms challenging traditional family structures, and the rapid movement of people within borders. The notion of being born, living and dying within the same community is a thing of the past. As the Law Commission observed, the practice of calling banns to announce an impending marriage is desperately outdated, as people no longer live 'in small, rural communities in which social life focused on the church', where 'announcing the marriage during divine service was a guaranteed way of bringing it to the attention of the community and ensuring that any potential problems were identified'.[14] Today, while such practices hold traditional significance, they no longer reflect social realities.

Modern family formation challenges the state, from how we marry and who we marry to the complex pathways to parenthood and the recognition of parental rights. The rights of both parents and children are a part of this dynamic. Access to family justice is dependent on the effective functioning of the FJS, which, as Resolution notes, stands at a 'crucial turning point'.[15]

The statutory framework governing the family court in England and Wales is set out in the Crime and Courts Act 2013, which introduced Part 4A to the Matrimonial and Family Proceedings Act 1984. This established a 'single, unified' family court 'within which almost all family proceedings are conducted'.[16] However, ensuring that this system meets the needs of increasingly diverse and mobile populations remains a significant challenge.

The FJS is hampered by overstretched courts, significant delays, limited access to legal advice, and inadequate legal protections from outdated laws.[17] In such circumstances, even where the intersectional needs of users are acknowledged,

---

[13] M Maclean and J Eekelaar, *Managing Family Justice in Diverse Societies* (Hart Publishing 2013) 1.
[14] Law Commission (n12) 32.
[15] Resolution, 'Vision for Family Justice' (2023) https://resolution.org.uk/wp-content/uploads/2023/11/Resolution-Vision-for-Family-Justice-full-221123.pdf, accessed 9 December 2024.
[16] *K (Children) (Powers of the Family Court)* [2024] EWCA Civ 2, [35].
[17] A Speed, 'Just-Ish? An Analysis of Routes to Justice in Family Law Disputes in England and Wales' (2020) 52(3) Journal of Legal Pluralism and Unofficial Law 276. Family Court Statistics Quarterly: October to December 2023, Ministry of Justice https://www.gov.uk/government/statistics/family-court-statistics-quarterly-october-to-december-2023/family-court-statistics-quarterly-october-to-december-2023, accessed 14 July 2025.

the system's ability to respond effectively and accommodate these needs is likely to be obstructed. In 2022, a frontline briefing by Research in Practice for legal practitioners and others working within FJS highlighted these systematic challenges:[18]

> Multiple needs and aspects of identity need to be considered, which can indicate how an individual can experience multiple levels of discrimination and oppression, based on their gender, class, immigration status, race, ethnicity and religion, for instance. These all need to be considered in terms of how family proceedings may further impact a child or family member's feelings of oppression.[19]

The 'Equal Treatment Bench Book' also highlights the difficult task faced by judges,[20] guiding them on approaches to children and parents in the courtroom:

> Multi-faith, multi-cultural and multi-ethnic communities make special demands on judges and others in the family justice system. Balancing respect for different approaches to parenting within potentially diverse cultural norms and, at the same time, aiming to protect all children from parental maltreatment is a difficult task. It is also important to hold the confidence of the parents that they have had a fair hearing.[21]

By contextualising the differing experiences of state welfare and legal systems for new arrivals in the country, the guide addresses 'notions of pride and honour' prevalent among minority ethnic communities, including those established as second or third generation, to underscore the importance of engaging with cultural differences. This is an attempt to engage with crucial diversity presented within the courtroom, yet clearly oversimplifies and potentially essentialises differences.[22] Put simply, notions of pride and honour will not resonate with all ethnic minority individuals or families, and even where they do, their significance may vary widely from person to person. While such guidelines signal a recognition of the varied experiences within family law, they fail to address a more fundamental issue – the lack of diversity within the legal profession itself, encompassing judges, lawyers, and, in some cases, social workers.

---

[18] Research in Practice, 'Ensuring Equality, Diversity, and Inclusion in the Family Court: Frontline Briefing' (July 2022) https://www.researchinpractice.org.uk/children/publications/2022/july/ensuring-equality-diversity-and-inclusion-in-the-family-court-frontline-briefing-2022/, accessed 9 December 2024.

[19] Ibid.

[20] Judicial College, 'Equal Treatment Bench Book' (September 2022) https://www.judiciary.uk/wp-content/uploads/2022/09/Equal-Treatment-Bench-Book.pdf, accessed 9 December 2024.

[21] Ibid, para 168.

[22] Ibid, paras 169–71.

Judges, in particular, tend to be drawn from privileged backgrounds,[23] and are unlikely to have experienced the types of marginalisation faced by the most vulnerable courtroom users.[24] Barriers to diversity within the upper echelons of the legal profession are linked to several systematic issues, including the dominance of Oxbridge and Russell Group universities producing legal professionals, the demanding work hours that disproportionately impact women, and structural inequities stemming from socio-economic differences, ethnic disparities, and disabilities.[25] This lack of representation has significant consequences. A 'homogenous' judiciary and legal profession can lead to a lack of empathy, understanding, and nuanced responses to challenges faced by diverse courtroom users. Without diverse voices and lived experiences integrated into the fabric of the FJS, even the most well-intentioned guidebooks will only provide limited solutions to the complexities of modern family law.

A brief review of recent case law illustrates the array of complex issues family courts are called upon to address, with judges required to navigate diverse needs of modern families. In *Re G (Children)*,[26] concerning twin girls and two same-sex parents – only one of whom had parental responsibility, while the gametes were from the other – Black LJ observed that 'Families are formed in different ways these days and the law must attempt to keep up and to respond to developments.'[27] Similarly in *Re A (2015)*,[28] Judge Bellamy reflected on the 'different ways in which modern family life is formed' when adjudicating child arrangements for nine-year-old Alice, conceived by donor insemination with sperm from a known donor, so consequently having four parental figures.[29] The challenges of transnational family dynamics were evident in *NF v EB*, where Mr Justice Peter Jackson considered an 'application under the Hague child abduction convention brought in London on behalf of a Bosnian father living in Copenhagen against a Slovakian mother living in Newcastle for the return of a child removed from Denmark and brought to the United Kingdom via Slovakia and the Czech Republic'.[30] In *AS v (1) BT, (2) CT, (3) S, A Child by His Guardian*,[31] HHJ Robin Tolson QC addressed the breakdown of an arranged marriage between the birth parents, stating: 'I as a judge am not to be heard to say that arranged marriages do not work or necessarily offend against modern

---

23 L Barmes and K Malleson, 'The Legal Profession as Gatekeeper to the Judiciary: Design Faults in Measures to Enhance Diversity' (2011) 74(2) Modern Law Review 245.

24 J Barton-Crosby and others, 'Judicial Diversity: Barriers & Initiatives' (NatCen Social Research, February 2023) https://natcen.ac.uk/sites/default/files/2023-02/Judicial%20div ersity_barriers%20&%20initiatives%20report_0.pdf, accessed 9 December 2024.

25 Ibid, 74–5.

26 [2014] EWCA Civ 336.

27 Ibid [30].

28 *Re A (A Child: Application for Leave to Apply for a Child Arrangements Order)* [2015] EWFC 47

29 Ibid [2].

30 *NF v EB* [2014] EWHC 484 (Fam).

31 [2016] EWFC B112.

Western ideas of freedom of choice or informed consent. That this arranged marriage did not work, however, is plain.'[32] In *Akhter v Khan*, Mr Justice Williams spoke at length of the unsatisfactory 'non-marriage' category:

> [A] couple who have lived together and had children but who have never as between themselves or held themselves out as married would rightly be treated as cohabitees without any of the remedies available to those who have married. But at the other end of the spectrum are cases where the application of the term 'non-marriage' seems inapt and indeed pejorative. The parties may have undergone a public marriage ceremony conducted by an official, witnessed by others, in which they confirmed there was no impediment to them marrying, that they consented and that they committed themselves to each other which they, their family and communities accepted led to them being married. They may have lived a married life and been accepted as married by their communities and the state. They may have had children. To all intents and purposes, they have been married. To characterise all of that as a non-marriage in law feels instinctively uncomfortable in 2018 and might rightly be regarded as insulting by many (although not all) of the participants.[33]

While the cases cited above relate to relatively routine issues, and high-profile sensational cases are generally unhelpful for family law students as they skew narratives, the Al Maktoum and Al Hussein divorce proceedings offer a compelling example of a case with multiple hearings and layers of complexity. One appeal, challenging earlier case management decisions, involved the court dealing with 'the mobile phones of the mother, two of her solicitors, her personal assistant and two members of her security staff' being 'the subject of either successful or attempted infiltration by surveillance software. The software used is called Pegasus software and was that of an Israeli company, the NSO Group.'[34] In the appeal, Lady Justice King, Lady Justice Macur, and Sir Julian Flaux upheld the earlier decision, confirming that the phones were indeed hacked at the appellant's request. These cases demonstrate how family law cases are seldom 'ordinary', and judges must be prepared to preside over a wide range of issues.

To facilitate this role, family court judges have wide ranging powers, and in *K (Children)*,[35] Sir Andrew McFarlane (President of the Family Division) used the opportunity brought in this case to:

---

[32]   Ibid [2].
[33]   [2018] EWFC 54 [8].
[34]   *His Highness Sheikh Mohammed Bin Rashid Al Maktoum v Her Royal Highness Princess Haya Bint Al Hussein and Al Jalila Bint Mohammed Bin Rashid Al Maktoum Zayed Bin Mohammed Bin Rashid Al Maktoum (by their Guardian)* [2021] EWCA Civ 1216.
[35]   *K (Children) (Powers of the Family Court)* [2024] EWCA Civ 2.

... reaffirm the wide and flexible powers of the family court. Where proceedings have been properly issued, the judge or magistrates to whom the case has been allocated may make incidental and supplemental orders of a kind that could be made under the inherent powers of the High Court where the purpose of such orders is to give effect to their substantive decision.[36]

While this approach allows cases to be handled efficiently, takes account of litigants in person who may not be aware of their full legal rights, and facilitates the implementation of wide-ranging domestic abuse protection provisions, when necessary, it also presents risks. Judges who may not fully understand the needs of litigants could either over-regulate or under-regulate their family matters.

Away from the courts, added to family law complexities are faith- and belief-based marriages (and potentially divorces), found across communities in England and Wales.[37] These marriages often raise questions of legal recognition, with non-legally binding marriages categorised as non-qualifying ceremonies,[38] which leave parties without access to family law remedies. For such couples, the concept of privatised family justice emerges, where the absence of state-prescribed remedies often results in the adoption of alternative normative frameworks, such as religious dispute-resolution mechanisms.[39] Described as 'Minority Legal Orders' by Maleiha Malik,[40] these refer to distinct cultural or religious norms which are systematically identified, interpreted, and enforced. While Minority Legal Orders are subordinate to the state legal system and not subject to any applicable regulations, their authority and legitimacy are derived from the minority community itself. Although commonly associated with Muslim communities, faith-based dispute resolution is also found in other traditions. Douglas and others explored examples including a Jewish Beth Din, a matrimonial tribunal of the Roman Catholic Church, and a Muslim Shariah Council.[41] Such Minority Legal Orders are often described as 'parallel legal systems',[42] yet they occupy the same informal dispute resolution space that the

---

[36] Ibid, para 3.

[37] See R Probert, R Akhtar, and S Blake, 'When is a Wedding Not a Marriage? Exploring Non-Legally Binding Ceremonies' (Nuffield Foundation 2021) https://lawandreligionuk.com/2021/01/12/when-is-a-wedding-not-a-marriage-exploring-non-legally-binding-ceremonies/, accessed 9 December 2024.

[38] *Attorney General v Akhter and Khan* [2020] EWCA Civ 122 [7] and [64].

[39] Eg see RC Akhtar, 'Plural Approaches to Faith-Based Dispute Resolution by Britain's Muslim Communities' (2019) 31(3) Child and Family Law Quarterly 189; F Ahmed, 'Religious Norms in Family Law: Implications for Group and Personal Autonomy' in M Maclean and J Eekelaar, *Managing Family Justice in Diverse Societies* (Bloomsbury Publishing 2015).

[40] M Malik, *Minority Legal Orders in the UK: Minorities, Pluralism and the Law* (British Academy 2012).

[41] R Sandberg and others, 'Britain's Religious Tribunals: "Joint Governance" in Practice' (2013) 33(2) Oxford Journal of Legal Studies 263.

[42] Malik (n40) 4.

FJS actively encourages individuals to use for resolving disputes. Their existence highlights the pluralistic reality of family law in England and Wales, where the interaction between state law and community-based norms continues to evolve.

Diverse families

National statistics reveal that family structures are more diverse than ever. This diversity spans various family types – married, cohabiting, or in non-legally binding marriages – and differences in children's living arrangements (eg in married or civil-partnered households, unmarried households, separated households, or state care). When coupled with rapid changes in faith and belief, alongside economic disparities between couples, family life can be fraught with tensions and the possibility of legal and quasi-legal interventions.

The 2021 census data revealed significant demographic shifts in the population of England and Wales, with important implications for family law.[43] For the first time, less than half of the population identified as 'Christian', a sharp decline from 71.7 per cent in 2001 to 59.3 per cent in 2011, and finally 46.2 per cent in 2021. This rapid decline in Christianity is particularly significant as key aspects of English family law were historically derived from canon law, with the validity of marriage once dependent on its performance by an ordained Anglican clergyman.[44] Statutory regulation of marriage began with the Clandestine Marriages Act 1753, followed by various iterations of the Marriage Act, culminating in the consolidated Marriage Act 1949, which remains in effect today, albeit amended.[45] In light of the changing religious and cultural landscape, the suitability of the current legal framework for marriage in an increasingly diverse society is called into question.

The second-largest group in the population identify as having 'no religion', accounting for 37.2 per cent (comprising 22.2 million people). This marks a significant shift from 25.2 per cent in 2011, highlighting a major change in belief and self-identification. The trend underscores the need for family law to accommodate a diversity of beliefs that do not fit within traditionally defined faith categories. The third-largest group are 'Muslims', comprising 6.5 per cent (3.9 million people), further emphasising the need to accommodate alternate family justice frameworks. Other faith groups include 0.5 per cent Buddhist, 1.7 per cent Hindu, 0.5 per cent Jewish, 0.9 per cent Sikh, and 0.6 per cent identifying as 'other religions'.[46] In this context, the rise of independent

---

[43] ONS (n2).

[44] R Probert, *Marriage Law and Practice in the Long Eighteenth Century: A Reassessment* (CUP 2009).

[45] R Probert, 'Valid, Void and Non-Qualifying Marriages' in Akhtar, Nash, and Probert (eds), (n4).

[46] Comprising Pagans (74,000), Alevi (26,000), Jain (25,000), Wicca (13,000), Ravidassia (10,000), Shamanism (8,000), Rastafarian (6,000), Zoroastrian (4,000), Agnostic (32,000), Atheist (14,000), and Humanist (10,000).

celebrant-led weddings is unsurprising, as couples increasingly seek ceremonies that align more closely with their personal beliefs.[47]

In terms of family structures, there have been notable changes. As of 2023, there were 19.5 million families in the UK, the majority being married or civil-partnered (66 per cent).[48] Cohabiting couples represented 18 per cent of all families, while lone-parent families accounted for 16 per cent. Although the overall number of married couples has slightly increased, as a proportion of all families they have decreased in number, signalling a slight shift away from marriage (or civil partnership) in favour of other relationship types, such as cohabitation. This shift is perhaps unsurprising, as marriage is no longer socially expected for many communities in England and Wales. The number of cohabiting families has grown by 42 per cent since 2013.[49] Thus, while marriage (or civil partnership) still marks the formation of the majority of family households, the lack of legal protections for cohabitants – compared to those who choose to commit through a formal marriage – fails to respond to the changing family justice needs of the population.

Dependent children were present in 43 per cent of households, with an additional 16 per cent having adult children living at home. The remaining 42 per cent either had no children or had children who did not reside in the household.[50] Among families with dependent children, the majority had one child (45 per cent), while 41 per cent had two and 14 per cent had three or more.[51] A significant social change occurred in 2021, when 320,713 (51.3 per cent) of all live births in England and Wales were to women who were not married nor in a civil partnership.[52] While this does not differentiate between children born to couples who are together and single parents, it nonetheless highlights the need for legal reforms to protect children from the poverty often associated with single-parent households, alongside the introduction of more robust child support mechanisms.

In 2022, there were 80,057 divorces in England and Wales, of which 78,759 involved opposite-sex couples.[53] The introduction of the Divorce, Dissolution and Separation Act 2020, which established no-fault divorce, has simplified and

---

[47]   S Blake and others, 'Independent Celebrant-Led Wedding Ceremonies: Translating, Tweaking and Innovating Traditions' (2023) Sociological Research Online https://journals.sagepub.com/doi/10.1177/13607804231211443, accessed 14 July 2025.

[48]   ONS, 'Families and Households in the UK: 2023' (2023) https://www.ons.gov.uk/peoplepopulationandcommunity/birthsdeathsandmarriages/families/bulletins/familiesandhouseholds/2023, accessed 9 December 2024.

[49]   Ibid.

[50]   Ibid.

[51]   Ibid.

[52]   ONS, 'Provisional Births in England and Wales: 2021' (2022) https://www.gov.uk/government/statistics/provisional-births-in-england-and-wales-2021, accessed 9 December 2024.

[53]   ONS, 'Divorces in England and Wales: 2022' (2023) https://www.ons.gov.uk/peoplepopulationandcommunity/birthsdeathsandmarriages/divorce/bulletins/divorcesinenglandandwales/2022, accessed 9 December 2024.

streamlined the divorce process. The divorce rate for all couples was 6.7 for men and 6.6 for women per 1,000 male or female married population. These are the lowest divorce rates since 1971,[54] likely influenced by the new law and requirement for couples to complete a waiting period. The ONS describes trends in divorce as follows:

> The cumulative percentages of marriages ending in divorce before their 25th (silver) wedding anniversary has increased over time. For couples who married in 1963 (the first cohort with data available), 23% had divorced before their 25th anniversary. This has steadily risen to 41% for couples who married in 1997 (the latest marriage cohort to potentially reach their 25th anniversary).
>
> The percentage of marriages ending before their 10th anniversary can give an indication of divorce trends for those marrying more recently, and this has also changed over time. This has increased from 1 in 10 couples married in 1965 (10%) to 1 in 4 couples in 1995 (25%). For couples married more recently, however, there has been a decrease, with less than 1 in 5 (18%) marriages in 2012 ending in divorce before their 10th wedding anniversary (the most recent cohort to reach their 10th anniversary).[55]

These statistics should be viewed in the context of an aging population, where decisions about marriage and divorce are increasingly influenced by longer life expectancy. However, the rise in divorces carries significant implications for the FJS, for children, and for families.

The context provided in the first part of this introductory chapter offers students a lens through which to engage with the diverse voices presented in this volume, highlighting the urgent need to incorporate a range of perspectives in family law to reform a FJS that is struggling to cope.

Diverse voices

The contributors to this volume represent a wide range of disciplines, including family law, critical feminist legal studies, law and society and socio-legal studies, property law, criminology, gender, violence and work, family violence and abuse, and psychology. This interdisciplinary diversity reflects the inherently multifaceted nature of family law, highlighting its connections to various fields and underscoring the need for diverse approaches and innovative solutions. This volume is structured in three parts and maps onto the traditional family law

---

[54]   Ibid.
[55]   Ibid.

syllabus, covering marriage, divorce, and parenthood; dispute resolution in family law; and domestic abuse.

Part I presents diverse voices in Marriage, Divorce, and Parenthood with six chapters exploring the colonial definitions of marriage laws; notions of equality for same-sex marriage and civil partnerships; the financial realities of divorce; prosecution for forced marriages (FMs), legal parenthood and same-sex couples; and public law child protection disparities for racially minoritised and asylum-seeking children. This part delves into the challenges encountered within families, exploring the dynamics that impact family life across diverse family forms. The authors critically examine prevalent myths, dismantle misconceptions with evidence-based perspectives, and survey barriers to family justice. By highlighting the evolving landscape of family justice, Part I emphasises the need for inclusive and flexible solutions that recognise and accommodate diverse relationships, along with the cultural, religious, and economic contexts that shape them.

In Chapter 2 ('Exposing Marriage Law: Colonial Definitions and Legacies'), Zainab Batul Naqvi focuses on the definition of a legally binding marriage in England and Wales, arguing that current legal understandings of marriage are stagnant and exclusionary, with legal recognition or a lack of it having sweeping implications for communities with varied forms of marriage ceremonies. Ultimately, an exclusionary law serves to invisibilise the parties and their communities, imposing a hierarchy of communities in which only some are preferred by the law. Using polygamy as a case study, Naqvi charts the colonial foundations of English law's conception of marriage and the 'othering' of non-monogamous practice despite its presence in family formation since time immemorial. The strong connection between law and religion during the colonial eras explains the influence of religion on the formation of marriage laws, to uphold and enforce Anglican values. Through the lens of coloniality, Naqvi sets out the influence of domination and suppression of non-Christians in British colonial history on the development of marriage laws and which ceremonies were excluded from recognition.

In Chapter 3 ('Assimilation or Difference? Same-Sex Relationship Recognition in England and Wales'), Andy Hayward explores the legal and social landscape for same-sex couples seeking legal recognition of their relationships. From historical criminalisation to the Same Sex Marriage Act (Marriage (Same Sex Couples) Act 2013), the journey for equal recognition remains ongoing and, in this chapter, Hayward explores how far genuine substantive equality has been achieved. In scrutinising this, Hayward deliberates on the extent to which legal recognition of same-sex couples is contingent on their relationships 'mimicking' that of heterosexual couples. While arguments are made concerning both assimilationist and differential models of family, the judiciary and legislature has framed 'family' in light of heterosexual norms and behaviours, perhaps in the absence of a structured alternative framework. The journey to marriage 'equality' is often phased and the chapter charts the

Civil Partnership Act 2004, which acted as a stepping stone towards same-sex marriage in England and Wales. With an emphasis on civil registration and the dissolution of a partnership as opposed to the celebration of marriage and divorce, these distinctions were key to passing the Act. This is considered by some to be a missed opportunity to explore couple innovation, instead seeking to mirror marriage in all but name.

In Chapter 4 ('The Financial Realities of Getting Divorced in England and Wales'), Emma Hitchings, Caroline Bryson, and Gillian Douglas focus attention on the economic disengagement between couples on divorce. With headline-grabbing 'big-money' cases, our understanding of the true financial reality of divorce for the vast majority of divorcing couples is often misunderstood. In this chapter, Hitchings and others provide a grounded perspective using findings from their much-lauded Fair Shares project to explore the experiences of financial resolution for the 'everyday' couple. For such couples, household income is incredibly modest and equity in homes which are owned are, on average, not enough to enable the purchase of two similar homes following divorce. Overall, the Fair Shares findings portray a very different financial reality for the everyday couples than big-money cases might lead one to assume, with almost a quarter of participants walking away with nothing or debts, portraying a reality of post-divorce financial hardship. Where intersectional character traits are introduced, the gender disparity in post-separation financial outcomes is stark, with parenthood – especially motherhood – and older age of wives being linked to greater financial hardship, with reduced income levels. Younger women without childcare responsibilities fare better financially compared to older women or those with children. Thus, parenthood, and particularly motherhood, has the most substantial impact on meeting a divorcee's immediate financial needs and long-term prospects.

In Chapter 5 ('Forced Marriage in the UK: How Intermediaries and Expert Witnesses Help Successful Prosecutions'), Aisha K. Gill provides a compelling account of the first successful criminal prosecution of a parent responsible for the FM of their child. The many criticisms of the criminalisation of FMs are brought to the fore in this exploration of family values and norms which hinder prosecutions, and how the use of experts can help empower victims through the legal process. Gill situates forms of violence – such as so-called honour-based violence – as part of a broader systematic violence by society against women, rather than being specifically or entirely culturally based. Consequently, FMs should be viewed as individual cases rather than a lens through which entire communities are mislabelled, especially as it tends to be found among women from minoritised communities. Gill's first-hand experience of the case *Regina v RB* (2018) takes us through the key stages of investigation, conviction, and sentencing, providing a detailed analysis of the legal process. Successful prosecutions, according to Gill, are reliant on the development of a trusting relationship between police and the victim, coupled with expert witness testimony, in recognition that victims often face a stark choice between complying with wishes of family on the one hand

and being completely ostracised from both family and community on the other. Even where significant external support exists, the loss of long-term close familial relationships and support structures are devastating, and no level of intervention can replace this.

In Chapter 6 ('Legal Parenthood and Same-Sex Couples'), Brian Sloan explores the pathways to legal parenthood for couples who do not fit into the 'traditional' cisgender heterosexual paradigm originally envisaged by the law. Within same-sex couples, the gender of the parties has a significant impact on the route to parenthood, particularly due to the law's notion of legal motherhood. Adoption, parenthood under the Human Fertilisation and Embryology Act 2008, and parenthood through a parental order relating to a baby born through surrogacy are the three pathways to legal parenthood for same-sex couples. Sloan's analysis of the law reflects the endurance of a gendered and heteronormative conception of family present in English law, in which the ideal is framed as a monogamous, heterosexual relationship with biologically related children. As such, the conferring of legal parenthood on individuals without a genetic relationship to the child seems to conflict with the emphasis traditionally placed on genetic connections in the context of non-assisted reproduction by heterosexual couples. Calls for reform recognise the differential treatment of same-sex couples by the law, resulting from the law's attachment to the biology of child conception and birth.

In Chapter 7 ('Child Protection Intersectionality: Disparities in Racially Minoritised and Asylum-Seeking Backgrounds'), Rachel Pimm-Smith focuses attention on the public child law regime for removing children from the care of parents and the disparities in the experiences of children from certain backgrounds. The over-representation of unaccompanied asylum-seeking children and children from racialised backgrounds in the social care system reflects deep-rooted structural inequalities. Differences in parenting styles further complicate these disparities, as non-Western collectivist approaches are often misunderstood or devalued in favour of Western individualist norms by social workers. Pimm-Smith scrutinises how cultural misunderstandings and racial biases, such as adultification bias, further exacerbate inequities. This bias, particularly affecting Black children, leads to their being perceived as more independent and less in need of nurturing, contributing to harsher interventions. The social care system's reliance on Eurocentric norms risks misinterpreting culturally diverse practices as neglect, creating mistrust between families and services. Addressing these disparities requires systemic reforms, essential to creating a social care system that recognises and respects diversity while ensuring equitable outcomes for all children.

Part II of this volume focuses on 'Dispute Resolution in Family Law', with four chapters exploring mediating family disputes and breakdown for diverse relationships; accessing family justice without lawyers, sharia councils as Muslim family dispute resolution forums; and the participation of children in family justice processes.

In Chapter 8 ('Family Dispute Resolution: Meeting the Challenge of Diversity'), Maria Federica Moscati analyses how mediation and alternative family dispute-resolution processes accommodate family diversity. This chapter addresses the dual issues of diversity in family disputes and the impact this has on the disputes and their resolution forums, arguing that access to justice for all requires dispute resolution processes that reflect the diversity of family structures. This requires consideration of intersecting identities of those involved and the rejection of stereotypical, binary, and heteronormative views of family. Taking a much broader approach to 'family', disputes considered here range from dissolution of marriages and arrangements for children to intergenerational disputes, sexual orientation and gender identity, and special needs of children. In disrupting the norms and expectations of disputants involved in family dispute-resolution processes, Moscati encourages a reimagining of family disputes and the notion of access to justice and emphasises the limitations of the dual disputant expectations found within mediation and other non-court dispute resolution (NCDR) processes.

In Chapter 9 ('Accessing Family Justice without Lawyers'), Rachael Blakey assesses the contemporary FJS in England and Wales and sets out an operational framework largely absent of widespread use of lawyers, which poses significant challenges for families navigating the law. The Legal Aid, Sentencing and Punishment of Offenders Act 2012 drastically reduced access to legal aid, particularly for private family law matters, leaving many litigants to represent themselves. This shift disproportionately affects groups more prone to vulnerabilities, including women, ethnic minorities, individuals with disabilities, and children, as predicted in the Ministry of Justice's 2010 Equality Impact Assessment and confirmed in subsequent reviews following implementation. These groups face compounded barriers, with limited access to affordable legal representation, rendering justice both inaccessible and perhaps even irrelevant for many. The absence of legal aid exacerbates power imbalances, especially in cases where one party is represented, exposing significant flaws in the system's ability to deliver equitable outcomes.

In Chapter 10 ('Religious Communities and Family Dispute Resolution: The Sharia Councils Debate'), Rehana Parveen delves into faith-based dispute resolution forums used specifically by Muslim communities. Serving the second-largest faith group, accounting for 6.5 per cent of the population (3.9 million people), sharia councils are often presented as contentious due to the (ill-)framing of these bodies as operating within a parallel legal system outside of the state law. These bodies operate in a hybrid manner, occupying a space in which the state is largely absent, and providing Muslim individuals, couples and communities with the freedom to navigate family law and cultural and religious norms. Parveen examines the experiences of Muslims marrying and divorcing in England and Wales, offering an analysis of the interplay between English marriage and divorce laws and the practices of Muslim communities. How these communities engage with the legal framework and how the law responds in turn has been an issue of much policy debate and is centred in the analysis. The chapter encourages critical reflection on the intersection of family law, divorce processes, and the lived experiences of Muslim couples, shedding light on the broader relationship between state law and Muslim family practices.

In Chapter 11 ('Participation of Children in Family Justice Processes'), Connie Healy journeys through private family justice processes, critically appraising the right of children to be heard within the myriad of legal, quasi-legal, and non-legal processes, concluding that the rights of the child to have their voice heard are not upheld in NCDR processes. In exploring the extent of children's participation in private family justice processes, Healy highlights the gap between legal expectations and practical realities during family transitions. In court processes, judges may lack the contextual understanding of litigants' socio-economic and cultural backgrounds and may overly rely on the assumption that parents always act in their child's best interests. Factors such as financial constraints, cultural barriers, health issues, addictions, or inadequate support can hinder parents' ability to advocate effectively for their child's wishes. Children emphasise the importance of their participation with adequate support systems in place, clear communication about the processes, and reassurances that meetings can be paused if needed. The Lundy participation model remains the standard for upholding children's right to be heard, underlining the need for structured approaches to ensure meaningful child participation.

Part III of this volume presents diverse voices on domestic abuse in families, with three chapters exploring how domestic abuse impacts on private law child arrangements proceedings; understanding the experiences of racially minoritised women victims; and the invisibilisation of male victims of domestic abuse.

In Chapter 12 ('It Can Happen to Anyone, But Not Everyone Has the Same Experience: The Need for Better Legal Responses to Domestic Abuse in the Family Justice System'), Mandy Burton focuses on child arrangements where there are allegations of domestic abuse. With up to two thirds of child arrangement cases potentially involving abuse allegations, the FJS faces grave concerns about its ability to recognise and respond appropriately to the risks posed by domestic abuse to children and the non-abusive protective parent. The voices of children are often ignored or minimised, overshadowed by a system focused on maintaining contact with both parents, seemingly at all costs. Recent case law has begun to address this, emphasising the need to consider the full spectrum of abuses defined under the Domestic Abuse Act 2021, including financial and emotional abuse. Despite these developments, studies show that the safety of women and children experiencing domestic abuse remains compromised. Racially minoritised mothers face additional disadvantages, including institutional racism, language barriers, and heightened isolation, which make them particularly vulnerable to control and manipulation during proceedings. These systemic issues underscore the need for a justice system that better balances the interests of all parties while prioritising the safety and well-being of children and protective parents.

In Chapter 13 ('In the Shadow of Hostile Environments and Bordering Regimes: Understanding Migrant Women's Experiences of Domestic Abuse and Legal-Institutional Responses'), Sundari Anitha exposes the risks of abuse faced by this marginalised and highly vulnerable section of society. Anitha focuses on the issue of migrant women's visa status allowing no recourse to public funds and the problems which can specifically arise with transnational marriage abandonment. The probationary period linked to immigration statuses exacerbate gendered power imbalances where wives are from abroad. Abusers can exploit the victim's insecure immigration status, threatening deportation or separation from their children to maintain control. For victims of transnational marriage abandonment, immigration reforms provide an avenue for applying for indefinite leave to remain under the Victim of Domestic Abuse rule (Appendix VDA) in order to escape the abusive spouse and visa limitations. However, Anitha presents research which demonstrates that gaps in funding during application processes have the potential to leave women destitute. Thus, immigration and welfare border policies form part of a matrix of structural inequalities sustaining domestic violence and abuse (DVA), creating conducive contexts for such abuse. This vulnerability is evidenced by statistics which show an increased risk of DVA for Black and minoritised women and girls which cannot be explained solely by factors such as socio-economic disadvantages arising from poverty, deskilling and class dislocation upon migration, and racism.

In Chapter 14 ('The Invisibilisation of Male Victims in the Family and Criminal Courts: Domestic Abuse, Honour-Based Abuse, and Parental Alienation'), Mohammad Mazher Idriss, Elizabeth Bates, and Ben Hine tackle the diverse experiences of male victims of domestic abuse. This under-explored area of domestic abuse necessitates a paradigmatic shift that moves beyond the predominant focus on female victimhood. While gendered experiences of abuse are interrelated, they are inherently distinct, with male and female survivors facing differing challenges and manifestations of abuse. Such differences need to be acknowledged and analysed independently, allowing for a nuanced understanding that respects the unique experiences and responds accordingly. Idriss, Bates, and Hine focus on a range of key issues which speak to male victimhood including post-separation abuse, parental-alienating behaviours, 'honour'-based abuse and FM. The perpetrators of domestic abuse against male victims are broad, including ex-partners and male and female relatives. Men continue to be less likely to report abusive behaviours due to gender stereotypes, a fear of disbelief and ridicule, and discrimination within the legal system. These all act as barriers to accessing help and support, while a lack of institutional recognition of male victimhood results in a lack of policy focus on the ways in which abuse against male victims manifests, ultimately affecting recognition, disclosure, and the availability of services and policies. This oversight contributes to the invisibility of male victims, effectively erasing them from intervention and support frameworks.

Conclusion

The three parts of this volume examine the diverse experiences of family justice and injustice in England and Wales. As this volume consists of 'Diverse Voices', the style hegemony one might usually expect from an edited volume is deliberately missing. Each author approaches the topic through their own lens and using their own voice. As a reader, this is a pedagogic exercise in 'hearing' the diversity both in views and voice. As editor of this volume, I have tasked myself with overseeing the arguments being made by the authors, while deliberately disengaging from the 'voices' and reflections therein.

Although this volume provides a rich array of diverse voices, there is always room for further inclusivity. In exploring this topic, the stark reality of a lack of racialised diversity within family law academia in England and Wales became evident. Alongside contributions from early career researchers to well-known scholars, this volume highlights narratives and perspectives that are often absent or underrepresented in the family law syllabus. I invite students to engage with this material as critical, decolonial scholars of family law, approaching the subject with nuance, sensitivity, and a commitment to challenging traditional paradigms in their future professional endeavours.

PART I

Marriage, Divorce, and Parenthood

2

Exposing Marriage Law: Colonial Definitions and Legacies

Zainab Batul Naqvi

Introduction

Undergraduate English family law modules often start with a discussion about the concept of 'family'.[1] What is the family? How do we conceptualise it in general? And how is it defined in law? At the heart of these discussions where we talk about parents, children and pets is the key relationship of marriage. Marriage and being a spouse are universally included in definitions of the family. That's not to say that marriage features in every family structure but just that it is always encompassed within global understandings of the family. Marriage, its celebration, and its breakdown therefore form a significant part of the family legal framework. In this chapter I focus on the definition of a legally binding marriage in England and Wales. I show how current legal understandings of marriage are stagnant, exclusionary, and still rooted in colonial ideals of domesticity. The effects of this are more sweeping than we might think. Marriage and its legal recognition give relationships a public and state-sanctioned status. Being legally recognised as married therefore confers certain benefits and privileges on married couples, which means that it can send a wider message about not only the status of the parties but also the community of which they are a part.

Legal recognition of a marriage, and the marriages occurring within any given community at the national level, increase the likelihood of recognition at the international level. If marriage ceremonies are recognised, the families and communities that practise them are also likely to be publicly recognised and acknowledged. Marriage is a powerful symbol: a symbol of family, of community

---

[1] When I use the phrase 'English law' I am referring to the law of England and Wales. Scots family law has its own framework.

and belonging. When it is recognised, this sends a strong message about public support and acceptance to that community. We accept you, your families and your ways of living and being with one another. Denying recognition can have devastating effects, whether symbolic or practical.

I start this chapter with an outline of the current legal framework for a valid marriage in England and Wales as well as how marriage might be legally defined. I then move on to explore the colonial legacies that influence this area, as well as ideals of marriage in English law, and explain how ideals of domesticity that pre-date the British Empire were solidified during colonialism and have led to the emphasis on Christian monogamy that the UK has in the law today.

Following this, I explore how marriage law operates to invisibilise and emphasise the foreignness of polygamy and non-marriage or non-qualifying ceremonies; this is a colonial strategy against minoritised communities. This strategy works in an expansive way to other and invisibilise the parties and also their communities. Their relationships and ways of being with one another are thus regarded as not belonging and, therefore, neither they nor their people belong. Marriage law creates a hierarchy of marriages which leads to a hierarchy of communities in the UK. This reinforces the use of the law as a force to divide UK society into those who are acceptable and recognised and those who are not.

English marriage law: an overview

The first and perhaps most surprising thing for us to note is that there is no authoritative definition of 'marriage' in English law. There is nothing in the statutes explicitly defining or describing a marriage. That being said, there is what could be termed an 'historical' definition worth mentioning. In the 19th-century case of *Hyde v Hyde and Woodmansee*, Lord Penzance stated:

> I conceive that marriage, as understood in Christendom, may for this purpose be defined as the voluntary union for life of one man and one woman, to the exclusion of all others.[2]

Scholars have demonstrated how this definition has always been unrealistic. Marriage may not be voluntary; it can end in divorce so is not lifelong; and infidelity means that it is not always a union to the exclusion of all others.[3] This is true now and was also true in 1866. Further, with the recognition of same-sex marriage, it is also not necessarily practised between one man and one

---

[2]   *Hyde v Hyde and Woodmansee* [1866] LR 1 P&D, 133.
[3]   R Probert, 'Hyde v Hyde: Defining or Defending Marriage?' (2007) 19(3) Child and Family Law Quarterly 322; G Calder, 'Penguins and Polyamory: Using Law and Film to Explore the Essence of Marriage in Canadian Family Law' (2009) 21 Canadian Journal of Women and the Law 55; ZB Naqvi, *Polygamy, Policy and Postcolonialism in English Marriage Law: A Critical Feminist Analysis* (Bristol University Press 2023).

woman. Nevertheless, this statement of a judge from over 150 years ago has left its traces on modern family law. In much later cases it has been termed 'classic'[4] and 'hallowed',[5] while a variation on these words have been read out before civil ceremonies for decades.[6] In the recent case of *Secretary of State for Work and Pensions v Akhtar*,[7] we are told that *Hyde* is 'often cited for the definition of marriage given by Lord Penzance'. The case, and the definition it provides, are still being used by judges as a notable part of the background to marriage in English law. So, how historic is this definition? And can we really claim that it has not influenced the way marriage is seen in English law today?

On top of this, there is a distinction to be made between marriage itself and what is termed 'weddings law'. Recently, the Law Commission explained that while marriage can be seen as the 'legal status of being married and the legal consequences that flow from it', weddings law is the framework that tells us 'how and where couples can get married'.[8] From this, we only know that marriage is a status and it has legal consequences. Marriage is the relationship; the wedding is the ceremony. So why, despite the lack of a legal marriage definition, am I homing in on marriage rather than wedding ceremonies? Because there is a lot to learn from what the law does *not* explicitly tell us, alongside what it does. We learn much more from the gaps and silences than we think.

The relationship between weddings law and marriage is significant because without a wedding (as set out by the law), there is no marriage. No recognised ceremony means no recognised marriage. In this way, the law which tells us what makes a valid wedding, tells us by extension what makes a marriage. If the law does not include a certain ceremony in its framework, that relationship is also not included. Therefore, if we know how to legally contract a marriage through the ceremony, we can then surmise how marriage is defined and constructed by law.

The law telling us what makes a wedding is considered 'ancient', with the principles remaining mostly unchanged since the 18th and 19th centuries.[9] Unsurprisingly, the social and cultural values of those times, along with how marriage was perceived, have shaped the various routes towards celebrating a legally recognised marriage. In England and Wales, wedding ceremonies can be either civil or religious.[10] Civil ceremonies are celebrated in a register office or approved premises and do not contain any religious content or rituals. There are

---

[4] *Corbett v Corbett (otherwise Ashley)* [1971] [83], [86].

[5] *Bibi v Chief Adjudication Officer* [1998] 1 FLR 375, 379.

[6] As recently as March 2014, a form of this statement was included in the wedding script templates for registrars by Haringey City Council. See 'Wedding Scripts' (2014) no longer available online.

[7] *Secretary of State for Work and Pensions v Akhtar* [2021] EWCA Civ 1353 [66].

[8] Law Commission, *Getting Married: A Consultation Paper on Weddings Law* (Law Com No 247, 2020) para 1.11.

[9] Ibid, para 1.14.

[10] The aim of this chapter is to look at minoritised marriage practices with more focus on racialised communities, for this reason I do not have the space to include practices that are more associated with the dominant community like same-sex marriage and civil partnerships.

four categories of religious ceremony: Anglican (Church of England/Church of Wales), Jewish, Quaker, and any other religious group. For the ceremony, whether civil or religious, to be valid, the parties must have the capacity to enter the marriage,[11] and must comply with the formal requirements in the Marriage Act 1949.[12] The requirements cover the entire ceremony process, which includes the public notice of the intention to marry either at the register office or through an Anglican church, the holding of the ceremony in a specified building registered for the purpose of celebrating weddings in the presence of an authorised person, registering the marriage once it has been celebrated and having two witnesses present.

This seems like a consistent list but does not tell the full story. The different pathways to marriage, whether civil or religious, are subject to a different combination of these requirements for validity. If we take Jewish ceremonies for example, the parties must profess the same religion, the ceremony must be according to the usages of the Jews and there is no restriction on place.[13] There are only three conditions. Quaker ceremonies are treated very similarly to Jewish ones.[14] If the ceremony is Anglican, it has to be according to the rites and ceremonies of the church, with two witnesses, conducted by a person in Holy Orders, and celebrated in a church, chapel or authorised place, which is four conditions.[15] By contrast, a ceremony of any other religion besides Jewish, Quaker or Anglican involves a form and ceremony that the parties wish, public access to witness the ceremony, two witnesses, prescribed form of words in the ceremony, and the presence of an authorised person, in a registered place of worship.[16] We can see how much longer the list is for the latter weddings. The Law Commission has observed that these 'different levels of regulation can ... be perceived as unfair' (2015, para 2.90), but is there an explanation?[17]

As we might expect, Anglican Christianity is the state religion in England and Wales and since the weddings laws of today have changed very little since their formation with the Anglican Church in mind, the legal infrastructure around

---

[11] Matrimonial Causes Act (MCA) 1973, s 11 sets out the conditions under which a marriage would be void because the parties lack the capacity to enter into it. These include being too closely related to one another, being underage, or already being lawfully married to someone while domiciled in England and Wales.

[12] Marriage Act 1949, s 49.

[13] See further ibid, s 26.

[14] See further ibid, s 47.

[15] Law Commission, *Getting Married: A Scoping Paper* (2015), figure 7. Part II Marriage Act 1949 provides the requirements for marriages performed according to Rites of the Church of England.

[16] Part III Marriage Act 1949 covers the requirements for all the other pathways including civil marriages carried out in a register office or on approved premises as well as Jewish, Quaker and other religious marriages, which are all conducted under the Superintendent Registrar's Certificate.

[17] Law Commission (n15) para 2.90.

marriage remains geared towards these ceremonies and this community. The law's hands-off approach to Jewish and Quaker ceremonies on the other hand is for a different reason. Both of these communities and their wedding ceremonies have a long-standing presence in England and Wales but legal attitudes towards them are captured in the condition that their ceremonies be celebrated 'according to the usages' of their people. By saying that a ceremony should be celebrated by people according to their usages, there is a distancing process at play. These 'alien' ceremonies are kept at arm's length and treated as 'foreign' weddings that are governed by foreign usages and laws.[18] There is therefore no need for the law to pay attention to them or care about their structures and processes.[19] It is possible to argue that the law is being deferential towards Jews and Quakers and even that the effect of this distance means that these communities are left to celebrate their weddings with much more freedom than any other religious group in the UK. However, the ways in which Quaker ceremonies were treated historically as pretend and the ways that Jewish marriage issues were seen as a matter for foreign law, suggests there is another story being told here.[20]

The less prescriptive and restrictive approach to Jewish and Quaker ceremonies is also reflected in the legal approach to the validity of ceremonies celebrated overseas (other foreign weddings). Very simply, if a wedding is celebrated overseas and complies with the legal requirements of the place it was celebrated in, that wedding would be considered valid in the English courts and the parties would be recognised as married for all relevant purposes.[21] We can keep this in mind for the discussion of polygamy and non-marriage later, where there are international considerations around their validity with which the courts are faced.

Summary

Marriage is not defined in the current English legal framework. Instead, there is statutory and common law guidance on what should form a part of the process for the various pathways to marrying. However, the historical definition from the 1866 case of *Hyde* has been mentioned a lot. To understand what makes a marriage in English law, we can look to the requirements for a legally binding ceremony in the Marriage Act 1949. Ceremonies can either be religious or civil in nature. The number and type of requirements for a religious ceremony

---

[18] HSQ Henriques, 'Jewish Marriages and the English Law' (1908) 20(3) The Jewish Quarterly Review 391.

[19] See also Naqvi (n3).

[20] In the statute An Act for granting to his Majesty certain rates and duties upon marriages, births and burials, and upon bachelors and widowers, for the term of five years for carrying on the war against France with vigour 1694 6 & 7 W 3 c 6, s 202, Quaker marriages were described as 'pretended'.

[21] Lord Collins of Mapesbury and others, *Dicey, Morris and Collins: The Conflict of Laws* (5th edn, Sweet & Maxwell 2012) 964.

to be legally binding differ according to your background. There is a hierarchy and religious ceremonies that are not Jewish, Quaker, or Anglican have more requirements. However, that does not mean Jewish and Quaker ceremonies are necessarily more accepted, but rather that the hands-off approach to these communities was due to perceptions of them being alien. Overall, the law around marriage has changed very little since it was originally developed with the Anglican Church ceremony in mind.

Colonial influences

Coloniality is the sexual, political, epistemic, economic, spiritual, linguistic, and racial domination and exploitation of racialised and minoritised groups by the dominant majority. This used to happen because of colonial rule over foreign lands, but manifests itself today across the European/non-European divide.[22] Racialised and minoritised groups are those who are oppressed and dehumanised because they are not White or associated with whiteness and they are often linked to the colonies.[23] Initially, European colonisation involved landing in other places and declaring them a part of the empire before taking over their resources, lands, and people. In 1900, the British Empire covered 11 million square miles and included 390 million people.[24] The imperial administration was not just interested in physical domination but full ideological control: it was not enough to control colonised people's bodies and possessions, they also wanted to control their minds and spirits. Two of the key tools for achieving this were law and religion. By forcing colonial laws on people, not only did this give the impression that the colonisers were acting lawfully and therefore their oppressive actions were valid, but it also forced the colonised people to regulate their behaviour according to what the colonisers wanted.[25] Related to this, forcing the ideal Christian religion on the colonies was another way to legitimise the imperial mission. Christian beliefs were deemed superior, thus portraying the colonisers as superior and civilised. By converting the colonised to their way of life and faith, by telling them how they should behave, by governing their sense of morality and ideals, the colonisers convinced themselves and imposed the narrative that this improved the colonised people. Moreover, the connection between law and religion is a strong one. Religion has often been used as the foundation for legal systems, which is true of England and Wales. The King is both head of the church and the state – there is no separation between the

---

22   R Grosfoguel, 'The Epistemic Decolonial Turn' (2007) 21(2–3) Cultural Studies 211.

23   N El-Enany, *(B)ordering Britain: Law, Race and Empire* (Manchester University Press 2020).

24   S Huntington, *The Clash of Civilization and the Remaking of World Order* (Simon & Schuster 1996).

25   L Benton and L Ford, *Rage for Order: The British Empire and the Origins of International Law 1800–1850* (Harvard University Press 2016); D Klerman and others, 'Legal Origin or Colonial History?' (2011) 3(2) Journal of Legal Analysis 379.

two. English law is therefore mostly compatible with Anglican Christianity and marriage law even more so.[26]

As an institution, marriage also had a larger ideological role to play in colonial processes. Marriage and domestic life are usually situated in the so-called private sphere.[27] They are therefore seen as something that happens behind closed doors and the state is not meant to get involved or intervene heavily with them. So why was marriage such an important site of struggle in the colonial administration? Alongside gender equality and the status of women, marriage was used by the coloniser as a marker for social advancement.[28] The structure and practice of marriage determined how socially advanced and therefore how civilised a community was. And it was the imperial society that decided what the ideal standard for marriage was before measuring colonised communities' practices against it. Additionally, marriage was an important building block for organising a community's relationships, families, and households. Interfering with how marriages are conducted or structured within communities is one of the quickest ways to break down their social structures and therefore leave them more vulnerable than ever. And this is exactly what the British colonisers did. They imposed a 'cult of domesticity',[29] inspired by Victorian family morals and ideals, to civilise and improve the colonies and their peoples. In doing so, they aimed to stamp out any difference or diversity in families and family practices. Marriages and the communities that celebrated them were therefore held up to the invader's standards and their differences were marked out before being dismissed as inferior. They were subjected to orientalist 'othering' processes where stories were made up by the coloniser about their inferiority and their lack of humanity because their marriages and relationships differed.[30] Their differences made them 'other': too strange and foreign. Marriage, in the past and today, has played a central role in struggles for power and control over minoritised groups. To challenge the colonial standard and practise marriage differently, to celebrate marriage differently, can therefore be seen as an act of revolution that defies the oppressor.[31] 'Other' marriages are resistance, they are a reclamation of minoritised ways of being, living and loving.

---

[26] J Rivers, 'Is English Law Christian?' Religion and Law Theos Thinktank (2012) 143 https://www.theosthinktank.co.uk/cmsfiles/archive/files/Religion%20and%20Law%20FINAL.pdf, accessed 14 July 2025; J Rivers, 'Could Marriage Be Disestablished?' (2017) 68(1) Tyndale Bulletin 121.

[27] S Thompson, *Quiet Revolutionaries: The Married Women's Association and Family Law* (Hart Publishing 2022).

[28] C Hall, 'Of Gender and Empire: Reflections on the Nineteenth Century' in P Levine (ed), *Gender and Empire* (OUP 2004) 50.

[29] A McClintock, *Imperial Leather: Race, Gender and Sexuality in the Colonial Contest* (Routledge 1995).

[30] E Said, *Orientalism* (Pantheon Books 1978).

[31] S Pearsall, *Polygamy: An Early American History* (Yale University Press 2019); Naqvi (n3).

Marriage is a powerful symbol and English legal understandings of wedding ceremonies and marriage are currently built to ensure that any difference, any resistance, any revolution are dismissed. They promote imperial values and ideals: whether it is by making it more cumbersome to undergo a religious wedding which is not Anglican, Jewish, or Quaker or to deny equal recognition to marriages that fail to fit the Christian template. If we go back to the case of *Hyde* I mentioned earlier, there is an important detail in Lord Penzance's definition as well as the timing of the judgment. The case was heard in 1866 when the British Empire was in its prime and British rule and colonisation were spreading far and fast. This meant that judges, lawmakers, and other institutional actors were operating as part of an imperial superpower. They were not just hearing cases and making laws that affected the inhabitants of a small island in Europe. Their words and actions were being exported around the world to be imposed as part of colonial administrations and orders.[32] The *Hyde* judgment declared that its definition of marriage applied to marriages 'as understood in Christendom'.[33] Christendom was an interesting choice here because it is broader and more encompassing than Britain or England and Wales.[34] Christendom is also used as a contrast against 'infidel nations' in the judgment.[35] So, the discourse here was around those in Christendom who believed in the true faith and those who did not: the infidels. This dividing line formed the difference between the empire (including its true subjects) and the disbelieving colonised peoples. And marriage could act as a test to decide which side of the line you were on. It asked: are you on our side or the other side? Finally, the petitioner in *Hyde* was an Englishman who had celebrated his Mormon marriage in Utah which was annexed to the US by colonial settlers. The classic, historic, and hallowed definition of marriage which lingers in legal conceptions of marriage even today was therefore formed as part of an English judge's encounter with a colonial-related marriage. Penzance LJ was not just defending English marriage with his definition in *Hyde*, he was defending *imperial* marriage.

Summary

English marriage law is influenced by coloniality, which signifies the domination and oppression of people across the European/non-European divide today. Law and religion were both used as key tools to oppress colonised people by imposing the imperial faith and order on them. Law and religion are also strongly connected in England and Wales because there is no separation between the Anglican Church and the state. This means the law has been shaped and influenced by the church to uphold and enforce Anglican values. Marriage is viewed as a test

---

32   Benton and Ford (n25).
33   *Hyde v Hyde and Woodmansee* [1866] LR 1 P&D 130 [133].
34   Naqvi (n3) 7.
35   *Hyde v Hyde and Woodmansee* [1866] LR 1 P&D 130 [135].

to measure the civility of a people – if your marriage does not match the ideal Anglican image well enough, it is dismissed as inferior. In English law, marriage recognition is designed to diminish any difference or resistance to how the state thinks a wedding should be celebrated and therefore what a marriage should look like.

Polygamous marriages in English law

I now turn to the case study which shows how the colonial foundations of English legal conceptions of marriage affect minoritised communities in practice.[36] Polygamy, or being married to more than one person at the same time, has been practised around the world, including in Europe, for millennia.[37] However, it has come to be typically associated with only certain people and places: Muslims living in the oriental imaginary inside and outside the West.[38] In this way, polygamy is seen as strange, alien, and other. It is only practised and celebrated over there not here. Polygamy is also mistakenly portrayed as being common and prevalent in those alien communities when it has always only ever been a minority form of marriage. The majority of Muslims, of racialised people, of colonised people have always been monogamous throughout history and into the present day. These misconceptions about polygamy are threaded throughout legal responses to this form of minoritised marriage practice. But what has the approach to polygamy been in England and Wales? Going very far back into the history of England, there is evidence of the Christian monk Augustine coming across polygamous Britons in 579 AD and being told to tolerate their practice. Taking a leap to the Tudors in the 1500s, we had one of the most famous divorces that changed the course of English history. King Henry VIII's desire to divorce Catherine of Aragon and marry Anne Boleyn caused a lot of concern. Some of his advisors hoped to avoid it all together by suggesting that he marry Anne as a second wife since the Roman Catholic Church might prefer that to allowing the great evil of divorce. As we know, the divorce still happened but the willingness to consider polygamy as an option shows us how it was acknowledged (although perhaps reluctantly) by serious political actors in those times. It was legitimate, and even preferable than divorce and remarriage to some. These historical snapshots demonstrate how polygamy has not always been as strange

---

[36] Lack of space means this discussion is limited to an exploration of the larger themes of legal and judicial approaches to this form of marriage, but I have written far more extensively on polygamy in English law in other work. See ZB Naqvi, 'A Contextualised Historical Account of Changing Judicial Attitudes to Polygamous Marriage in the English Courts' (2017) 13(3) International Journal of Law in Context 408; Naqvi (n3); ZB Naqvi, 'Polygamy in English Marriage Law: Critical Postcolonial Perspectives' in R Probert and S Thompson (eds), *Research Handbook on Marriage, Cohabitation and the Law* (Edward Elgar 2024).

[37] J Witte Jr, *The Western Case for Monogamy over Polygamy* (CUP 2015).

[38] MK Zeitzen, *Elite Malay Polygamy: Wives, Wealth and Woes in Malaysia* (Berghahn Books 2017).

or distant from England and Wales as we might assume. Therefore, when the law behaves as though polygamy is unheard of and too foreign for these shores, it is enacting a form of orientalist othering against it.

And what is the current legal framework regulating the courts' approach today? There is only one way for a polygamous marriage ceremony to be valid in England and Wales: if it was not celebrated here. In line with the rules around international ceremonies, a polygamous ceremony celebrated in a place legally permitting polygamy which complied with all the legal requirements of that place will be valid. This is only the case as long as the parties were not domiciled, resident or citizens of England and Wales at the time of the ceremony.[39] A citizen, resident or domiciliary of England and Wales therefore cannot enter into a valid polygamous marriage either in the UK or abroad. If the overseas polygamous marriage meets these conditions, the courts are permitted (but not compelled) to give the parties matrimonial relief or make a declaration about its validity. They can therefore recognise it for all purposes.[40]

As mentioned earlier, for a ceremony that is celebrated in England and Wales to be legally binding, the parties must have the capacity or ability to enter into the marriage. One of the reasons why a party may not have such a capacity is because they are already legally married to someone else. In such cases, the marriage would be void, which means it never existed.[41] It is therefore not possible to conduct a legally binding polygamous ceremony in England and Wales for anyone, regardless of citizenship, domicile, or residence. What's more, a person who is domiciled in the UK also cannot enter into a valid polygamous marriage anywhere else in the world – it would also be void in English law. A void marriage can still attract some remedies from the courts when they grant a decree of nullity. Finally, a polygamous marriage ceremony in England and Wales conducted outside of the legal framework can be considered a non-qualifying or non-existent ceremony (also known as non-marriage). If the ceremony was performed overseas, it would be non-existent if it failed to meet the legal requirements of the place it was being celebrated in. At this stage, we should be aware that parties to a non-qualifying ceremony are seen as nothing more than cohabitants in English law. They are legal strangers and not spouses in any legally recognised form. This category allows people to practise polygamy outside of legal regulation by first having a legally binding ceremony and then having further informal and non-legally binding ceremonies.[42]

---

[39]   Lord Collins of Mapesbury and others (n21) 964.

[40]   MCA 1973, s 47.

[41]   Ibid, s 11(b). This situation of already being married and marrying another person is typically framed as bigamy when the ceremonies could both have been legally binding in their own right if not for their contemporaneous nature.

[42]   See *A- M v A- M (Divorce: Jurisdiction: Validity of Marriage)* [2001] 2 FLR 6 for an example of where a polygamous ceremony celebrated in London was treated as a non-marriage. Further discussion of this case can be found in: ZB Naqvi, 'The Racialising Effects of Non-Marriage

Long before we had the common-law descriptor of 'non-marriage' there were several instances where the courts held that a polygamous marriage could not count as a marriage in the first place.[43] One of the most prominent examples yet again is found in *Hyde*, which was not just about a colonial marriage but also indicated legal attitudes to polygamy. John Hyde was an Englishman who was living in Salt Lake City, Utah, as a member of the Mormon community. He was also married to a woman there. He left Utah and Mormonism to return to England, which led to his being excommunicated from the community. His wife, in line with local custom, married again. Having returned to England, Hyde petitioned for a divorce from his Mormon wife and Lord Penzance's definition of marriage was a reaction to being faced with this strange, colonial, and polygamous marriage. Hyde was in a monogamous marriage up until he left his wife and Utah, but he clearly considered himself still married, which is why he asked the courts to grant him a divorce. This meant that at the time of the judgment his marriage was in fact polygamous since the wife had a second husband. But the judge would not even recognise Hyde's foreign marriage as a marriage at all, because the Mormon polygamous marriage did not match the colonial definition of marriage and so there was no marriage to dissolve:

> Now, it is obvious that the matrimonial law of this country is adapted to the Christian marriage, and it is wholly inapplicable to polygamy.[44]

This was despite the petitioner arguing that his overseas marriage was contracted according to the law of its place of celebration. It should have therefore been a valid overseas marriage. Polygamy was the sticking point here and whether *Hyde* was actively practising it or not did not matter since the law was not adapted to this foreign marriage. Therefore, it simply did not exist for the purpose of getting a divorce. The foreignness was marked out and then used to invisibilise Hyde's marriage in the courts.[45]

In subsequent cases seeking judicial remedies, we see the same pattern of polygamy being used against parties to a monogamous marriage. In cases like *Re Bethell; Bethell v Hildyard*, for example,[46] the widow of a wealthy, landowning Englishman and her daughter with the deceased were denied recognition for inheritance purposes because she was a member of the Rolong community in Bechuanaland,[47] which is where she lived with her husband. The couple had

---

in English Law: A Critical Postcolonial Analysis' (2023) 19(4) International Journal of Law in Context 578.

43 The concept of non-marriage as we use it today can be traced from *R v Bham* [1966] 1 QB 159. See Naqvi (n42).

44 *Hyde v Hyde and Woodmansee* [1866] LR 1 P&D 130 [135].

45 See also Naqvi, 'Polygamy' (n36).

46 *Re Bethell; Bethell v Hildyard* [1887] 38 Ch D 220.

47 British Bechuanaland was a short-lived colony located in what is now the Republic of Botswana.

married in a Rolong ceremony and the fact that the community permitted polygamy was reason enough for the English courts to dismiss it. It was a marriage 'in the *Baralong* sense ... not a valid marriage according to the law of England'.[48] Elsewhere I have argued that the possible polygamy of the Rolong was used by the courts to block this colonised wife and her colonised child from benefitting from the imperial wealth and assets of the Bethell family who were located in England. Her community and its foreignness were brought into stark relief through the tool of polygamy, denying legitimacy to her and her child.[49] The couple in this case were in a monogamous marriage, neither of the parties was practising polygamy at all and there was no suggestion that they intended to, but the mere association of their marriage with polygamy was enough to declare this not valid in English law. Again, it should have been possible to argue that this was a valid, overseas marriage but the courts could not see past the practice of polygamy.

Bethell looked at a marriages that was monogamous in reality but celebrated in a place that allowed polygamy. In the English legal gaze, it had the *potential* to be polygamous which meant it might as well be polygamous in practice. The characterisation of such foreign marriages was another strategy to prevent foreign relationships from corrupting Christian English marriage and law. It further allowed the courts to wriggle out of dealing with foreign, and mostly colonial marriages. However, this was not a long-term viable solution, because what would the courts do if they wanted to intervene in a potentially polygamous marriage? The *Sinha Peerage Claim* presented this problem because the late Lord Sinha had married in a Hindu ceremony in India and although he had lived monogamously all his life, the location of his wedding meant that it was potentially polygamous.[50] Sinha was the first Indian member of the English House of Lords, and the issue was whether his foreign marriage affected the son's legitimacy and ability to inherit his father's seat. It was held that since the case had nothing to do with the divorce court, this situation was not concerned with the *Hyde* definition. On the date that the Crown issued the patent permitting Lord Sinha to join the House of Lords, he was a member of a religious sect that only practised monogamy and so he was prohibited from being polygamous. In this way, his potentially polygamous marriage could be reframed as monogamous. The marriage was sanitised and converted from foreign polygamy to domestic monogamy. The foreignness of the marriage and its associated polygamy were wiped away to allow Lord Sinha's son to succeed to his peerage. This almost religious-like conversion of a potentially polygamous marriage has since continued. If a person now enters into a potentially polygamous marriage, but later changes their domicile to the UK or changes their religion to one that

---

48   *Re Bethell; Bethell v Hildyard* [1887] 38 Ch D [221].
49   Naqvi, 'Contextualised' (n36); Naqvi (n3); Naqvi, 'Polygamy' (n36).
50   *Sinha Peerage Claim* [1946] 1 All ER 348.

forbids polygamy, their marriage can be converted.[51] However, this does not mean that potential polygamy has disappeared from legal discourse. Until we have a statutory rule to tell us otherwise, a potentially polygamous marriage will still be seen as actually polygamous by default.[52] So, even with the courts engaging in these legal gymnastics with the rules of private international law, any marriages celebrated in a place which allows polygamy are still considered polygamous. Not much has changed for these foreign marriages and polygamy remains a tool to separate and distance them from English marriage.

Another discussion around polygamous marriages, which shows how it is used to 'other' racialised communities and their practices, relates to whether parties to these marriages can be included in the meaning of the words 'husband', 'wife', and 'widow' in various statutes. These cases span many areas of legal regulation, from inheritance to immigration, welfare benefits, and other state funding. What is the relevance of this discussion around such terms? We now have more expansive labels for the parties to a marriage and relatedly their children, but the judicial interpretations of these terms are crucial for telling us who is married and who is the child of such a marriage. And if we know who is married, we know what kind of relationship leads to that status of being married. For this reason, knowing who is and is not covered by these labels indicates to us again what English marriage constitutes and who is then accepted as a party to or a child of it.

There are plentiful examples of the courts deciding that polygamous spouses could be included within these labels while interpreting statutes but the motivations for this are revealing. In *Cheang Thye Phin and Others v Tan Ah Loy (since Deceased)*,[53] we see an early instance of the courts recognising a Chinese secondary wife or t'sip as a legitimate widow who can inherit from her husband's estate along with her child. This was an appeal from the Supreme Court of the Straits Settlements in Penang, which 'recognises and applies the Chinese law of marriage. It is not disputed that this law admits of polygamy.'[54] We can distinguish this from *Re Bethell* because here the court was dealing with a Chinese marriage practice in a Chinese settlement which was governed by Chinese marriage law.

---

51   Law Commission, *Family Law Report on Polygamous Marriages* (Law Com No 42 1971) 5. Some of these cases include *Sinha Peerage Claim* (HL Deb 12 December 1935), vol 99, cols 224–32; *Cheni v Cheni* [1965]; *Ali v Ali* [1966] 2 WLR 620; [1968] P 564; *Mirza v Mirza* (1966) 110 SJ 708; *Parkasho v Singh* [1967] 2 WLR 946; [1968] P 233; and *Hassan v Hassan* [1976] 28 RFL 121. MCA 1973, s 47 now tells us that the courts are not prevented from granting matrimonial relief or making a declaration of validity for marriages that are polygamous or were polygamous at some point in the past. See also Naqvi, 'Polygamy' (n36).

52   Lord Collins of Mapesbury and others (n21) 964. This is supplemented by the concession in s 5(1) Private International Law (Miscellaneous Provisions Act) 1995 that these foreign potentially polygamous marriages are no longer *automatically* void. Overall, even though they are not automatically void they are still viewed as potentially polygamous.

53   *Cheang Thye Phin and Others v Tan Ah Loy (since Deceased)* [1920] AC 369.

54   Ibid [373]–[4].

All of the parties were overseas, the secondary marriage was overseas, and so was the estate, along with the law that was being interpreted. This made it easier for the English Court of Appeal to accept the secondary marriage in that situation because it would not affect English marriage or people. This can be contrasted with the later *Khoo Hooi Leong Appellant v Khoo Hean Kwee Respondent*,[55] where the secondary marriage of the appellant's t'sip grandmother was not recognised (among other reasons) because she was a Christian who had not left the religion. Being Christian meant that this foreign marriage practice could not apply to her. Thus the appellant, along with his father, could not be included in the phrase 'my sons and grandsons' in the deceased grandfather's will. The Christian faith of the grandmother played a role in forcibly distancing her from her relationship and left her child and grandchild without recognition as legitimate heirs. It is almost as if the courts could not bear the idea of a Christian woman being in anything other than a Christian marriage. To accept this threatened Christian marriage and its idealised aesthetic.

In later cases, we have examples of polygamous wives and their children falling within the scope of statutes like the Statute of Distributions 1670 (*Matthew Olajide Bamgbose, Appellant v John Bankole Daniel and Other Respondents*);[56] the Married Women's Property Act 1882 (*Chaudhry v Chaudhry*);[57] and the Administration of Estates Act 1925 (*Official Solicitor v Yemoh and Others*).[58] Like *Cheang Thye Phin*, these cases which allowed polygamous wives to inherit from their husbands' estates can be distinguished from *Re Bethell* because they are again about overseas foreign marriages and foreign estates. When these women are being recognised as spouses in faraway lands to inherit assets 'over there' rather than 'here', the English courts have no issue with acknowledging polygamy. But when there is a threat to resources or conceptions of marriage in England or even Christianity, the courts are less willing to recognise this minoritised practice.[59]

The threat to resources is one that the courts take extremely seriously where polygamy is concerned and undercuts many cases reaching into the present day. State resources are an important priority for obvious reasons: they concern public spending and funding. However, the rhetoric around this towards immigrants, refugees, and racialised communities in general is also steeped in the imperialist government's agenda to blame a lack of public resources on these vulnerable sections of the population. This creates a dividing line between the deserving and undeserving and also protects the imperial wealth that was robbed from the colonies.[60] The group of people who should benefit from state aid (and colonial

---

55 *Khoo Hooi Leong Appellant v Khoo Hean Kwee Respondent* [1926] AC 529.

56 *Matthew Olajide Bamgbose, Appellant v John Bankole Daniel and Other Respondents* [1955] AC 107.

57 *Chaudhry v Chaudhry* [1975] 3 WLR 559; [1976] Fam 148.

58 *Official Solicitor v Yemoh and Others* [2010] EWHC 3727 (Ch).

59 Naqvi, 'Polygamy' (n36).

60 El-Enany (n23).

wealth) is confined to those who are from the cultural majority and therefore not a burden. This characterisation of certain people and groups as a burden on the state is reflected in legal and policy responses to polygamous spouses (mostly wives) and their children. We can start here with cases explicitly looking at public money.

As the 20th century progressed, colonial subjects were increasingly migrating into the imperial centre of the empire and arriving in Britain to settle and live. This led to a forced awareness of these communities and their practices in the courts. The courts were no longer dealing with foreign marriages happening in foreign places but were seeing them at home. Faced with polygamy on their home turf, they now had to decide what the approach would be when public money was at stake. In *Iman Din v National Assistance Board*,[61] a man abandoned his second wife and their children, so she received financial help from the National Assistance Board. This help was cut off and the husband was ordered to pay back the board and support his family. The husband appealed. The polygamous marriage was recognised and he was considered liable to maintain them under the National Assistance Act 1948,[62] because they were included within the meaning of the phrase 'wife and children'. More importantly, it was confirmed that the husband could not be allowed to 'avoid all responsibility and thereby throw the whole burden of maintaining his wife and children upon the public'.[63] Maintaining this family was seen as a burden that the public should not carry. Here, the polygamy in the situation was overlooked to protect public money but it was also foregrounded to emphasise what a burden this second wife and her children were. It is possible that the same decision would be reached even when the marriage was monogamous, but this still feeds into the wider stereotypes about women and children being a burden, especially when they come from 'elsewhere'.

Another case that highlights the imperative to protect public money from polygamous outsiders is *Nabi (Ghulam) v Heaton (Inspector of Taxes)*.[64] A man was prevented from claiming tax relief for maintaining his second wife during the years that he was still married to his first wife. It would be too 'violent' to read the term 'wife' in the Income and Corporation Taxes Act 1970 as including polygamous wives.[65] Here, the appellant husband's second overseas polygamous marriage hit too close to home. Despite being conducted elsewhere, it generated consequences that affected the domestic tax system and revenue. The polygamy was therefore recognised but to prevent rather than permit the second marriage's tax relief. Interestingly, this decision was later successfully appealed because there

---

[61]   *Iman Din v National Assistance Board* [1967] 2 WLR 257.
[62]   National Assistance Act 1948.
[63]   Naqvi, 'Contextualised' (n36) 218.
[64]   *Ghulam Nabi v Peter Richard Heaton (HM Inspector of Taxes)* [1983] 1 WLR 626.
[65]   Ibid [1058].

were implications for people who had more than one spouse during their life through multiple monogamous marriages.

This change of heart was not so much about polygamy but about the potential issues for people on the right side of the line, the deserving ones who had lived monogamously. The same attitude is echoed in cases around widowed parent's allowance. In *Bibi v Chief Adjudication Officer*,[66] a polygamous wife's claim for widowed mother's allowance as it was then known was rejected because the legislation did not intend for such an allowance to be divided between more than one widow so it must be limited to those in monogamous marriages. In the much more recent *NA v Secretary of State for Work and Pensions*,[67] the widow of a marriage that was polygamous when it was contracted was allowed to claim this allowance along with a bereavement payment. The marriage in this situation was also polygamous at the start and the husband had also divorced his wife earlier on. So far, so similar. The husband in both cases was even domiciled in the UK at the time of the second marriage so it was void in both cases. The main factor which led to a different outcome here is that the marriage was monogamous for many years before the husband passed away since he had divorced his first wife quite early on. In this way, the marriage was seen as more monogamous than polygamous – it had crossed over the line into respectability as a result. That being said, the government successfully appealed against this decision, with the judgment addressing the policy reasons for this approach:

> maintaining a legal structure which discourages bigamous marriages and makes bigamous marriages void for those domiciled in England and Wales cannot be said to be without reasonable foundation, let alone manifestly without reasonable foundation. Indeed, as set out above, I consider that the structure and effect of the legislation is clearly justified.[68]

This reveals once more that law and policy are so focused on the ideological implications of permitting polygamy that they will reduce all such marriages to bigamy. Bigamy is a specific legal category of polygamy, one which involves the attempt to celebrate multiple ceremonies that would be legally valid in the UK.[69] There is always an element of deception involved, to one of the parties and/or the authorities. There is no indication in any of these cases that there was an attempt to hide the polygamy or commit bigamy, but this is still being used to explain the interpretation of social security legislation in ways that exclude polygamy. The foreignness of these marriages leads to them being falsely linked to a criminal offence which not only makes these relationships inferior but could

---

[66] *Bibi v Chief Adjudication Officer* [1998] 1 FLR 375.
[67] *NA v Secretary of State for Work and Pensions* [2019] 1 WLR 6321.
[68] *Secretary of State for Work and Pensions v Akhtar* [2021] EWCA Civ 1353, para 236.
[69] See s 57 Offences Against the Person Act 1861.

panic the minoritised communities where polygamy is practised lawfully (with a lack of state recognition) and openly.[70]

Again, there are cases that seem to go against this grain such as *R v Department of Health Ex p Misra*, which gives us another story around money.[71] Here, the courts allowed the two widows of a doctor to receive an equal share of their deceased husband's NHS pension. Both widows had applied to the state pension scheme and the NHS scheme. For state pension purposes, it was decided that the first marriage was valid but the second was not so the first wife was treated as a widow and received the pension. However, for the NHS scheme both marriages were found valid and, under National Health Service Superannuation Regulations 1980, the entitlement was divided equally between them. The first wife appealed this decision because she presumably wanted the whole sum, but her claim was dismissed. The NHS scheme was not bound by the state pension scheme's findings and could make an independent decision to give both widows the money. This is interesting but the two schemes are distinguishable because the NHS scheme was an employer pension which arguably involved funds that were not considered as public or state-funded in the same vein as the state pension scheme. When the money is not as connected with the public purse, it is possible to take a more flexible and open approach to polygamy. The stakes are not so high for English marriage, especially since the state pension scheme preserved the right ideals.

The final area which gives insight into the ways that polygamy is treated to uphold the optics around English marriage is around immigration. Immigration, like the public money cases, is concerned with the protection and preservation of state resources. In this line of cases, the emphasis is on stopping the entry of polygamous spouses and their children into the UK.[72] Broadly speaking, if you already have a spouse here, you cannot be joined by any subsequent ones while you are still married to the spouse already living here.[73] This is extended to children of those subsequent marriages as well. In *Azad v Entry Clearance Officer, Dhaka*, the appellant's son of his third marriage was denied entry into the UK.[74] The third marriage was valid in Bangladesh where it was celebrated

---

[70] For example, during their fieldwork interviewing people in non-legally binding marriages, at times Probert, Akhtar, and Blake (2022) had to reassure participants that their ceremonies were not illegal: R Probert, R Akhtar, and S Blake, 'When is a Wedding Not a Marriage? Exploring Non-legally Binding Ceremonies' Nuffield Foundation (2022) https://www.nuf fieldfoundation.org/wp-content/uploads/2020/11/When_is_a_wedding_not_a_marriage_ A_briefing_paper_for_the_Law_Commission-FINAL.pdf.

[71] *R v Department of Health Ex p Misra* [1996] 1 FLR 128.

[72] I have discussed various aspects of these cases previously in Naqvi, 'Contextualised' (n36); (n3); and 'Polygamy' (n36).

[73] See for example: *ECmHR Appl 19628/ 92, Bibi v UK* (Dec) 29 June 1992; *Zeenat Bibi v Secretary of State for the Home Department* [1994] Imm AR 550; and *R v Immigration Appeal Tribunal Ex p Begum (Hasna)* [1995] Imm AR 249. For a detailed discussion of these cases, see Naqvi (n3).

[74] *Azad v Entry Clearance Officer, Dhaka* [2000] WL 1918688.

but void in English law because the father was domiciled in the UK at the time of the ceremony. This was considered a test case for all children of second and third marriages. The question here was whether at the time of the child's conception both or either of the parents believed their marriage was valid. If so, even though the marriage was void, the child would still be treated as legitimate under section 1 Legitimacy Act 1976 (as amended). This reasonable belief was not established, the son could not be treated as legitimate, and the appeal failed. This case is significant because of what it says about legitimacy. This child of a valid marriage in Bangladesh cannot be considered legitimate because of the nature of his parents' marriage. This is a troubling message from the state about the status of children from polygamous marriages. There has always been a strong resistance to considering children illegitimate because of the stigmas attached to it. The fact that the courts are willing to consider a child illegitimate to prevent them entry into the UK because of polygamy tells us how far they are able to go to protect English marriage and resources.[75]

Like the public money cases, the immigration case law has also advanced a policy of preventing polygamy because it is undesirable. For example, in *ECO New Delhi v SG* the child of a man's third valid overseas marriage was denied entry into the UK for several reasons, including that her biological mother was caring for her and would continue to do so in Nepal where they lived. Another important reason for this decision was rooted in policy: the legitimate aim of excluding an actually polygamous wife from the UK, which in turn justified the indirect effect of excluding her children:

> Equally the fact that anyone who is lawfully resident in the United Kingdom, whether a British national or otherwise can live in a relationship akin to a polygamous household with more than one partner, does not mean that it is illogical and inconsistent to deny aliens the right to come to the United Kingdom for the purpose of establishing such a household.[76]

This excerpt tells us a lot about the ways that certain lifestyles and relationship choices are viewed in judicial discourse. It dismisses any comparison or equivalence to be drawn between living informally in a polygamous relationship in the UK and being in a lawful overseas polygamous marriage. Simply put, if it is happening unofficially, the courts are not concerned but when it is practised openly by *aliens* it is logical and consistent to prevent such households from forming. The key term here is aliens – these aliens coming from overseas should not live or be legally recognised as living in this type of household and

---

75 See *MB (Bangladesh) by Her Mother and Litigation Friend, JB v Secretary of State for the Home Department* [2013] EWCA Civ 220 for another case that looked at the legitimacy of children in polygamous marriages.

76 *ECO New Delhi v SG* [2012] UKUT 00265 (IAC), para 39.

relationship. This also extends to their children who had no part in their parents' relationship choices. They are not just aliens because of where they have come from but also because of their relationships. There is no clearer way to send the message of dehumanisation than by openly using such a derogatory and orientalist term that confirms they are other. The foreign polygamy in this case was at the heart of such a disturbing characterisation and there should be no room in the law or policy for such attitudes. This tells minoritised communities that their very humanity can be determined by the structure of their marriages, household, and family. What marriage is in English law, how it is structured, and why it is structured in this way therefore have far more significant effects than we can imagine.

Summary

Polygamous marriage has always been framed in dominant legal narratives as something that only happens in foreign communities in faraway places but there have been traces of it on British shores for a long time. A polygamous ceremony can only be legally binding in England and Wales if it was not celebrated here and the parties to it were also not based here. However, polygamy is still practised in an informal sense through what the courts have called 'non-marriages'/non-qualifying ceremonies. Furthermore, polygamy is recognised by the courts but usually to prevent the parties from accessing financial support or remedies. In earlier cases, we see that even monogamous marriages were treated as polygamous if they were celebrated in a place that allows polygamy. And while the courts eventually started to convert these potentially polygamous marriages to monogamous ones, the rule remains the same that these marriages are seen as polygamous by default. This upholds the emphasis on Anglican Christian monogamy in English family law. In other contexts, such as inheritance or welfare aid, the courts are again keen to focus on the polygamy in a marriage if it protects the public purse and state ideals of marriage. Finally, we see the courts' naked motives to protect imperial monogamy in the immigration cases concerning polygamous families. Protecting the state's borders and resources from *aliens* and their marriages is a top priority. Communities that practise minoritised forms of marriage are dehumanised while their relationships are manipulated to protect the colonial aims of civilising the colonised.

Conclusion

In this chapter, I looked at English legal definitions and understandings of marriage from the perspective of what is not covered by them. I argued that English weddings law is designed to restrict and dismiss any marriages that fail to fit within the colonial and Christian template that tells us how to get married and who can get married. Marriage creates a dividing line between people and communities who belong and are accepted and, crucially, those who are not. Drawing from the legislative framework and case law around the minoritised marriage practice of polygamy, I showed that this relationship is often acknowledged to emphasise the foreignness of communities. It is highlighted and used as a convenient excuse to deny these already vulnerable people their inheritance, state funding, and entry into the UK if there is a perceived threat to the idealised vision of English marriage. At its most extreme, marriage law can even operate to dehumanise people purely based on their relationship choices and family structure. In this chapter, I have not engaged with the question of whether polygamous marriage should be indiscriminately recognised in English law because there is no 'easy' answer to this question. However, a first step to dealing with the orientalising work of English marriage law is to acknowledge the forces that have shaped it in the first place. I therefore end this chapter with a question: how can we stop marriage law from being used as a tool to dehumanise the most marginalised in our communities?

Further questions to consider

- How do you think marriage should be defined in English law? What would be the key components of an 'ideal' definition?
- What kinds of requirements should a marriage ceremony involve as a minimum to be legally binding?
- Can you think of any other minoritised marriage practices being practised in England and Wales? What about around the world?
- How do you think the law around marriage can be changed to tackle its imperialist underpinnings?
- Are there any other problematic influences that you can see shaping ideals of marriage and marriage law in England and Wales?

Further materials

Akhtar RC, Nash P, and Probert R (eds), *Cohabitation and Religious Marriage: Status, Similarities and Solutions* (Bristol University Press 2020)

Bailey C, 'Love Multiplied: Sister Wives, Polygamy and Queering Heterosexuality' (2015) 32(1) Quarterly Review of Film and Video 38.

Brake E, *Minimizing Marriage: Marriage, Morality and the Law* (OUP 2012)

Calder G, and Beaman LG (eds), *Polygamy's Rights and Wrongs: Perspectives on Harm, Family and Law* (University of British Columbia Press 2014)

Ertman MM, 'Race Treason: The Untold Story of America's Ban on Polygamy' (2010) 19(2) Columbia Journal of Gender and Law 287

Franke K, *Wedlocked: The Perils of Marriage Equality* (New York University Press 2015)

Majeed D, *Polygyny: What It Means when African American Muslim Women Share their Husbands* (University Press of Florida 2015)

Roy A, 'Postcolonial Theory and Law: A Critical Introduction' (2008) 29(1–2) Adelaide Law Review 315

School of Law, Warwick University, 'Non-Legally Binding Weddings: Having a Nikah? Legal Things You Need to Think About' YouTube (4 May 2022) https://www.youtube.com/watch?v=k0OJHG5IbhY&t=2s, accessed 14 April 2024

Shah VA (director and producer), *Namastey London* [film] (2007)

True Vision TV, 'The Truth about Muslim Marriage' [TV documentary] (21 November 2017)

Wing AK, 'Polygamy from Southern Africa to Black Britannia to Black America: Global Critical Race Feminism as Legal Reform for the Twenty-First Century' (2001) 11(2) Journal of Contemporary Legal Issues 811

3

Assimilation or Difference? Same-Sex Relationship Recognition in England and Wales

Andy Hayward

Introduction

Same-sex relationships have existed throughout history yet their legal recognition in England and Wales is a relatively new phenomenon. For centuries marriage was seen as the gold standard relationship and, most importantly for this chapter, it was available to mixed-sex couples only. The glamourisation and romanticisation of marriage in art, literature, and culture created a strong societal attachment to this institution, which was buttressed by the church promoting the view that marriage was the only acceptable form of union for adult relationships. Indeed, it was the only union in which legitimate children could be born. Unsurprisingly, mixed-sex couples were encouraged, and financially incentivised, to marry.

Historically, same-sex relationships were subject to the full force of the criminal law, shifting from male sexual activity resulting in the death penalty in the Tudor period to life imprisonment in the Victorian.[1] However, following the process of decriminalisation of sexual activity between consenting adults in the Sexual Offences Act 1967, precipitated by the Wolfenden Report,[2] the state adopted an increasingly more tolerant approach. Towards the end of the 20th century, specific protections were created that recognised same-sex relationships in certain contexts. These, however, fell short of recognising same-sex couples as a family unit; this was only achieved through the introduction of the Civil Partnership Act 2004 (CPA). This created a registration regime that was 'marriage in all

---

[1] See eg S Cretney, *Same Sex Relationships: From 'Odious Crime' to 'Gay Marriage'* (OUP 2006).
[2] Committee on Homosexual Offences and Prostitution, *Report of the Committee on Homosexual Offences and Prostitution* (London 1957).

but name', conferring virtually the same rights and responsibilities of marriage. Crucially, parliamentarians and policy makers were keen at that time to stress that civil partnership was not 'gay marriage'.

Same-sex marriage was introduced following the Marriage (Same Sex Couples) Act 2013. With the first ceremonies taking place in March 2014, same-sex couples were finally granted access to what many view as a key institution embodying societal acceptability and citizenship. Interestingly, unlike many jurisdictions that phased out their registration regimes following marriage equality, England and Wales retained civil partnerships for same-sex couples from 2014 onwards and later opened that institution to mixed-sex couples in December 2019.

The position now reached could be said to be 'full equality'. Both same- and mixed-sex couples have a choice as to two relationship statuses – they can either marry or register a civil partnership. However, this chapter poses the more difficult question of how far genuine substantive equality has been realised. As will be revealed, legal distinctions between same- and mixed-sex couples do still exist and some of these are quite striking. More importantly, this chapter questions whether same-sex relationships are recognised in law on their own terms or if instead they have been assimilated into the institutions and practices of mixed-sex couples through their need to emulate a 'heterosexual' paradigm. Put differently, how far is legal recognition contingent on same-sex couples mimicking the relationship practices and marital norms associated with mixed-sex couples?

The first part of this chapter explores global trends and theoretical perspectives on same-sex couple recognition. It identifies different mechanisms used to confer legal protection and queries how far they pursue assimilation of same-sex couples or recognise their difference. The second part analyses civil partnerships, noting key debates surrounding their creation and questioning how far they challenge marital norms. The final part critiques same-sex marriage, exploring how far it can be said marriage equality exists and the future of civil partnerships as an alternative relationship status.

Summary of the relevant law

Same-sex couples in England and Wales presently have two ways of obtaining formal legal recognition of their relationship. Introduced in 2005, civil partnerships give couples virtually the same rights and responsibilities as spouses. Rather than divorcing, civil partners dissolve their union but the legal basis remains the same as that used by spouses, namely where the relationship has irretrievably broken down. Since December 2019, mixed-sex couples have been able to register civil partnerships. The other route to legal recognition is same-sex marriage, which, like civil partnership, largely equates the legal position with that of spouses. Religious exemptions apply, meaning that Church of England and Church in Wales clergy cannot officiate same-sex ceremonies and other religious organisations must opt in. Outside of formal recognition, same-sex couples can use contracts, trusts, and transfers of property to give legal effect to their relationship, while those who cohabit, rather than register a civil partnership or marry, will, in some circumstances, be recognised in law, for example, in the context of domestic abuse or succession.

Global trends in same-sex relationship recognition

At a global level, all countries permit mixed-sex couples to marry. In contrast, a comparatively small number of countries permit same-sex marriage. As of 2025, only 38 countries offer marriage to same-sex couples, with the Netherlands beginning this trend in 2001. In general, we see across the globe, and particularly in Europe, a gradual trend of countries extending marriage to same-sex couples. However, whether motivated by religion, conservatism, or right-wing populism, some countries staunchly refuse to permit same-sex marriage and may resist these trends by defining marriage in their constitutions as available to mixed-sex couples only.[3]

Countries rarely jump from no recognition of same-sex relationships to marriage equality. Rather, a common reform pattern is to introduce a registration regime,[4] known by various names, such as civil or registered partnerships or civil unions. They are often a compromise between the need for same-sex couples to gain some form of legal recognition while 'sidestepping or altogether avoiding the granting of marriage itself'.[5] When available to same-sex couples only, reform is often a stepping stone to marriage, with the registration regime then being phased out once same-sex marriage is ultimately introduced. Take Denmark, for example, which was the first country in the world to introduce same-sex registered partnerships in 1989 but then in 2012 phased out that regime once same-sex marriage was made available.[6]

Within this reform model, slight variations exist. Some alternatives are true 'functional equivalents to marriage' or 'marriage mimics',[7] replicating the rights and obligations of mixed-sex marriage, such as the UK CPA 2004. Others might confer most of the rights associated with marriage but omit particularly controversial ones such as those relating to child law, especially access to adoption or assisted reproductive technologies, pensions, and social security.

---

[3] See eg H Fenwick and D Fenwick, 'Finding "East"/"West" Divisions in Council of Europe States on Treatment of Sexual Minorities: The Response of the Strasbourg Court and the Role of Consensus Analysis' (2019) 3 European Human Rights Law Review 247.

[4] See JM Scherpe and A Hayward, *The Future of Registered Partnerships: Family Recognition Beyond Marriage?* (Intersentia 2017) and JM Scherpe, 'Why Registered Partnerships? A Comparative Overview' in R Probert and S Thompson (eds), *Research Handbook on Marriage, Cohabitation and the Law* (Edward Elgar 2024).

[5] E Aloni, 'A Queer Perspective on Property Protections in Marriage and Other Registered Partnerships' in M Briggs and A Hayward (eds), *Research Handbook on Family Property and the Law* (Edward Elgar 2024) 121, 125.

[6] See I Lund-Andersen, 'Registered Partnerships in Denmark' in Scherpe and Hayward (n4).

[7] See Aloni (n5) 127.

Some countries might create specific regimes for both same- and mixed-sex couples. This caters for the need for some type of recognition for the former and, at the same time, an alternative to marriage for the latter. Generally, these regimes operate even once same-sex marriage is created and so offer an alternative means of recognition for all couples. Variation exists here too. Some regimes confer identical rights to marriage, like the New Zealand civil union, whereas others, like the French pacte civil de solidarité or the Belgian cohabitation légale, confer lesser rights.[8] It is crucial to appreciate this distinction when questioning how far registration regimes might cater for the differing needs of couples.

What motivates the legal recognition of same-sex relationships?

Impetus for reform is often political. Concerted lobbying and activism by LGBT+ campaign groups and organisations lead to reform proposals that are then passed in accordance with a jurisdiction's political processes. This is often motivated by changing societal attitudes and public concerns as to discrimination and inequality. But that route to reform is not always the case. Some countries introduced same-sex marriage via a public referendum, such as Ireland,[9] whereas others obtain recognition through litigation. The right to same-sex marriage is constitutionally protected in the United States following the landmark US Supreme Court decision of *Obergefell v Hodges*,[10] and, following *Minister of Home Affairs v Fourie*, the Constitutional Court of South Africa used constitutional protections relating to sexual orientation discrimination to extend the common law definition of marriage to same-sex couples.[11]

At an international level, there is no right to same-sex marriage contained within a treaty or convention and its introduction is highly contingent on the political processes of any given state. However, within supranational organisations, positive obligations have been developed. For example, the European Convention on Human Rights (ECHR) protects the right to marry and found a family in Article 12 but it applies to mixed-sex couples only.[12] Despite this, Article 8 of the ECHR that protects to the right to respect for private and family life has been interpreted incrementally by the Strasbourg Court to impose a positive obligation on all member states to offer some form of legal protection

---

[8]   See chapters by L Francoz-Terminal, 'Registered Partnerships in France' and G Willems, 'Registered Partnerships in Belgium' in Scherpe and Hayward (n4).

[9]   See eg B Tobin, *The Legal Recognition of Same-Sex Relationships: Emerging Families in Ireland and Beyond* (Hart Publishing 2023). A variation is Australia where same-sex marriage was introduced following a postal vote.

[10]   576 US 644 (2015).

[11]   *Minister of Home Affairs and Another v Fourie and Another; Lesbian and Gay Equality Project and Others v Minister of Home Affairs and Others* [2005] ZACC 19.

[12]   See P Johnson and S Falcetta, 'Same-Sex Marriage and Article 12 of the European Convention on Human Rights' in C Ashford and A Maine (eds), *Research Handbook on Gender, Sexuality and the Law* (Edward Elgar 2018).

to same-sex couples. Falling short of requiring the introduction of same-sex marriage, principles derived from *Oliari and Others v Italy*,[13] and from *Fedotova and Others v Russia*, require member states to offer same-sex couples a means of formal legal recognition, like a civil or registered partnership.[14] However, the shape and content of such regime is left to the discretion of the state in question but must be adequate in terms of the legal effects conferred.

Theoretical perspectives on same-sex couple recognition

Protection of same-sex relationships is highly contingent on political processes. However, it is not as simple as persuading policy makers and politicians as to the merits of reform. It requires careful consideration of not only the political climate but also a regime's legal content and how far it meets the needs of the LGBT+ community. Just like the diversity of viewpoints possessed by mixed-sex couples, there is an equally diverse range of viewpoints among same-sex couples. Indeed, some same-sex couples applaud the advent of civil partnerships and same-sex marriage as a victory for equality, while others are more ambivalent and questioning of how far they are genuinely progressive innovations.

A tension is created between 'assimilation' of same-sex relationships within the existing legal structures utilised by mixed-sex couples and recognising 'difference' through acknowledging the lived experience of same-sex relationships. Calls for reform premised on assimilation largely arise from equality-based arguments and the need to treat same- and mixed-sex couples equally. The ban on same-sex marriage was discriminatory, as too was the ban on mixed-sex couples being able to register a civil partnership. Thus, as Wintemute notes, and referencing the 'separate but equal' motif used to justify racial segregation,

> There is no longer any justification for excluding same-sex couples from civil marriage and different-sex couples from civil partnership. It's like having separate drinking fountains or beaches for different racial groups, even though the water is the same! The only function of the twin ban is to mark lesbian and gay people as inferior to heterosexual people.[15]

Consequently, once same-sex couples had access to both institutions, demands had been met. In addition, some same-sex couples see equal access to such regimes

---

[13]   (Appl nos 18766/11 and 36030/11) Judgment of 21 July 2015. Discussed in A Hayward, 'Same-Sex Registered Partnerships: A Right to Be Recognised?' (2016) 75(1) Cambridge Law Journal 27.

[14]   (Appl nos 40792/10, 30538/14 and 43439/14) Judgment of 17 January 2023. Discussed in N Palazzo, 'Fedotova and Others v. Russia: Dawn of a New Era for European LGBTQ Families?' (2023) 30(2) Maastricht Journal of European and Comparative Law 216.

[15]   Equal Love Campaign 2010.

as important societal acknowledgement and validation of their relationships.[16] Inclusion speaks to their citizenship in society, dignity, and equal treatment by the law. Quite memorably, when faced with the argument that same-sex couples might undermine or challenge the foundations of marriage in the United States, the Supreme Court in *Obergefell* exemplified the trend of assimilation, with Justice Kennedy remarking, to the contrary, that 'It would misunderstand these men and women to say they disrespect the idea of marriage' and that 'Their plea is that they do respect it, respect it so deeply that they seek to find its fulfilment for themselves.'[17]

However, others might see these 'victories' differently and question the need for same-sex couples to 'assimilate'. Or, put differently, they might feel '[e]quality is granted, but only on heterosexual terms'.[18] That concern had long been present in England and Wales prior to civil partnerships being introduced in a line of cases concerning the definition of family for the purpose of succession to a tenancy.[19] In *Fitzpatrick v Sterling Housing Association*, a surviving same-sex partner sought to succeed to his deceased partner's tenancy after they lived together for 18 years. The House of Lords by a majority allowed the partner to succeed as 'a member of the tenant's family' based on how that relationship emulated marriage. Crucially, that generosity has been criticised because legal recognition was contingent on the relationship mimicking a heterosexual one. Lord Slynn, in particular, was highly influenced by the fact that the parties were in a 'longstanding, close, loving and faithful, monogamous, homosexual relationship'.[20] If that particular same-sex relationship had not emulated such features, it was highly likely recognition would have been denied. Diduck expressed a degree of ambivalence towards the judicial reasoning in *Fitzpatrick*, both welcoming legal recognition but questioning 'the extent that it supports the privilege of one particular image of family over others as worthy of that social benefit'.[21] This speaks to a much broader debate, identified by Herman, who asked whether, once lesbians and gay men can call themselves families or spouses, 'are the meanings of those words radicalized or are we simply accommodating ourselves to the existing structures and ideologies without subverting them?'[22]

---

[16] See HR Kennedy and RL Dalla, ' "It May Be Legal, But it is Not Treated Equally": Marriage Equality and Well-Being Implications for Same-Sex Couples' (2019) 32(1) Journal of Gay & Lesbian Social Services 67.

[17] 576 US 644 (2015) 681.

[18] K McK Norrie, 'Marriage is for Heterosexuals: May the Rest of Us Be Saved from It' (2000) 12(4) Child and Family Law Quarterly 363, 365.

[19] See also Notes, 'Looking for a Family Resemblance: The Limits of the Functional Approach to the Legal Definition of Family' (1991) 104 Harvard Law Review 1640.

[20] [2001] 1 AC 27, 32.

[21] A Diduck, 'A Family by Any Other Name ... or Starbucks™ Comes to England' (2001) 28(2) Journal of Law and Society 290, 309.

[22] D Herman, 'Are We Family? Lesbian Rights and Women's Liberation' (1990) 28(4) Osgoode Hall Law Journal 789, 790.

Broader questions arise as there are some same-sex couples opposed to any legal regulation of their relationship. They might argue that the state should not be involved in their private relationship and thus may be content with the lack of legal protections flowing from that decision.[23] Others might adopt a more ideologically informed stance, noting the longstanding oppression and institutionalised homophobia same-sex couples have endured.[24] Here, parallels exist with critiques of marriage by some feminists, who have argued that marriage represents a patriarchal and anti-egalitarian institution that oppresses women.[25] These perspectives prompt us to consider whether these statuses recognise the lived experience and relationship dynamics of same-sex couples. After all, the gendered division of labour within marriage between breadwinning and homemaking or concepts such as fidelity and monogamy may not necessarily align with the vision of an interpersonal relationship that some same-sex couples possess. The same could equally be said for mixed-sex couples, revealing a plurality of viewpoints regarding relationship recognition.

Summary

Marriage between mixed-sex couples is recognised across the globe, with comparatively few countries permitting same-sex marriage. The position is changing, with some countries creeping towards greater recognition through initially permitting civil partnerships as a precursor to marriage. Some of these regimes confer the same rights as marriage whereas others are less generous. This reform process generates fundamental questions regarding whether the regime should mimic marriage or offer something different. In turn, this forces us to reflect on whether same-sex couples should assimilate into structures traditionally conceived for mixed-sex couples and, by doing so, emulate norms and practices that may not align with how they view their own relationships.

The introduction of civil partnerships

Civil partnerships were introduced by the CPA 2004. The government stressed the rather problematic leitmotif of 'separate but equal'; thus, civil partnerships would operate in parallel to marriage but be distinct in terms of terminology. For example, marriages would be 'celebrated' whereas civil partnerships would be 'registered'. Civil partners would 'dissolve' their relationship unlike spouses who

---

23   A Rolfe and E Peel, 'It's a Double-Edged Thing: The Paradox of Civil Partnership and Why Some Couples are Choosing Not to Have One' (2011) 21(3) Feminism & Psychology 317.

24   See H Fenwick and A Hayward, 'From Same-Sex Marriage to Equal Civil Partnerships: On a Path towards "Perfecting" Equality?' (2018) 30(2) Child and Family Law Quarterly 97, 115–16.

25   See N Barker, *Not the Marrying Kind: A Feminist Critique of Same-Sex Marriage* (Palgrave Macmillan 2013) and C Chambers, *Against Marriage: An Egalitarian Defence of the Marriage-Free State* (OUP 2017).

would 'divorce'. Bigamy did not apply, instead it was 'perjury'.[26] This desire to differentiate helped with the passage of the Act and, as Browne and Nash note, there was 'little organised and mobilised opposition' to reform.[27]

Civil partnerships are a formal relationship status.[28] To create a civil partnership, couples must not be within the prohibited degrees, must be over the age of 18,[29] and cannot already be married or in a pre-existing civil partnership.[30] A failure to comply with these formalities will render the civil partnership void.[31]

This scheme was, until very recently, limited to same-sex couples. This was justified on the basis that mixed-sex couples had long been able to access religious and civil forms of marriage and, since same-sex marriage was not a politically viable option in 2004, a mechanism was needed to grant same-sex couples some legal recognition of their relationship.[32]

In a legal sense, civil partnerships are 'marriage in almost all but name' and, with few exceptions, civil partnership and civil marriage are similar in terms of the formalities for creation, legal consequences upon registration and dissolution.[33] Distinctions did exist when first introduced in relation to pension entitlements and the basis for dissolution.[34] For example, civil partners were unable to seek a dissolution based on adultery because that concept was defined in the common law as only applicable to sexual intercourse between mixed-sex couples. Instead, civil partners had to seek a dissolution based on their partner's 'behaviour'. Thankfully this distinction has now been removed by the Divorce, Dissolution and Separation Act 2020 (DDSA) that streamlines dissolution and divorce for all types of couples.

Interestingly, some distinctions remain. Unlike mixed-sex spouses, civil partners are unable to obtain a nullity order relating to the sexual elements of their relationship, for example incapacity or wilful refusal to consummate or on the

---

[26]   Section 80 Civil Partnership Act amends section 3(1) Perjury Act 2011 encompassing making a false statement.

[27]   K Browne and C Nash, 'Opposing Same-Sex Marriage, By Supporting Civil Partnerships: Resistances to LGBT Equalities' in N Barker and D Monk (eds), *From Civil Partnerships to Same-Sex Marriage: Interdisciplinary Reflections* (Routledge 2015) 61, 65.

[28]   See A Hayward, 'Registered Partnerships in England and Wales' in Scherpe and Hayward (n4) 187 and A Hayward, 'Civil Partnerships and the Repurposing of Relationship Formalisation: from Creating a Space to Developing a Script' (2025) 47(1) *Journal of Social Welfare and Family Law* 28.

[29]   Originally this was 16 but the age increased following section 3 of the Marriage and Civil Partnership (Minimum Age) Act 2022.

[30]   As mandated by the Civil Partnership Act 2004, section 3(1)(a)–(d).

[31]   Civil Partnership Act 2004, section 49.

[32]   See Department of Trade and Industry, 'Civil Partnership: A Framework for the Legal Recognition of Same-Sex Couples' (2003) 13.

[33]   B Hale, 'Homosexual Rights' (2004) 16(2) Child and Family Law Quarterly 125, 132. See also *Wilkinson v Kitzinger (No 2)* [2006] EWHC 2022 (Fam) [88] (Sir Mark Potter P).

[34]   *Walker v Innospec Limited and Others* [2017] UKSC 47.

basis that the respondent was suffering from a venereal disease at the time of the registration. These elements expose a tension with how far civil partnerships mirrored marriage in terms of expectations of intimacy and conjugality.

When introduced in England and Wales in December 2005, civil partnerships were very popular among the LGBT+ community. There were 1,227 registrations in the first three days of the Act coming into force, with 1,857 concluded by the end of that year (1,228 concluded between men and 629 between women). This is unsurprising given the pent-up demand for some form of legal recognition. The following full year of data (2006) saw 14,943 registrations, with 9,003 between men and 5,940 between women. As the regime became more established the total number of civil partnerships entered each year gradually decreased to around 6,000. Same-sex marriage was introduced in March 2014 and this precipitated a dramatic decrease in civil partnership registrations. Nevertheless, registrations have gradually increased and, interestingly, the demographic makeup of civil partners has changed too. In 2022 there were 1,119 registrations, with 58.2 per cent between male couples and 41.8 per cent between female couples.[35]

Civil partnerships in England and Wales have evolved too. Noting the potential of an alternative status to marriage, mixed-sex couples sought civil partnerships. Some campaigned believing that marriage was not the right 'fit' for them, whereas others rejected it on ideological grounds, viewing marriage as patriarchal, sexist, heteronormative, and exclusionary. Pressure for reform intensified once same-sex marriage was introduced, especially because same-sex couples could marry or enter a civil partnership while mixed-sex couples could only marry. In *R (on the Application of Steinfeld and Keidan) v Secretary of State for International Development*, the Supreme Court ruled that the ban on mixed-sex civil partnerships constituted discrimination under Articles 14 and 8 of the ECHR.[36] Change materialised via the Civil Partnerships, Marriages and Deaths (Registration etc) Act 2019 that compelled the Secretary of State to amend the CPA, by way of regulations. The Civil Partnership (Opposite-Sex Couples) Regulations 2019 came into force at the end of December 2019, granting mixed-sex couples access to civil partnerships in the same manner as same-sex couples. While the primary focus of this chapter is on same-sex couples, this development forces us to consider broader trends in relationship recognition.

---

[35] Office for National Statistics (ONS), 'Civil Partnerships in England and Wales: 2022' https://www.ons.gov.uk/peoplepopulationandcommunity/birthsdeathsandmarriages/marriagecohabitationandcivilpartnerships/bulletins/civilpartnershipsinenglandandwales/2022, accessed 29 February 2024.

[36] [2018] UKSC 32. See A Hayward, 'Taking the Time to Discriminate: *R (on the Application of Steinfeld and Keidan) v Secretary of State for International Development*' (2019) 41(1) Journal of Social Welfare and Family Law 92 and A Hayward, 'Equal Civil Partnerships, Discrimination and the Indulgence of Time' (2019) 82(5) Modern Law Review 922.

Evaluation

Civil partnerships generate important questions that go to the heart of how we regulate adult relationships. The first issue is why a separate registration regime was adopted and the associated symbolism of that choice. Indeed, creating a separate regime (of substantively the same rights and entitlements) seems to contradict equal treatment under the law and loftier notions of equality, more generally. It is particularly difficult to reconcile with the government's position that billed civil partnerships as an 'important equality measure'[37] introduced on the basis of 'general equality and social justice'.[38]

When civil partnerships were first mooted, some commentators favoured the simpler solution of extending marriage to same-sex couples. Peter Tatchell, a well-known human rights and LGBT+ activist, advocated for same-sex marriage and argued that reserving marriage for mixed-sex couples and civil partnership for same-sex couples created a system of segregation.[39] He argued that 'By legislating a two-tier system of relationship recognition Labour has, in effect, created a form of legal apartheid based on sexual orientation.'[40] The difficulty, however, with this argument is that the type of reform introduced was always a political choice subject to diverse opinions among the public. Many religious groups opposed same-sex marriage at that time, with some even rejecting civil partnerships too, believing them to be a form of 'counterfeit marriage'.[41] Thus, while with hindsight and to modern eyes it might appear strange that same-sex marriage was not sought originally, there were, arguably, political justifications for the government's approach.

Similarly, pragmatism and compromise were considerations too – indeed, Stychin viewed the CPA as 'a victory for the politics of compromise' rather than 'an achievement of the legal imagination'.[42] Although Kitzinger and Wilkinson saw civil partnerships as a 'painful compromise between genuine equality and no rights at all',[43] they and other activists also accepted that they were a step towards same-sex marriage. Introducing civil partnerships as a precursor to marriage can be seen as a tactical move too. By creating a regime conferring near identical rights to marriage, it becomes very difficult to resist same-sex marriage

---

[37]   Department of Trade and Industry (n32) 13.

[38]   Department of Trade and Industry, 'Responses to Civil Partnership: A Framework for the Legal Recognition of Same-Sex Couples' (2003) 21 https://www.rightsnet.org.uk/pdfs/Civil_partnership_Nov_2003.pdf, accessed 23 July 2025.

[39]   P Tatchell, 'Civil Partnerships Are Divorced from Reality' *The Guardian* (19 December 2005).

[40]   Ibid.

[41]   See eg The Christian Institute, *Counterfeit Marriage: How Civil Partnerships Devalue the Currency of Marriage* (The Christian Institute 2002).

[42]   C Stychin, 'Not (Quite) a Horse and Carriage: The Civil Partnership Act 2004' (2006) 14(1) Feminist Legal Studies 79.

[43]   S Wilkinson and C Kitzinger, 'In Support of Equal Marriage: Why Civil Partnership is Not Enough' (2006) 8(1) Psychology of Women Review 54.

in the future because all that change would involve is modifying the specific label attached to a relationship rather than the rights conferred.[44] It would be a semantic, rather than substantive, change. That said, some did not share that optimism at that time and felt that civil partnerships were effectively 'marriage-lite'[45] or a 'consolation prize'.[46] This reveals how same-sex couple recognition goes much further than the ability to access legal entitlements; it speaks to broader concepts of public acceptance, citizenship, and dignity.

A further issue is the paradoxical nature of civil partnerships; that is, they are both different from marriage while, at the same time, effectively a carbon copy of it. This tension led Barker and Monk to note that modelling the CPA on marriage law meant that it too could be open to attack, just in the same way that marriage had been attacked by feminist and queer scholars.[47]

Within the process of differentiation, we also see potential discrimination and contradictions, especially regarding sexual intimacy between civil partners. When civil partnership was first introduced, a civil partner was unable to obtain a dissolution based on their partner's 'adultery' because that concept, informed by religion, was defined in heterosexual terms.[48] In a similar vein, civil partners remain unable to dissolve their relationship on the basis of grounds relating to sexual activity such as non-consummation. When questioned on these omissions, Baroness Scotland explained it was the state not wishing to 'look at the nature of the sexual relationship' because civil partnership was 'totally different in nature' to marriage.[49] Other less explicitly articulated justifications might be the uneasiness of judges having to enquire, let alone define, how same-sex couples consummate their relationship. However, this approach, as Maine has argued, is problematic because it 'unjustifiably reinforces a notional sexual hierarchy by enshrining heterosexual sex as natural and necessary – and dismissing all other sexual acts as at best irrelevant'.[50]

As a potential solution, Crompton argued that we should adopt a broader concept of 'sexual intimacy' capable of embracing same-sex couples.[51] This would favour inclusivity because '[i]f gay people are to be viewed as capable of

---

[44]   See eg S Cummings and D NeJaime, 'Lawyering for Marriage Equality' (2010) 57(5) UCLA Law Review 1235.

[45]   See R Harding, *Regulating Sexuality: Legal Consciousness in Lesbian and Gay Lives* (Routledge 2010) 68.

[46]   *Wilkinson v Kitzinger (No 2)* [2006] EWHC 2022 (Fam) [5] (Sir Mark Potter P).

[47]   N Barker and D Monk, 'From Civil Partnership to Same-Sex Marriage: A Decade in British Legal History' in Barker and Monk (n27) 5.

[48]   See *Clarkson v Clarkson* (1930) 143 LT 775 and *Dennis v Dennis* [1955] P 153. See also the Matrimonial Causes Act (MCA) 1973, s 1(6).

[49]   HL Deb 17 November 2004, col 1479.

[50]   A Maine, 'Queer(y)ing Consummation: An Empirical Reflection on the Marriage (Same Sex Couples) Act 2013 and the Role of Consummation' (2021) 33(2) Child and Family Law Quarterly 143, 160.

[51]   L Crompton, 'Where's the Sex in Same-Sex Marriage' (2013) 43(5) Family Law 564.

having a committed relationship equivalent to marriage, it needs to be overtly acknowledged that they have sex'.[52] However, arguably a preferable solution would be instead for the law to remove consummation as a nullity basis entirely. Instead, as Herring has argued, we should shift our focus away from conjugality and to other more pressing concerns of family law such as, for example, the provision and recognition of care.[53] Here we see an instance of 'difference' as distinct from assimilation, albeit on questionable grounds.

Another issue regarding infidelity is that this approach failed to recognise bisexual civil partners. Such individuals could have actually fallen within the common law definition of 'adultery' under the old law if one partner had sexual intercourse with a member of the opposite sex. Indeed, the approach adopted to same-sex spouses prior to the introduction of the DDSA could have been applied to same-sex civil partners, whereby sexual intercourse with a member of the opposite sex would constitute as adultery while intercourse with a member of the same sex would not and should fall under behaviour. Nevertheless, the approach taken was to send mixed messages about sexual intimacy by not outrightly denying its existence in civil partnerships yet failing to acknowledge it. That position continued after mixed-sex civil partnerships were permitted in December 2019. Prior to the DDSA coming into force in April 2022, mixed-sex civil partners could not petition for adultery (thus denying a sexual dimension to the relationship) but where a female civil partner gave birth to a child, the male civil partner was presumptively treated as the father (thus suggesting a sexual dimension).

These examples expose much broader tensions between recognising difference and assimilation. Given that civil partnerships are effectively a replication of marriage, it would be difficult for same-sex couples to create a brand-new regime recognising their relationship cognisant of their lived experiences. For example, a regime could have permitted more than two individuals registering, which would respond to empirical data showing considerable engagement with non-monogamy and non-dyadic relationships among same-sex couples.[54] But civil partnerships, like marriage, can only be entered into by two individuals. While there is less of a cultural script surrounding civil partnerships seeing as they are a 'construct of statute' and thus, at face value, possess greater scope for couple innovation,[55] their derivation from marriage law restricts creativity. For Glennon, this aspect is disappointing because civil partnerships could have been more radical

---

[52] Ibid, 573.

[53] J Herring, 'Why Marriage Needs to Be Less Sexy' in J Miles, P Mody, and R Probert (eds), *Marriage Rites and Rights* (Hart Publishing 2015).

[54] See eg C Klesse, 'Non-Monogamy, Heteronormativity and the Marriage Debate in the Bisexual Movement' (2006) 7(2) Lesbian & Gay Psychology Review 162 and CH Hoff and SC Beougher, 'Sexual Agreements among Gay Male Couples' (2010) 39(3) Archives of Sexual Behaviour 774.

[55] *R v Bala and Others* [2016] EWCA Crim 560 [38] (Davies LJ).

than they are by recognising a much broader range of relationships.[56] Platonic relationships, carers, or siblings could have been included within the regime.

Since the extension of civil partnerships to mixed-sex couples, there may be early signs of creativity. However, this lies not in relation to the legal framework, which is unyielding and not capable of personalisation by the parties, but instead in relation to how civil partners view their status. Couples, especially mixed-sex ones, are embracing the idea that civil partnerships can be conceptualised as 'a blank slate on which people can inscribe their own hopes and dreams'.[57] Couples are, for example, developing their own traditions and rites in relation to proposals and engagements,[58] and revisiting/reclaiming the ceremony itself.[59] This trend is also present within marriage too, with recent research showing how couples who used independent celebrants sought to tweak traditions or innovate and personalise ceremonial elements.[60]

A similar hope of recognising difference was expressed regarding how civil partners might divide assets. Like spouses, Schedule 5 of the CPA allows civil partners to have their property divided by a court using a structured judicial discretion with the aim of achieving fairness. The first reported case, *Lawrence v Gallagher*, saw the Court of Appeal adopt the exact same approach to division of assets as that used between mixed-sex spouses.[61] In one sense, that choice emphasised equality of treatment between spouses and same-sex civil partners and aligns with the central message of civil partnerships as a parallel institution to marriage. However, it can be viewed as a disappointment. Rather than recognising same-sex relationships and how same-sex partners might hold their property on their own terms, the court applied a set of principles that were created, and developed by the courts, for mixed-sex couples. It applied principles of sharing that were created in response to a longstanding gendered division of labour, whereby traditionally the husband would be the breadwinner and the wife the homemaker. This is a dynamic that may not align with same-sex relationships. These principles were largely devised to protect the economic

---

56   L Glennon, 'Displacing the "Conjugal Family" in Legal Policy: A Progressive Move?' (2005) 17(2) Child and Family Law Quarterly 141.

57   R Steinfeld and C Keidan, 'Our Fight for Right to Civil Partnership is Finally Won', *Evening Standard* (29 November 2019).

58   See A Jowett and E Peel, 'Reshaping Relational Scripts? Marriage and Civil Partnership Proposals among Same-Gender Couples' (2019) 10(4) Psychology & Sexuality 325.

59   See N Hayfield and others, 'Exploring Civil Partnership from the Perspective of Those in Mixed-Sex Relationships: Embracing a Clean Slate of Equality' (2023) 45(8) Journal of Family Issues 1925 and A Hayward, 'Mixed-Sex Civil Partnerships: A Blank Canvas or Painting by Numbers?' in Probert and Thompson (eds), (n4) 237.

60   See S Blake and others, 'Independent Celebrant-Led Wedding Ceremonies: Translating, Tweaking, and Innovating Traditions' (2023) Sociological Research Online https://doi.org/10.1177/13607804231211443, accessed 5 June 2025.

61   [2012] EWCA Civ 394. Discussed in R George, '*Lawrence v Gallagher* [2012] EWCA Civ 394: Playing a Straight Bat in Civil Partnership Appeals?' (2012) 34(3) Journal of Social Welfare and Family Law 357.

position of wives as they were statistically more likely to make domestic, rather than financial, contributions to the marriage. The emerging literature shows that same-sex couples adopt more varied and egalitarian patterns of owning, enjoying, and dividing assets, with one study revealing that female same-sex couples are more likely to share domestic tasks equally than male same-sex couples.[62] While acknowledging distinct practices among same-sex couples, the study also reinforced the important point that 'Partners in same-sex relationships have also been raised in mostly heterosexual house-holds in heteronormative societies, exposing them to the same normative forces as heterosexuals.'[63]

Summary

Civil partnership is a formal status introduced in December 2005 via the CPA 2004. This regime confers upon the couple largely identical rights and responsibilities to those obtained through marriage. Same-sex couples are subject to virtually the same legal protections as spouses. While originally civil partners could not end their relationship based on their partner's adultery (through a process called dissolution), since 2020 civil partnerships can be dissolved in the exact same way and on the same basis as spouses when they divorce.[64] Civil partnerships were originally conceived as an institution intended for use exclusively by same-sex couples at a time when marriage was not available; however, campaigning by mixed-sex couples paved the way for civil partnerships being extended to these couples too. This occurred via regulations created pursuant to the Civil Partnerships, Marriages and Deaths (Registration etc) Act 2019. While statistically more same-sex couples marry, a proportion of same-sex couples continue to register civil partnerships each year.

Introducing same-sex marriage

Shortly after the introduction of civil partnerships there were calls to introduce same-sex marriage and in 2012 a consultation was undertaken.[65] At this point in time, a marriage between two people of the same sex would be treated as void *ab initio*,[66] and would be considered contrary to the common law definition of marriage as a union of one man and one woman.[67] The consultation received

---

[62]   M van der Vleuten, E Jaspers, and T van der Lippe, 'Same-Sex Couples' Division of Labor from a Cross-National Perspective' (2021) 17(1) Journal of GLBT Family Studies 1.

[63]   Ibid, 1.

[64]   See the Divorce, Dissolution and Separation Act 2020.

[65]   Government Equalities Office, 'Equal Civil Marriage: A Consultation' (2012) https://assets.publishing.service.gov.uk/media/5a7acf6840f0b66a2fc02f5b/consultation-document_1_.pdf, accessed 23 July 2025.

[66]   MCA 1973 section 11(c).

[67]   See *Hyde v Hyde & Woodmansee* (1866) LR 1 P&D 130.

the highest ever response rate from members of the public, which indicates that it was a topic which generated strong opinions. On the question of whether same-sex civil marriage should be introduced, 53 per cent of the respondents were in favour.

The consultation exercise and government response revealed concerns regarding religious freedoms. This was to be expected as most mainstream religious organisations, such as the Church of England, Catholic Church, and Muslim Council of Britain, were opposed to same-sex marriage. After reflecting on the responses received, the government stated its commitment to propose new legislation to enable same-sex marriage while being mindful of the need to protect religious organisations.

Key to balancing those aims was what was termed the 'quadruple lock', which was a set of religious exemptions. These exemptions ensured that religious organisations were required to 'opt in', with the Church in England and Church in Wales being statutorily prohibited from doing so. A religious marriage ceremony of a same-sex couple would only be possible if the governing body of the religious organisation had opted in, the individual minister was willing to conduct the marriage, and the ceremony took place in a place of worship. No religious organisation would be compelled to celebrate a same-sex marriage and it would not be unlawful discrimination under the Equality Act 2010 for an organisation or individual to refuse to marry a same-sex couple. The final element of the 'quadruple lock' was that the legislation would not affect the Church of England's canon law meaning that, for those purposes, marriage would remain defined as a union between a man and a woman and the common law duty to marry parishioners does not extend to same-sex couples. The government was confident that this position would be compatible with the UK's obligations under the ECHR, particularly as that Convention does not recognise a right to same-sex marriage under Articles 8 or 12 and Article 9 expressly protects religious freedom. Ultimately, it would be for the General Synod to determine whether religious same-sex marriages should take place in the future.

Same-sex marriage was introduced in England and Wales through the Marriage (Same Sex Couples) Act 2013, with the first ceremonies taking place from midnight on the 29 March 2014. The introduction proved popular, with 4,850 same-sex marriages celebrated in 2014.[68] On average there has been a yearly increase in the number of same-sex marriages celebrated. Interestingly, it has always been the case that more female couples marry than male couples. In 2022 there were 4,896 female same-sex marriages in comparison to 2,904 male same-sex marriages.

The legal effects of same-sex marriage are virtually identical to those for mixed-sex marriages. However, a distinction was drawn in relation to adultery (which

---

[68]   ONS, 'Marriages in England and Wales: 2021 and 2022' https://www.ons.gov.uk/peoplepop ulationandcommunity/birthsdeathsandmarriages/marriagecohabitationandcivilpartnerships/ bulletins/marriagesinenglandandwalesprovisional/2021and2022, accessed 20 June 2024.

was later removed by the DDSA 2020) and same-sex spouses cannot obtain a nullity of marriage order because of incapacity of either party or wilful refusal of the respondent to consummate. Section 9 of the Act offers same-sex civil partners the ability to convert their civil partnership to marriage, with section 9(6) stipulating that the parties will be treated as married from the date of the civil partnership and not the marriage. It is not possible for same-sex spouses (or mixed-sex spouses) to convert their marriage to a civil partnership.

An interesting dimension in the introduction of same-sex marriage was the approach taken to civil partnerships. In contrast to other countries that phased out their same-sex civil partnership regimes after introducing same-sex marriage, the UK government sought to evade this issue, preferring to secure same-sex marriage at all costs. The strategy adopted compelled the Secretary of State to conduct a review as to the future of civil partnerships. The Department for Culture, Media and Sport undertook this review, but the level of public engagement was far from that seen in the earlier Equal Civil Marriage consultation.[69] Findings of the review revealed that same-sex civil partnerships were valued and 55 per cent of respondents opposed them being phasing out. However, there was little support for extending civil partnerships to mixed-sex couples (only 22 per cent of respondents were in favour). The review accepted that there was no 'united call for change',[70] and no further action was taken. Since the consultation exercise was concluded only months after the introduction of same-sex marriage it is perhaps unsurprising that the results were inconclusive: more time was needed to analyse the uptake of same-sex civil partnerships following the availability of same-sex marriage in March 2014.

Evaluation

The introduction of same-sex marriage can, in many ways, be seen as an important victory for LGBT+ rights. However, there are remaining issues, notably the position of same-sex couples of faith wishing to marry in accordance with their religious beliefs and the relationship between same-sex marriage and civil partnerships.

Religious exemptions and same-sex marriage

Religious exemptions can be seen as antagonistic to the realisation of full equality between mixed- and same-sex couples. Marrying in accordance with

---

[69] Department for Culture, Media and Sport, 'Civil Partnership Review (England and Wales): A Consultation' (2014) https://assets.publishing.service.gov.uk/media/5a7c6ef4ed915d696ccfc bf4/140122_CP_con_doc_pdf__docx.pdf, accessed 23 July 2025.

[70] Department for Culture, Media and Sport, 'Civil Partnership Review (England and Wales): Report on Conclusions' (2014) 4 https://assets.publishing.service.gov.uk/media/5a75a a0a40f0b67b3d5c8405/Civil_Partnership_Review_Report_PDF.pdf, accessed 23 July 2025.

one's religion is significant in that it allows individuals to enact traditions, obtain acceptance within a broader community, and evidence commitment in a manner sacred to the couple.[71] Religious same-sex couples wishing to marry but belonging to a religious organisation that refuses to celebrate such unions must find a religious organisation that has opted in. The difficulty here is that very few religious organisations have opted in, with the Law Commission noting that of the 22,334 places of worship in England and Wales, only 292 places (amounting to 1.3 per cent) are registered for same-sex marriages.[72] Another study revealed that where couples belonged to a denomination that had not opted in, they often engaged in a difficult process of 'church shopping', potentially being met with hostility.[73] Couples with fervent religious convictions were in a particularly difficult position, potentially having to enter a civil marriage as no suitable religious option was available to them.

It is not unusual for religious exemptions to exist and they are present in other European countries.[74] Similarly, even when same-sex marriage is introduced, there is sometimes evidence of distinctions drawn in relation to legal entitlements too. Greece, for example, introduced same-sex marriage in February 2024 but the law does not go so far as permitting such couples access to assisted reproduction technologies or surrogacy. While some might find this an afront to equality, others may see this as an inevitable consequence of balancing competing interests and evidences family law and policy developing incrementally.

The position of religious organisations is, however, beginning to change. In July 2024 the General Synod of the Church of England voted in favour of proposals to allow gay members of the clergy to marry. This builds on developments in 2023 where the General Synod voted in favour of permitting standalone blessings for same-sex couples that would look and feel like a church wedding.[75] Crucially, this would not be treated in law as a same-sex marriage and a couple would need to enter a civil marriage for legal recognition of the union. Interestingly, respondents to the aforementioned study by Falcetta, Johnson, and Vanderbeck

---

[71] See eg R Sandberg, *Religion and Marriage Law: The Need for Reform* (Bristol University Press 2021) chapter 3.

[72] Law Commission, *Celebrating Marriage: A New Weddings Law* (Law Com No 408, 2022) 280–1, para 8.22. See also R Probert, 'Why Universal Civil Marriage Is Not the Answer' (2024) 36(1) Child and Family Law Quarterly 15.

[73] S Falcetta, P Johnson, and RM Vanderbeck, 'The Experience of Religious Same-Sex Marriage in England and Wales: Understanding the Opportunities and Limits Created by the Marriage (Same Sex Couples) Act 2013' (2021) 35(1) International Journal of Law, Policy and the Family 1, 15.

[74] P Johnson and RM Vanderbeck, 'Sacred Spaces, Sacred Words: Religion and Same-Sex Marriage in England and Wales' (2017) 44(2) Journal of Law and Society 228.

[75] The Church of England Press Release, 'Synod Signals Support for "Anglican Way Forward" on Same-Sex Relationships' (8 July 2024) https://www.churchofengland.org/media/press-releases/synod-signals-support-anglican-way-forward-same-sex-relationships, accessed 12 August 2024.

did not favour legal reform compelling 'overtly homophobic churches' to marry same-sex couples, believing instead that religious freedom and tolerance should be respected.[76] These more tentative developments may see religious organisations changing their position over time resulting in further equalisation of the legal treatment between mixed- and same-sex couples.

The relationship between same-sex marriage and civil partnerships

Introducing same-sex marriage prompted another important discussion as to the continuing need for same-sex civil partnerships. When compared to other jurisdictions, England and Wales took the rather unusual step of retaining same-sex civil partnerships while extending marriage to same-sex couples, thus reviving debates surrounding assimilation and difference. Were civil partnerships needed now that same-sex couples could marry? Similarly, could 'difference' be recognised by same-sex civil partnerships developing in a separate and ideologically different manner to marriage? Multiple positions were adopted but three key themes emerged.[77]

First, same-sex civil partnerships were seen by some as redundant because the long sought-after prize of same-sex marriage had finally been achieved. The language of equality was very noticeable in the debates on the Marriage (Same Sex Couples) Bill, with Yvette Cooper MP considering same-sex marriage as 'the next step for equality'.[78] Similarly, academic commentary acknowledged how same-sex couple recognition was often an incremental process, with same-sex marriage as the 'final stop for "full equality" for lesbian and gay men'.[79] Baroness Hale, writing extra-judicially, noted these stages in LGBT+ history, beginning from a position of criminal punishment and moving to legal recognition, remarking that '[t]he final steps are taken by family law' encompassing a state 'providing for registered civil partnerships, and finally … for civil marriage'.[80] Adopting this perspective, it can be questioned why same-sex couples might want a civil partnership when they served, as one judge noted, an 'essentially transitional purpose, designed to alleviate the disadvantages which then affected same-sex couples, but do not now'.[81]

The difficulty with this argument is the way that it homogenises same-sex relationships and channels them towards marriage, which is a status that some same-sex couples do not want to access. Moreover, the belief that there

---

[76]   Falcetta, Johnson, and Vanderbeck (n73) 24.
[77]   See eg A Hayward, 'Relationships with Status: Civil Partnerships in an Era of Same-Sex Marriage' in F Hamilton and G Noto La Diega (eds), *Same-Sex Relationships, Law and Social Change* (Routledge 2020) 189.
[78]   HC Deb 5 February 2013, vol 558, col 136.
[79]   See Barker (n25) 2.
[80]   Hale (n33) 125.
[81]   *Steinfeld and Keidan v Secretary of State for Education* [2017] EWCA Civ 81 [172] (Briggs LJ).

is a standard reform model or universally followed path for same-sex couple recognition can be challenged too. While most countries phase out same-sex-only civil partnerships once marriage is available, that is not always the case. For example, Austria introduced same-sex marriage in 2019 and, at the same time, both retained their same-sex-only civil partnership regime while opening it up to mixed-sex couples. Similarly, countries that offered civil partnerships to both same- and mixed-sex couples often retain them once same-sex marriage is introduced. This reveals that the inevitability that a certain reform pattern will occur can be questioned and countries are now embracing the idea that formalisation can encompass a range of options for couples. This reflects what Eskridge has termed a 'sedimentary' approach whereby the drive towards same-sex marriage has created the potential for pre-existing regimes to evolve, with new institutions developing on top of existing ones.[82] Equality need not be achieved through marriage alone.

A second argument present in the discourse surrounding reform was the assumed inferiority of civil partnerships versus the more established and superior status of marriage. Indeed, it was questioned why same-sex couples might want what some considered a weak carbon copy of marriage. Contrasting civil partnerships with marriage naturally created this division of opinion. Harding, for example, saw civil partnerships as 'marriage-lite: same great taste, half the respect of regular marriage'.[83] Similarly, Waaldijk conceptualised civil partnerships as poorer versions of marriage, creating a typology of non-marital institutions that were 'quasi-marriage' or 'semi-marriage'.[84] In addition, retaining this status could also be viewed as furthering *inequality* because it would act as a painful reminder that civil partnerships were originally conceived to *segregate* same-sex couples from mixed-sex couples. As Wiseman notes, civil partnerships are 'still smoky with the stench of its history as a consolation prize to gay couples when a homophobic society, under pressure to modernise, was still unable to bring itself to fling open the doors to "actual" marriage'.[85]

However, these status-based arguments can also be countered. It is true that when first introduced, some judges emphasised how civil partnerships were merely a registration regime.[86] Their discussion conceptualised civil partnerships as almost sterile or purely administrative in nature, which perhaps was to be expected given the policy position adopted of repeatedly emphasising how civil

---

[82] WN Eskridge Jr, *Equality Practice Civil Unions and the Future of Gay Rights* (Routledge 2013) 121.

[83] R Harding, ' "Dogs are 'Registered', People Shouldn't Be": Legal Consciousness and Lesbian and Gay Rights' (2006) 15(4) Social and Legal Studies 511, 524.

[84] K Waaldijk, 'Others May Follow: The Introduction of Marriage Quasi-Marriage, and Semi-Marriage for Same-Sex Couples in European Countries' (2003–04) 38(3) New England Law Review 569, 583.

[85] E Wiseman, 'New Ways to Say I Love You: Without Slavery and Homophobia' *The Guardian* (8 July 2018).

[86] See *Ghaidan v Godin-Mendoza* [2004] UKHL 30 [96] (Lord Nicholls).

partnerships were distinct from, and thus not a direct threat to, marriage. The stance could be anticipated too, as from their inception civil partnerships are a 'construct of statute'[87] without a historical legacy, ceremonial rites, or an ideology like that associated with marriage. But arguably, that position no longer is the case and civil partnerships have now been elevated to a meaningful status for couples to express commitment.[88] In 2014 the Department for Culture, Media and Sport stated that civil partnership had now become a 'well-understood legal institution' playing 'an important role in the lives of many couples'.[89]

More recent empirical studies show that while some same-sex couples see civil partnerships as redundant owing to the availability of marriage, others embrace the status as 'a modern form of relationship recognition free from the cultural and historical "baggage" of marriage'.[90] These sentiments align with those expressed by mixed-sex couples in their campaign for civil partnerships to be extended to them. Although Miles and Probert have questioned how far some of these desires can be recognised in law (given the close similarity between civil partnership and marriage),[91] a nascent ideology of civil partnership is emerging, emphasising differentiation from marriage.[92]

A final argument questioning the need for civil partnerships was their uptake after same-sex marriage was introduced. In 2013, there were 5,646 civil partnership registrations but after the introduction of same-sex marriage in March 2014, this number decreased to 1,683.[93] The following year that number dropped to 861. Clearly this shows that the availability of same-sex marriage impacted the civil partnership rate. For some, civil partnerships had become a 'legacy relationship' and that when same-sex couples are confronted with a choice, they opt for marriage.[94] However, this picture is complicated by the fact that from 2016 onwards there has been a gradual, albeit small, increase in civil partnership

---

[87]   *R v Bala and Others* [2016] EWCA Crim 560 [38] (Davies LJ).

[88]   See eg *Bull v Hall* [2013] UKSC 73 [26] and *Radmacher v Granatino* [2010] UKSC 42.

[89]   Department for Culture, Media and Sport (n69) para 1.4 https://assets.publishing.service. gov.uk/media/5a7c6ef4ed915d696ccfcbf4/140122_CP_con_doc_pdf__docx.pdf, accessed 23 July 2025.

[90]   A Jowett and E Peel, ' "A Question of Equality and Choice": Same-Sex Couples' Attitudes towards Civil Partnership after the Introduction of Same-Sex Marriage' (2017) 8(1–2) Psychology and Sexuality 69, 75.

[91]   J Miles and R Probert, 'Civil Partnership: Ties That (Also) Bind?' (2019) 31(4) Child and Family Law Quarterly 303.

[92]   See A Hayward, 'New Models of Registered Partnership Reform: Embracing Family Recognition beyond Marriage?' in M Breger (ed), *Exploring Norms and Family Laws across the Globe* (Lexington Publishers 2022) 35.

[93]   ONS, 'Civil Partnerships in England and Wales: 2016' (26 September 2017) https://www. ons.gov.uk/peoplepopulationandcommunity/birthsdeathsandmarriages/marriagecohabitationa ndcivilpartnerships/bulletins/civilpartnershipsinenglandandwales/2016, accessed 23 July 2025.

[94]   Department for Culture, Media and Sport (n69) para 3.10 https://assets.publishing.service. gov.uk/media/5a7c6ef4ed915d696ccfcbf4/140122_CP_con_doc_pdf__docx.pdf, accessed 23 July 2025.

registrations. In 2016, for example, 890 civil partnerships were formed in England and Wales, representing an increase of 3.4 per cent compared with the previous year.[95] More recently, in 2022, there were 1,119 same-sex civil partnerships registered.[96] While this figure, when compared to 7,800 same-sex marriages celebrated that year, appears low, it does indicate that some same-sex couples still wish to register civil partnerships.[97]

Another dimension to appreciate is conversion data. Conversion from a civil partnership to marriage was permitted by the 2013 Act but relatively few same-sex couples have converted their civil partnership. In 2016, approximately one in eight civil partnerships were converted to marriages,[98] leading to Tim Loughton MP to observe that 'more than 80% of same-sex couples who have committed to a civil partnership do not think that they need to or want to convert that into marriage'.[99] This offers another piece of evidence indicating a cohort of same-sex couples that still value retaining their status as civil partners.

Summary

Same-sex marriage was introduced in March 2014 following the Marriage (Same Sex Couples) Act 2013. The Act renders same-sex marriage lawful and same-sex spouses are treated the same way in law as mixed-sex spouses. Owing to concerns of religious organisations, significant exceptions were created in that Act. For example, while all same-sex couples can enter civil marriages, Church of England and Church in Wales clergy are statutorily banned from officiating same-sex ceremonies. Other religious organisations are not expressly banned by the Act but have instead been given the ability to opt in to the framework, if they wish to do so. In practice, very few religious organisations have agreed to celebrate same-sex weddings.[100] Same-sex civil partners may convert their relationship to a same-sex marriage. However, this ability is not available for mixed-sex civil partnerships nor can either same- or mixed-sex spouses convert their marriage to a civil partnership. Same-sex marriage has proved very popular, particularly among younger same-sex couples, and in 2022 there were 7,800 marriages celebrated (in comparison to 239,097 marriages between mixed-sex couples).[101]

---

[95] ONS (n93).

[96] ONS, 'Civil Partnerships in England and Wales: 2022' https://www.ons.gov.uk/peoplepop ulationandcommunity/birthsdeathsandmarriages/marriagecohabitationandcivilpartnerships/ bulletins/civilpartnershipsinenglandandwales/2022, accessed 29 February 2024.

[97] ONS (n68).

[98] See J Haskey, 'Civil Partnerships and Same-Sex Marriages in England and Wales: A Social and Demographic Perspective' (2016) *Family Law* 44 and J Haskey, 'Perspectives on Civil Partnerships and Marriages in England and Wales: Aspects, Attitudes and Assessments' (2021) Family Law 816.

[99] HC Deb 2 February 2018, vol 635, col 1142.

[100] Falcetta, Johnson, and Vanderbeck (n73).

[101] ONS (n68).

Conclusion

The approach to the legal recognition of same-sex relationships has evolved dramatically over a comparatively short period of time. In the space of 20 years, we have moved from a position of very limited legal recognition of same-sex couples as a family unit to the introduction of same-sex marriage. While further work is needed to strengthen the legal position of same-sex relationships and tackle homophobia in society, from a legal perspective some might argue that the position is resolved.[102] Others might question whether the arguably discriminatory position of religious exemptions needs to be removed so that we can fully realise the goal of 'equal' marriage.

The law itself, however, is just one aspect of the lived experience of LGBT+ couples. Questions arise as to the level of engagement of same-sex couples with formalisation, whether through civil partnership or marriage, and how far those statuses give authentic and meaningful recognition of their relationship. Put differently, do the current options force LGBT+ couples to 'mimic straight lifestyles' or be 'lumbered with the legal straitjacket of wedlock'?[103] Should more progressive approaches to relationship recognition be developed that go beyond the existing models to embrace non-conjugal couples, non-dyadic relationships, or even friendship?[104] These are the frontiers of 21st-century family law and the future challenges for the legal recognition of same-sex couples.

Further questions to consider

- What is the purpose of relationship formalisation? What interest does the state have in couples formalising their relationship?
- Why might same-sex couples prefer to register a civil partnership than marry?
- How far are religious protections in relation to the celebration of same-sex marriages justified?
- Do civil partnerships serve any purpose now that same-sex marriage is available?

Further materials

Barker N and Monk D (eds), *From Civil Partnership to Same-Sex Marriage: Interdisciplinary Reflections* (Routledge 2015)

Haskey J, 'The New Unions of Civil Partnerships and Same-Sex Marriages in England and Wales: A Demographic Approach to Developments' (2023) Family Law 554

---

[102]   See eg S Gilmore and others, 'Reflections on Future Directions in Family Law' (2023) 35(2) Child and Family Law Quarterly 99, 105.

[103]   Tatchell (n39).

[104]   See eg F Swennen, 'Un-Coupling Family Law: The Legal Recognition and Protection of Adult Unions Outside of Conjugal Coupledom' (2020) 28(1) Feminist Legal Studies 39.

Jowett A and Peel E, ' "A Question of Equality and Choice": Same-Sex Couples' Attitudes towards Civil Partnership after the Introduction of Same-Sex Marriage' (2017) 8 Psychology and Sexuality 69

Palazzo N and Redding J, *Queer and Religious Alliances in Family Law Politics and Beyond* (Anthem Press 2022)

Swennen F, 'Un-Coupling Family Law: The Legal Recognition and Protection of Adult Unions Outside of Conjugal Coupledom' (2020) 28(1) Feminist Legal Studies 39

4

The Financial Realities of Getting Divorced in England and Wales

Emma Hitchings, Caroline Bryson, and Gillian Douglas

Introduction

The process of divorce includes, among other things, couples disengaging economically from one another and/or organising ongoing financial ties between themselves where required. The consequences of these financial decisions have the potential to be wide-reaching, affecting immediate and long-term outcomes for the parties and any children.

In England and Wales, approximately 100,000 couples divorce each year.[1] These couples do so within a legal framework which confers wide powers and broad discretion on the courts to allocate money and property between them.[2] However, it is not mandatory for a divorcing couple to obtain a court order and only around one-third of the divorcing population obtain some form of court order for their financial and property arrangements upon divorce, with the vast majority of these made by consent.[3] This results in approximately two thirds of the divorcing population remaining outside of the formal legal system when it comes to their financial and property arrangements. Much of the reported case law involves couples with significant wealth, which is far from typical of the socio-economic circumstances of the majority of the divorcing population. However, while much of the analysis and criticism of the current law governing finances on divorce has been based on these 'big-money' cases,[4] there has been

---

[1] Ministry of Justice, 'Family Court Statistics Quarterly: January to March 2024', table 12 https://www.gov.uk/government/statistics/family-court-statistics-quarterly-january-to-march-2024, accessed 23 July 2025.

[2] Matrimonial Causes Act 1973 (MCA 1973).

[3] Ministry of Justice (n1) table 14.

[4] For example, in recent years, a focus for the media has been on the 'meal ticket for life' myth of lifelong spousal periodical payments: '"Meal Ticket for Life" Bid Backfires as Divorcee Loses

a major gap in our knowledge and understanding of how divorcees from right across the financial spectrum sort out their arrangements.

Despite the fact that the legal framework governing the financial consequences of divorce has existed for 50 years, very little has been written about the smaller money financial remedy cases, particularly what arrangements couples made, how they were made, and how these worked in practice.[5] Drawing on data generated for the Fair Shares study, the first nationally representative survey of recent divorcees in England and Wales, with responses from 2,400 divorcees divorced in the previous five years together with interview data from 53 divorcees,[6] this chapter provides a more diverse perspective by shedding light on the financial and property arrangements made on divorce for the majority of the divorcing population and the key issues of concern for the 'everyday' couple. The chapter considers the implications of these findings with respect to gender and socio-economic circumstances and, in doing so, it explores the extent to which the current legal system helps couples to achieve fair financial arrangements.

Summary of the law governing finances on divorce

The law governing finances on divorce is contained in the Matrimonial Causes Act 1973 (MCA 1973). The Act's wide-ranging powers enable the court to make orders encompassing options such as periodical payments,[7] lump sum payments,[8] transfers of property,[9] and pension

---

£175,000 a Year from Ex-husband' *The Telegraph* (11 April 2018). Academic commentary has also had a tendency to focus on issues of relevance in the larger money cases. See T Cummings, 'Compensation: Rejuvenated? A Critical Re-appraisal of the Principle of Compensation in the Award of Financial Remedies upon Divorce' (2024) Child and Family Law Quarterly 133 and Emma Hitchings, 'Reconsidering the *Duxbury* "Default"' (2021) Child and Family Law Quarterly 275.

[5] For research on the financial consequences of divorce, see H Fisher and H Low, 'Divorce Early or Divorce Late? The Long-Term Financial Consequences' (2018) 32 Australian Journal of Family Law 6. For research into the legal process concerning financial remedies, see E Hitchings, J Miles, and H Woodward, 'Assembling the Jigsaw Puzzle: Understanding Financial Settlement on Divorce' (University of Bristol, 2013) https://www.bristol.ac.uk/media-libr ary/sites/law/migrated/documents/stage%201%20report%202018%20amends.pdf, accessed 5 June 2025. For research into substantive outcomes, see E Hitchings and J Miles, 'Financial Remedies on Divorce: The Need for Evidence-Based Reform' (2018) https://www.nuffieldfou ndation.org/sites/default/files/files/briefing%20paper%20Jun%202018%20FINAL.pdf, accessed 5 June 2025, and in relation to pensions, H Woodward with M Sefton, '*Pensions on Divorce: An Empirical Study*' Cardiff University (2014) https://orca.cardiff.ac.uk/id/eprint/56700/, accessed 5 June 2025.

[6] For a more detailed outline of the study's methods and aims, see the full report: Emma Hitchings and others, 'Fair Shares? Sorting out Money and Property on Divorce' Bristol University (2023) https://www.bristol.ac.uk/media-library/sites/law/news/2023/Fair%20Shares%20report%20-%20final.pdf, accessed 5 June 2025.

[7] Section 23(1)(a) MCA 1973.

[8] Section 23(1)(c) MCA 1973.

[9] Section 24(1)(a) MCA 1973.

sharing.[10] These powers enable the courts to deal with both capital and income issues together, and to achieve an overall package of arrangements, rather than having to treat future 'maintenance' of an ex-spouse as a matter separate from the distribution of assets.[11]

The legal framework providing the basis on which such orders are made is contained in section 25 of the MCA 1973. Section 25(1) requires the court to give 'first consideration ... to the welfare while a minor of any child of the family' under the age of 18, while section 25A provides for the court to consider the desirability and feasibility of a 'clean break' – that is, the ending of any continuing financial ties between the divorcing spouses and the avoidance of ongoing financial support by way of spousal periodical payments, where possible.

Section 25(2) contains a 'checklist' of factors to which the court must have regard, the importance of each of which varies from case to case and these powers are exercised according to a wide discretion.

Reported case law provides additional guidance on how the statutory criteria should be applied. Through a number of leading judgments, the higher courts have kept the operation of the law in tune with current norms and attitudes, most importantly the view that marriage is a partnership of equals in which each spouse plays an equally important role. In *White v White*,[12] Lord Nicolls outlined that the implicit objective is to achieve a fair outcome and in seeking to do so, 'there is no place for discrimination between husband and wife and their respective roles'.[13] However, it was left to the subsequent House of Lords combined appeal of *Miller v Miller; McFarlane v McFarlane* to outline the underlying principles that should guide the courts in their consideration of the section 25 exercise.[14] Lord Nicholls and Baroness Hale gave the leading opinions and laid down three core elements of fairness: needs, compensation, and sharing.

Meeting the parties' needs will include the provision of a home for each spouse and the income they will require to live on, including into retirement. As this chapter demonstrates, most divorcing couples will be unable to go beyond this principle (ie to consider sharing and compensation), due to the limited amount of assets and income at their disposal. Instead, the focus for the parties is to try to divide assets which could just about meet the needs of one household into two new households.

In cases where the available assets go beyond meeting the parties' needs, the other principles may be relevant. The compensation principle recognises the 'relationship-generated disadvantage' that may arise when one spouse gives up a well-paying career to meet family-focused priorities, such as bringing up children. However, although we live in a society where women still undertake

---

[10] Section 21A(1) MCA 1973.

[11] By contrast, this is the norm in civil jurisdictions.

[12] [2001] 1 AC 596, HL.

[13] Ibid, 599ff.

[14] [2006] UKHL 24, [2006] 2 AC 618.

the larger share of childcare and homemaking,[15] very few divorcees will be in marriages where the other spouse is earning enough to compensate them for their ongoing loss. Indeed, it has proved difficult for the courts to determine when or how compensation should be awarded, with a general view that this will be subsumed by an award that meets the party's needs,[16] or under the third principle of 'sharing'.

The sharing principle derives from *White v White*, where Lord Nicholls had stressed that equal sharing of the parties' available wealth should be regarded as a 'yardstick' by which to assess fairness, but not a 'presumption'. In *Charman v Charman (No 4)*,[17] the Court of Appeal went further by holding that equal shares should be the court's starting point, or presumption. In the relatively rare 'big-money' case where there is a surplus left over after satisfying each of the parties' respective needs (and any compensation), equal division of the total pool may be the 'fair' outcome.[18] But where the pool is inadequate to meet the parties' respective needs, an unequal division may be fairer. For example, this may be the case in situations where a full-time carer of young children has limited options in terms of paid work going forward. The spouse in such a case may potentially require all or a larger share of the former matrimonial home to rehouse themselves and their children compared with the spouse who is able to work full-time and build up savings towards another home.

Context and outcomes: the economic reality

When considering the law on financial remedies, it is important to have an awareness of the economic context in which couples enter the divorce process as this is crucial to understanding the financial arrangements that emerge at the end of the divorce process, as well as being relevant to the level of financial security divorcees will experience after they are divorced. This section provides an overview of the economic circumstances of divorcees at the end of their marriage using the Fair Shares data.[19] It also provides a summary of the overall outcomes reached. In particular, it provides evidence as to the low to medium levels of wealth and income that the majority of the divorcing population experience in

---

15 R Wishart and others, 'Changing Patterns in Parental Time Use in the UK' (NatCen 2018) https://www.ksh.hu/iatur2018/iatur40_wishart_dunatchik_speight_mayer.pdf, accessed 23 July 2025.

16 *SA v PA (Pre-Marital Agreement: Compensation)* [2014] EWHC 392 (Fam). For a rare example of an award, see *RC v JC* [2020] EWHC 466 (Fam).

17 [2007] EWCA Civ 503.

18 For discussion of the case law concerning how to determine which of the parties' assets should be 'counted' in the sharing exercise, see N Lowe and others, *Bromley's Family Law* (12th edn, OUP 2021), ch 9.

19 Hitchings and others (n6).

the period before their divorce and provides a direct contrast to the 'big-money' reported case law which is the focus for much textbook discussion of the law.[20]

The family economic context

Most divorcees do not enjoy significant wealth during their marriage. Figure 4.1 shows the breakdown of divorcees' monthly household incomes, after tax, prior to separation. Two in five divorcees (43 per cent) reported that their net household income was under £2,000 a month when they separated, and only 8 per cent had a disposable monthly income of £5,000 or more.

Figure 4.1: Household income prior to separation

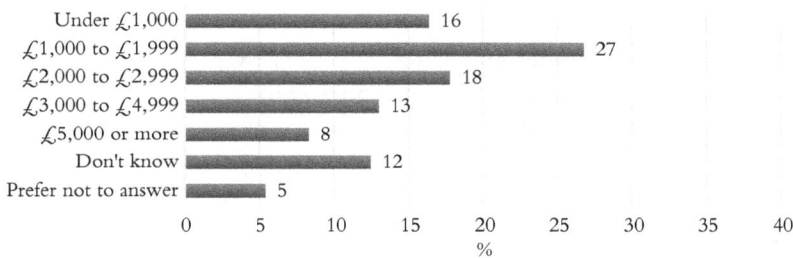

Unweighted bases: All divorcees (2,415).
Note: Where the percentages do not add up to exactly 100 per cent, this is due to rounding to the nearest percentage point.

Moving away from income to assets, while seven in ten (68 per cent) divorcees owned their matrimonial home, this was most often with a mortgage, and sometimes with a shared ownership arrangement. Only 15 per cent owned their home outright. As a result, the equity in the home (that is, the value of the home minus any mortgage to pay off) was often modest. In addition, three in ten (28 per cent) divorcees were renters, with the majority in private tenancies, meaning that there was no equity to divide for this group and therefore less capital available to meet both parties' needs on divorce.

Figure 4.2 shows the estimated equity in the matrimonial home among homeowners at the point of divorce. A third (34 per cent) of divorces where the matrimonial home was owned involved an equity of under £100,000.[21]

---

[20] See for example, Lowe and others (n18) chs 8 and 9; R George and others, *Family Law: Text, Cases and Materials* (5th edn, OUP 2023) ch 6.

[21] For information on the average cost of housing for the five-year period preceding August/September 2022 (the period in which the survey data was collected), see Office for National Statistics (ONS), 'UK House Price Index' (December 2023) figure 2 https://www.ons.gov.uk/economy/inflationandpriceindices/bulletins/housepriceindex/december2023, accessed 5 June 2025.

Figure 4.2: Equity in the matrimonial home

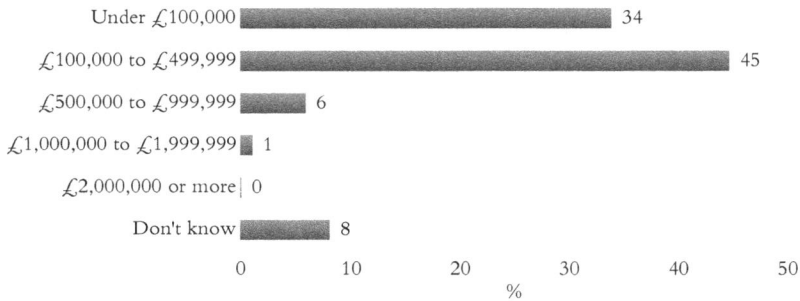

Unweighted bases: All homeowners (1,691).

As is to be expected, home ownership in general was associated with higher incomes, and outright ownership with longer marriages and being older. The opposite was true for renting, particularly private renting, where tenants were more likely to be younger (eg 25 per cent of those under 35 were private renters compared to 10 per cent of those aged 60 or over), with shorter marriages (28 per cent of those married for fewer than six years were private renters compared to 7 per cent of those married for 20 years or more) and lower incomes (43 per cent of divorcees with a net monthly income of under £1,000 were private or social renters compared to 14 per cent of those with a monthly income of £5,000 or more).

Another key asset to consider is the parties' pensions. Alongside family homes, pensions are usually the largest asset to consider on divorce. Pensions are complex; not only in terms of understanding the different types of state and private pension,[22] but also in terms of valuation,[23] the legal mechanisms available to address differences in pension wealth and deal with pensions fairly on divorce,[24] and the differences in the treatment of pensions in 'needs' and 'sharing' cases.[25] In seven in ten (70 per cent) divorces in the Fair Shares study, one or both spouses had a pension other than the state pension. For two in five (40 per cent), both spouses had pensions, but for three in ten (30 per cent) only one spouse had a pension. Those without pensions included younger divorcees

---

[22] For a very helpful overview of the different types of pensions designed for individuals going through divorce, see AdviceNow, 'A Survival Guide to Pensions on Divorce' (2024) ch 2 https://www.advicenow.org.uk/pension, accessed 6 June 2025.

[23] See Pension Advisory Group, 'A Guide to the Treatment of Pensions on Divorce' (2nd edn, 2024) part 3 https://www.nuffieldfoundation.org/wp-content/uploads/2023/A-guide-to-the-treatment-of-pensions-on-divorce-2nd-edition.pdf, accessed 6 June 2025.

[24] Ibid, parts 3, 6, and 7.

[25] Ibid, part 4.

and the self-employed, as well as those with low earnings. For example, one of the wives in our interview sample commented of her self-employed husband that:

> I'm pretty sure he didn't [have a pension] ... I just think he never bothered to organise anything. ... [T]he fact that we did have a little bit of savings and we, you know, we were getting the mortgage gone, he probably didn't consider that it was an absolute necessity really. (Wife 9)

This wife's uncertainty in this quotation reflected the fact that a good proportion (24 per cent) of divorcees did not know whether their ex-spouse had a pension and were therefore presumably unable to take this into account in the negotiation of any financial arrangements.[26] This raises questions as to the overall fairness of any outcome where the parties are uncertain as to the overall 'pot' to be divided.

However, for the 70 per cent of divorcees that did have a pension other than the state pension, it is important to consider the value of these pensions. Figure 4.3 splits divorcees into those already drawing their pension and those with a pension pot yet to be used. Those already drawing their pension were asked the monthly amount they received, after any deductions, while those not yet drawing their pension were asked the value of the pot. We look at the gender split in relation to pension amounts in the next section when considering the gender issues, but for now, there are two key issues to pull out from the pension value figure.

Figure 4.3: Pension value

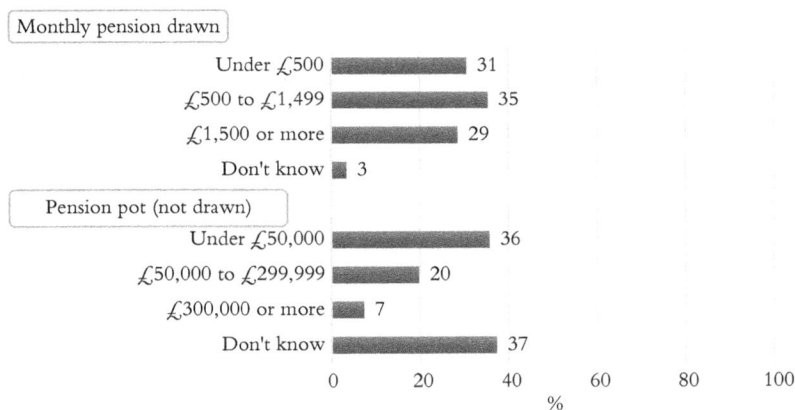

Unweighted bases: All divorcees drawing a pension (276); all divorcees with a pension pot (1,464).

First, the bar chart emphasises the low value of pensions in payment and future pension pots for many divorcees. A third (36 per cent) of divorcees not yet

---

[26]   This degree of ignorance as to the pension position of their ex means that our analysis is based on participants' responses in respect of their own pensions only.

drawing their pension had a pension pot that was worth less than £50,000, while three in ten (31 per cent) divorcees already in receipt of a pension were receiving less than £500 per month.[27] Secondly, the last row of the figure provides an indication as to the large number of divorcees who did not know the value of their pension pot. Just over a third (37 per cent) of all divorcees not yet drawing their pension did not know the value of their own pension pot. In addition (not shown in the figure), a quarter (23 per cent) of those who had an employer pension did not know what type of pension it was – whether it was a defined benefit or defined contribution pension scheme.[28] An example of this lack of knowledge of the value of a spouse's pension pot can be seen through the following interview quote. One wife knew that her husband had various valuable pensions, but had 'no idea' how much they were actually worth:

> He's worth an absolute fortune when he dies ... [but] if there was a way around him not giving me any money, he would find that way. So I didn't look into it. If you don't know what you're missing, you don't mind. (Wife 27)

This lack of awareness and understanding in pensions fed through, as one would expect, into how, if at all, pensions were taken into account when couples sought to make their financial arrangements, particularly the gendered aspect of this, and will be looked at in the next section.

When making decisions about finances and property on divorce, couples need to consider all of their assets and debts if they are to arrive at a truly fair outcome. In taking all assets and debts together, Figure 4.4 provides a breakdown of the total net value of the assets from the marriage, including the matrimonial home and pensions, savings and other assets, with any debts deducted from the total. Most divorcees in the study had relatively modest amounts of wealth to divide at the end of their marriage. The median value of divorcing couples' total asset pool including home and pension was £135,000. Nearly one in five (17 per cent) had no assets to divide and two thirds (63 per cent) had total assets worth under £500,000. So, the picture of couples' financial position at the point of divorce was quite contrary to the impression given by the media's reporting of divorces. Most divorcees did not enjoy lives of luxury during their marriage and had relatively modest amounts of wealth to divide at the end.

---

[27] For a useful guide to how much retirees will need in retirement for an 'essential', 'comfortable', or 'luxurious' retirement, see Which?, 'How Much Will You Need to Retire?' https://www.which.co.uk/money/pensions-and-retirement/planning-your-retirement/how-much-will-you-need-to-retire-aNmlv7V7sVe9, accessed 5 June 2025.

[28] A defined benefit pension is where an income will be paid in retirement which is based on a proportion of the pension holder's salary. A defined contribution pension is a scheme whereby the pension pot is build up by regular contributions over time, which are invested. The final pension is then determined by the value of the contributions and investment returns at retirement.

Figure 4.4: Total net value of assets

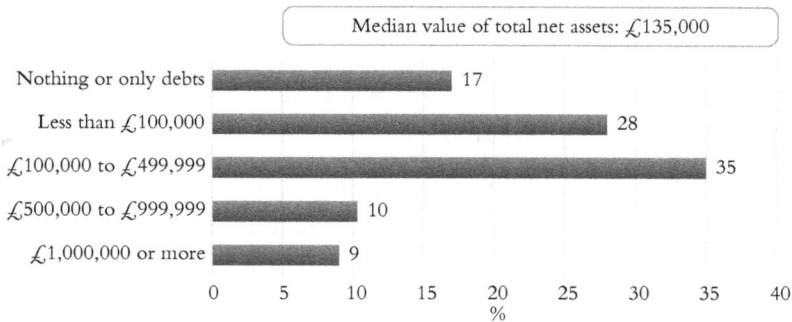

Median value of total net assets: £135,000

	%
Nothing or only debts	17
Less than £100,000	28
£100,000 to £499,999	35
£500,000 to £999,999	10
£1,000,000 or more	9

Base: All divorcees with an estimation of the value of their assets (2,283).

Dividing the overall assets

In *White v White*,[29] the House of Lords held that, to determine a 'fair' outcome in the financial arrangements a couple make on divorce, a 'yardstick' of equality should be used, but that where the needs of the parties so require a 'departure' from equal sharing will be the correct – and fair – result. Indeed, the data from the Fair Shares study found that only around three in ten (28 per cent)[30] divorcees who had divided their assets at the point of the survey reported receiving roughly half (between 40 and 59 per cent) of the total asset pool (see Figure 4.5). This meant that the majority shared out their assets unequally, with a third (32 per cent) of divorcees reporting receiving a percentage share of less than 40 per cent, including 3 per cent who took on more by way of debts than they received in assets and a further 3 per cent who received nothing. Two in five (40 per cent)[31] divorcees

Figure 4.5: Percentage of the total asset value received by divorcee

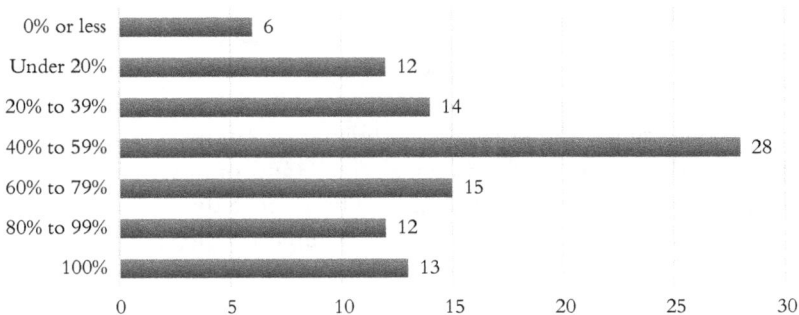

	%
0% or less	6
Under 20%	12
20% to 39%	14
40% to 59%	28
60% to 79%	15
80% to 99%	12
100%	13

Base: All divorcees who had divided assets (excluding those with only debts) for whom a calculation could be made (1,280).

---

29   [2001] 1 AC 596, HL.
30   Percentage slightly different to figure due to rounding to nearest whole percentage point.
31   Percentage slightly different to figure due to rounding to nearest whole percentage point.

reported receiving more than 60 per cent of the total asset pool, including 7 per cent who received all of the pool and a further 5 per cent who received more than 100 per cent, possibly as a result of their ex-spouse taking on debts.

The reasons for divorcees sharing out their assets unequally were explored through the interview data and reflected the parties' needs, individual circumstances, and differing motivations, such as wanting a clean break. One wife who was still waiting for the sale of the marital home to go through and the equity to be split, explained that she had agreed to take less equity than she originally expected in the hope of having a clean break:

> I wanted to end up comfortable, that I could afford to buy a property, which I am in the process of [although] not the one I wanted. I've taken less but I feel now I can have a clean break, by taking less, as long as he keeps his side of the bargain, fingers crossed that he will. (Wife 7)

Many interviewees also spoke about compromising or conceding when it came to the division of finances in order to spare their children from the emotional upheaval of divorce as far as they could or in order to protect their own mental health:

> [W]hen [pensions] came into the negotiations in mediation, he only offered to give me that menial amount providing I don't try to touch his pension and he had a massive pension. Again, my mental health just wanted, I just wanted it off my mind, so I just gave into everything then. (Wife 3)

Since the median value of divorcees' total asset pool was £135,000, it is unsurprising that half of divorcees who had made arrangements across all of their assets received less than £50,000. Figure 4.6 breaks down the value of the money and assets that divorcees received when they had settled all their finances, net of debts. It highlights both the fact that many divorcees came out of their marriages with nothing, and the modest value of the money and assets that other divorcees received. Almost a quarter (23 per cent) ended up with nothing (10 per cent) or only debts (13 per cent).[32] A further one in five (21 per cent) ended up with money or assets worth under £25,000 and only 9 per cent came out of the marriage with £500,000 or more. The picture that is painted is thus of many divorcees ending up with very little. Therefore, the 'everyday divorce' is

---

[32] Previous research examining court files has highlighted that in some cases where the divorcee ends up with nothing, the other spouse will also have been left in a similar position, that is, where the parties have no capital or pension assets and there is a clean break 'of nothing'. J Miles and E Hitchings, 'Financial Remedy Outcomes on Divorce in England and Wales: Not a "Meal Ticket for Life"' (2018) 32(1 and 2) Australian Journal of Family Law 43, fn 36.

one marked by relative financial hardship for both parties, and their children, as they set out on the 'road to independent living'.[33]

Figure 4.6: Value of the assets and money received by divorcee

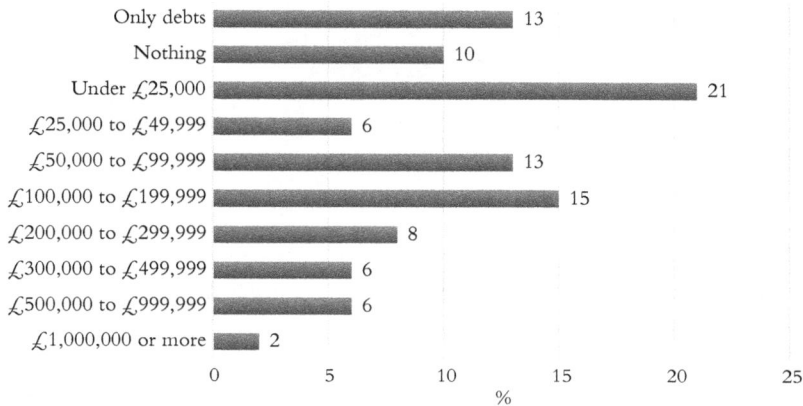

Base: All divorcees who had divided assets (including only debts) for whom a calculation could be made (1,449).

Summary

Most divorcees do not enjoy significant wealth during their marriage. Alongside family homes, pensions are usually the largest asset to consider on divorce, although the study emphasises the low value of pensions in payment and future pension pots for many divorcees.

A large proportion of divorcees do not know the value of their pension pot. In the Fair Shares study, just over a third (37 per cent) of all divorcees not yet drawing their pension did not know the value of their own pension pot.

In taking all assets and debts together, the median value of divorcees' total asset pool including home and pension was £135,000. It is therefore unsurprising that half of divorcees who had made financial and property arrangements across all of their assets received less than £50,000.

The majority of divorcees shared out their assets unequally, with a third (32 per cent) reporting receiving a percentage share of less than 40 per cent and with only around three in ten (28 per cent) receiving roughly half (between 40 and 59 per cent) of the total asset pool.

The reasons for divorcees sharing out their assets unequally reflected the parties' needs, individual circumstances, and differing motivations, such as wanting a clean break.

---

[33] *Miller v Miller; McFarlane v McFarlane* [2006] UKHL 24, para 144 (Baroness Hale of Richmond).

Context and outcomes: the implications of gender

This section provides an outline of how the roles taken on by women and men during a marriage can have financial implications both during, and in particular, on the breakdown of any relationship. The language used in section 25 of the MCA 1973 is gender neutral and the statute and subsequent case law should ensure that there is 'no discrimination between the respective roles of husband and wife' when it comes to division of assets on divorce. However, gender is a key issue when it comes to considering financial and property outcomes on divorce, particularly in relation to work and ongoing caring responsibilities, pensions, and the potential implications for parties in the longer term.

Gender and the family context

On average, women were bringing less income into the household prior to separation, being less likely than men to be in paid work (78 per cent compared to 86 per cent), especially full-time work (46 per cent compared to 62 per cent) and earning less on average than men (Figure 4.7).[34] Three in ten (28 per cent) working women had a take-home pay (after deductions for tax, etc) of less than £1,000 per month, compared with one in ten (10 per cent) men. At the other

Figure 4.7: Paid work at point of separation, by gender

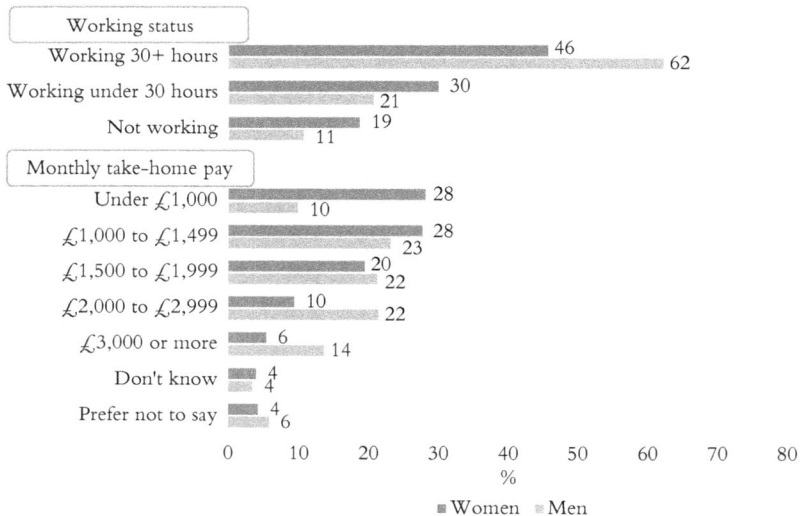

Unweighted bases: Female divorcees (1,380); male divorcees (1,035); female divorcees working at point of separation (1,125); male divorcees working at point of separation (903).

---

[34]   Two per cent of women and 2 per cent of men who were working did not give information about their hours.

end of the spectrum, only 6 per cent of women earned £3,000 or more per month, compared to 14 per cent of working men.

While mothers and women without children were equally likely to have been in paid work at the point of separation, women without children were more likely than mothers to have been working full-time (61 per cent compared to 42 per cent of mothers with dependent children and 23 per cent of those with older children). Overall, and likely reflecting their higher rate of part-time employment, the salary levels of mothers in paid work were somewhat lower than those of women without children. Among women in paid work, mothers were far more likely (32 per cent of those with dependent children and 39 per cent of those with older children) than women without children (20 per cent) to have a net monthly take-home pay of less than £1,000. At the other end of the earning spectrum, one in five (21 per cent) women without children took home £2,000 a month or more compared to 13 per cent of mothers with dependent children and 8 per cent of those with older children.

These figures suggest that, at least in the immediate aftermath of the separation or divorce, women's – and particularly mothers' – earnings, and earnings potential, make them more likely to be vulnerable financially than men. An example of this financial vulnerability for some mothers is provided by this wife, who emphasised her ongoing care responsibility for the couple's children:

> I've spent a good 15 years with him, raising his children who both have autism and I'm still having to be a full-time mum because of their special needs, so it's not easy for me to go out and get a job because I've always got to go to different meetings and different places … so obviously my pension, I will have hardly anything. (Wife 8)

As we have discussed, pensions are a key issue when considering and dividing assets on divorce due to the prospective wealth contained within them alongside the potential to generate a future income stream. Even if, for many divorcees, the size of their pension is relatively modest, it could constitute a valuable asset alongside any equity in a matrimonial home. A share of such a resource has the potential to make a significant contribution to longer-term financial stability for a financially vulnerable spouse.

The Fair Shares study found that women had accumulated poorer pension provision than men. Although women were as likely as men to have a pension, men were more likely to have paid into it for longer, probably due to women having periods out of the labour market while they were looking after children. For instance, a third (36 per cent) of women with pensions had been paying in for fewer than ten years, compared with 26 per cent of men. At the other end of the spectrum, a quarter (23 per cent) of women and two in five (39 per cent) men had been paying in for 20 years or more. Also, men's pensions were worth more than those of women.

Figure 4.8 presents a stark picture of women being more likely to have a lower value pension than men. Among women with pension pots, four in ten women had a pot worth less than £50,000, compared to three in ten men. And among men with pension pots, 13 per cent had a pot worth at least £300,000 compared to only 2 per cent of women. However, it is important to note that a number of other factors, most of which would be expected, are also associated with higher pension values. For example, those with larger pension pots were,[35] unsurprisingly, more likely to have higher earnings and to be older.[36]

Overall, this highlights a particular financial vulnerability for women. Their lower-value pension pots are likely to impact on their financial security in retirement, particularly if they have taken the main responsibility for childcare post-divorce and are unable to make decent contributions to a pension scheme over the coming years.

Figure 4.8: Pension value, by gender

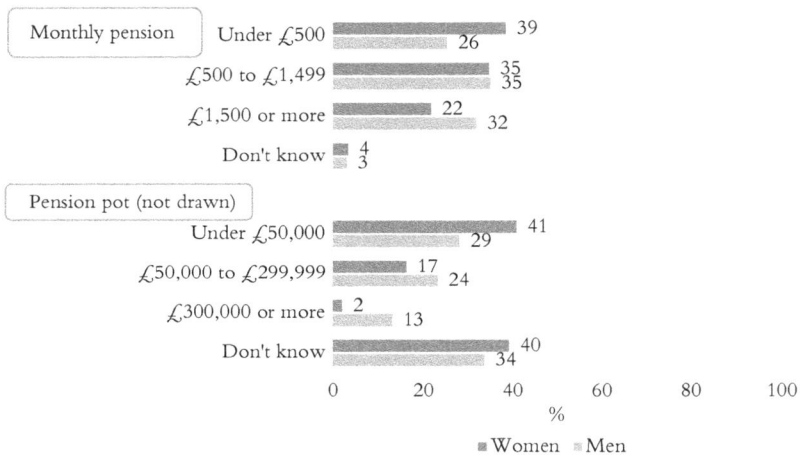

Unweighted bases: Female divorcees drawing a pension (104); male divorcees drawing a pension (172); female divorcees with a pension pot (854); male divorcees with a pension pot (610).

As noted previously, over a third of divorcees with a pension not yet in payment did not know the value of their own (let alone their ex-spouse's) pension pot, but Figure 4.8 also highlights the gender discrepancy, with women (40 per cent) more likely than men (34 per cent) to say that they did not know. This lack of awareness and understanding of pensions fed through, as one would expect, into

---

35   Here, because of the larger sample sizes, the focus is on the value of the pension pot for those not yet drawing their pension.

36   In addition, another indicator of wealth which was significant was being an owner-occupier rather than renting.

how, if at all, pensions were taken into account when couples sought to make their financial arrangements.

Gender and division of assets

As noted earlier in the chapter, half of divorcees who had made arrangements across all of their assets received less than £50,000, but when dividing their asset pool, fewer than three in ten divorcees did so in broadly equal (between 40 and 60 per cent) shares, with the majority sharing out their assets unequally.

While there was no notable difference between men and women in the shares they received, or their net value, what did differ between them were the factors which tended to lead to them receiving the larger share in any unequal division. For men, being less enmeshed in the marriage, such as having no children, or being younger, married for a shorter time, and having fewer assets, pointed towards doing better than their ex-spouse. For women, the reverse pattern was exhibited, though more weakly, with the analysis showing that women tended to receive a larger share of the pool where there was more value in the matrimonial home.[37]

Finally, the findings confirmed the limited extent to which pensions were shared on divorce. Reflecting earlier research,[38] the Fair Shares study found very low levels of pension sharing. Only 11 per cent of divorcees had an arrangement that one or both parties' pensions should be shared.[39] In the majority (71 per cent) of these divorces, the arrangement was to share only one pension, with the remaining three in ten (29 per cent) involving pension sharing of both ex-spouses' pensions. Where a pension not yet in payment was shared, there was an equal split of the participant's pension in only 22 per cent of cases. In nearly half of cases the recipient received less than half and in 18 per cent over half.

Interviewees frequently noted that pensions 'had not come up' in discussions over financial arrangements, even when solicitors had been involved.[40] But this was not necessarily only due to ignorance. A spouse might not actually *want* a share of the other's pension. A husband noted that although his wife

> could take 50 per cent of [the pension] She decided not to. I don't know why. ... [I]t's been a bonus, like the whole pension thing, that she hasn't ... I was prepared to like, lose half my pension, but the fact that she said she didn't want it, that's been a bonus. (Husband 25)

---

37   See Hitchings and others (n6) chs 6 and 7 for further detail and breakdown of outcomes in relation to the matrimonial home.

38   Woodward with Sefton (n5).

39   Within divorces where one or both parties had a pension that they were not yet drawing.

40   For the solicitor's duty of care in relation to advice about pensions on divorce, see *Joanne Lewis v Cunningtons Solicitors* [2023] EWHC 822 (KB).

The prevailing view appeared to be that pensions are entitlements of the individual concerned and generally to be preserved by that person, rather than 'marital assets' available to be shared.

> [T]he property ... it's practical, you need a roof over your head ... is the first thing, but the property is something you've paid for jointly; your pension is something that you've taken out of your salary every month, right, that's a very personal thing, even though you don't think about it at the time, it's very, very personal. ... You do think about it differently [from the home] because you've – I suppose part of your pension is what you've earnt because it's your contribution. (Husband 14)

This no doubt reflects a variety of factors: the fact that a person may start contributing well before they meet their spouse; that the contributions may continue for many years; that they usually come out of a person's salary and are recorded on the payslip, or the fact that employers may make contributions too. But another reason for keeping away from the pension was to avoid complexity and dispute and to ensure a complete clean break:

> I initially wanted a share of his pension, 'cause I thought, well hang on a minute I've got responsibilities here, I have a child and everything. He has to support his child, so I thought the pension was part of that ... but the reason why I agreed to separate it was because it would have been protracted, more documentation to present, it would have extended the divorce period and I just wanted to be completely free and in the end I just thought, okay. (Wife 7)

It is clear that sharing the pension itself is still a comparatively rare outcome. The strength of the view that pensions 'belong' to the contributor, coupled with a need (and wish) to resolve the matter of housing for the couple and any children, mean that 'offsetting' the pension by taking a larger share in the former matrimonial home, or transferring other assets, could be a useful strategy where the question of the pension *is* raised in negotiations,[41] and this was reflected in some of the interviews:

> I'd been in the house and had spent an awful lot of money on an extension to the house and things, so I didn't feel at the time that a 50/50 split was completely fair ... I also felt at the time in terms of what we'd each put into it at all, that I should have something more.

---

[41] See G Lazarus, '"You Need the House, Love – Let Him Keep His Pension"' (2019) 49 Family Law 373.

> [But] I came down to splitting it 50/50 in the end on the basis of, she
> then gave up any claim to ongoing part of my pension. (Husband 20)

Given the limited proportion of pension sharing among divorcees, it is therefore
not surprising that offsetting in the form of trading shares in the matrimonial
home was the preferred alternative for many couples, as reflected by the extent to
which wives received a transfer of, or a larger share of, the equity in the home. In
terms of the combined pool of assets, while there were no significant differences
in either the proportionate share of the assets received or the monetary value of
this between husbands and wives, husbands tended to receive more of the value
of the combined pension pool and wives of the matrimonial home.[42]

It therefore appears from the data that divorcing couples with children are, to
a large extent, prioritising the housing of the parent with care and the children,
which sits with the law's priority to provide first consideration to the welfare
of any minor children of the family under section 25(1) of the MCA 1973. In
addition, the finding chimes with previous research, which has noted that mothers
of dependent children are more likely to demonstrate a 'present bias', prioritising
rehousing in their financial and property arrangements.[43] With women's pension
pots smaller than men's, the longer-term situation for women is therefore more
precarious due to their potentially more limited incomes in retirement.

Gender and ongoing financial support

While the allocation or division of capital assets (and debts) is a key part of the
financial package that couples make on divorce, ongoing payments in the form
of spousal periodical payments can also play an important role. The issue of
spousal maintenance has received particular attention over the last few years in
England and Wales. Claims that the current law provides ex-wives with a 'meal-
ticket for life' have been used as a rationale to suggest reforms which would limit
the spousal maintenance period. However, research has shown that within the
population that obtain a financial remedies order through the court, lifetime
spousal periodical payments are rare.[44] The Fair Shares findings confirmed
this: only 22 per cent of divorcees reported having had a spousal maintenance
arrangement at the point of divorce (and by the time of the survey, up to five
years later, this percentage had dropped to 14 per cent).

A number of reasons came through from the interview data as to why most
couples have no ongoing spousal maintenance arrangement. For many divorcees,
the issue was simply not on their radar when going through divorce; others
mentioned the practical reality of affordability, the desire for a clean break, the
need to demonstrate financial independence from the other spouse, as well as

---

[42] See Hitchings and others (n6) ch 10.
[43] Hitchings and Miles (n5) 13.
[44] Ibid, 16.

domestic abuse issues, with the victim of the abuse wanting to cut ties with the perpetrator and not communicate with them going forward.

Figure 4.9: Period for which spousal maintenance to be paid

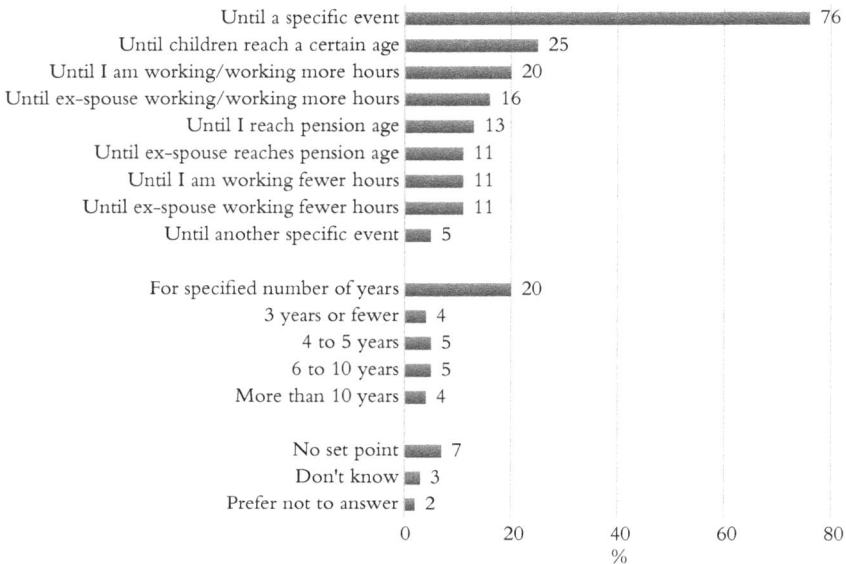

Base: Divorcees with a spousal maintenance arrangement (394).
Note: Participants could pick more than one response, hence the figures amounting to more than 100 per cent.

Where spousal maintenance was paid, women were more likely to receive maintenance than men, but this was nearly always for a fixed term, with 88 per cent of arrangements for a specified period, either defined by an agreed number of years (Figure 4.9) or a particular event. Only about one in five (20 per cent) arrangements specified a particular number of years for which spousal maintenance would be paid. For most divorcees (76 per cent), the arrangement was instead anchored to a particular event. A quarter (25 per cent) had an arrangement for payments to last until children reached a certain age, while others had arrangements linked to the earnings potential of either the maintenance recipient or the ex-spouse paying the maintenance. For example, one wife in the interview sample had made an informal agreement with her ex-husband that he would pay her mortgage until the youngest child finished education, although some uncertainty was expressed over the exact end date:

> [W]hen my youngest finishes education … [a]lthough this one is a little bit grey at the moment. I think this one may continue a little longer actually … because I earn significantly less, plus I'm self-employed

so the whole mortgage situation, I'm not entirely sure … this is the one thing that is very up in the air because it's such a long way away. (Wife 18)

The payment of spousal maintenance was also associated with a certain amount of vulnerability on behalf of the receiving spouse, often being connected with having (or having had) children or having an illness or disability. For instance, there was such an arrangement in three in ten (30 per cent) divorces involving dependent children, and two in five (43 per cent) with non-dependent children, compared with only 7 per cent of divorces not involving children. This association between spousal maintenance and having children was highlighted in the interview data, with one husband noting that in his case the spousal and child maintenance payments were merged together in one large payment:

> It was all covered in the child money, like whatever we thought she would need to run the house, pay electric, gas, mortgage, whatever, it's all taken from that. We could have broken it up into two separate payments, but what's the point? It's all in that one payment. (Husband 1)

However, spousal maintenance could also be paid in certain situations where there were no dependent children. For example, in the following case, the husband paid the wife £500 per month for approximately a year to 'get her going' on the path to independent living:

> He gave me that spousal maintenance to get me going. … So obviously I had to keep the house, the flat going. That was one thing that he had to pay the bills for the flat whilst I was there. I wasn't − I didn't work. … When it came to an end I had managed to get myself some sort of part-time job to just try and make ends meet. (Wife 10)

Therefore, there was nothing within these findings to suggest that maintenance was being used as a 'meal ticket for life' for the wife. Instead, payments appeared primarily to be used to address the adjustment to post-divorce living arrangements, such as meeting housing and household expenses.

Gender issues in the long term

This final section explores the financial vulnerability of many female divorcees, particularly mothers and those in older age, compared with men.

Two thirds of divorcees in the Fair Shares study had children and over half (54 per cent) had children of dependent age. The majority of parents reported that children were living with their mothers at the time of divorce, so that childcare responsibilities were falling primarily on divorced wives, potentially limiting their earning capacity and future pension contributions.[45] Importantly, a third (36 per cent) had children who were older and the large majority of such parents (84 per cent) continued to provide support to these children, even though they were classed by the law as 'non-dependents'.[46]

Despite little difference between the genders in terms of monetary shares received from the assets,[47] at the time of the survey, up to five years after the divorce, women, and in particular mothers with dependent children, were, on average, worse off financially then men. Not only were mothers more likely than fathers to be working part-time rather than full-time, more mothers than fathers with dependent children were in receipt of Universal Credit and Child Tax Credit. In addition, older wives without children had incomes that were significantly lower than men's. By contrast, women and men under 50 without children had similar living standards to each other at the time of the survey.[48]

An example of these longer-term gender differences can be seen in Figure 4.10.

Figure 4.10: Gross annual household income at time of survey

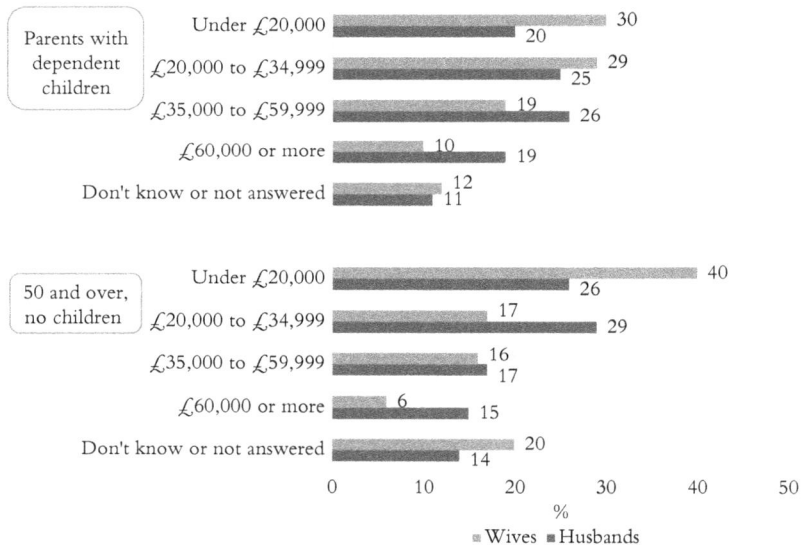

Base: Mothers (685) and fathers (504) with dependent children; women (255) and men (224) without children.

---

45 There were differences in the perceptions of mothers and fathers about what constituted their children living 'only or mainly' with one parent and what constituted 'roughly equal time' with each parent. Fathers were far more likely than mothers to say that their children stayed with them half the time. See Hitchings and others (n6) figure 9.1.

46 Mothers were more likely to have children living with them at home, while fathers were more likely to be providing financial support. See Hitchings and others (n6) ch 9 for further detail and discussion on this point.

47 See 'Gender and division of assets' subsection.

48 See Hitchings and others (n6) ch 10 for further detail and discussion.

This figure shows the gross annual household incomes of women and men at the time of the survey for the two groups where the incomes of men and women were significantly different: parents with dependent children and over 50s with no children. Among parents with dependent children (first set of bars) and older divorcees without children (second set of bars), women had significantly lower household incomes than men.

Women and men under 50 who had divorced with no children had similar living standards to each other at the time of the survey. This is in contrast with the findings that mothers and older female divorcees without children were generally worse off than men at the time of the survey. The reality when looking at the drop in living standards and income post-divorce for these groups is that mothers and older women are hit harder by their ongoing socio-economic circumstances and vulnerabilities associated with childcare, the gender pay gap, part-time work, and lower-value pension pots. In contrast, the picture painted for the divorcing population under 50 without children is of a group that is more independent, with no significant differences in assets and housing outcomes between the genders on divorce and with pensions largely ignored. Furthermore, there is almost no use of spousal maintenance within this group.[49] It appears that this autonomous, more egalitarian positioning of divorcees who are under 50 and have no children is a consequence of both the lack of dependency and related vulnerabilities associated with caring for dependents and being young enough to recover their economic position.

Overall, the Fair Shares data found that being a parent – especially a mother – and being older – especially an older wife – are associated with greater financial hardship in terms of the amount of income received. Indeed, younger women, unencumbered with childcare responsibilities, tended to do relatively well, in comparison to women who were older or had children. It is therefore parenthood, and particularly motherhood, that has the most significant impact in relation to meeting a divorcee's immediate financial needs and long-term prospects.

Summary

In the immediate aftermath of separation or divorce, women's – and particularly mothers' – earnings, and earnings potential, make them more likely to be vulnerable financially than men.

Women accumulate poorer pension provision. Among women with pension pots, four in ten women had a pot worth less than £50,000, compared to three in ten men. And 13 per cent of men had a pot worth at least £300,000 compared to only 2 per cent of women.

Pension sharing on divorce is still comparatively rare. Among divorces where one or both parties had a pension they were not yet drawing, only 11 per cent

---

[49]   See ibid, ch 10.7, 293–6, for further detail and discussion of this point.

of divorcees had an arrangement that one or both parties' pensions should be shared. Offsetting in the form of trading shares in the matrimonial home is the preferred alternative for many couples. In terms of the combined pool of assets, husbands tend to receive more of the value of the combined pension pool and wives of the matrimonial home.

Only 22 per cent of divorcees had a spousal maintenance arrangement at the point of divorce, with 88 per cent of these for a fixed term. Women were more likely to receive maintenance than men. The arrangement was usually connected with having children or the recipient having an illness or disability.

The majority of parents reported that children were living with their mothers at the time of divorce, so that childcare responsibilities were falling primarily on divorced wives, potentially limiting their earning capacity and future pension contributions. Being a parent – especially a mother – and being older – especially an older wife – are associated with greater financial hardship in terms of the amount of income received.

Conclusion: Fair shares on divorce?

The current financial remedies regime in England and Wales is highly discretionary and enables a very wide range of solutions to be arrived at to meet the individual parties' needs and circumstances. Although legal finality can only be achieved by way of a court order, couples are not obliged to obtain one and many do not. This means that they have a free hand to shape outcomes as they wish, with the risk that the stronger party in the relationship may determine the arrangements made. Nonetheless, the situation is not chaotic nor a free-for-all.

For the majority of divorcing couples in England and Wales, the situation is generally one of constrained financial circumstances. Not only are the majority of the divorcing population very far from being well-off before their divorce, but there are gender implications as an additional issue, with women, as one would expect, tending to have lower incomes and (hence) lower-value pension pots than men, as well as ongoing caring responsibilities.

For 'everyday divorcees', the breakdown of their marriage will present a severe challenge as they seek to reorganise and adjust their finances to their new post-marital situation. The Fair Shares findings have shown that the vast majority constitute what the law describes as 'needs' cases,[50] where the available resources of the parties, including earning capacity and assets, are at best able to meet core requirements for housing and future support. Almost always, they do not stretch sufficiently to prevent a diminution in living standards, at least for a time, and the more vulnerable financial position of women leaves them more likely to be worse off than men for longer.

---

[50]   See *Miller v Miller; McFarlane v McFarlane* [2006] UKHL 24.

Furthermore, general lack of interest in the pension, and a strong sense that it should remain with the spouse who has been contributing to it, were the main reasons for the failure to see it as a potential sharing resource in most divorces. It is therefore not surprising that offsetting in the form of trading shares in the matrimonial home was the preferred alternative for many couples. Yet offsetting does not adequately redress the imbalance in the total pool of financial resources (in the form of income and earning capacity as well as capital) available to the husband and wife. Neither does it redress the differences in divorcees' living standards up to five years after their divorce, with women, on average, worse off financially than men. It is clear, therefore, that both parties to a divorce need to be made more aware of the potential importance of pension wealth as a part of their entire asset pool. In particular, the issue of how to deal with pensions needs to be re-examined to consider how it should be made easier for pensions to be fully factored into the financial arrangements that couples make.

One proposed reform option is to narrow the current broad discretion the law provides to the courts (and by extension, to all divorcees), to a more formulaic and stronger presumption of 'equal sharing'.[51] The Fair Shares findings suggest this would be unlikely to deliver substantive 'fairness', given that many couples recognised that it would not be appropriate to their circumstances. Nor would it necessarily achieve objective 'equality', because, regardless of couples' intentions, even when the asset pool looks as if it has been shared equally, the nature of the assets assigned to each spouse may result in future economic inequality by leaving the bulk of pension wealth to the husband and the bulk of the value of the former matrimonial home to the wife. Moreover, there would be a particular challenge in achieving such equality in the case of those couples who had rented the matrimonial home and had no other substantial asset to split or to 'offset', especially where the tenancy was retained by the primary carer in accordance with social housing criteria. Achieving a fair outcome should therefore be about enabling parties to emerge from their marriage in a broadly substantively equal position to move to financial independence – which may require unequal sharing – rather than formally equal in percentage or cash terms.

Further questions to consider

- What should the principles, or the overall objective, of the financial remedies jurisdiction be?
- The financial consequences of the ending of the marriage are likely to land unequally between the parties. To what extent, as a matter of justice, should one party be required to redress that?

---

51 Baroness Deech's Divorce (Financial Provision) Bill [HL] Session 2021–22, HL Bill 45 proposed to amend the MCA 1973 by setting a presumption that 'matrimonial property' would be shared equally between the spouses https://bills.parliament.uk/publications/42276/documents/566, accessed 6 June.

- What is the foundation (if any) on which an ex-spouse can expect to have their needs met by their former spouse into the future?

Further materials

Fair Shares report launch, YouTube video, https://www.youtube.com/watch?v=cLTLL77qvW8, accessed 6 June

Hitchings E and Miles J, 'Financial Remedies on Divorce: The Need for Evidence-Based Reform' (2018) https://www.nuffieldfoundation.org/sites/default/files/files/briefing%20paper%20Jun%202018%20FINAL.pdf, accessed 6 June

Hitchings E and others, 'Fair Shares? Sorting Out Money and Property on Divorce' Executive Summary (Bristol University 2023) https://www.nuffieldfoundation.org/wp-content/uploads/2021/03/Fair-Shares-Executive-summary_web.pdf, accessed 6 June

Manchester University, Pensions on divorce, YouTube video https://www.youtube.com/watch?v=ouEnvDmo7U4, accessed 6 June

Woodward H with Sefton M, 'Pensions on Divorce: An Empirical Study' (Cardiff University 2014) https://orca.cardiff.ac.uk/id/eprint/56700/, accessed 6 June

5

Forced Marriage in the UK: How Intermediaries and Expert Witnesses Help Successful Prosecutions

Aisha K. Gill

Introduction

Forced marriage (FM) affects many communities in the UK and has far-reaching consequences for individuals and society. The UK introduced FM legislation in 2007 and 2014, and this chapter analyses the UK's first successful FM prosecution, which concerned a mother who had forced her daughter into marriage overseas. The case study highlights the importance of understanding the role of family values and norms in FM if we wish to both achieve successful prosecutions and provide effective assistance to victims. The best way to develop such understanding is to involve intermediaries in police investigations and expert witnesses in court. The chapter also explores how expert witnesses and intermediaries help to fulfil the law's potential to empower victims.

What is a forced marriage?

An FM is an illegal and invalid marriage that takes place without the consent of one or both parties. It is a serious violation of an individual's human rights, including the right not to marry and the right to freely consent to marry. Children and adults alike can be forced into marriage; forcing a child to marry is a form of child abuse.

Current definitions of FM specify that it involves the exercise of explicit force by an agent – usually a parent, but sometimes other family members – who is seeking to control or subjugate the victim, often through coercion. *The Oxford English Dictionary* (2023) defines coercion as 'persuading' an individual to do something through two important means: (a) acts of force or active pressure, and/or (b) physical and/or non-physical forms of explicit and/or implicit force and threats, particularly psychological pressure. Numerous influences intersect to shape the nature of coercion in relation to marriage, including socio-cultural norms regarding gender and sexuality, disability and associated caring needs, state policies (particularly immigration policies), and familial and community diasporic contexts. For example, a growing body of research indicates that these gendered processes generally involve the treatment of women and girls in order to direct/control their behaviour.[1]

Controlling and coercive behaviours are the product of complex relationship dynamics, personality traits, personal histories, and individual choices. However, socio-cultural factors can affect and contribute to the ways in which controlling and coercive behaviours present.[2] Coercive and controlling tactics are often used in concert to create an environment where the victim feels there is no meaningful alternative but to submit to the demands of others.[3] Coercive behaviour is legally recognised in the UK as a criminal offence and a form of domestic abuse within an intimate or family relationship.[4] This provides statutory recognition that a perpetrator can cause serious emotional and psychological harm even when the abuse stops short of physical or sexual violence. The statutory guidance on this legislation acknowledges that such behaviour is primarily targeted at women and girls and is 'underpinned by wider societal gender inequality'.[5] However, coercive control has been studied predominantly in the context of intimate partner violence; it remains underexamined in relation to FM.[6]

The limited extant research shows that controlling and coercive behaviour is often used to force women and girls into marriage, which in turn can – and often does – lead to a range of other serious harms, including abduction, domestic violence, rape, forced pregnancy, and domestic servitude.[7] Refusing or trying to escape an FM often puts victims at risk of 'honour' killings or other

[1] K Chantler and M McCarry, 'Forced Marriage, Coercive Control, and Conducive Contexts: The Experiences of Women in Scotland' (2019) 26(1) Violence Against Women 89.

[2] AK Gill and S Anitha, 'An Exploration of Survivors' Lived Experiences of Coercion and Coercive Contexts in Forced Marriage' (2025/6) International Journal of Law, Crime and Justice (forthcoming).

[3] J Callaghan and others, 'Beyond "Witnessing": Children's Experiences of Coercive Control in Domestic Violence and Abuse' (2018) 33(10) Journal of Interpersonal Violence 1551.

[4] Section 76, Serious Crime Act 2015.

[5] UK Government, 'International Women and Girls' Strategy, 2023 to 2030' https://www.gov.uk/government/publications/international-women-and-girls-strategy-2023-to-2030/international-women-and-girls-strategy-2023-to-2030, accessed 6 June 2025.

[6] S Walklate and K Fitz-Gibbon, 'Why Criminalise Coercive Control? The Complicity of the Criminal Law in Punishing Women through Furthering the Power of the State' (2021) 10(4) International Journal for Crime, Justice and Social Democracy 1.

[7] S Anitha, 'Understanding Economic Abuse through an Intersectional Lens: Financial Abuse, Control and Exploitation of South Asian Women's Productive and Reproductive Labour' (2019) 25(15) Violence Against Women 1854; Chantler and McCarry (n1).

forms of 'honour'-based violence.[8] While all violence against women and girls (VAWG) is underpinned by the patriarchal notion of women/girls as property, it manifests in different ways depending on the cultural context in which it occurs and the specific socio-cultural factors at play. However, it is vital to understand some forms of VAWG, such as 'honour'-based violence, are part of the broader, systemic violence wrought by so-called liberalisation and structural adjustment policies in the UK that have had adverse effects on particular communities, rather than as specific to a particular culture or as entirely culture-based. When the media reports on such crimes against women from Black and minoritised communities in this way, they may misrepresent entire cultures. Furthermore, support services may also risk essentialising such crimes by viewing them only through the lens of culture.

In the UK, FM largely affects women and girls from Black and minoritised communities. Most are women of South Asian origin, with the next largest group being women of Middle Eastern origin.[9] While the UK government's Forced Marriage Unit (FMU) supports 1,200–1,400 victims per year, that figure does not include those who do not or cannot seek support, so the true number of victims is believed to be significantly higher.[10] However, the latest data also indicate recent changes in the ethnic profile of those affected: since 2016, there has been a 100 per cent year-on-year increase in the number of cases involving Somali children and teenagers.[11]

Forced marriage legislation in England and Wales

Efforts to counter FM are increasingly visible in British criminal justice. In June 2014, FM became a specific offence in England and Wales under section 121 of the Anti-Social Behaviour, Crime and Policing Act, carrying a maximum seven-year prison sentence.[12] Before this, prosecutors had used more general legislation covering false imprisonment, kidnapping, and violence for FM cases.

In civil legislation, the Forced Marriage (Civil Protection) Act 2007 enables courts to issue forced marriage protection orders (FMPOs), a form of injunction that prohibits persons from committing acts that might lead to a named individual being forced into marriage. Breaching the terms of an FMPO is a criminal offence carrying a maximum five-year sentence. Pursuant to section 63A(1) of the Family Law Act 1996, a potential victim, a 'relevant third party', or any other

---

[8]   Gill and Anitha (n2).

[9]   Forced Marriage Unit (FMU), 'The Right to Choose: Government Guidance on Forced Marriage (2023) https://www.gov.uk/government/publications/the-right-to-choose-gov ernment-guidance-on-forced-marriage, accessed 6 June 2025.

[10]   AK Gill and H Harvey, 'Examining the Impact of Gender on Young People's Views of Forced Marriage in Britain' (2017) 12(1) Feminist Criminology 72.

[11]   FMU (n9).

[12]   Gill and Harvey (n10).

person with the court's leave (or the court itself) may seek an FMPO to protect someone who may be or has already been forced into marriage. Between 25 November 2008, when the provision came into force, and 31 December 2018, 1,943 FMPO applications were made – 1,598 of them for women – and 1,856 applications were granted. The number of FMPOs issued subsequently increased year on year, from 109 in 2009 to 346 in 2022.[13]

FMPO applications are primarily about risk management. They require the court to weigh the need for state intrusion into family life against the need to protect an at-risk person from harm. The court must therefore consider an individual's circumstances and collate evidence to determine the level of risk. The evidence can come from a number of sources: a victim might disclose directly to the police or another statutory agency, resulting in a paper trail (often digital nowadays); or they might provide records of invitations from extended family to travel overseas, the purchase of wedding-related items, and so forth. Similarly, a GP, teacher, therapist, or charity worker might provide witness evidence. Police may also have encounters with family members that trigger concern. The arrest of a potential perpetrator, particularly for offences such as assault or kidnap, may result in the victim disclosing the risk of FM; under current policy, this should lead to a proactive risk assessment. In other cases, FMPOs may be used to facilitate the repatriation of victims who are overseas but have disclosed to parties in the UK that they are at risk of being or have already been forced into marriage.

The key issue is that victims and potential victims can come to the attention of authorities in a range of ways involving a variety of sources of evidence, some of them confidential. It is therefore vital that professionals are able to recognise indicators and risk factors for FM so that they can effectively evaluate potentially disparate, incomplete, and even inconsistent evidence. Despite such challenges, two key successful FM convictions were secured in 2018 after the victims disclosed their situation to the authorities: *Regina v RB* in Birmingham and *Regina v M and B* in Leeds.[14]

---

13 Ministry of Justice, 'Family Court Statistics Quarterly: July to September 2022' https://www.gov.uk/government/statistics/family-court-statistics-quarterly-july-to-september-2022, accessed 6 June 2025.

14 *Regina v M and B* came before Leeds Crown Court in May 2018 and involved a young woman who was 19 at the time of the attempted FM. The young woman, who was studying for her A-levels, was taken out of college during term time for what she thought would be a six-week family holiday to Bangladesh. However, while overseas her parents revealed that she was to marry her first cousin – a marriage that had been planned for some time. The young woman refused and sought the support of her mother, but her mother made it clear that this was a shared parental plan. She told her daughter that refusing was not an option and that, if necessary, violence would be used; the young woman's stepfather also issued a threat when she refused to cooperate. Days before the wedding, the young woman's sister alerted the British High Commission in Bangladesh, who worked with the UK's FMU and the Bangladeshi police to protect the young woman and bring her back to the UK. Her parents were found guilty of using violence and coercion to force her to marry against her will. They were sentenced on 30 July 2018, the father to four and a half years and the mother to three

Regina v RB came before Birmingham Crown Court on 30 April 2018. It involved the mother of a teenage girl being prosecuted under two FM-specific subsections of the Anti-Social Behaviour, Crime and Policing Act: practising deception to cause the victim to leave England and Wales, pursuant to section121(2), and using coercion to force her daughter into marriage upon the latter's arrival in Pakistan, pursuant to section 121(1) (the Act has extraterritorial jurisdiction). Throughout the trial the defendant denied the charges, asserting that her daughter had 'agreed' to the marriage and was 'ready'. However, on 22 May 2018, she was found guilty on two counts of FM, for which she was sentenced to three and a half years, and one count of perjury, for which she was sentenced to one additional year.[15] This case illustrates not only the key elements of a successful FM investigation but also how a conviction can be secured using FM-specific legislation. Moreover, it offers a powerful demonstration of the importance of understanding the role that cultural and family dynamics, traditions, and values play in FM cases and how the UK legislation can empower victims.

Regina v RB

The insights presented here are based on direct knowledge and experience of *Regina v RB*'s progress from disclosure to investigation, conviction, and sentencing. For legal reasons, the defendant cannot be named. The defendant was born in Pakistan and immigrated to the UK in the 1990s to join her then-husband, who was from the village in which she had grown up. Before divorcing acrimoniously, the defendant and her husband had four children. The children resided with their mother until she returned to Pakistan for five months in 2005, leaving the children in the permanent care of their father. While overseas, the defendant married a Pakistani national. When she returned to the UK, only two of the children resumed living with her, including her youngest daughter – the victim. Her new husband remained in Pakistan until he was granted a spousal visa and joined his wife in the UK in 2009.

In 2012, the defendant took the victim, then aged 13, to Pakistan to stay with her second husband's family. During this time, a ceremony was conducted to marry the victim to her stepfather's 29-year-old nephew. Given the victim's age, this marriage was not lawful under either Pakistani or British law. Nonetheless, the groom took advantage of what he considered his marital 'rights' to have sex with the victim and she became pregnant.

---

and a half years. See F Perraudin, 'UK Couple Found Guilty of Trying to Force Daughter to Marry' *The Guardian* (2018) https://www.theguardian.com/uk-news/2018/may/29/cou ple-found-guilty-attempted-forced-marriage-daughter, accessed 6 June 2025.

15   H Summers, 'Birmingham Woman Jailed for Duping Daughter into Forced Marriage' *The Guardian* (23 May 2018) https://www.theguardian.com/uk-news/2018/may/23/birming ham-woman-jailed-duping-daughter-forced-marriage, accessed 2 May 2025.

When the victim returned to the UK, she told a school counsellor that her mother was taking her to the GP because she had missed her period. Although the victim did not recognise the significance of this, the counsellor and the GP did, and both independently alerted children's services. The police were not informed at this stage, but a social worker interviewed the mother and daughter informally to determine whether there were any child protection issues. The child was not removed from her mother's care prior to this interview, nor was her father informed of the situation. Neither the victim nor the defendant told the social worker about the marriage ceremony. Instead, the defendant told the social worker that the father of the unborn child was himself a teenager. She claimed that although she had considered him a prospective husband for her daughter, because they had had sex while her daughter was underage, all ties with him and his family had been severed once the family had returned from Pakistan.

Social services accepted this explanation without challenge. They undertook no wider investigation of the defendant's family structure, the age of the man who had impregnated the victim, or the relationship between the defendant, the victim, and the father of the unborn child. They also did not explore the veracity of the mother's assertion that a relative in Pakistan was terminally ill and that this was why they had been there when the victim became pregnant. Since the supposedly sick relative was the defendant's new mother-in-law, and therefore unrelated to the victim, social services should have questioned why the victim was required to accompany her mother when this involved being taken out of school during term time – something the school was not made aware of in advance. Moreover, rather than applying for a holiday visa for her British daughter, the defendant had applied for a Pakistani identification card, giving an address in Pakistan as her daughter's place of residence. Thus, social services either misunderstood or ignored significant warning signs.

The victim underwent an abortion in 2012. Her behaviour changed markedly over the following year: she began drinking, taking drugs, and engaging in sexual behaviours that placed her at serious risk of exploitation. In 2013, the victim was deemed 'beyond parental control' and her mother agreed to her being accommodated by the local authority under section 20 of the Children Act 1989. Although children's services had not appeared to appreciate the significance of the 2012 Pakistan trip, or the implications of what had occurred afterwards, the victim's subsequent entry into the care system did offer her some level of protection: the defendant was forced to wait for a new opportunity to remove the victim from the UK so that the marriage could be legalised in both jurisdictions when the victim turned 18.

In December 2015, the victim was moved from a children's home to semi-independent accommodation close to her mother's residence and she began visiting her mother daily. In early 2016, the defendant returned to Pakistan. The victim struggled to cope with her mother's absence and the lack of boundaries afforded by her new living arrangements, repeatedly absconding from her accommodation. Upon her mother's return, the victim chose to spend most nights at her mother's home and made it apparent that she wanted to live with her again. The defendant told children's services that she wanted her daughter back home and threatened legal action if they refused.

During the trial in May 2018, the Crown Prosecution Service (CPS) argued that the defendant had used her daughter's attachment and fear of abandonment to encourage her to resist accepting independent accommodation. The defendant's subsequent offer to take the victim on a family holiday to Pakistan in August 2016 was a significant inducement to ignore what had happened on the previous trip, given that the victim was a young person who had been separated from her family for four years. The defendant also told the victim that she would receive an iPhone 6 on her birthday if she went on the trip. Since the victim's eighteenth birthday was approaching, children's services did not think it appropriate to apply for an interim care order when they were informed of the trip. Therefore, when the defendant requested the return of her daughter's passport, it was provided.

The defendant and victim left for Pakistan two weeks before the victim's eighteenth birthday, using airline tickets that the police later discovered were transferable – meaning the defendant could change the return date without her daughter's knowledge. The day the victim turned 18, she attended what she thought was going to be a birthday party. Instead, she found herself being congratulated on her forthcoming marriage. The man involved in the ceremony that had taken place when she was 13 appeared, bearing the promised iPhone. Over the next ten days, the defendant used psychological and emotional pressure to coerce her daughter into marrying him. When her daughter resisted, the defendant threatened to destroy her passport and disown her. The victim eventually, but unwillingly, participated in a *mehndi* (pre-wedding celebration), a marriage ceremony, and a *walima* (post-wedding party); she was then sent to live with her new husband and in-laws.

Children's services had previously given the victim a prepaid phone in case of emergencies, but this had disappeared before she left the UK. The defendant had also encouraged her daughter to leave her usual phone at home, despite the fact that the victim would have no easy access to the internet or other phones in Pakistan. Secretly using her mother's mobile phone, the victim managed to send WhatsApp calls and messages to her sister asking for help. The victim's sister alerted their father, who in turn alerted children's services and the police.

Two months after the 2016 marriage, the defendant returned to the UK without her daughter. She was immediately summonsed to attend the High Court, as children's services had initiated proceedings for an FMPO. Under oath, the defendant denied that her daughter had been forced into marriage. However, this statement was proven to be false when the victim's sister provided the court with the WhatsApp messages. An FMPO was then made ordering the defendant and her second husband to secure the victim's immediate return to the UK. The defendant complied, contacting the family in Pakistan and directing the groom to take the victim to the airport the following day, where a plane ticket purchased by children's services was waiting. The fact that the Pakistani groom and his family made no effort to assert the validity of the marriage demonstrates the extent of the defendant's control, although their immediate compliance also shows that they had colluded in the FM.

The role of expert witnesses in forced marriage prosecutions

The successful prosecution of *Regina v RB* depended on the strategic use of evidence, the development of trusting relationships between the police and the victim, and expert witness testimony. Expert witnesses feature prominently across many areas of criminal and civil law, and a large body of scholarship shows that they are effective at swaying jury decisions in both contexts. For example, in a series of simulated murder trials, jurors who heard expert testimony for the defence were consistently more lenient towards defendants.[16] However, the research also suggests that expert testimony does not affect all jurors equally:[17] jurors' responses to expert testimony are mediated by their beliefs about forensic science, as measured by individuals' exposure to television crime dramas.[18]

In the case of *Regina v RB*, the CPS was conscious of the importance of explaining the cultural and religious pressures, nuances, and unwritten rules at play in terms of how and why the victim was forced into marriage, including the complexities of the dynamic between the defendant and victim. An expert report for the prosecution was produced for this case, explaining the victim's socio-cultural background and how it might have affected her belief system, as well as how the defendant's remarriage would have been culturally, socially, and legally organised within her second husband's family and community in Pakistan.

The prosecution's case was that the defendant had sought to impose control over her daughter to curb behaviours that challenged her as a parent and caused familial shame (eg her daughter's awakening sexuality). Her response had been to arrange what she perceived to be a suitable, even attractive, marriage using her extended family network, thereby meeting familial expectations and strengthening existing kinship ties. It is noteworthy that the victim's parents' marriage had been arranged by their respective families. However, in sharp contrast to the defendant, the victim's father described in court how 'in those days' he had felt unable to challenge his parents' choice of wife; he also stated that the two children who had lived with him since 2005 had both made 'love'

---

[16]   R Schuller and S Rzepa, 'Expert Testimony Pertaining to Battered Woman Syndrome: It's Impact on Jurors' Decisions' (2002) 26(6) Law and Human Behaviour 655.

[17]   L Hudspith and others, 'Forty Years of Rape Myth Acceptance Interventions: A Systematic Review of What Works in Naturalistic Institutional Settings and How This Can Be Applied to Educational Guidance for Jurors' (2023) 24(2) Trauma, Violence, & Abuse 981.

[18]   C Kearney, 'Crime in TV, the News, and Film: Misconceptions, Mischaracterizations, and Misinformation' (2024) 68(4) Journal of Broadcasting & Electronic Media 641.

choices when selecting their marriage partners. Thus, while the defendant's 'solution' to what she perceived as the difficulties arising from her daughter's burgeoning sexuality were no doubt shaped by her cultural background, the approach of her former husband (who shared the same cultural heritage) makes clear that her choice to force her daughter into marriage was not an inevitable product of her background. This demonstrates how vital it is to avoid essentialising cultures – an issue that expert witnesses are able to speak to eloquently – and instead to look at the range of choices, behaviours, and values present in all cultural groups.[19]

An expert witness explained to the court why the 2016 marriage ceremony might not be recognisable as such to those unfamiliar with the community concerned: the 'marriage' had consisted of an imam visiting the victim at a beauty salon while she was being dressed for her wedding. In the presence of her mother, but not the groom or any independent witnesses (although there were other women present, preparing for their own weddings), the victim was asked if she wished to marry. Against the backdrop of her mother's threats – including the familiar coercive tactic 'after all I've done for you …' – she was pressured into saying yes. As she and the groom saw the imam and signed the wedding certificate separately, the victim next met the groom only after the marriage had been contracted and announced at the *walima*, where the couple were presented to 250 guests as husband and wife.

Upon arrival back in the UK in October 2016, after the FMPO had been issued, the victim was met by police and a social worker. In an attempt to protect her mother, she initially denied that any marriage had occurred; however, once reunited with her sister, she produced photographs of the wedding and explained how she had been forced into it. On 1 November 2016, the victim attended a High Court hearing where the fact of the marriage was established and the defendant admitted having lied under oath at the initial hearing. The judge then directed that the CPS be informed of the defendant's lies in his court so that prosecutors could also consider investigating this act of perjury. Following the issuance of the FMPO, the police had already initiated an independent investigation regarding the FM.

As the police investigation proceeded, the significance of what had occurred in 2012 became apparent. The police then sought expert advice from an experienced officer in the Metropolitan Police Service and from academic experts and charity workers, as well as obtaining records from GPs, the victim's school, children's services, and counselling services. The victim was assessed as having 'early experience trauma' arising from lengthy absences from formal schooling as well as significant attachment issues, resulting in difficult and often risky behaviours. There had clearly been inadequate investigation of the victim's

---

[19]   AK Gill and D Gould, 'The Role of Family Coercion, Culture, Expert Witnesses and Best Practice in Securing Forced Marriage Convictions' (2020) 4(1) Journal of Gender-Based Violence.

situation when she became pregnant at age 13. This shows the importance of collecting all relevant records through cross-agency cooperation: once collated, the body of information available to police enhanced their understanding of the socio-cultural context of the case.[20]

Having experts to assist law enforcement and legal practitioners with understanding of the socio-cultural contexts and marriage traditions of different countries, cultures, and religions proved invaluable in this case, as it has in similar cases, such as that of Shafilea Ahmed.[21] In the investigation and trial of *Regina v RB*, experts were able to shed light on broad issues concerning cultural life in Pakistan and the Pakistani diaspora, offering insights into factors such as gender inequalities, 'honour' systems, patriarchal values and traditions, immigration concerns, and how and why control over female sexuality is manifested in general and specific forms of gender-based violence. Understanding these factors was critical for grasping the effectiveness of the coercive means used by the defendant.

Without expressing it directly, in court the victim revealed a genuine sense of powerlessness in the environment where her mother had placed her, both in 2012 and in 2016. Thus, the jury was able to understand that even though the victim had signed the marriage certificate, attended the wedding party immaculately dressed, and participated in a photoshoot with her husband, she had not chosen to do any of those things of her own free will. Rather, she had been unable to challenge what was happening because her mother had undermined her attempts to assert her own agency through the consistent application of various forms of coercion, both in the UK and in Pakistan.[22]

For a coercive threat to be recognised as such in a legal context, the coercer must be in a position to carry out the negative consequences threatened, or

---

[20] AK Gill and H Begum (eds), *Child Sexual Abuse in Black and Minoritised Communities: Improving Legal, Policy and Practical Responses* (Palgrave 2023); M Skidmore and others, 'Organised Crime and Child Sexual Exploitation in Local Communities' *The Police Foundation and Perpetuity Research* (2016) https://www.police-foundation.org.uk/wp-content/uploads/2017/06/organised_crime_and_cse.pdf, accessed 23 July 2025.

[21] In February 2003, Iftikhar and Farzana Ahmed took their daughter Shafilea to Pakistan against her will for the purpose of forcing her into marriage. In an effort to prevent the marriage, Shafilea ingested bleach. As a result of her injuries, she was no longer considered eligible for marriage and was brought back to the UK. Shafilea then disappeared from her family's home on the night of 11 September 2003. The circumstances of her disappearance were treated as suspicious from the start for many reasons, not least the documented history of parental abuse. On 4 February 2004, the decomposed remains of a human body were found on the banks of the River Kent near Force Bridge in Cumbria. Both Iftikhar and Farzana were eventually convicted of Shafilea's murder and they received life sentences on 3 August 2012. AK Gill, 'Murder in the Family: Why Culture is an Insufficient Explanation for "Honour"-Based Violence' in J Devaney and others (eds), *The Routledge Handbook on Domestic Violence and Abuse* (Routledge 2021).

[22] Gill and Gould (n19); S Husain, *The Stigma Matrix: Gender, Globalization, and the Agency of Pakistan's Frontline Women* (Stanford University Press 2024).

the coerced party must reasonably believe that the coercer is in a position to do so. However, this does not mean that the coercer must be able to carry out the threat directly: critically in this case, the victim believed that her mother was in a position of sufficient authority, with effective control over the threatened consequences and the situation in general. For instance, the victim was afraid of the possible consequences of challenging her mother in Pakistan, including potential abandonment and the certainty that the wider community would see a rejection of the marriage as a source of considerable shame for the entire family. It is not the existence of choice, but the ability to freely engage in the *process* of choice, that is key to determining consent versus coercion.[23] In this case, the mother actively interfered in this process by using threats and other coercive and deceptive measures such that her daughter was not in a position to consent.

Indeed, at sentencing the judge suggested that the defendant had viewed the victim's FM as akin to a commercial transaction in which the victim was the commodity. In cultural terms, the groom and his family would have considered the victim to be wholly unsuitable: following her return from Pakistan in 2012, she had a series of sexual encounters, used drugs, smoked, drank alcohol, and was not a practising Muslim. For marriage to such an unsuitable girl, the judge suggested, the trade-off for the groom and his family would be a spousal immigration visa to the UK. As yet, there are no sentencing guidelines for this form of offence, and the Sentencing Guidelines Council will need to tackle the transnational nature of such crimes in future. Factors marking culpability in such cases should include the deliberate use of marriage to secure immigration status for a spouse and perhaps extended family members, other motivating factors behind the use of FM, whether sexual activity and childbirth follow the FM, and the nature of the coercion applied.

Summary

The case of *Regina v RB* demonstrates the importance of understanding family and cultural dynamics and empowering victims in the process of securing an FM conviction. The case highlights how essential it is that support services pay close attention to warning signs and undergo thorough investigations to collect key evidence; that the police work closely with experts and facilitate cross-agency cooperation to grasp the complexity of the victim's experience, gain their trust, and gather relevant evidence; and that expert witnesses are involved in court proceedings to elucidate the necessary cultural, religious, and familial background and thus help the court avoid essentialising particular forms of gender-based violence.

---

[23] Gill and Anitha (n2).

Achieving best evidence: victim care and the use of intermediaries

A fundamental challenge in preventing (or at least improving outcomes in) FM cases is victims' inability to access appropriate services. Although the police in *Regina v RB* directed the victim to charity-sector partners, their skilled intervention was hampered by the fact that the situation had been ongoing for so many years: the victim required intensive, long-term assistance to address the trauma and other difficulties caused by her experiences between 2012 and 2016. A further complication was that the victim displayed challenging behaviours: she was particularly suspicious of the police, lawyers, and various legal processes involved in the case.

The victim chose to provide her pretrial evidence in the form of police statements rather than a pre-recorded interview, and her initial statement was taken without the benefit of an intermediary. After the defendant had been charged, the CPS requested a conference with the police during which they recommended that an intermediary be engaged to assess the victim, report on her vulnerabilities, and advise the police on how they could most effectively obtain further evidence through additional statements. Counsel also directed the police to collect and collate third-party materials, including documentation from social services, the victim's school, GPs, and children's services, to create a full picture of the victim and her situation. Given that the victim's reliability and credibility would inevitably be called into question by the defence, this strategy of proactive disclosure management and active case-building meant that the police and CPS could establish a comprehensive understanding of the victim's experiences from 2012 onwards.

Over the years, the victim had experienced high levels of intervention from statutory services. Gathering, collating, and assessing all this material proved key to the successful prosecution of the case, but this work only commenced after the October 2016 investigation had begun. The materials gathered provided rich evidence of a controlling mother struggling to deal with her daughter's burgeoning sexuality and the impact of the former's subsequent 'solution' on an already vulnerable child. The victim's response had been to engage in risky behaviours, which in turn cemented the defendant's belief that the best way to control her daughter's sexuality was to formalise the 2012 marriage as soon as her daughter turned 18.

The police worked hard to build trust with the victim, separating investigative and safeguarding roles by appointing an intermediary to undertake all safeguarding duties. The separation of these roles enabled investigators to focus on their enquiries while a police liaison officer took ownership of the victim's care. The police liaison officer provided consistent and reliable ongoing support for the victim, with continued contact and clear boundaries. This helped to develop the victim's confidence in the legal process, which was critical to her remaining involved throughout the trial. Considerable care was taken to handle interactions appropriately, and the police devised a contact protocol to ensure transparency and full compliance with disclosure obligations.

The police liaison officer assisted this process in numerous ways, including by helping the prosecution to recognise specific trauma triggers that resulted in reactive and often self-sabotaging behaviours in the victim. This process also allowed the liaison officer to outline the victim's linguistic and cognitive abilities, helping counsel formulate effective questions to elicit reliable, accurate testimony while reducing the risk of secondary trauma.[24] Engaging the police liaison officer as an intermediary made plain the need for examination and cross-examination to be carefully managed; as a result, a 'ground rules' hearing was held to determine the parameters and form of questioning best suited to securing the victim's best evidence in court.[25]

Under the Criminal Procedure Rules 2015, courts preparing for trial must take every reasonable step to facilitate the participation of witnesses and defendants. In addition, section 29 of the Youth Justice and Criminal Evidence Act 1999 provides for any and all examinations of a vulnerable witness to be conducted through an intermediary, who will communicate questions to the witness and (if required) communicate the witness's answers to the questioner in turn, explaining those answers where necessary.[26] During the 'ground rules' hearing in *Regina v RB*, the questions the CPS and defence were planning to ask the victim were subject to stringent judicial scrutiny. The CPS also decided to change the traditional order in which witnesses appeared, presenting the victim's evidence after that of other witnesses so that the jury would be fully apprised of the victim's history, background, and reasons for certain behaviours before hearing from her. The defence's cooperation with this tactic further demonstrated how a collaborative working relationship between professionals in such cases can help to minimise secondary victimisation without undermining the fairness of the trial process.[27]

Thanks to these measures, and despite the victim's considerable trauma and the significant distress caused by testifying against her mother, she was able to clearly describe for the jury her situation in the UK and Pakistan, the methods of coercion used, and how they made her feel. Although the victim lacked sophisticated language and conceptual skills, she was still able to explain the deception and manipulation her mother had employed to secure her agreement

---

[24] E Henderson, '"A Very Valuable Tool": Judges, Advocates and Intermediaries Discuss the Intermediary System in England and Wales' (2015) https://journals.sagepub.com/doi/abs/10.1177/1365712715580535, accessed 23 July 2025. M Outtara, P Sen, and M Thompson, 'Forced Marriage, Forced Sex: The Perils of Childhood for Girls' (1998) 6(3) Gender and Development 27; J Plotnikoff and R Woolfson, *Intermediaries in the Criminal Justice System: Improving Communication with Vulnerable Witnesses and Defendants* (Policy Press 2015).

[25] Henderson (n24).

[26] Ibid.

[27] Plotnikoff and Woolfson (n24).

to leave the UK in 2016. She detailed her reliance upon her mother as she had approached the end of her time in care and how her mother had encouraged her to return home and hand over her passport. The victim also told the jury about how her mother had created conflict between her and her social workers, noting the mother's anger and hostility towards children's services and her undermining of various protective measure put in place by them. She then explained how the trust she had placed in her mother – trust that the 'holiday' to Pakistan signified her mother's love and acceptance – had been betrayed.

The victim told the court that when she arrived in Pakistan, her mother had convinced her that it was unsafe for her to leave the house alone because she was a Western female. She also explained the psychological impact of being part of a new family group with different social rules and behaviours, particularly regarding gender roles and expectations. She had no money, her mother was holding her passport, and she did not know where she was geographically, only that she was a considerable distance from the airport. Without access to her usual support structures, the victim did not know which institutions she could turn to for help. Moreover, she had no independent internet or phone access, relying instead upon sporadic and surreptitious use of her mother's phone. Her lack of self-confidence and low self-esteem were major factors in how her mother was able to coerce her into marriage in this situation. The mother had also refused to listen to the victim's protests, threatening to disown her and asserting her disappointment in her for not wanting to do this 'one small thing'.

The victim's description of the marriage process and celebrations made a strong impact on the jury's verdict, including on the count of perjury; naturally, it also had a significant impact on the jury's appraisal of the veracity of the defendant's testimony as a whole. Conducted over a number of days at a variety of venues, and involving elaborate traditional clothing, the marriage celebrations had culminated in a *walima* attended by 250 guests. The jury found the defendant's claims that these arrangements had all been made just two weeks after their arrival in Pakistan, as well as the reasons she gave for excluding all family members in the UK, not credible. The defence had supplied the police with video footage of the celebrations, but the footage was later proven to have been significantly edited; it then became part of the prosecution's case, as it provided evidence of the defendant's controlling and manipulative behaviour. Similarly, the marriage certificate that the victim had signed, which the defendant subsequently gave to police as evidence of her daughter's willing consent, supported the prosecution's contention about the level of deception the defendant had employed. The certificate asserted that the victim's address was in Pakistan and that her stepfather (who was in the UK when the wedding occurred) was acting as her guardian (a role that must be undertaken by the bride's natural father under Islamic law). In fact, all the roles formally required by the Pakistani wedding process were undertaken by members of the defendant's second husband's family.

These disclosures and explanations show that as the victim's trust in the police and criminal justice system grew – largely through a shrewd choice of police liaison officer and the diligence of the investigating officers – she was able to present a more comprehensive narrative. Indeed, the clarity of the victim's evidence developed in parallel with the police and prosecution's knowledge and understanding of the case. Thus, in FM cases such as *Regina v RB*, the importance of building trusting relationships, separating investigative and safeguarding functions, and making the right choice of police liaison officer (ie one who offers continuity, consistency and reliability) cannot be overstated.

Key learnings: protecting and supporting victims

FM victims often face a stark choice between complying with familial wishes or being completely ostracised by their family and community.[28] Some are at risk of physical violence or even (as in the Shafilea Ahmed case) murder.[29] Even when the victim has significant external support, the effects of losing long-term relationships and support structures are devastating:[30] the police cannot provide an alternative for a lifetime of relationships. Therefore, once the criminal justice process has concluded, significant ongoing support and assistance are required to help victims build new lives.[31]

Regina v RB demonstrates that one of the key challenges for prosecutions is to overcome the barriers that prevent victims reporting either FM itself or concerns about the risk of FM.[32] Proper awareness of such reports, and effective responses to them, must become the norm. The victim in this case did not report what was happening to the authorities herself; instead, it was her sister who brought the FM to the attention of the relevant statutory agencies. However, although children's services actively considered applying for an FMPO in 2016, they did not do so, and the police had not been made aware of their concerns. Even when the police were finally informed, the information came through a third party. Indeed, the success of the prosecution was largely due to the fact that police were able to access considerable evidence of the defendant's alarming behaviours because the victim had been in the care system. Women and girls without access to support services, those whose family members and/or community are complicit, and those whose lives do not intersect with statutory agencies are unlikely to be identified by third parties; in such cases, victim disclosure offers the only realistic prospect of assistance. However, as FM can also be committed by British citizens and residents travelling to other jurisdictions to marry, serious questions arise as to how those whom they 'marry' can be identified and informed of their fundamental right to choose their own marriage

---

[28]   Gill (n21).

[29]   Ibid.

[30]   H Love and others, 'Navigating an Unclear Terrain: Challenges in Recognizing, Naming, and Accessing Services for "Forced Marriage"' (2019) 25(9) Violence Against Women 1138.

[31]   Gill (n21).

[32]   Ibid.

partner. Therefore, going forward, best-practice guidelines need to be developed to improve statutory agencies' ability to recognise risk factors and warning signs, and to act on them accordingly, in order to increase the rate of prevention, or at least early intervention.

Understanding the role of socio-cultural factors and transnational elements

The fact that FM is a mechanism through which one person is controlled by one or more others is central to understanding this crime. While the desire for control plays out in many different ways, FM most often arises in families and communities where patriarchal power systems are the norm.[33] The defendant in *Regina v RB* was part of the Mirpuri diaspora in Britain and maintained close links with Pakistan; her second husband was a Pakistani national from the Punjab, a place she visited regularly and where she had a home. The defendant's background and the relevant socio-cultural norms, values, and traditions are thus crucial to understanding her decision to force her daughter to marry a Pakistani national overseas. Indeed, the defendant was only *able* to commit the offences thanks to her knowledge of the local community in Pakistan, her extended family network there, and the failure of UK statutory agencies to robustly address the risks they had identified in early 2016. The partnership between the expert witness and the prosecution team was essential in illuminating and explaining all this for the jury.[34]

Regina v RB is a clear example of how a transnational FM 'exploits boundaries and jurisdictions as strategic advantages'.[35] These strategic advantages gave the defendant the means to exert control over her daughter in Pakistan that she did not have in the UK, particularly given the protection afforded by the UK care system (notwithstanding the criticisms to be made of the care system's actions, particularly in 2012). Although the victim spoke fluent Urdu, was culturally Muslim and of Pakistani heritage, she was also a British teenager who had been raised in the UK and had visited Pakistan only occasionally. By taking her daughter to a different environment in which different legal and social rules and values applied – as well as removing her support network and denying her access to money, means of communication, and any exit from the situation – the defendant was able to exploit her daughter's vulnerabilities and coerce her into marriage.

To bolster the likelihood of successful FM prosecutions, victims must be empowered to come forward. To help enable this, support services must become more attuned to FM dynamics in order to adequately assess and address risk factors. For example, there is a general reluctance in children's services to use

---

[33] Gill (n21).

[34] Gill and Gould (n19).

[35] A Jamieson, 'Transnational Organised Crime: A European Perspective' (2001) 24 Studies in Conflict and Terrorism 377.

care proceedings for older children[36] – but since the victims in most FM cases are over 16, this approach needs to change for those at potential risk of FM and related crimes.[37] There is also an assumption that young people trying to escape abuse are likely to leave their family home. However, it is rare for South Asian teens and young adults to move out of the family home before marriage; doing so often has long-term implications for family and community acceptance, and even for the young person's ability to marry within the community.[38] Understanding FM and the contexts in which it is most likely to occur will better equip services to offer victims the support they need. It will also enable services to recognise the specific forms of risk and coercion involved and the particular ways in which victims might respond because of their socio-cultural values and experiences.[39]

Summary

FM often takes place in cultural and familial contexts with patriarchal power systems. A better understanding of these factors is key to developing best practice to assist victims more effectively.

The successful prosecution of FM cases relies on victims feeling empowered to come forwards. The presence of specialist intermediaries to support them during police investigations is critical to victims' empowerment. Intermediaries can explain to police and support services the socio-cultural dynamics involved and how those dynamics may have affected the victim's mind-set and behaviour, especially with regard to coercive family tactics.

Expert witnesses play a vital role in helping law enforcement and legal practitioners to understand the religious and socio-cultural contexts (eg marriage practices and traditions) underpinning individual FM cases in order to ensure that effective prosecutions can be brought.

Conclusion

Until recently, forms of violence experienced primarily by Black and minoritised women, including FM, were neglected in both academic literature and policy debates. Now they are often hyper-visible without necessarily being well understood.[40] Traditionally, domestic violence has been understood as primarily perpetrated by male partners and ex-partners; today, increasing attention is

---

[36]   J Dickens and others, 'Courts, Care Proceedings and Outcomes Uncertainty: The Challenges of Achieving and Assessing "Good Outcomes" for Children after Child Protection Proceedings' (2019) Child & Family Social Work 1.

[37]   Gill and Anitha (n2).

[38]   T Mayeda, S Cho, and R Vijaykumar, 'Honor-Based Violence and Coercive Control among Asian Youth in Auckland, New Zealand' (2019) 25(2) Asian Journal of Women's Studies 159.

[39]   Gill and Anitha (n2).

[40]   Gill (n21).

being directed to forms of VAWG committed by relatives (including female relatives) from the wider kin group rather than just the immediate family. As the discussion of *Regina v RB* has demonstrated, although cultural specificities must be recognised when one is shaping legislation and prosecuting offenders, such recognition does not mean that minority *cultures* should be blamed.[41] There is a difference between wholesale condemnation of the culture of a socio-ethnic group and condemnation of the harmful, illegal practices undertaken by some members of that group. Understanding the violence experienced by Black and minoritised women in Britain requires us to take account of the continuities between different forms of VAWG, irrespective of the cultural context in which it is perpetrated, while also addressing the specificity of particular forms of VAWG such as FM.[42] Only then will efforts to address VAWG in general, and FM in particular, move beyond the simplistic cultural essentialising of certain ethnic groups.

The causal factors behind *Regina v RB* are far more complex than the common British media tale of backward immigrant parents and progressive British society. Looking ahead, it will be important to address the harmful effects of patriarchal cultural practices, no matter which culture they are associated with. Preventing these harmful practices will only be possible if the current mono-focus on culture is replaced by a more complex, nuanced, and intersectional understanding that looks at the various types of inequality that lie behind not just FM but all forms of VAWG.

In this case, the prosecution argued that the defendant's compliance with the legal proceedings was based on her expectation that her daughter would not disclose the FM because of her love for, and desire to protect, her mother. This belief seemed to be borne out by the victim's stance upon her return from Pakistan in 2012, and initially in 2016, demonstrating that one of the key barriers to reporting and prosecution is the strength of familial loyalty and affection. Despite the defendant's belief that her daughter would not testify against her, she eventually did so with the help of an intermediary; this led to the defendant being convicted of two offences of FM and an offence of perjury, for which she received a total sentence of four-and-a-half years' imprisonment.

When an investigation and subsequent trial are handled well, as they were in this case (at least as regards the response of statutory agencies after the second 'marriage' in 2016), the legal system can both protect and empower women. This sends a strong message that women who are subjected to deception and coercion during the process of an unwanted marriage will be supported if they feel able (or are enabled) to challenge these practices. A key lesson is the need to improve victims' awareness of, access to, and confidence in the protections afforded by criminal and civil law. In this case, the sensitive way in which police officers dealt

---

[41]   Ibid.
[42]   Ibid.

with the victim, the early investigative advice provided by an experienced CPS lawyer, the early involvement of counsel, and the clear division of safeguarding and investigative functions were critical in securing a successful prosecution.

The case also demonstrates the value of multiagency collaboration, including looking to other sectors (including the charity sector and academia) for the expertise needed to shed light on the cultural, social, religious, and legal contexts of the actors involved. Following her mother's conviction, the victim spoke of her pride at having participated in the criminal proceedings, demonstrating the value of enabling the victim to be part of challenging the serious offences her mother had committed against her. However, a better understanding of risk factors and warning signs might have enabled statutory agencies to intervene in 2012, protecting the victim from years of additional trauma. While successful prosecutions are vital, the best outcomes are when we prevent FMs in the first place by empowering those at risk so that they can avoid victimisation by accessing support and protective measures such as FMPOs.

Further questions to consider

- Consider the value of civil orders in FM cases – what are the benefits and drawbacks of these orders?
- Critically explore the intersectional responses to FM risk factors. How would you offer a holistic overview in dealing with such complex cases when working with support services, the police, and the wider legal system?
- How would you assess the impact of living in a coercive family environment that may contribute to victims/survivors at risk of FM on children living within this?
- Explore the most effective ways to protect victims of FM, sharing innovative practice for dealing with these kinds of cases across diverse communities.

Further materials
Forced Marriage Unit (FMU), 'The Right to Choose: Government Guidance on Forced Marriage (2023) https://www.gov.uk/government/publications/the-right-to-choose-government-guidance-on-forced-marriage, accessed 10 June 2025

Love H and others, 'Navigating an Unclear Terrain: Challenges in Recognizing, Naming, and Accessing Services for "Forced Marriage"' (2019) 25(9) Violence Against Women 1138–59

Outtara M, Sen P, and Thompson M, 'Forced Marriage, Forced Sex: The Perils of Childhood for Girls' (1998) 6(3) Gender and Development 27–33

6

Legal Parenthood and Same-Sex Couples

Brian Sloan

Introduction

A cisgender heterosexual couple who are able and willing to procreate through natural sexual intercourse will have little difficulty in being recognised as the resulting child's legal parents in England and Wales.[1] The woman who gives birth to the child will be the child's legal mother.[2] The man will use his status as biological father to assert *legal* fatherhood, usually straightforwardly using DNA testing if necessary.[3] If he is in a marriage or civil partnership with the mother, he will also benefit from a presumption that he is the legal father.[4] Only subsequent adoption of the child could remove that couple's parenthood.[5]

For 'same-sex' couples, and others who do not fit within the 'traditional' paradigm, establishing legal parenthood will often be more complicated. That is the concern of this chapter, and it is significant given the distinct consequences of the status of legal parenthood per se.[6] At the outset, it is important to note

---

[1] For a general account of the law of parenthood in England and Wales written by the author, see B Sloan, 'The law of parenthood in England and Wales' in C Fenton-Glynn (ed), *The Law of Parenthood: A Comparative Guide* (Edward Elgar 2025).

[2] *Ampthill Peerage* [1988] AC 547; *R (McConnell) v Registrar General for England and Wales* [2020] EWCA Civ 559.

[3] Cf, eg, B Sloan, 'The "Chimera" of Parenthood' (2021) 84(3) Modern Law Review 503.

[4] Legitimacy Act 1976, s A1(2).

[5] The use of assisted reproduction is a pre-requisite for a parental order giving effect to a surrogacy arrangement (see further later in this chapter), so there is no realistic scope for such an order to be made in favour of third parties where a child has been conceived naturally by a couple.

[6] Sloan (n1).

that the interests and welfare of the child concerned do and should play some role in the allocation of legal parenthood to a same-sex couple.

An important preliminary point is that the law does not always adopt a consistent approach to whether the relevant concept is 'sex' or 'gender' in referring to an individual, and by extension a couple, in the context of personal relationships. For example, the assisted reproduction provisions in the Human Fertilisation and Embryology Act (HFEA) 2008 repeatedly refer to a 'woman' who has an embryo placed in her, is artificially inseminated, or carries a child as being the 'mother'.[7] The clear implication of the decision in *R (McConnell) v Registrar General for England and Wales*,[8] however, is that someone who is legally a male (by virtue of the Gender Recognition Act 2004) and is so inseminated and gives birth will be treated as the child's legal 'mother'. Similarly, despite the Act's name, the Marriage (Same Sex) Couples Act 2013 effectively introduced same-*gender* marriage.[9] This chapter will often use the standard terminology of 'same-sex' couples, but highlight instances where a party's transgender status could make a difference.

Some of the difficulties experienced by same-sex/same-gender couples in relation to parenthood are arguably connected to biology itself, but it is the law's attachment of significance to that biology, together with the two-legal-parent limit currently operative in England and Wales,[10] that produces the differential treatment. It is also arguable that some of the hurdles faced by same-sex couples in becoming legal parents are justified by factors such as the child's identity rights. The differential treatment, the complexity, and the potential for controversy not routinely faced by our paradigm cisgender heterosexual couple nevertheless remain. As Jennings and colleagues asserted in 2014, 'gay and lesbian individuals must navigate discriminatory practices on their journey to parenthood'.[11]

This chapter will begin by summarising the relevant law on parenthood as it applies to same-sex couples, focusing specifically on adoption, assisted reproduction, and surrogacy, and then provide a critical overview of same-sex couples' treatment by the legal system in their attempts to become parents. As will be explored, the sex/gender of the parties concerned can have a profound impact on their route to parenthood.

---

[7] See, eg, HFEA 2008, ss 33, 35, 36, 42, and 43.

[8] *McConnell* (n2).

[9] See, eg, Marriage (Same Sex) Couples Act 2013, s 12. Cf, generally, *For Women Scotland Ltd v Scottish Ministers* [2025] UKSC 16.

[10] Cf, eg, JM Scherpe, 'Breaking the Existing Paradigms of Parent–Child Relationships' in G Douglas, M Murch, and V Stephens (eds), *International and National Perspectives on Child and Family Law: Essays in Honour of Nigel Lowe* (Intersentia 2018).

[11] S Jennings and others, 'Why Adoption? Gay, Lesbian, and Heterosexual Adoptive Parents' Reproductive Experiences and Reasons for Adoption' (2014) 17(3) Adoption Quarterly 205, 209.

Summary of the relevant law

A cisgender same-sex couple unable to conceive naturally may become parents via adoption. Under section 50 of the Adoption and Children Act (ACA) 2002, an adoption order can be made in favour of 'a couple',[12] defined in section 144(4) as a married or civil partnership couple, who may now be any combination of genders,[13] or 'two people (whether of different sexes or the same sex) living as partners in an enduring family relationship'.[14] In addition, the female partner of a woman who gives birth can be treated as the child's second female parent under the HFEA 2008. Under section 41, 'if at the time of the placing in her of the embryo or the sperm and eggs or of her artificial insemination', the (birthing) mother 'was a party to a civil partnership with another woman or a marriage with another woman', then essentially 'the other party to the civil partnership or marriage is to be treated as a parent of the child unless it is shown that she did not consent to the placing in' the mother 'of the embryo or the sperm and eggs or to her artificial insemination (as the case may be)'. If the mother is not married or in a civil partnership with the intended second parent, second female parenthood can be conferred by virtue of the 'agreed female parenthood conditions' (governed by sections 43 and 44). Finally, a same-sex couple who were party to a surrogacy arrangement could become a child's legal parents after the birth by obtaining a parental order under section 54 of the 2008 Act, which allows applicants to be spouses, civil partners, or partners 'in an enduring family relationship'. The rest of this chapter will provide a more detailed and critical account of the position of same-sex couples with regard to adoption, assisted reproduction, and surrogacy respectively. It will be seen that despite the basic eligibility of same-sex couples to become parents via all three methods, each presents barriers as compared to the position of the naturally reproducing couple described in the introduction.

Same-sex couples and adoption

The road to eligibility

The history of the law's treatment of LGBT+ (would-be) parents is an unhappy one from the perspective of those individuals. Even where an LGBT+ person became a legal parent as part of a heterosexual relationship *before* becoming a member of a same-sex couple, they faced prejudice in applications for what would now be called child arrangements orders specifying that their children

---

[12] ACA 2002, s 50(1).

[13] Marriage (Same Sex Couples) Act 2013; Civil Partnerships, Marriages and Deaths (Registration etc) Act 2019.

[14] Relatives are excluded: ACA 2002, s 144(5).

would live with them.[15] In *C v C (A Minor) (Custody: Appeal)*, decided by the Court of Appeal in 1990, for example, it was held that the ideal environment for a child's upbringing is the home of their mother and father and, where that is impossible because of separation, the court's task is 'to choose the alternative which comes closest to that ideal'.[16] Despite changing social attitudes, it was asserted that 'a lesbian relationship ... is an unusual background in which to bring up a child'.[17] In 1999, however, the European Court of Human Rights held in *Salgueiro da Silva Mouta v Portugal* that it was a breach of Article 8 of the European Convention on Human Rights in conjunction with Article 14 to have granted custody of a child to her mother on the basis that her father was a gay man living in a relationship with another man.[18]

Whatever the changing approach to residence, at the end of the 20th century there was still no mechanism in England and Wales for a same-sex couple jointly to adopt a child. It was in principle possible for one member of a same-sex couple to adopt solely, with the possibility of a 'joint residence order'. Such an order would specify that the child would live with both partners, while also giving the non-adopting partner a measure of practical authority over the child by conferring parental responsibility.[19] But only one member of the couple would have the status of legal parent.

Same-sex adoption was finally legislated for when the Adoption Act 1976 was effectively replaced by the ACA 2002. As Ball put it:

> The [Adoption and Children] Bill originally mirrored the restrictions on eligibility to adopt in the 1976 Act. However, sustained, well-articulated pressure from [the British Association for Adoption and Fostering] and almost all the leading child care organisations persuaded the Government to allow a free vote on a private members' amendment which lifted the restriction at third reading in the House of Commons. An opposition attempt subsequently to restrict the definition of 'couple' to heterosexual couples was defeated by a large majority. Intense lobbying by individuals and organisations opposed on religious or other grounds to adoption by unmarried couples, combined with the natural conservatism of many peers, initially succeeded in getting the amendment reversed in the House of Lords. It was then reinstated by the Commons and a further attempt to reverse it in the Lords was narrowly defeated

---

15 Such orders were called 'residence orders' until Children Act (CA) 1989, s 8 was amended by Children and Families Act 2014, s 12.

16 [1991] 1 FLR 223, at 228.

17 Ibid.

18 (2001) 31 EHRR 47.

19 See, eg, *Re AB (A Minor) (Adoption: Unmarried Couple)* [1996] 1 FLR 27; CA 1989, s 3. Such orders would now be child arrangements orders.

when several peers, who had previously resisted the change, were persuaded of the strength of the case.[20]

Same-sex couples were ultimately included as eligible adopters in the 2002 Act. Despite the difficult history, it is highly significant that legislation facilitating same-sex joint adoption was passed *before* the Civil Partnership Act 2004 was. By virtue of an adoption order, the child effectively acquires new legal parents,[21] usually in place of the previous ones.[22] The adoptive parents will be registered in the Adopted Children Register as the 'parent(s)' of the adopted child.[23]

The realities of the adoption process

The fact that one or more people are in principle *eligible* to adopt by virtue of the statutory qualifications does not in itself mean that they will have their wish to adopt fulfilled. In one sense, a same-sex couple are formally in no worse a position than a heterosexual couple who undergo the adoption process. It would be actionable discrimination for a same-sex couple to be disfavoured as prospective adopters on the basis of their gender/sexual orientation alone.[24] But two points should be made. First, subtler discrimination is inherently possible in practice. For example, the 2002 Act expressly permits the making of regulations 'for the purpose of securing that, in determining the suitability of a couple to adopt a child, proper regard is had to the need for stability and permanence in their relationship',[25] and this has been done.[26] This sort of measure could facilitate de facto discrimination.[27] Secondly, a cisgender same-sex couple are perhaps more likely to opt for adoption, with all its hurdles and complexities, precisely because they are unable to conceive naturally.

Even if a particular same-sex couple successfully complete an adoption agency's vetting procedures and convince the agency that they are plausible prospective adopters of a hypothetical child in principle, that is far from the end of the process. Fundamentally, and I would argue correctly, adoption is a practice ostensibly undertaken for the benefit of children, not primarily a service intended to benefit prospective adopters.[28] The welfare of the child potentially

---

[20] C Ball, 'The Adoption and Children Act 2002: A Critical Examination' (2005) 29(2) Adoption & Fostering 6, 10.

[21] ACA 2002, s 67.

[22] Cf, eg, the possibility that a child can be adopted by the partner of an existing legal parent without terminating the parenthood of that parent: ibid, s 46(3)(b).

[23] Adopted Children and Adoption Contact Registers Regulations 2005/924, sch 1.

[24] See, eg, *EB v France* [2008] 1 FLR 850.

[25] ACA 2002, s 45(2).

[26] Suitability of Adopters Regulations 2005/1712, r 4(2).

[27] See, eg, U Kilkelly, 'In *Re P*: Adoption, Discrimination and the Best Interests of the Child' (2010) 22(2) Child and Family Law Quarterly 115, 130.

[28] See, eg, P Hodgkin and R Newell, *Implementation Handbook for the Convention on the Rights of the Child* (3rd edn, UNICEF 2007) 295.

to be adopted, throughout their life, is the 'paramount' consideration 'whenever a court or adoption agency is coming to a decision relating to the adoption of a child'.[29] The relevant checklist of factors to be taken into account when that principle is being applied include, inter alia, the child's relationship with both existing relatives and any prospective adopters.[30]

Significantly, since the 1970s, there has been a broad change in the dominant character of adoption, from an ostensibly voluntary process whereby 'trouble-free' babies were relinquished in secrecy by potentially stigmatised unmarried mothers, to the more open, but also involuntary, character of adoption today as a solution for older, potentially troubled children with experience of the care system.[31] A same-sex couple may be faced with a difficult decision as to whether to embark on the process. The preliminary step is placement of the child with prospective adopters. In the absence of parental consent, this requires a placement order.[32] Such an order, in turn, generally requires a finding that the child is suffering, or likely to suffer, significant harm attributable (in most cases) to the standard of parental care.[33] Parental consent to the order can be dispensed with on the basis that 'the welfare of the child requires the consent to be dispensed with'.[34] Following a minimum period of residence with the child,[35] together with appropriate assessments,[36] the prospective adopters can apply for the final adoption order transferring parenthood to them.[37] Even where (birth) parental consent was dispensed with at the placement order stage, the parents can seek to oppose the final order if there has been a change in circumstance since the placement order was made.[38] Significantly, however, in *Re J and S (Children)*, the parents unsuccessfully argued that the fact that the prospective adopters were a same-sex couple (*inter alia*) was a relevant change of circumstance for this purpose.[39] Even if the parents are given permission to oppose the order, their consent can still be dispensed with as before,[40] and the order will be made (or refused, albeit that this is unlikely at that stage of the process)[41] on the basis of the paramountcy of the child's welfare.

---

29   ACA 2002, s 1.
30   Ibid, s 1(4)(f).
31   See, eg, N Lowe, 'The Changing Face of Adoption: The Gift/Donation Model versus the Contract/Services Model' (1997) 9(4) Child and Family Law Quarterly 371.
32   The relevant consent is that of all parents with parental responsibility and legal guardians (including special guardians): ACA 2002, s 52(6).
33   Ibid, s 21.
34   Ibid, s 52(1)(b).
35   Ibid, s 42.
36   Ibid, s 43.
37   Ibid, s 46(1).
38   Ibid, s 47(5)–(7).
39   [2014] EWFC 4.
40   ACA 2002, s 47(2).
41   B Sloan, 'Adoption Decisions in England: *Re B (A Child) (Care Proceedings: Appeal)* and Beyond' (2015) 37(4) Journal of Social Welfare and Family Law 437.

Successive 21st-century governments have sought to increase the number and speed of adoptions from state-supported foster care, with adoption perceived as a potentially more desirable alternative to a child remaining in such care.[42] But the Supreme Court in *Re B (A Child) (Care Proceedings: Appeal)* emphasised 'adoption of a child against her parents' wishes should only be contemplated as a last resort – when all else fails',[43] meaning that 'before making an adoption order ... the court must be satisfied that there is no practical way of the authorities (or others) providing the requisite assistance and support'.[44] The judiciary have since taken a rigorous approach to whether adoption is appropriate for a given child.[45] I have argued that this is admirable in itself, in light of the draconian nature of adoption, the risk of social engineering, and the rights (including under Article 8 of the European Convention on Human Rights) and interests of both the child and their birth parents.[46] But with this background, same-sex couples relying on adoption to build their family may find adoption to be a stressful or even frustrating experience for a variety of reasons, even if ultimately a positive one for both the adopters and the child.[47] Complex issues may arise in relation to post-adoption contact and access to information about origins.[48]

'Step-parent' adoption

If one member of a same-sex couple is *already* a parent of a child, the other partner may also become a parent through a 'step-parent' adoption. Under the ACA 2002, the partner of an existing parent can become a parent in addition,[49] excluding the non-partner existing parent to give a measure of security to the relationship between the child and their former step-parent/ new parent. The issue of step-parent adoption is in some ways very different from that of the more typical 'public law' adoption with which we have mainly been concerned so far. A parent may be particularly keen for their new partner to be given formal recognition and status in relation to their children, and it may reflect the reality of the 'blended' family's lives. On the other hand, it is arguably precisely because there is no need to provide the child with a secure

---

[42] See, eg, B Sloan, 'Adoption versus Alternative Forms of Care' in JG Dwyer (ed), *The Oxford Handbook of Children and the Law* (OUP 2020).

[43] [2013] UKSC 33, para 104.

[44] Ibid, para 105.

[45] See, in particular, *Re B-S (Children) (Adoption Order: Leave to Oppose)* [2013] EWCA Civ 1146.

[46] See, eg, Sloan (n42).

[47] See, eg, J Doughty and others, 'The Legal and Administrative Processes in Adoption: Views and Experiences of Newly Formed Adoptive Families' (2017) 39(4) Journal of Social Welfare and Family Law 473. F Tasker and C Bellamy, 'Adoption by Same-Sex Couples – Reaffirming Evidence: Could More Children Be Placed?' (2019) 2 Family Law 171, 177.

[48] B Sloan, 'Post-Adoption Contact Reform: Compounding the State-Ordered Termination of Parenthood?' (2014) 73(2) Cambridge Law Journal 378.

[49] ACA 2002, s 46(3)(b).

home completely *outside* the family that the issue of step-parent adoption is difficult. It might be questioned whether it is truly justifiable to terminate the parenthood of one of the child's parents to enhance the legal status of a step-parent, whether part of a same-sex couple or not, given that there are other mechanisms through which the step-parent could be granted parental responsibility to enable participation in care and decision making.[50] In *Re P (A Child) (Adoption: Step-Parent)*, however, it was held to be wrong to say that every case required a finding that 'welfare would be prejudiced significantly if the [adoption] order were not made'.[51]

Evaluation

As stated, it could be argued that same-sex couples and heterosexual couples are in principle treated in the same way by the law of adoption. Adoption, however, is a particularly controversial and potentially arduous process, which is rightly focused on the needs of the child. The reality is that a same-sex couple may be more likely to subject themselves to that process because they are less likely to be able to reproduce naturally. Some prefer adoption to assisted reproduction techniques because it gives them an equal non-biological and legal connection to the child concerned.[52] In addition, Mellish and colleagues found that same-sex couples were more likely to feel that they had experienced negative reactions as they journeyed through the adoption system,[53] although this situation may have improved more recently.[54] In any event, it is clear that a significant number of same-sex couples *do* successfully become parents by adoption: for the quarter October to December 2023, 14 per cent of all adoption orders were made in favour of same-sex couples, as compared to the 57 per cent issued to mixed-sex couples, 18 per cent to sole applicants, and 10 per cent to step-parents.[55] This is despite the fact that same-sex couple families made up only 1.7 per cent of all couple families in England and Wales according to the 2021 census.[56]

---

[50] See, eg, CA 1989, s 4A.

[51] [2014] EWCA Civ 1174, para 31.

[52] Tasker and Bellamy (n47) 177.

[53] L Mellish and others, *Gay, Lesbian and Heterosexual Adoptive Families: Family Relationships, Child Adjustment and Adopters' Experiences* (British Association for Adoption & Fostering 2013).

[54] Tasker and Bellamy (n47) 178.

[55] Ministry of Justice, 'Family Court Statistics Quarterly: October to December 2023' (2024) https://www.gov.uk/government/statistics/family-court-statistics-quarterly-october-to-december-2023/family-court-statistics-quarterly-october-to-december-2023#adoptions, accessed 15 May 2024.

[56] Office for National Statistics (ONS), 'Families in England and Wales: Census 2021' (2023) https://www.ons.gov.uk/peoplepopulationandcommunity/birthsdeathsandmarriages/families/articles/familiesinenglandandwales/census2021#same-sex-families, accessed 15 May 2024.

Summary

Same-sex couples have in principle been able to adopt children jointly since 2005, under the ACA 2002. They are eligible even if not in a marriage or civil partnership, provided they are in a relevant 'enduring family relationship' with each other. Significant numbers of same-sex couples do adopt children and it would be unlawful to discriminate against such a couple on the basis of their sexual orientation. That said, adoption is primarily, and rightly, seen as a process undertaken for the benefit of children rather than as a service for prospective adopters, with the child's welfare ultimately treated as the paramount consideration. Most adoptions in England and Wales now concern children who have some experience of the care system, many of whom will have complex histories and needs and are being adopted without the consent of their birth parents. Same-sex couples may find the adoption process to be a stressful one, and it is a more arduous route to parenthood as compared to that experienced by a heterosexual couple able and willing to conceive naturally.

Same-sex couples and assisted reproduction

Legal parenthood and assisted reproduction

One of the most significant, and controversial, features of the HFEA 2008 was its facilitation of legal parenthood for a mother's *female* partner in an assisted reproduction context (inevitably involving donor sperm in the case of a cisgender lesbian couple). While we have seen that joint adoption had been available to same-sex couples for several years, the 2008 Act was novel in allowing the creation of children who would have two female parents from birth.[57] As explained earlier in the chapter, it presumptively treats the female spouse or civil partner of the mother as the child's second parent, which mirrors the mechanism through which the mother's husband or male civil partner becomes the child's father under the Act.[58] The Act contains a general principle that '[a]ny reference (however expressed)'[59] in 'any enactment, deed or any other instrument or document (whenever passed or made)'[60] 'to the father of a child who has' a second female parent by virtue of the Act 'is to be read as a reference to the woman who is [thus] a parent of the child'.[61]

We have seen that the 'agreed female parenthood conditions' apply where the mother is not in a marriage/civil partnership with the intended second female

---

[57] Ignoring the possibility of legal gender change.

[58] Compare HFEA 2008, ss 41 and 35.

[59] Ibid, s 53(2).

[60] Ibid, s 53(1).

[61] Ibid, s 53(2). The general principle does not apply where a statute makes express reference to second female parenthood: s 53(4)–(5).

parent, and again these are equivalent to the 'agreed fatherhood conditions' applied to a *male* informal partner.[62] In order for an *informal* partner to become the parent, the artificial insemination or placement of sperm and eggs or embryo must occur 'in the course of treatment services provided in the United Kingdom' by a licensed person.[63] The agreed female parenthood conditions require the intended second female parent to give to the person responsible for supervising the licensed treatment a notice that she 'consents to being treated' as the second parent of 'any child resulting from treatment provided to [the mother] under the licence'.[64] The person who is to give birth must also give the responsible person 'a notice stating that she consents' to the intended second parent 'being so treated'.[65] The conditions require that neither party have given a further notice withdrawing consent,[66] and the person who gives birth has not given a subsequent notice that someone else is to be treated as the second parent.[67]

Access to treatment for same-sex couples

Whatever the possible controversies, a survey of 40 years' worth of empirical evidence by Golombok suggests that

> the number, gender, sexual orientation, and biological relatedness of parents matters less for children than previously thought. The presence of a father, or a mother, or two parents, is not essential for children to thrive. What matters most for children is the quality of relationships within their family, the support of their wider community, and the attitudes of the society in which they live.[68]

Despite this, the starting point as regards access to treatment is that there is no absolute right to become a parent or to fertility treatment in English law. In fact, the proportion of treatment cycles funded by the NHS has been decreasing in recent years.[69] There has been controversy over a requirement that same-sex couples pay for private treatment cycles before being eligible for NHS treatment, while heterosexual couples merely had to attempt natural conception for two

---

[62]   Compare ibid, ss 43 and 44 with ss 35 and 36.
[63]   Ibid, s 36(a).
[64]   Ibid, s 44(1)(a).
[65]   Ibid, s 44(1)(b).
[66]   Ibid, s 44(1)(c).
[67]   Ibid, s 44(1)(d).
[68]   S Golombok, 'The Psychological Wellbeing of ART Children: What Have We Learned from 40 Years of Research?' (2020) 41(4) Reproductive Biomedicine Online 743, 745.
[69]   Human Fertilisation and Embryology Authority, 'Fertility Treatment 2021: Preliminary Trends and Figures' (2023) https://www.hfea.gov.uk/about-us/publications/research-and-data/fertility-treatment-2021-preliminary-trends-and-figures/, accessed 15 May 2024.

years before being similarly eligible, albeit that the practice is apparently being changed.[70] In any event, female same-sex couples are increasingly using IVF.[71]

Irrespective of funding considerations, under section 13(5) of the HFEA 1990, '[a] woman shall not be provided with treatment services unless account has been taken of the welfare of any child who may be born as a result of the treatment (including the need of that child for supportive parenting), and of any other child who may be affected by the birth'. The legislative history of that sub-section, itself curious because of its suggestion that a hypothetical child might be better off not having been born at all, is indicative of the changes in law and society since the 1990 Act was enacted. The original section referred to the need *for a father* rather than for supportive parenting, but was changed by the 2008 Act against a backdrop of considerable debate,[72] including opposition from religious groups.[73] In one sense, a change was inevitable in light of the fact that one of the purposes of the Act was to confer parenthood on people who were not technically fathers but 'second female parents'. But for some it was contentious to remove the express reference to the heterosexual, two-parent 'ideal', while Wallbank and Dietz highlighted that even the gender-neutral formulation settled upon was still concerned with 'regulating parentage within prescribed parameters'.[74]

An insight into the welfare assessment is provided by the Human Fertilisation and Embryology Authority's Code of Practice.[75] Clinics are advised to assess both the intended mother and any partner to ascertain whether there is a risk of significant harm or neglect in respect of any child produced,[76] though there is an emphasis on a fair assessment in which 'patients should not be discriminated against on grounds of age, disability, gender reassignment, marriage and civil partnership, pregnancy and maternity, race, religion or belief, sex or sexual orientation'.[77]

It should be noted, however, that the Act's assisted reproduction provisions per se are based around the person who gives birth being the child's mother and any partner being the father/second parent. This means that (subject to legal gender

---

[70] A Hutton, 'NHS Group Changes Same-Sex Fertility Rules after Couple's Campaign', *The Guardian* (22 July 2023) https://www.theguardian.com/world/2023/jul/22/nhs-group-changes-same-sex-fertility-rules-couples-campaign, accessed 15 May 2024.

[71] Human Fertilisation and Embryology Authority (n69).

[72] See, eg, J McCandless and S Sheldon, '"No Father Required"? The Welfare Assessment in the Human Fertilisation and Embryology Act 2008' (2010) 18 Feminist Legal Studies 201.

[73] See, eg, S Kettell, 'Did Secularism Win Out? The Debate over the Human Fertilisation and Embryology Bill' (2009) 80(1) The Political Quarterly 67.

[74] J Wallbank and C Dietz, 'Lesbian Mothers, Fathers and other Animals: Is the Political Personal in Multiple Parent Families?' (2013) 25(4) Child and Family Law Quarterly 451, 456.

[75] Human Fertilisation and Embryology Authority, 'Code of Practice' (9th edn, 2023) https://portal.hfea.gov.uk/media/yrkn55xa/2024-10-01-hfea-code-of-practice-v9-4.pdf, accessed 4 July 2025.

[76] Ibid, para 8.3.

[77] Ibid, para 8.6.

change), a male same-sex couple cannot use those provisions, albeit that they do have access to both parental orders giving effect to surrogacy arrangements and adoption.

Trans★ parents

Where a trans★ man has retained female reproductive capacity, it is possible for that person and his male partner to become a child's legal parents under the HFEA 2008. Controversially, however, because of the decision in *R (TT) v Registrar General for England and Wales*,[78] upheld in *R (McConnell) v Registrar General for England and Wales*,[79] a trans★ man who gives birth will be treated as the child's *mother*, irrespective of a gender recognition certificate giving him the legal gender of male. On the President's analysis at first instance:

> being a 'mother' is to describe a person's role in the biological process of conception, pregnancy and birth; no matter what else a mother may do, this role is surely at the essence of what a 'mother' undertakes with respect to a child to whom they give birth. It is a matter of the role taken in the biological process, rather the person's particular sex or gender.[80]

Strictly speaking, not all same-gender couples will need to make use of the HFEA 2008 in order to become legal parents. It would in principle be possible, for example, for a trans★ man who retained the ability to gestate a child to become pregnant via sexual intercourse with his cisgender male partner. Even here, however, by virtue of *McConnell* the trans★ man would be the mother of the child. Conversely, if a trans★ woman was able to inseminate her female partner, the trans★ woman would be the legal 'father' by virtue of *McConnell*, even if legally female.

The outcome in *McConnell* has been criticised. On Fenton-Glynn's analysis, the President's judgment laid bare the extent to which 'a gendered, heteronormative, conception of the family' remains in operation in English law.[81] This 'binary conception of the parental role privileges a certain form of "family life" rooted in the sexual family ideal, consisting of one (cisgendered) man and one (cisgendered) woman in a monogamous, heterosexual, relationship, who raise their own genetic children'.[82] Even as 'alternative' family forms have been recognised, this has been done using what Fenton-Glynn calls an 'assimilationist approach', which involves

---

[78]   [2019] EWHC 2384 (Fam).
[79]   *McConnell* (n2).
[80]   *McConnell* (n2) para 139.
[81]   C Fenton-Glynn, 'Deconstructing Parenthood: What Makes a "Mother"?' (2020) 79(1) Cambridge Law Journal 34, 36.
[82]   Ibid.

'taking the traditional family model as the starting point and working outwards to encompass emerging relationship forms'.[83] The result is that '[n]ew forms of parenthood are not recognised in their own right, but in terms of how they fit with conventional understandings of family relationships'.[84] The issue of gender neutrality in this context is complex, however: it is arguable that the conclusion in *McConnell* was gender neutral since it involved a recognition that either males or females could in certain circumstances be mothers (or indeed fathers).

Davis has emphasised that 'the law's insistence that trans men be termed a "mother" is a clear refusal to acknowledge the social reality of families outside the "traditional" ideal'.[85] With reference to empirical research, Davis argues that '"mother" is clearly a highly gendered term, illustrating that "male mothers" ... is a poorly constructed legal fallacy'.[86] It should be noted, however, that substantive differences in the treatment of mothers and fathers may have to be resolved before a fully equal approach to the labels can realistically be taken, even if it would be possible to distinguish between the label of 'motherhood' and the substantive status. For example, the Court of Appeal noted that under the current law, only the mother will automatically have initial parental responsibility for a child at birth in all circumstances,[87] and that it could create practical difficulties surrounding decision making about the child's upbringing if no person had parental responsibility accordingly because no one was recognised as a 'mother'.[88]

Children and sperm donors

Many same-sex couples will have to use donor sperm to conceive children through assisted reproduction. We have seen that the mother's partner can be treated as the parent, irrespective of the absence of a genetic link, provided the 2008 Act's requirements are met. If the mother's partner is so treated, no other person (such as a sperm donor) will be treated as the child's other parent.[89] Even if the mother's partner is *not* treated as the other parent, this does not in itself mean that the sperm donor will be the other parent instead. Section 41 of the Act makes clear that, if the donor validly consented to the use of his sperm under schedule 3 of the 1990 Act, the donor is not to be treated as the father. Where the mother's partner is not to be treated as a parent under the Act, the mother will be the sole legal parent.

---

[83] Ibid.

[84] Ibid.

[85] L Davis, 'Deconstructing Tradition: Trans Reproduction and the Need to Reform Birth Registration in England and Wales' (2021) 22(1–2) International Journal of Transgender Health 179, 188.

[86] Ibid, 185.

[87] CA 1989, s 2.

[88] *McConnell* (n2) para 64.

[89] HFEA 2008, s 45(1).

Where valid consent is given by an ostensibly 'anonymous' donor under the Act, the framework for the limited disclosure of information relating to a donor-conceived child may nevertheless come into play. At the age of 16,[90] such a person can access *inter alia* a donor's physical description, year and country of birth, ethnicity, marital status, medical history, and any goodwill message left,[91] except in limited circumstances.[92] At 16, the applicant can also ask for limited information about any genetic siblings they may have,[93] and there is provision for information to be provided about a prospective partner.[94] At 18, the applicant can access 'identifying information' in the form *inter alia* of the donor's name, date of birth, and last known address.[95] Donors themselves are generally able to access information about the number, year of birth, and sex of any children produced by their gametes,[96] and they may also be notified of any application for information by any such children.[97] The 'disruptive' potential of this framework for the parenthood of a same-sex couple is relatively minimal, even if a child will likely know that their conception will have involved donation if their parents are a cisgender same-sex couple. In any event, and whatever the same-sex parents themselves may think, knowing the truth about genetic origins is particularly important for the purposes of the child's identity, relevant to the right to respect for private life under Article 8 of the European Convention on Human Rights and for developments in individualised medicine.[98]

More difficult circumstances can be faced by a same-sex couple who use a 'known' sperm donor, such as a friend, to conceive a child, particularly outside the context of a licensed clinic. Where, for example, one partner and the so-called donor choose to conceive the child through sexual intercourse, the 'donor' will be a legal parent to the exclusion of the other same-sex partner.[99] The same would be true where the conception is 'artificial' but is done outside a licensed clinic and the mother's partner was an informal one or did not consent to the conception. From the perspective of the same-sex couple, the legal parenthood of the person they see as the 'donor' may be undesirable. This is particularly true where the biological father acquires parental responsibility, effectively conferring a prima facie entitlement to be involved in important decisions concerning the

---

[90]   HFEA 1990, 31ZA; Human Fertilisation and Embryology Authority (Disclosure of Donor Information) Regulations 2004/1511, r 2(3A).

[91]   Human Fertilisation and Embryology Authority (Disclosure of Donor Information) Regulations 2004, r 2(2).

[92]   Ibid, s 31ZA(6).

[93]   Ibid, s 31ZE.

[94]   Ibid, s 31ZB.

[95]   HFEA 1990, s 31ZA(4); Human Fertilisation and Embryology Authority (Disclosure of Donor Information) Regulations 2004, r 2(3).

[96]   HFEA 1990, s 31ZD.

[97]   HFEA 1990, s 31ZC.

[98]   See, eg, Sloan (n3) 520–2.

[99]   *M v F (Declaration of Parentage: Circumstances of Conception)* [2013] EWHC 1901 (Fam), para 27.

child's upbringing and (again from the same-sex couple's perspective) potentially 'interfering' in the substantive parenting of the same-sex couple. In *Re D (Contact and Parental Responsibility: Lesbian Mothers and Known Father)*, Black J granted parental responsibility to a legal father who had agreed to help the mother and her long-term female partner to have a child, albeit via sexual intercourse with the mother.[100] At the time, it was not possible for even a female same-sex couple to be recognised as legal parents from birth. Black J viewed it as essential for the child, D's, welfare that she continue her relationship with the applicant. The judge also recognised the reality that the applicant was D's father. At the same time, Black J was 'anxious' about

> whether making a parental responsibility order would be in D's interests [in view of] the potential threat to the stability of D's immediate family from what I may loosely call 'interference' from [the father] as well as the impact on society's perception of the family if he were, in fact, to use it to become more visible in D's life.[101]

The judge resolved the difficulty via the father's willingness to be bound by conditions on his exercise of parental responsibility. In *R v E and F (Female Parents: Known Father)*, however, a sperm donor for a lesbian couple who was the child's legal parent was denied parental responsibility altogether.[102] The reality for the child was held to be that his mother and her partner were the true 'parents' and the father's perception that the child had a single family that also included himself and his partner was considered mistaken. Granting the father parental responsibility in those circumstances would generate conflict with the female 'parents' and distress them.

Even if the same-sex couple do establish themselves as the relevant child's two legal parents, they may still be faced with applications for parental responsibility or child arrangements orders (governing with whom the child is to live and have contact) from the 'known' donor.

An example of the role that can be played by a child arrangements order in regulating parental responsibility is provided by *A v B and C (Lesbian Co-Parents: Role of Father)*.[103] A lesbian couple agreed with a male friend that he would provide the sperm through which they conceived a child. The mother and the 'donor' father had gone through a marriage ceremony to placate her religious family, making the donor a legal father with parental responsibility. A disagreement arose between the three about the father's future role in the child's life, with the female partner who lacked legal parenthood feeling marginalised. The Court of Appeal held that the judge had made a

---

[100] [2006] EWHC 2 (Fam).
[101] Ibid, para 89.
[102] [2010] EWHC 417 (Fam). See also *Re B (Role of Biological Father)* [2007] EWHC 1952 (Fam).
[103] [2012] EWCA Civ 285.

fundamental error in suggesting a general rule that a donor father's role would be 'limited' in such a case. All cases were fact-specific and subject to the paramountcy principle.[104] Thorpe LJ rejected the concept of 'principal' and 'secondary' parents,[105] which had been suggested in an earlier case as a means of deciding cases involving 'alternative' families.[106] He was conscious that '[i]t has the danger of demeaning the known donor and in some cases they may have an important role'.[107] The case was remitted for a rehearing involving more detailed analysis of the child's welfare. Black LJ emphasised that '[t]he adults' preconception intentions were relevant factors in this case but they neither could nor should be determinative'.[108] The important factor was the source of the child's nurture, stability, and security. This conclusion is arguably consistent with the requirement to treat the child's welfare as the paramount consideration, albeit that Smith has criticised the reasoning in *A v B and C* on the basis that welfare is consistent with parties normally being held to their original plans in such disputes.[109] On her account, it is 'precisely because the parties to known donor arrangements are liable to change their minds about the nature of the relationships they want that a principle restricting their ability to do so is needed'.[110]

In *Re G; Re Z (Children: Sperm Donors: Leave to Apply for Children Act Orders)*, 'known' sperm donors were granted leave to apply (albeit by no means guaranteed success) for contact orders in relation to children born to lesbian couples,[111] notwithstanding the fact that the biological fathers were *not* legal parents of the children. Baker J held that while '[t]he 2008 Act denies the biological father the status of legal parent', 'it does not prevent the lesbian couple, in whom legal parenthood is vested, from encouraging or enabling the biological father to become a *psychological* parent' and 'it empowers the lesbian couple to take that course as the persons in whom parental responsibility is vested'.[112] A fact-sensitive approach will be taken, however, and if a same-sex couple were to take steps to *avoid* the donor father becoming a psychological parent, such leave is less likely to be granted. Unlike substantive decision about whether to grant a child arrangements order, leave decisions, as recognised in *Re G; Re Z*, do not involve paramountcy, but require consideration of the nature of the proposed application, the applicant's connection with the child,

---

[104] CA 1989, s 1.
[105] *A v B and C* (n103) para 30.
[106] *AR v RWB and SWB* [2011] EWHC 3431 (Fam).
[107] *A v B and C* (n103) para 30.
[108] Ibid, para 44.
[109] L Smith, 'Tangling the Web of Legal Parenthood: Legal Responses to the Use of Known Donors in Lesbian Parenting Arrangements' (2013) 33(3) Legal Studies 355.
[110] Ibid, 372.
[111] [2013] EWHC 134 (Fam).
[112] Ibid, para 118.

any risk there might be of that proposed application disrupting the child's life to such an extent that they would be harmed by it,[113] as well as the merits of the application.[114]

Evaluation

As with adoption, then, same-sex couples are in a similar position to heterosexual couples using assisted reproduction, but are more likely to face the complications associated with such reproduction because they are inherently more likely to make use of it. As commentators such as Bainham and Callus have pointed out,[115] however, the conferral of legal parenthood on those who lack a genetic relationship with the child under the 2008 Act is potentially at odds with the importance attached to genetic links in the context of non-assisted reproduction.[116] In the context of adoption, Fenton-Glynn and I have argued in favour of the involvement of biological fathers in the adoption process, even where the person giving birth wishes the child to be adopted by strangers.[117] We did so with reference to the child's welfare and international human rights norms, including *prima facie* rights to respect for identity and family relations and to know and be cared for by (biological) parents. We advocated a general approach whereby a father should be presumptively entitled, for the benefit of the child, to know that his child exists and have some level of involvement in the adoption proceedings, unless there is an objective finding that such involvement would be contrary to the child's best interests. Many of the same arguments will apply where a child is conceived using genetic material from others at the instance of a same-sex couple, although genuine (initial) agreement between the parties that the same-sex couple are to be the legal parents may distinguish the situation in some respects.

The assisted reproduction provisions we have considered in this section cannot be used by cisgender male same-gender couples to become parents: they rely on one of the intended parents giving birth. Surrogacy will therefore be considered later in this chapter.

---

[113] CA 1989, s 10(9).

[114] *Re G; Re Z* (n111) paras 61–2.

[115] A Bainham, 'Arguments about Parentage' (2008) 67(2) Cambridge Law Journal 322, 334; T. Callus, 'First "Designer Babies", Now à la Carte Parents' (2008) 2 Family Law 143, 147.

[116] For a general discussion, see L Smith, 'Clashing Symbols: Reconciling Support for Fathers and Fatherless Families after the Human Fertilisation and Embryology Act 2008' (2010) 22(1) Child and Family Law Quarterly 46.

[117] C Fenton-Glynn and B Sloan, 'Fathers and the Adoption Process' in N Lowe and C Fenton-Glynn (eds), *Research Handbook on Adoption Law* (Edward Elgar 2023).

Summary

The HFEA 2008 was significant in allowing a cisgender female same-sex couple to be considered a child's legal parents from the moment of the child's birth. The person giving birth will be the child's mother and the mother's partner will presumptively be the child's second parent if in a marriage or civil partnership with the mother, or if the agreed female parenthood conditions (equivalent to the agreed fatherhood conditions) are met. The agreed female parenthood conditions impose consent-based formalities and can apply only where relevant treatment is provided by a licensed clinic. There is no absolute right to such treatment, and despite the risk of unlawful discrimination, there is evidence that same-sex couples have faced difficulties in accessing treatment as compared to heterosexual couples. If a same-sex couple attempt to become parents outside the context of a licensed clinic, they may find that the person they consider a 'mere' sperm donor is considered the child's legal father. Whether the sperm donor is a legal parent or not, his existence may complicate the same-sex couple's relationship with the child in a manner not experienced by a naturally reproducing heterosexual couple. The child's welfare and identity-related rights are, however, legitimate considerations in this context.

Same-sex couples and surrogacy

An introduction to surrogacy in England and Wales

The Law Commissions of England and Wales and Scotland defined surrogacy as

> the practice of a woman[118] (… the 'surrogate') becoming pregnant with a child that may, or may not, be genetically related to her, carrying the child, and giving birth to the child for another family (… the 'intended parents').[119]

Unlike the other assisted reproduction provisions in the 2008 Act, then, it is a method through which a single person or a couple can acquire exclusive legal parenthood without (either of them) having given birth to the child. Most significantly for present purposes, surrogacy is therefore the only method through which a cisgender male couple can become legal parents under the 2008 Act,[120]

---

118   The *McConnell* decision suggests that in principle a surrogate could be a legal male, though cf Law Commission and Scottish Law Commission, *Building Families through Surrogacy: A New Law: A Joint Consultation* Paper (2019) Consultation Paper 244/Discussion Paper 1670, para 1.82.

119   Law Commission and Scottish Law Commission (n118) para 1.1.

120   They could also use adoption.

and the Law Commissions have reported recent increases in the number of such couples using surrogacy.[121]

It should immediately be made clear that surrogacy is a particularly controversial issue even in the modern world, facing objections distinct from those aimed at same-sex adoption or the treatment of the mother's same-sex partner as a second parent under the 2008 provisions already considered. The Warnock Committee, a Committee of Inquiry into Human Fertilisation and Embryology reporting in 1984, were concerned about the serious dangers of exploitation of the surrogate mother,[122] and such concerns are ever-present in contemporary debates on surrogacy. In *XX v Whittington Hospital NHS Trust*, Lady Hale recognised that there is a 'spectrum of surrogacy arrangements' in practice.[123] At one end, she described the 'desperately poor women who are induced to sell one of the few things they have for sale, their wombs, and are often grossly exploited by the agents and middlemen who make serious profits from the large sums which desperate commissioning parents are prepared to pay.'[124]

At the other end sit the 'altruistic women who enjoy being pregnant and are happy to make a gift of their child-bearing capacity to people who need it'.[125]

As a result of the surrounding debate, English law currently adopts a contradictory approach to surrogacy, which same-sex couples would have to navigate. In *XX*, Lady Hale described the UK approach to surrogacy as one that is 'fragmented and in some ways obscure'.[126] The starting point is that '[i]n essence, the arrangement is completely unenforceable'.[127] Under section 1A of the Surrogacy Arrangements Act 1985, '[n]o surrogacy arrangement is enforceable by or against any of the persons making it'. Under the current law, the surrogate is thus not bound by an agreement made, as the Law Commissions put it, 'before the possibly life-changing event of the birth takes place, at a time when she may not have been able to anticipate the implications'.[128]

Under the 1985 Act, it is also an offence to do a range of acts relating to a surrogacy arrangement on a commercial basis in the UK,[129] unless the act is performed by the commissioning parents or the intended surrogate.[130] The model ostensibly adopted in practice in the UK was described as a 'friendship model of altruistic surrogacy arrangements' by Lady Hale, whereby the surrogate

---

121   Law Commission and Scottish Law Commission (n118) para 3.20.
122   Department of Health and Social Security, 'Report of the Committee of Inquiry into Human Fertilisation and Embryology' (1984) https://wellcomecollection.org/works/pxgeeqnf/items, accessed 23 July 2025.
123   [2020] UKSC 14, para 39.
124   Ibid.
125   Ibid.
126   *XX* (n123) para 9.
127   Ibid.
128   Law Commission and Scottish Law Commission (n118) para 8.99.
129   Surrogacy Arrangements Act 1985, s 2. See also s 3.
130   Surrogacy Arrangements Act 1985, s 2(2).

chooses the commissioning parents rather than the other way around.[131] While the privileged position of the surrogate would be supported by many, it is at the expense of a same-sex couple (often a cisgender male same-sex couple) wishing to become legal parents via this method.

As Lady Hale made clear, however, 'the details are more complicated' than the basic position, as regards both legal parenthood and attitudes to commercial surrogacy.[132] While it is true that '[t]he surrogate mother is always the child's legal parent unless and until a court order is made in favour of the commissioning parents',[133] the parental order is a specific mechanism (introduced by the HFEA 1990 and now governed by the 2008 Act) precisely designed to give effect to a surrogacy arrangement.[134] It can remove parenthood from the surrogate and her partner (if relevant) and confer it on the commissioning parents, albeit (subject to very limited exceptions) not without the consent of, *inter alia*, the surrogate mother.

International surrogacy is popular amongst couples based in the UK because of the more relaxed attitude taken to it in some other jurisdictions, despite the immigration problems potentially faced when a child is brought into the country by people who are not recognised here as the child's legal parents.[135] English law's somewhat conflicted attitude to surrogacy thus continues and we will see that the Law Commissions have recommended significant reforms.[136]

Parental orders and surrogacy

As elsewhere in English law, the starting point in a surrogacy situation is that the person giving birth to the child (the surrogate) will be the mother. The general law, including that on assisted reproduction, will also determine the child's father or second female parent (if any) in the first instance.

That said, a 'parental order' made after the child is born confers legal parenthood on the commissioning parent(s) who apply for it and extinguishes the default parenthood of the surrogate and any non-applicant who would otherwise have it, such as the surrogate's spouse. Such orders are governed by sections 54 (for joint applicants) and 54A (for sole applicants) of the 2008 Act. The effect of the order is to 'provid[e]… for a child to be treated in law as the child' of the applicant(s),[137] with essentially the same consequences as an adoption order.[138] A number of ostensibly stringent requirements must be satisfied before such an order can

---

[131] *XX* (n123) para 22.
[132] Ibid, para 9.
[133] Ibid.
[134] HFEA 2008, ss 54–54A.
[135] Law Commission and Scottish Law Commission (n118) ch 16.
[136] Law Commission of England and Wales and Scottish Law Commission, 'Building Families through Surrogacy: A New Law' (2023) Law Com No 411/Scottish Law Com 262.
[137] HFEA 2008, s 54(1); s 54A(1).
[138] Ibid, s 55; Human Fertilisation and Embryology (Parental Orders) Regulations 2018/1412.

be made, though Lady Hale has noted that the courts have been 'remarkably sympathetic' in applying some of them.[139] Importantly, the Law Commissions have recommended, *inter alia*, that, where before the child is conceived, the intended parents, the surrogate, and a regulated surrogacy organisation have made a regulated (domestic) surrogacy statement and have met certain screening and safeguarding and eligibility requirements, then on the birth of the child the intended parents should be the child's legal parents.[140]

Under the original 2008 Act, there had to be two applicants for the parental order (ie commissioning would-be parents).[141] It is still the case that where there are two applicants they must (as we have seen) be spouses, civil partners, or people 'living as partners in an enduring family relationship' (but who are not within the prohibited degrees of relationship).[142] Significantly, the 1990 Act limited parental order applicants to spouses only.[143] This prevented cisgender same-sex couples from applying for a parental order altogether, since even civil partners were initially excluded when civil partnerships became available in 2005. It was the 2008 Act that brought eligibility essentially into line with the law of adoption (as it applies to couples), using the same phrasing to describe those not in a marriage or civil partnership.[144] The courts have been generous in their interpretation of what amounts to an 'enduring family relationship'.[145] Section 54A was inserted in 2018 to allow applications by single applicants.

The gametes of at least one of the applicants must have been used to bring about the creation of the embryo that was carried by the surrogate,[146] who must not herself be one of the applicants for the parental order.[147] Even in the law of surrogacy, then, genetics remain key,[148] such that only the longer and more arduous route of adoption is available to those who are not genetic parents. It is notable that although assisted reproduction must be used for the order to be made,[149] the commissioning parents can make use of either a sperm donor or an egg donor but not both.[150]

---

[139] B Hale, 'What Do We Mean By a Family?' (2021) Bridget Lindley Memorial Lecture, Family Justice Council, 13 https://www.judiciary.uk/wp-content/uploads/2021/03/Family-Justice-Council-Bridget-Lindley-Memorial-Lecture-2021-.pdf, accessed 15 May 2024.

[140] Law Commission of England and Wales and Scottish Law Commission (n136) Recommendation 1.

[141] HFEA 2008, s 54(2).

[142] Ibid.

[143] HFEA 1990, s 30.

[144] ACA 2002, s 144(4).

[145] See, eg, *Re A (A Child: Surrogacy: Section 54 Criteria)* [2020] EWHC 1426 (Fam).

[146] HFEA 2008, s 54(1).

[147] Ibid, s 54(1)(a).

[148] Ibid, s 54(1)(b).

[149] Ibid, s 54(1)(a).

[150] From the perspective of both the *surrogate* and some of the assisted reproduction provisions of the 2008 Act, both commissioning parents could be 'donors' in circumstances where section 54 remains applicable.

In addition to imposing requirements about the would-be parents' relationship, the Act also requires the child to have their home with the applicant(s) at the time of the application.[151] Consistently with their approach to the 'enduring family relationship', the courts' view of the 'home' requirement has also been generous and welfare-focused.[152]

According to the text of the legislation, the application for a parental order must be made within six months of the child's birth.[153] It is perhaps in this respect that the courts have been most generous in their willingness to interpret the legislation for the benefit of the applicants and the perceived welfare needs of the child. The situation is complicated by the popularity of international surrogacy and the fact that some jurisdictions will recognise the commissioning parents as the legal parents.[154] In *Re X (A Child) (Surrogacy: Time Limit)*, the commissioning parents applied for a parental order over two years after the child's birth in India.[155] Sir James Munby P held that he was able to grant the order despite the delay and did so on the basis of the child's welfare, and it could be argued that the requirement is now effectively ignored.

Provided they can be found and are capable of giving it,[156] the consent of the surrogate mother and any non-applicant who is the child's legal parent must be obtained.[157] It is significant that the surrogate's husband or other partner may *prima facie* be considered the child's legal parent by virtue of the principles contained earlier in this chapter, such that their consent is needed in addition to that of the surrogate. The surrogate's consent is ineffective if given less than six weeks after the birth.[158]

In contrast to adoption, there is in principle no scope for the court to dispense with the need for consent on the basis of the child's welfare. This is significant. In a situation where the surrogate decides not to 'hand over' the child after birth, it would in principle be possible for the court to make a child arrangements order to the effect that the child should live with the commissioning parents so that in theory the 'home' requirement considered earlier is satisfied. Even if this practice is by no means universal,[159] a residence order was made in favour of the commissioning parents in *Re P (Surrogacy: Residence)*, where the surrogate had

---

[151]   HFEA 2008, s 54(4). There are also provisions relating to domicile.
[152]   See, eg, *Re X (Parental Order: Death of Intended Parent Prior to Birth)* [2020] EWFC 39.
[153]   HFEA 2008, s 54(3).
[154]   See, eg, C Fenton-Glynn, 'England and Wales' in JM Scherpe, C Fenton-Glynn, and T Kaan (eds), *Eastern and Western Perspectives on Surrogacy* (Intersentia 2019) 117.
[155]   [2014] EWHC 3135 (Fam).
[156]   HFEA 2008, s 54(7).
[157]   Ibid, s 54(6).
[158]   Ibid, s 54(7).
[159]   See, eg, *Re Z (A Child) (Surrogacy Agreements: Child Arrangements Orders)* [2017] EWCA Civ 228.

falsely claimed a miscarriage and was caring for the child herself.[160] But despite the extreme flexibility shown in relation to other aspects of section 54, it is not apparently possible to circumvent the 'consent' requirement in order to make a parental order in these circumstances. Adoption per se would be the only option for the transfer of parenthood.[161]

When making the order the court must be satisfied that 'no money or other benefit has been given or received by either of the applicants' in consideration of the making of the order, consent to it, the handing over of the child, or the making of arrangements relating to the order.[162] That said, the payment of reasonable expenses is excepted and the court can authorise the making of other payments.[163] The legislation is structured in such a way that the court cannot make the parental order at all unless it authorises any payments exceeding reasonable expenses made.[164]

It has already been seen that the welfare of the child has permeated the judicial application of many of the formal requirements of section 54. Although not present within section 54 itself, the welfare of the child is made the paramount consideration for the court via Human Fertilisation and Embryology (Parental Orders) Regulations 2018. The particular 'version' of the welfare principle applied is that in the ACA 2002, so that the emphasis is on lifelong welfare.[165] But it is noteworthy that the impact of the 'paramountcy' of welfare has been essentially to soften the application of the strict statutory criteria rather to impose any additional requirement. If the section 54 criteria are satisfied, it is extremely unlikely that the court would refuse the order on the basis of the child's welfare. In fact, the Law Commissions were 'not aware of any decision where the court, having the power to do so, has refused to make a parental order solely on the basis of the child's welfare'.[166]

Evaluation

Jennings and colleagues reported that the financial accessibility of adoption was 'especially relevant for gay fathers as an impetus to select adoption over surrogacy, as most considered they would most likely have had to turn to international surrogates given that commercial surrogacy is prohibited in the United Kingdom'.[167] Their finding was that 'gay fathers in particular selected adoption as it appeared the simplest, most predictable and secure of the available

---

[160] [2007] EWCA Civ 1053.

[161] *Re AB (Surrogacy: Consent)* [2016] EWHC 2643 (Fam).

[162] HFEA 2008, s 54(8).

[163] Ibid.

[164] *Re X & Y (Foreign Surrogacy)* [2008] EWHC 3030 (Fam), para 18.

[165] ACA 2002, s 1.

[166] Law Commission and Scottish Law Commission (n118) para 7.67.

[167] Jennings and others (n11) 217.

options'.[168] If the Law Commissions' recommendation of a pathway whereby the intended parents can be the legal parents from birth is implemented, surrogacy may become a more attractive route to parenthood for same-sex couples. English law's antipathy to commercial surrogacy is still likely, however, to deter many. The indirectly differential treatment of same-sex couples, and in this instance particularly cisgender male same-sex couples, must again be acknowledged.

Summary

Unlike the other assisted reproduction provisions in the HFEA 2008, the making of a parental order to give effect to a surrogacy agreement under the Act can confer legal parenthood on a cisgender male same-sex couple. A surrogacy agreement is not, however, straightforwardly enforceable in England and Wales and English law has an ambivalent attitude to surrogacy, especially commercial surrogacy. There remain concerns about the potential exploitation of the surrogate mother. She will remain the legal parent at birth and the parental order transferring parenthood to the commissioning parents (whether a same-sex couple or not) requires her consent (among other things). The Law Commissions of England and Wales and Scotland have recently recommended a pathway whereby the commissioning parents can be considered the legal parents from the child's birth. For the moment, however, surrogacy is another challenging route to parenthood for a same-sex couple.

Conclusion

By definition, an evaluation of the position of same-sex parents cannot begin and end with the parents themselves. There is inevitably a third party in the relationship, the child themselves, whose welfare is treated as 'paramount' in several areas of the law. However unfairly same-sex would-be parents may feel they have been treated because (in the case where both are cisgender) they are unable to conceive a child naturally, such a child will have their own rights and interests, to which their (prospective) same-sex parents' interests might reasonably be expected to give way on occasion. It nevertheless must be recognised that attaching significance to biology is a choice made by the law and not necessarily an inevitable one. Reform would be conceivable: Herring, for example, argues that 'parenthood should shift from focusing on blood ties to focusing on the caring relationship between child and other',[169] such that '[p]arental status should be earned by the care and dedication to the child, something not shown simply by a biological link'.[170] Such a change may well benefit same-sex couples unable to conceive, albeit potentially creating difficulties relating to certainty,

---

[168] Ibid.
[169] J Herring, *Caring and the Law* (Hart 2013) 202.
[170] Ibid, 200.

practicality, social engineering, and identity. The differential treatment of same-sex couples under the current law, highlighted in this chapter, ought in any event to be acknowledged.

Further questions to consider

- Should any restrictions be placed on the ability of same-sex couples to become legal parents?
- What are the relative advantages and disadvantages of adoption, assisted reproduction, and surrogacy as methods of becoming parents for same-sex couples?
- What weight should the rights and interests of the child concerned carry where a same-sex couple (propose to) become their parents?
- Should the law permit a child to have more than two legal parents and what would the implications of such a change be for same-sex couples?

Further materials

Callus T, 'First "Designer Babies", Now à la Carte Parents' (2008) 2 Family Law 143

Golombok S, 'The Psychological wellbeing of ART children: What Have We Learned from 40 Years of Research?' (2020) 41(4) Reproductive Biomedicine Online 743

Jeffs L and Oakley S, 'Some Families' (2020–21) (podcast) StoryHunter

Smith L, 'Tangling the Web of Legal Parenthood: Legal Responses to the Use of Known Donors in Lesbian Parenting Arrangements' (2013) 33(3) Legal Studies 355

Tasker F and Bellamy C, 'Adoption by Same-Sex Couples – Reaffirming Evidence: Could More Children Be Placed?' (2019) 2 Family Law 171

7

Child Protection Intersectionality: Disparities in Racially Minoritised and Asylum-Seeking Backgrounds

Rachel Pimm-Smith

Introduction

Child protection is the state's legal regime for removing a child from parental care if they are at risk of some form of significant harm. It is a difficult area of law because notions of protective intervention directly conflict with the fundamental principle that children are best brought up by their parents. The law aims to resolve this tension by carefully balancing the needs of children to have a stable upbringing within their families against their needs to be safeguarded from harm.

This balancing act is made more difficult by the fact that both intervention and non-intervention can lead to seriously negative outcomes.[1] A failure to act could lead to a child suffering serious injury, or death, as evidenced by some of the high-profile cases reported in the media where the authorities failed to intervene and a child died in appalling circumstances. Such cases sometimes trigger reviews into the effectiveness of the safeguarding framework so that areas of improvement can be identified.[2] Although these cases are undoubtedly tragic, it is important to

---

[1] See *F & L v A Local Authority and A* [2009] EWHC 140 (Fam) [14] in which Hedley J noted the 'dreadful conundrum' that a mistaken finding of non-accidental injury 'is to risk tearing apart an innocent family' while a failure to identify non-accidental injury is to 'risk returning a child a situation of high or even fatal risk'.

[2] A recent example is the Child Safeguarding Practice Review Panel, 'National Review into the Murders of Arthur Labinjo-Hughes and Star Hobson' (2022) https://assets.publishing.service. gov.uk/media/628e262d8fa8f556203eb4f8/ALH_SH_National_Review_26-5-22.pdf, accessed 23 July 2025.

understand that most children do not enter care following concerns of physical abuse or neglect. Instead, most children come to the attention of social workers following concerns about domestic violence against a parent or the mental health of a parent.[3] Physical abuse and neglect are comparatively less common.

Failing to protect a child who is at risk is indisputably problematic. However, it is also problematic for the state to intervene into the lives of families excessively or unnecessarily. The numbers of children entering care is increasing year on year and research has established that the experience of being in care is linked to substantial disadvantage in adult life.[4] This is particularly important in the context of racially minoritised and unaccompanied asylum-seeking children (UASC) who are some of the most over-represented groups within children's social care.

According to the 2021 census, 81.7 per cent of the population of England and Wales were White, and 18.3 per cent were racially minoritised.[5] The racially minoritised population were broken down into 14 reductive categories of ethnicity, which are also used by the Department for Education to classify children in social care and thus will be referred to throughout this chapter.[6] According to the census, 4 per cent of the population were classified as Black, 10 per cent as Asian, and the remainder as 'any other mixed ethnicity'.[7] And yet according to the Department for Education's 2023 statistics, 7 per cent of children in social care were classified as Black, 10 per cent as 'mixed ethnicity', and a further 10 per cent classified as either Asian or 'any other racially minoritised'.[8] It should be noted that these statistics include UASC, who were predominately classified as 'any other racially minoritised' or 'any other Black'.[9]

This chapter starts by summarising the relevant law as it applies to children in care and then goes on to explore the disparities experienced by racially

---

3   Department for Education, 'Children in Need' (2023): 'Data on factors identified at the end of assessment' https://explore-education-statistics.service.gov.uk/find-statistics/children-in-need/2023, accessed 23 July 2025.

4   Department for Education, 'Children Looked after in England (including Adoption)' (2023): 'Data on children looked after on 31 March', 'Data on convictions and health outcomes', 'Data on 17 to 21-year care leavers' https://explore-education-statistics.service.gov.uk/find-statistics/children-looked-after-in-england-including-adoptions/2023/, accessed 23 July 2025; Prison Reform Trust, 'Lord Laming Report: In Care, Out of Trouble' (2016) https://prisonreformtrust.org.uk/publication/in-care-out-of-trouble-how-the-life-chances-of-children-in-care-can-be-transformed-by-protecting-them-from-unnecessary-involvement-in-the-criminal-justice-system/, accessed 23 July 2025.

5   Office for National Statistics (ONS), 'England and Wales 2021 Census' https://www.ons.gov.uk/peoplepopulationandcommunity/populationandmigration/populationestimates/datasets/censusbasedstatisticsuk2021, accessed 23 July 2025.

6   Ethnic categories: Indian, Pakistani, Chinese, any other Asian, Caribbean, African, any other Black, White and Black Caribbean, White and Black African, White and Asian, Arab, any other mixed ethnicity; any other racially minoritised group.

7   ONS (n5).

8   Data on characteristics, Department for Education (n4).

9   Department for Education (n4): data on unaccompanied asylum-seeking children.

minoritised children and UASC before, during, and after the court process. Overall, this chapter aims to provide a critical exploration of the disparities faced by racially minoritised children and UASC under the care of the state and evaluates some of the possible reasons for their differential experience.

Summary of the relevant law

Local authorities have a duty to protect children and have a range of powers at their disposal to achieve this goal. The Children Act (CA) 1989 contains most of the provisions, but other statutes also play supplementary roles in the safeguarding framework. Protective action usually starts following a referral. At present, the police are the biggest source of referrals, but other agencies can also raise concerns about a child, such as schools or health professionals.[10] Once a referral is made, the local authority must determine if the child requires immediate protection or if other options are more appropriate.

At this stage, the local authority becomes bound by a general duty under section 17 of the CA 1989. This duty compels the local authority to safeguard and promote welfare and, so far as it is compatible with that duty, to promote the child being brought up by their family.[11] After a referral is made, social workers conduct an assessment to determine if the child should be classified as 'in need'. Once a child has the status of 'in need' the local authority can provide the child and their family with supportive services. This includes things such as advice, guidance, counselling, social/cultural recreational activities, and holidays.[12] Support can also be provided by way of cash payments or vouchers where appropriate.[13] It is important to note that this duty is general, not mandatory, which means local authorities cannot be compelled to provide supportive services if a child has 'in need' status. This is entirely understandable given there were 403,090 children classified as 'in need' in 2023 and this was a reduction from the previous year.[14] Factors such as budgetary constraints, administrative workability, and the demands of children's social care caseloads would render any non-mandatory duty at this stage unenforceable.

If the local authority has reasonable cause to believe the child is suffering, or is likely to suffer, significant harm, they have a duty to investigate those concerns. Section 47 of the CA 1989 gives local authorities the power to gain access to a child to determine if any action is necessary to safeguard or promote their welfare.[15] If the concerns are substantiated, a child protection conference will be held to determine if the child needs a child protection plan. Child

---

10   Department for Education (n3); data on referrals sources.
11   CA 1989 s 17(1)(b).
12   Ibid, sch 2, para 8.
13   Ibid, ss 17(6), 17A and 17B.
14   Department for Education (n3).
15   CA 1989 s 47(4).

protection conferences bring together numerous professionals within the social care framework along with the parents of the child to ascertain the likelihood that the child is experiencing, or likely to experience, significant harm. The goal of the conference is to discuss ways to safeguard and protect the child and clarify the roles and responsibilities of all the parties involved.

It is often at this stage that a voluntary arrangement might be suggested by the local authority under section 20 of the CA 1989. This provision requires the local authority to provide accommodation for any child who is abandoned, parentless, or has a parent who for whatever reason cannot provide suitable accommodation. But the local authority can also use this power to offer voluntary accommodation for children who are classified as 'in need' and/or subject to a child protection plan. These agreements do not give local authorities decision-making powers over the child and parents retain the right to withdraw their child at any time.[16] However, research indicates parents in this situation often feel pressured into agreeing to these arrangements in the hopes of avoiding care proceedings.[17]

Unfortunately, there is no available research about the ways that non-nationals or families with cultural factors feel about voluntary accommodation. The term 'cultural factors' is inherently vague but is used by the courts to describe families that have non-national, ethnic, or religious circumstances that cannot be ignored.[18] The courts have been highly critical of local authorities who misuse, or in some cases abuse, section 20 powers as an alternative to care proceedings because it bypasses judicial oversight.[19] But the latest statistics reveal that over half the children who entered care in 2023 came into the system via a section 20 agreement.[20] This is quite concerning because voluntary accommodation does not require a court order or any judicial scrutiny and it is highly debatable how voluntary these agreements really are if parents feel pressured to enter into them. Even more worrying is the use of these voluntary agreements for parents who do not understand English because it will invariably impact their understanding of the law and their rights as parents.

Crucially, none of these provisions empower the local authority to remove a child from parental care without consent. This can only be achieved by a court order if the threshold for significant harm is met.[21] There are five possible orders the court can make: a supervision order, a special guardianship order, a deprivation of liberty order, a care order, or an adoption order. Each of these orders represents

---

[16] Ibid, s 22.

[17] J Hunt and A McLeod, *Statutory Intervention in Child Protection* (Bristol University Press 1998).

[18] *Re K* [2007] 1 FLR 399 para 26.

[19] *N (Children) (Adoption: Jurisdiction)* [2015] EWCA Civ 1112; *Re W (Children)* [2014] EWCA Civ 1065; *Northamptonshire County Council v AS and Ors* [2015] EWHC 199 (Fam); *Medway Council v M & T* [2015] EWFC B164.

[20] Department for Education (n4); data on Children Looked After (CLA) starting during the year shows 56 per cent of looked-after children who entered care during 2023 were initially looked after under a section 20 agreement.

[21] CA 1989 s 31(2)(a) and (b).

an increasing degree of intrusion by the state into the relationship between a parent and their child.

Supervision orders are the least interventionist because the local authority does not obtain decision-making powers over the child and the child will most likely stay in their home.[22] These orders simply require the local authority to 'advise, assist and befriend' the child and they cannot run for longer than three years. Special guardianship orders by comparison are a bit more interventionist because they grant decision-making powers to the guardian, but also allow the parent to retain these rights.[23] These orders are most appropriate for children who are in kinship care where the carer needs legal recognition. Deprivation of liberty orders are arguably more intrusive.[24] They are used for children who are looked after by the local authority but present a risk of absconding. They are meant to prevent a child from running away and coming to harm and the courts have the discretion to impose any necessary timescales or restrictions on the child's liberty to promote their welfare.[25]

Care orders are substantially interventionist because parents are forced to share responsibility for the child with the local authority and their decision making can be modified or curtailed.[26] These orders allow the local authorities to determine if it is best to leave the child with their parent or place them in a children's home or foster home. A parent cannot override the local authority's decision and the local authority can place the child in alternative accommodation at any time without prior notice to the parent. Lastly, there are adoption orders, which are the most severe form of state intrusion into a parent–child relationship.[27] These orders permanently extinguish the parent–child relationship and transfer all parental authority to the adoptive parents. The law requires parental consent for these orders to be granted, unless a court decides that parental consent can be dispensed with to promote the welfare of the child.[28] Most children who become available for adoption from the children's social care system will fall under this latter category, which is why this is the most intrusive form of protective action.

Before court

This section will explore the differential experiences of racially minoritised and UASC children within the social care population compared to White children before going to court. It will explore the different ways these children come to

---

[22]   Ibid, s 35.

[23]   Ibid, s 14A.

[24]   Ibid, s 25.

[25]   Ibid, ss 3 and ss 4.

[26]   Ibid, s 33.

[27]   Adoption and Children Act 2002 s 46, s 50, and s 51.

[28]   Ibid, s 52(1).

the attention of the authorities and evaluate the disproportionate use of voluntary accommodation agreements for these groups.

Coming to the attention of social services

Children based in the UK come to the attention of social workers in very different ways from UASC. Social services are normally alerted to a possible child 'in need' following a referral and this will either lead to a decision of no further action or an assessment. Three out of every ten referrals made in 2023 were from the police, but more referrals were made in total by the combined efforts of schools, health services, and local authorities.[29] Most of these children were classified as 'in need' after their referral.[30]

The definition of 'in need' is clearly important and the law adopts a wide definition. A child will be classified as 'in need' if they are disabled or if their 'health and development' are likely to be affected without help from the local authority.[31] The number of children classed as 'in need' is increasing every year.[32] To give an idea of the scale of the task faced by local authorities, there were 640,430 referrals made to social services departments in 2023 alone.[33] From this group, 403,090 children were classified as 'in need', of which 51 per cent were male and 49 per cent were female.[34] The data shows 225,000 of these children were investigated under section 47 and a further 50,780 were placed on child protection plans.

There are significant racial disparities within this data that need to be acknowledged. To start, racially minoritised children who are 'in need' have higher rates of disability. White children have disability rates around 13 per cent across the social care population but this rises to anywhere between 17–20 per cent for children with Indian, Pakistani, Bangladeshi, or Chinese backgrounds.[35] Although this disparity accounts for some of the over-representation of these groups within the social care population, it certainly does not account for all.

Other groups of racially minoritised children are more likely to experience intervention by social services as an initial response to a referral rather than supportive services. Children from Asian (42 per cent) and Black (37 per cent) backgrounds were more likely to enter care after coming to the attention of social services for the first time, whereas children from White and mixed ethnic

---

[29] Department for Education (n3); data on referrals.
[30] Ibid.
[31] CA 1989 s 17(10).
[32] There was more than a 3 per cent increase between 2021 and 2023.
[33] Department for Education (n3): data on referrals.
[34] Ibid.
[35] Nuffield Family Justice Observatory, 'How Might Our Ethnicity Affect Our Experience of the Family Justice System?' Inequalities Project (July 2023).

backgrounds were more likely to enter care following prior involvement from social services.[36] This means children from White and mixed ethnic backgrounds are more likely to be supported in their homes prior to removal than children from Asian and Black backgrounds.

Children from Black African, Black Caribbean, and 'any other black' backgrounds were also the most likely groups to be put on child protection plans which led to care orders compared to all other ethnic groups collected by the Department for Education.[37] By comparison, children from Asian backgrounds were the least likely to be put on child protection plans or be taken into care.

Lastly, racially minoritised children tend to be older and from non–deprived areas when they first come to the attention of social services, whereas White children tend to be younger and from the most deprived areas.[38] Most children from Black and Asian backgrounds came to the attention of social services as teenagers following concerns of unacceptable behaviour or gang involvement, whereas White children typically presented as infants or toddlers following concerns of domestic violence against a parent or mental health concerns of a parent.

UASC by comparison come to the attention of social services in very different ways from children based in the UK. Social workers are alerted to the presence of an unaccompanied asylum-seeking child after they present themself at a point of entry into the UK, rather than a referral from an internal source. Once presented, social workers must assess the child and the general duty for the local authority to provide supportive services is invoked until an order is made by a court. UASC currently account for 9 per cent of the total care population, which is a 2 per cent rise from 2022.[39] Given refugees account for less than half of a percent of the total population of England and Wales, it is fair to say UASC are the second most over-represented group within the social care population after White gypsy/Roma children.[40]

Factors identified during assessment

Domestic violence and concerns about the mental health of a parent are the most common factors identified during an assessment across the whole of the children's social care population. But there are notable disparities in the factors identified for children from certain racially minoritised and UASC backgrounds.

---

[36] Ibid 3.

[37] Ibid.

[38] Ibid, 27; P Bywaters and the Child Welfare Inequalities Project Team, 'The Child Welfare Inequalities Project: Final Report' University of Huddersfield (2020) https://pure.hud.ac.uk/ws/portalfiles/portal/21398145/CWIP_Final_Report.pdf, accessed 23 July 2025.

[39] Department for Education (n4): data on unaccompanied asylum-seeking children.

[40] UNHCR statistics, November 2022, https://data.unhcr.org/en/documents/details/97980, accessed 23 July 2025.

For example, children from Black ethnic backgrounds presented with higher levels of extra-familial harms compared to any other group. This type of harm is defined as the occurrence of one or more of the following:

- socially unacceptable behaviour
- gangs
- trafficking
- child sexual exploitation
- going missing

The statistics show gangs were identified as a factor for 3 to 4 per cent of Black children, but the main extra-familial harm identified during assessment for Black children was socially unacceptable behaviour.[41]

UASC are a distinct group within the children's social care population and share a few notable characteristics. They are predominantly male (96 per cent), over 16 years of age (84 per cent), and their ethnicity is largely classified as 'any other ethnic' (44 per cent) or 'any other black' (21 per cent).[42] Unaccompanied children are immediately accommodated under section 20 irrespective of any asylum claim so that the local authority can carry out an assessment. The main factors identified during the assessment of UASC were absent parenting (88 per cent), abuse/neglect (7 per cent), or acute family stress (4 per cent). Once an assessment is completed, the child can be placed in any local authority throughout the UK under the National Transfer Scheme, which aims to share the responsibility for refugee children so that entry points are not disproportionately affected.[43]

It is important to note that UASC status is a specific form of immigration leave and thus automatically attracts protection under the safeguarding framework. But once a child reaches the age of 18, the situation changes quite drastically. Recent Home Office statistics reveal the vast majority of UASC applications were approved for those under the age of 18 (91 per cent) and, what few rejections there were, resulted from the Home Office disputing the age of the child.[44] However, the approval rate dropped to 13 per cent for UASC who turned 18 during the application process.

---

[41] N Ahmed and others, 'Ethnicity and Children's Social Care: May 2022' Department for Education 19.

[42] Department for Education (n4): data on unaccompanied asylum-seeking children.

[43] Department for Education, 'Care of Unaccompanied Migrant Children and Child Victims of Modern Slavery: Statutory Guidance for Local Authorities' (November 2017) https://assets.publishing.service.gov.uk/media/5a823a6e40f0b6230269b850/UASC_Statutory_Guidance_2017.pdf, accessed 23 July 2025.

[44] Ibid.

Voluntary accommodation

Children accommodated under section 20 are considered part of the social care population despite the absence of a court order. This means the local authority has a duty to promote the child being brought up within their family where possible. But data obtained in 2022 following a Freedom of Information request from the Department for Education suggests the racial disparities observed in other parts of children's social care also extend to the use of voluntary accommodation. The data showed 10 per cent of White and 10 per cent of mixed ethnic children were accommodated under section 20, whereas 16 per cent of Black children, 20 per cent of Asian children, and 21 per cent of 'any other ethnic' group were accommodated this way.[45] UASC are always accommodated under section 20 and thus were excluded from this data.

Researchers have suggested that a possible explanation for this racial disparity might be the fact the law does not require parental consent.[46] It is important to understand that a requirement to give consent is very different from the right to withdraw it. The courts have been very clear that the law does not require parental consent for voluntary accommodation,[47] presumably because it would hinder the ability of local authorities to accommodate abandoned or parentless children. But this can become problematic very quickly for children who have parents with limited or no spoken English who might not understand what they are agreeing to. Local authorities have been heavily criticised by senior courts for this practice and urged to follow best practice when accommodating children with cultural factors.[48] In 2018 the Supreme Court issued guidance to local authorities to consider the absence of a consent requirement as a question of 'delegating parental responsibility' rather than an issue of consent.[49] Meaning, local authorities should utilise section 20 powers when parents have delegated responsibility to them through their conduct, not as an alternative to care proceedings when parents do not understand the system.

But years on from this advice, racial inequalities within section 20 persist. An independent review of children's social care was conducted in 2022 which took indirect aim at this problem. It criticised the system's inability to see parents and families as part of the solution rather than the source of harm. The authors noted 'we are not curious enough about why families face challenges […] we slip into seeing the purpose of social care as rescuing children from their families and communities, without a real plan for what to do next'.[50] Considering most

---

45 C Edney, 'Ethnic Inequalities and Section 20 Voluntary Agreements' *Local Government Lawyer* (28 November 2023).

46 Ibid.

47 *Williams v Hackney LBC* [2018] UKSC 37 [36].

48 *Re N (Children) (Adoption: Jurisdiction)* [2015] EWCA Civ 1112 [171].

49 *Williams v Hackney LBC* (n47) [39] and [56].

50 J MacAlister, 'The Independent Review of Children's Social Care Final Report' Department for Education (May 2022) 35.

children enter care through a voluntary arrangement and there are substantial racial disparities within its implementation, this is an area of practice that requires urgent investigation to understand why differential treatment persists.[51]

Evaluation

Justifying state intrusion based on a child's unacceptable behaviour is arguably questionable because the boundaries of acceptability are naturally subjective and the law must allow for diverse parenting. Researchers have long argued that there is a real risk that children's social care practice prioritises White Euro-centric norms at the expense of racially minoritised and non-national families.[52] Fears have been expressed that a failure to understand that families from culturally diverse backgrounds might not share Western parenting ideals or agree with key definitional terms such as abuse or neglect, which could lead to differential treatment and cultural conflict.[53] The courts have called for social workers to implement a degree of cultural relativism in this context,[54] but the continued over-representation of racially minoritised children within children's social care suggests important questions remain unanswered.

We know that children from Black and UASC backgrounds typically come to the attention of social services for reasons other than domestic violence or mental health concerns. We also know they are usually older when social services first encounter them and typically find themselves under court orders without any form of prior intervention at much higher rates than children from other categories of ethnicity. Some of this might be attributable to a systematic prioritisation of Euro-centric norms coupled with a failure to adopt a culturally flexible approach to notions of ill-treatment and/or acceptable parenting. But there is the possibility of something even more sinister that researchers call the 'adultification bias'.

The 'adultification bias' has been explored in relation to children's social care as a possible explanation for racial inequalities, with specific focus on children from Black backgrounds.[55] It refers to situations where notions of innocence and vulnerability are not afforded to certain children based on racial characteristics and, thus, they are viewed as adults when in fact they are children. Researchers argue that when this happens outside the home, it is always founded on discrimination and racial injustice.[56] Academics argue that Black children are more likely to

---

51   Department for Education (n4): data on CLA starting during the year.

52   J Brophy, 'Child Maltreatment in Diverse Households: Challenges to Law, Theory and Practice' (2008) 35 Journal of Law and Society 75.

53   Ibid.

54   *A Local Authority v N, Y, K (by Her Children's Guardian)* [2007] 1 FLR 399 para 26.

55   J Davis, 'Adultification Bias with Child Protection and Safeguarding' Her Majesty's Inspectorate of Probation (2022) https://hmiprobation.justiceinspectorates.gov.uk/document/adultificat ion-bias-within-child-protection-and-safeguarding/, accessed 23 July 2025.

56   Ibid.

experience 'adultification bias' due to issues surrounding race, ethnicity, and racism, which hinder protective practice and the professional curiosity of social workers.[57] The historical legacies of dehumanisation and devaluation of Black people caused by slavery and colonialism have arguably created the preconditions for Black children to not have their safeguarding needs met.[58] The United Nations have expressed concerns that a similar form of dehumanisation is currently happening with respect to refugees.[59] Given the over-representation of Black children, the disproportionate emphasis on unacceptable behaviour as a basis for intervention, and the highly differential treatment of UASC within the care setting which will be discussed in the next section, the possibility of 'adultification bias' must be considered as an explanation for some of the racial disparities we currently see in children's social care.

Summary

Children from racially minoritised and asylum-seeking backgrounds come to the attention of social services for different reasons compared to White children. They are typically older when they make first contact with social services whereas White children are usually very young at the first point of contact. White children are also more likely to receive supportive services before being placed in care, whereas racially minoritised children are more likely to experience a child protection plan or a section 20 agreement as an initial response to a first referral. Racially minoritised children and UASC are also significantly over-represented within the children's social care system and yet there is no conclusive research that identifies all the factors contributing to this disparity.

Going to court

This section will explore the differential experience of racially minoritised children and UASC compared to White children during the court process and query the importance of cultural relativism in this context. It will explore racial disparities in the types of orders made by courts and the experiences of racially minoritised children who are placed in foster care.

---

[57] J Davis and N Marsh, 'Boys to Men: The Cost of "Adultification" in Safeguarding Responses to Black Boys' (2020) 8(2) Critical and Radical Social Work 255.

[58] Davis (n55).

[59] United Nations, 'Refugees, Migrants Branded "Threats", Dehumanized in Campaigns Seeking Political Gain, High Commissioner Tells Third Committee, Appealing for Return to Dignity' (18 October 2018) https://press.un.org/en/2017/gashc4247.doc.htm#:~:text=Refugees%20and%20migrants%20have%20become,left%20to%20perish%20at%20sea, accessed 18 June 2024.

Significant harm

If the local authority believes a child 'in need' is experiencing, or is likely to experience, significant harm without further intervention they can apply to the court for an order to protect the child. The law defines harm as the ill-treatment or the impairment of health or development, including for example, impairment suffered by seeing or hearing the ill-treatment of another.[60] This definition includes the impact on both physical and mental health. It is intentionally broad to reflect the growing concern that although children might not be victims of domestic violence themselves, they may witness such violence in their homes and the law considers this a form of harm.

Despite this broad statutory definition, the courts have consistently resisted attempts to firmly define what significant means. For example, in *Re MA* the court said 'significant' required a justification for removing a child from parental care,[61] whereas in *Re B* the court said 'significant' required removal be a proportionate response to the harm so that intervention was never excessive.[62] Arguably, a flexible understanding of significant promotes elasticity within the law, so that it can respond effectively to a range of situations, but it remains unclear how significant operates within the cultural context.

Unhelpfully, when faced with this question the courts have been dishearteningly inconsistent. For example, in *Re K* cultural factors were considered extremely important,[63] whereas in *Re D* the court doubted they were relevant.[64] Questions of this nature invariably fall within judicial discretion, which will most likely be heavily influenced by the personal experience of individual judges, with some being more sympathetic than others. Munby J described the situation as this:

> And the court should, I think, be slow to find that parents only recently or comparatively recently arrived from a foreign country – particularly a country where standards and expectations may be more or less different, sometimes very different indeed, from those which are familiar – have fallen short of an acceptable standard of parenting if in truth they have done nothing wrong by the standards of their own community.[65]

This suggests cultural sensitivity and relativism *should* feature into how social workers understand notions of significant harm. And yet the only research on this question revealed most social workers struggle with questions of cultural

---

[60] CA 1989 s 31(9).
[61] [2009] EWCA Civ 853 para 45.
[62] [2013] UKSC paras 85 and 186.
[63] [2005] EWHC 2956 (Fam).
[64] [1998] Fam Law 656.
[65] *A Local Authority v N, Y, K (by Her Children's Guardian)* [2007] 1 FLR 399 para 26.

diversity when implementing children's social care.[66] Issues such as different attitudes towards physical chastisement, school attendance, and suspicion towards health or welfare agencies were all cited as evidence of 'failed parenting' by most social workers.[67] Calls were made for a more intersectional approach whereby cultural factors could be approached contextually and holistically, rather than an opportunity to reinforce unhelpful stereotypes.[68] Unfortunately, years later there is little evidence the situation has improved, with recent surveys revealing that a third of social workers have witnessed racism towards families in care proceedings by colleagues and/or managers.[69]

Types of orders

Acknowledging the role of culture in care proceedings is important because there are disparities in the types of orders made for racially minoritised children and UASC compared to White and mixed ethnic children. Before these disparities are explored, it is important to note that the law requires wherever possible that a court make no order at all if that promotes the child's welfare.[70] This is called the 'no order principle' and the thinking behind it is that orders should be reserved for those cases where parental cooperation with the local authority is impossible. Those cases where cooperation is feasible can benefit from the flexibility of not having an order because the parents and local authority can work together. It is therefore significant that children from Asian (15 per cent) and Black (9 per cent) backgrounds were the most likely to receive no order, whereas White children were the least likely (4 per cent). It is possible this finding reflects the fact these children were typically older when their case went to court. This would mean the views of the child would be considered, which might have prompted the court to issue no order. However, it must also be considered that this finding indicates that Black and Asian families were more able to work in tandem with social workers for the benefit of the child despite being offered fewer supportive services prior to intervention. It also raises the inescapable question, why were these families in court in the first place?

Following from this, it is perhaps unsurprising that Asian (25 per cent) and Black (21 per cent) children experienced higher rates of supervision orders compared to White (12 per cent) and mixed ethnic (15 per cent) children in 2023.[71] Supervision orders rely on a certain amount of collaboration between parents and the local authority to work because they can require the child to live in a specified place, do certain activities, and/or report to a particular place at a set

---

[66]   Brophy (n52).
[67]   Ibid.
[68]   Ibid.
[69]   MacAlister (n50) 89.
[70]   CA 1989 s 1(5).
[71]   Nuffield Family Justice Observatory (n35).

time. This allows the local authority to monitor the child without the disruption of more interventionist power. Supervision orders typically last for a year but can be extended to a maximum of three years if necessary. Their temporary nature reflects the fact they are meant to be collaborative, not adversarial, but they do require the threshold of significant harm to be met.

Special guardianship orders, by contrast, do not need to satisfy the threshold of significant harm. Instead, they grant legal decision-making powers to a guardian so that they can provide equivalent care as a parent. These orders have the effect of formalising kinship care arrangements where a family member looks after a child on behalf of another family member. They are commonly used to remove a child from a foster care arrangement and place them with family when the court feels a kinship arrangement will promote the welfare of the child. Children from White (18 per cent) and mixed ethnic (17 per cent) backgrounds are more likely to benefit from these arrangements than children from Black (13 per cent) or Asian (7 per cent) backgrounds.[72] This disparity matters because informal kinship arrangements (those without court orders) are most prevalent among children from Black and Asian backgrounds, but they do not attract the financial support that is guaranteed by a special guardianship order.[73] Local authorities have a duty to provide financial assistance for special guardians for the duration of the order,[74] but informal kinship carers are not entitled to anything. This means the special guardians of White and mixed ethnic children are financially privileged over kinship carers of Black and Asian children.

The prevalence of care orders is broadly consistent across all ethnic groups.[75] However, there are notable racial differences in the use of deprivation of liberty and adoption orders. Deprivation of liberty is when a child is confined without their consent by the authority of the state.[76] Most children who are accommodated in this way are placed in secure accommodation, which are locked facilities that children cannot leave. This type of detention must be authorised by a court and any confinement that is not is unlawful.[77] The main consideration for the court when awarding these orders is the likelihood of the child absconding and the risk that they will experience significant harm if they succeed.[78] These

---

[72] Ibid.

[73] Kinship Foundation supported by KPMG Foundation, 'Kinship to Lead New Research on the Experiences of Kinship Families from Black, Asian and Minority Ethnic Communities' (2022) https://kinship.org.uk/our-work-and-impact/news/kinship-launches-major-new-research-on-the-experiences-of-kinship-families-from-bme-communities/, accessed 20 June 2024.

[74] Department for Education, 'Special Guardianship Guidance: Statutory Guidance for Local Authorities on the Special Guardianship Regulations 2005' (January 2017) 9 https://assets.publishing.service.gov.uk/media/5a8202c940f0b62305b92007/Special_guardianship_statutory_guidance.pdf, accessed 23 July 2025.

[75] Nuffield Family Justice Observatory (n35).

[76] *Storck v Germany* 61603/00 [2005] ECHR 406.

[77] *London Borough of Lambeth v L (Unlawful Placement)* [2020] ECHC 383 (Fam).

[78] CA 1989 s 25(1).

orders are quite often used for children who are suspected victims of trafficking. At present, Black (1.3 per cent) and Asian (1.3 per cent) children are more likely to be detained against their will than White (0.5 per cent) and mixed ethnic children (0.6 per cent).[79]

Some of this disparity can be explained by the increasing number of UASC who are consistently from racially minoritised backgrounds. While most UASC live in semi-independent (45 per cent) or fully independent (16 per cent) accommodation there are more UASC in secure accommodation than any other group within the care population.[80] Concerns have been raised about the differential treatment of UASC more broadly compared to other looked-after children. The courts recently determined that the Home Secretary had acted unlawfully by authorising Kent County Council to use hotels as a form of secure accommodation.[81] The court explained that the Home Secretary's actions had the effect of 'entrenching and normalising the practice of using hotels to accommodate UASC', which was an excessive use of power and a breach of the statutory duty to provide suitable accommodate for children in need under section 20.[82] Hotels were deemed unsuitable accommodation for local authorities to house UASC because of the risk that these vulnerable children could go missing, be trafficked, or be exposed to significant harm. At the time of writing, the Home Office responded to this judgment by pledging to end the use of hotels for UASC and to work with Kent County Council and local authorities throughout the UK to increase the number of appropriate placements to meet demand.[83] It remains to be seen how the increasing number of UASC will be accommodated in a way that is compatible with the obligations imposed on all local authorities by the CA 1989.

Given the extent of differential treatment experienced by racially minoritised children in the social care system it should come as no surprise that they are also the least likely to be adopted. White (17 per cent) and mixed ethnic (16 per cent) children are the most likely to be placed for adoption compared to Black (6 per cent) and Asian children (5 per cent).[84] Research confirms this disparity cannot be explained by the ages of the racially minoritised children, nor due to being part of a sibling group.[85] Older children and those who form part of a sibling group are harder to place for adoption than single infants, but these factors

---

[79] Nuffield Family Justice Observatory (n35).

[80] Department for Education (n4): data on characteristics.

[81] *ECPAT UK, R (on the Application of) v Kent County Council & Anor* [2023] EWHC 1953.

[82] Ibid, para 204.

[83] Home Office, 'Response to a Report on the Use of Hotels for Housing Unaccompanied Asylum-Seeking Children' (2024) https://www.gov.uk/government/publications/response-to-a-report-on-the-use-of-hotels-for-housing-unaccompanied-asylum-seeking-children/response-to-a-report-on-the-use-of-hotels-for-housing-unaccompanied-asylum-seeking-children, accessed 23 July 2025.

[84] Nuffield Family Justice Observatory (n35).

[85] Ibid.

were not relevant, and thus we still do not know why this racialised inequality is present in the adoption system.

Placement location and stability

Although the volume of care orders was broadly consistent across all ethnicities there were other areas of racial difference that are worthy of note before moving onto life after court. Namely, children from some ethnic minority backgrounds were more likely to be placed outside the boundary of their local authority and to experience higher rates of placement instability once they were accommodated compared to White children. Seventy per cent of the looked-after population experienced one placement in 2023 and 20 per cent experienced two placements.[86] This suggests disruption was relatively uncommon for most children in the care system. However, the figures reveal that most disruption was experienced by Black Caribbean and White traveller children. Fifteen per cent of both groups experienced three or more placements within one year, whereas children from Chinese and Bangladeshi backgrounds experienced comparatively little instability.[87] It is possible that the higher rates of instability experienced by Black Caribbean children is attributable to the fact they were more likely to be teenagers when they entered care, but in the absence of detailed research any correlations would be merely speculative.

Black Caribbean children were also significantly more likely to be placed outside the boundary of their local authority. The law requires local authorities to accommodate children in a way that is consistent with their welfare. This means they must ensure that any placement allows the child to be near their home and that they remain in the area managed by the local authority.[88] There are several reasons local authorities might struggle to meet this requirement, including but not limited to a substantial lack of resources. What is less clear is why there are clear racial disparities between children who are placed within the boundary and those who are not. Children from Black Caribbean (64 per cent) backgrounds were more likely to be placed outside their local area, compared to White (38 per cent) children, and yet they were also more likely to be returned to their families and never return to care.[89]

Evaluation

Academics and practitioners have expressed a range of possible explanations for the racial disparities arising during the court process. The Child Welfare Inequalities Project looked at thousands of children in care to better understand

---

[86] Department for Education (n4): data on placement stability.
[87] Nuffield Family Justice Observatory (n35).
[88] CA 1989 s 22(8) and (9).
[89] Nuffield Family Justice Observatory (n35).

why there are such pronounced inequalities based on ethnicity.[90] The study concluded that major causes for concern included a lack of attention from policy makers since the early 2000s and a lack of understanding about the racial disparities in deprivation throughout the UK. The study confirmed deprivation plays a real role in the rates that children enter care. Children in the most deprived areas were over ten times more likely to be looked after than children in the least deprived areas.[91] But deprivation is not experienced equally by all ethnicities and research indicates intervention rates fluctuate based on deprivation. There is a clear correlation between intervention and deprivation for White children that does not exist for Asian and Black children.[92] Although Black and Asian children are over-represented within the care system, they are not disproportionately drawn from deprived areas, whereas White children typically are. More research is needed into the intersection between deprivation and intervention with a specific line of enquiry focused on racial disparity.

There is very little research on why ethnic minorities are over-represented within the system. Barrister Olivia Edwards presented findings drawn from an analysis of casefiles from 18 St John Street Chambers on this question.[93] She concluded there were a range of issues contributing to racial disparities beyond discrepancies in economic deprivation. These included factors such as the difficulty some ethnic minorities face verbalising their case through interpreters, timescale pressures on document translation, unconscious bias throughout all levels of the court system, and a widespread lack of supportive services to help ethnic minority parents understand cultural expectations of parenting in the UK.[94] Edwards reasoned that there is a difference between 'individualist' and 'collectivist' parenting which is also causing problems. 'Individualist' parenting is practised in Western cultures where behaviours such as nurturing, supporting, affection, and curiosity towards social constructs are prioritised. 'Collectivist' parenting is practised in non-Western cultures where behaviours such as obedience, social responsibility, religious observance, and self-discipline are prioritised.[95] Edwards concludes that the imposition of 'individualist' parenting expectations on 'collectivist' parents might be a key reason why ethnic minorities are over-represented in the care system.

Different approaches to the important issues that often catch the attention of social workers, like physical chastisement, school attendance, and care giving, will obviously differ depending on parenting style. These differences, coupled with the ongoing apathy of successive governments about questions of ethnic

---

[90]   Bywaters and Team (n38).

[91]   Ibid, 4.

[92]   C Webb and others, 'Cuts Both Ways: Ethnicity, Poverty and the Social Gradient in Child Welfare Interventions' (2020) 117 Children and Youth Services Review 105299.

[93]   O Edwards, 'Race and Culture in Family Law' (2021) Family Law 1174.

[94]   Ibid.

[95]   Ibid.

over-representation and racial disparities in treatment all contribute to the worrying situation the UK is currently in. The only way to change the direction of travel is to invest in research to clearly establish the primary causes of these inequalities so that they can be directly addressed.

Summary

Clearly racially minoritised children have very different court experiences than White children. They are more likely to be granted 'no order', but if they are given an order it will probably be less interventionist. Kinship carers of racially minoritised children are more likely to have informal care arrangements that do not benefit from financial support whereas carers of White children are more likely to receive financial provision from the local authority. Racially minoritised children and UASC also experience more placement instability and geographical displacement than White children, but they are also less likely to return to care. There are many possible factors that might contribute to the racial inequality observed in the children's social care court system. What is clear is that there is not enough research currently available to draw meaningful conclusions or make informed decisions for change. This is a critical area that needs to be explored and a list of questions for further research are included at the end of this chapter.

After court

This section explores the outcomes for racially minoritised children after they leave the care system. There is specific focus on economic inactivity and criminal convictions because most of the data on care leavers outcomes focuses on these issues.

Convictions and offending

There is an unfortunate but well-established correlation between care experience and contact with the criminal justice system. More than half of looked-after (52 per cent) children who were born in 1994 and educated in England had a criminal conviction by the time they were 24 years of age compared to 13 per cent of the general population who were not in care.[96] This data excludes UASC because they were not educated in the UK, and it is worth noting that there is currently no published research on whether UASC experience higher rates of offending compared to the wider population.

---

96   ONS, 'The Education Background of Looked-After Children Who Interact with the Criminal Justice System' (December 2022) https://www.ons.gov.uk/peoplepopulationandcommunity/ educationandchildcare/articles/theeducationbackgroundoflookedafterchildrenwhointeractw iththecriminaljusticesystem/december2022, accessed 23 July 2025.

Although immediate imprisonment is an unusual outcome after an initial encounter with the criminal justice system, care-experienced young adults were ten times more likely to receive an immediate custodial sentence compared to other offenders.[97] Care leavers were also more likely to be cautioned or fined rather than given a warning, and yet again, racial disparities are present. Young people from Black (19 per cent) and mixed ethnic (21 per cent) backgrounds had higher rates of imprisonment than young people from White (15 per cent) and Asian (7 per cent) backgrounds.[98] White care leavers were also more likely (40 per cent) to receive non-custodial sentences if their cases went to court than racially minoritised care leavers.

This is significant because local authorities have a statutory duty to keep in touch with and provide assistance to young people who have been in their care until they reach the age of 21.[99] The law requires local authorities to maintain contact with care leavers even if they leave the area and to provide them with support, accommodation, advice, and/or money if needed.[100] This duty can also be extended to the age of 25 if required.[101] We need to better understand why Black and mixed ethnic children care leavers are more likely to be criminalised as young adults because they are also the most likely to be in touch with the local authority. The data reveals that Black (94 per cent) and mixed ethnic (92 per cent) care leavers were the most likely groups to keep in touch with the local authority, whereas Asian (89 per cent) and 'any other ethnic' (89 per cent) children were the least likely but also the least likely to be criminalised.[102] This suggests there is currently not a correlation between after-care supportive services and a reduction in the criminalisation of ethnic care leavers.

The over-representation of young Black and mixed ethnic care leavers in the criminal justice system raises serious questions about how the compulsory duty operates in relation to racially minoritised children. This is particularly alarming because we know children from these backgrounds have already experienced more disadvantage before and during the court process than White children. If Black and mixed ethnic care leavers are denied the same compassion and vulnerability afforded to White care leavers due to the 'adultification bias', local authorities should be able to mitigate this form of discrimination by fulfilling their duty to provide appropriate support and advice throughout criminal justice proceedings. Again, it is unclear why this is happening, but it is an important question that deserves further research so that supportive services can reduce the criminalisation of ethnic minority care leavers.

---

[97] Ibid.

[98] Ibid, data on gender and ethnicity.

[99] CA 1989 s 23C.

[100] Ibid, s 23B.

[101] Ibid, s 23CZB and s 23CA.

[102] Noor and others (n41) 38.

Not in education, employment, or training (NEET)

NEET is government terminology for young people aged 16 to 25 who are not in education, employment, or training. The government capture data on this question annually so that they can measure and differentiate between young people who are in some form of education or training and those who are seeking employment versus those who are economically inactive. Inactivity must be differentiated from those who are unemployed but seeking employment because there is always the possibility of becoming economically active once a job is obtained. Inactivity is a concern for any sitting government due to the wider economic consequences for the state.

The latest data shows that 12.5 per cent of all young people aged between 16 and 24 were NEET and that care leavers were ten times more likely to fall into this category than the general population.[103] Data is not available for the ethnicity of care leavers who are NEET but data is available for the ethnicity of the population of NEET young people as a whole. Again, racial disparities are present, but they are not as clearly divided between White and racially minoritised groups as some of the other issues explored in this chapter.[104] The data shows that young people from Bangladeshi (12 per cent), Pakistani (14.3 per cent), and White (11.7 per cent) backgrounds were more likely to be NEET, whereas young people from Black (11.5 per cent) Asian (11.3 per cent), and mixed ethnic (11 per cent) backgrounds were broadly consistent with the national average, and children from Chinese (4.5 per cent) and Indian (7.3 per cent) backgrounds were less likely.[105] Most of these young people were classed as economically inactive, rather than unemployed.

Given that we know children from minoritised backgrounds are more likely to experience social care intervention and this correlates with a substantially increased risk of being NEET in young adulthood it is perhaps unsurprising that most minoritised groups are either overrepresented or in line with the national average for economic activity. The only exception to this were UASC who were excluded from NEET data because the methodology defined a care leaver as children who were in care from the age of 14, while most UASC entered the UK

---

[103] ONS, 'Young people not in education, employment or training (NEET)' (May 2025) https://www.ons.gov.uk/employmentandlabourmarket/peoplenotinwork/unemployment/datasets/youngpeoplenotineducationemploymentortrainingneettable1, accessed 23 July 2025; N Harrison and others, 'Care Leavers' Transition into the Labour Market in England' Nuffield Foundation (2023) https://www.education.ox.ac.uk/wp-content/uploads/2023/01/CareLeaversLabourMarket.pdf, accessed 2 July 2025.

[104] Note that UASC were omitted from this study due to visa restrictions on their ability to work as young adults.

[105] ONS, 'Young people not in education, employment or training (NEET) by ethnicity' (February 2021) https://www.ethnicity-facts-figures.service.gov.uk/work-pay-and-benefits/unemployment-and-economic-inactivity/young-people-not-in-employment-education-or-training-neet/latest/, accessed 23 July 2025.

after the age of 16. UASC face different challenges as young adults from non-asylum-seeking care leavers because they have better educational outcomes but still lag behind the general population and face significant immigration challenges.[106]

Evaluation

A recent study tried to explore why care leavers are significantly more likely to be NEET in their 21st year compared to other children.[107] Major challenges were identified as reasons for economic inactivity, including disability and caring responsibilities along with the impact of early childhood trauma and disruption to education. However, other factors were also identified that had arguably been previously overlooked. Most care leavers (63 per cent) were identified as having special educational needs and only 20 per cent left school with five GCSEs compared to 65 per cent of the general population.[108] Poor educational attainment was directly correlated with economic inactivity due to the limited employment options available after education. As a result, a significant number of care leavers became reliant on a mixture of benefits and precarious employment in early adulthood. This study noted that these challenges were further exacerbated by the fact most care leavers did not have parental support for finance or accommodation that would have allowed them to take up work-related opportunities like other young people. The authors of the study made a range of recommendations for improvement including educational intervention, top-up financing, and improved pathways for training and employment specifically aimed at care leavers.[109] They also noted the unhelpfulness of the term NEET because it was unable to account for the nuanced reasons that many care leavers might be economically inactive (precarious work, short-term contracts, disability, etc).

Summary

It appears racially minoritised care leavers and UASC also have different experiences of young adulthood compared to the general population. Some racially minoritised groups were more prone to economic inactivity and others were more likely to be criminalised and/or receive custodial sentences. Most alarmingly, these disparities persist despite the fact these same groups are often the most likely to be in touch with the local authority and therefore able to access support and advice.

---

[106] A O'Higgins, 'Analysis of Care and Educational Pathways of Refugee and Asylum-Seeking Children in Care in England: Implications for Social Work' (2019) 28(1) International Journal of Social Welfare 53.

[107] N Harrison (n103).

[108] Ibid.

[109] Ibid.

Conclusion

There are innumerable possible factors that contribute to the widespread racial disparities discussed in this chapter and not enough research exists to identify them. Cultural difference, Euro-centric norms, racial bias, language barriers, gendered assumptions, and many others undoubtedly play a role in the differential treatment experienced by racially minoritised children and UASC in the care system. While fresh research into these issues is crucial for their resolution, this chapter concludes that the entire protective framework would benefit from a more intersectional approach. Intersectionality requires that the voices of all parties be heard, especially those voices which have been marginalised in the past. The voices of racially minoritised, non-national children and UASC need to be heard in addition to the parents of such children and/or their kinship carers. This is not a case of reforming the law but, instead, changing the way it is practised. Children's social care needs to embed diverse reasoning into decision making and display a true curiosity for notions of 'otherness' within family life. Child protection undoubtedly needs to be about safeguarding children, but if social workers continue to respond to notions of difference as safeguarding concerns there is a real risk the racial inequalities currently observed will become more entrenched and compound the disadvantage experienced by some communities in the UK even further.

Further questions to consider

• Why do racially minoritised children receive fewer supportive services prior to intervention compared to White children?
• Why do racially minoritised children experience more immediate intervention by social workers but less interventionist orders by courts?
• Should notions of significant harm be culturally relative?
• Do UASC experience higher incidents of criminal offending and/or convictions as young adults like other care leavers?
• Is bias playing a role in each stage of protective action to re-entrench the disparities discussed in this chapter?
• What role does deprivation play in the decision to intervene in White versus racially minoritised families?

Further materials

Brophy J, 'Child Maltreatment in Diverse Households: Challenges to Law, Theory and Practice' (2008) 35 Journal of Law and Society 75

Bywaters P and the Child Welfare Inequalities Project Team, 'The Child Welfare Inequalities Project: Final Report' University of Huddersfield (2020)

Harrison N and others, 'Care Leavers' Transition into the Labour Market in England' Nuffield Foundation (2023) https://www.education.ox.ac.uk/wp-cont ent/uploads/2023/01/CareLeaversLabourMarket.pdf, accessed 11 June 2025

O'Higgins A, 'Analysis of Care and Educational Pathways of Refugee and Asylum-Seeking Children in Care in England: Implications for Social Work', (2019) 28(1) International Journal of Social Welfare 53

Webb C and others, 'Cuts Both Ways: Ethnicity, Poverty and the Social Gradient in Child Welfare Interventions' (2020) 117 Children and Youth Services Review 105299

PART II

Dispute Resolution in Family Law

8

Family Dispute Resolution: Meeting the Challenge of Diversity

Maria Federica Moscati

Introduction

This chapter analyses whether and how mediation and other family dispute-resolution processes can accommodate family diversity. More specifically, the questions addressed are: in what ways does diversity manifest itself in family disputes and their resolution? And in what ways could dispute resolution processes accommodate family diversity? The arguments developed here are twofold. The first suggests that the combination of heterogeneity within family units and the intersecting personal characteristics of family members who are involved in a dispute influence the creation and resolution of a dispute. The second argument concerns the practice of mediation and other dispute resolution processes proposed by the Family Procedure Rules, arguing that to ensure access to justice for every kind of family member, dispute resolution processes should be shaped around the variety of family forms that exist, be mindful of the intersecting identities of the disputants, and avoid drawing on stereotypical, normative understanding of family (one that is binary, cis–heteronormative, monocultural, wealthy, and ableist).

The study of family mediation, and family dispute resolution more broadly, requires eschewing assumptions about this type of disputes. Needless to say, disagreements, conflicts, and disputes can be found in all families, in all cultures, and in all legal systems, and it is often through disputes that abuses and power imbalances become visible. Thus, it is important to avoid pathologising disputes and instead focus on the question of how disputes are resolved. Family disputes are resolved with recourse to a variety of means and processes including, litigation, negotiation, mediation, arbitration, collaborative law, asking for help from friends or community leaders, and so on,[1] though it should be noted that some disputes can remain unresolved, and parties might just avoid to engage. Depending on the nature, and characteristics of the dispute, it might be that parties need to attempt a range of different dispute resolution mechanisms. Similarly, sometimes other types of intervention like counselling, family therapy, and parenting training are required to help the parties to address broader conflict; though intertwined with the legal dispute, these concern emotional, psychological, and relational aspects. Thus, the learning point is not to assume that mediation (or any other dispute resolution process) is necessarily the most suitable process for all types of family disputes. As an additional learning point, this chapter, shows how the study of dispute resolution, including the resolution of family disputes, requires responsiveness to interdisciplinarity. Anthropology, sociology, psychology, and several other academic disciplines contribute to the study of dispute resolution and have unveiled the variety of ways disputes are dealt with outside courtrooms, thus, it is important to understand that the resolution of family disputes is not only a legal matter.

The chapter starts by discussing the meaning and nature of quarrels between family members before moving on to consider the developments of family mediation in England and Wales, including the latest reforms to the Family Procedure Rules that refer to non-court dispute resolution .Critical conversations then follow on the manner in which diversity shapes disputes and their resolution, including reflections on access to justice and whether family mediation as currently performed offers a suitable and inclusive arena for addressing family diversity. Finally, the chapter engages with the concept of fitting the *forum to the fuss* by discussing how decisions can be made to find the appropriate process for each dispute.

After reading this chapter and considering the questions and role play that it suggests, readers will gain broad critical knowledge of how diversity within family units influences disputes and their resolution through family mediation. They will also acquire general knowledge of the current legal framework concerning family dispute resolution.

Clarifying the terms and the scope

Using the appropriate terminology is particularly important during the resolution of disputes because lack of linguistic clarity and misunderstanding can trigger or exacerbate disputes. Therefore, to begin, we clarify some key terms used in this chapter, namely dispute, family disputes, and dispute resolution.[2]

Starting with dispute, it is common to believe that disputes start when lawyers are involved. However, this is a limited characterisation that overlooks the complexity of disputes as embedded in social contexts. As Palmer and Roberts

---

[1] For a comprehensive overview of the variety of responses to disputes see M Palmer and S Roberts, 'Disputes and Dispute Processes' in Palmer and Roberts, *Dispute Processes: ADR and the Primary Forms of Decision Making* (3rd edn, CUP 2020) 73.

[2] Mediation will be addressed later.

submit, 'in any social context, disputes are embedded in everyday life, arising from "a past" and emerging into "a future"'.[3] Similarly, Felstiner, Abel, and Sarat have suggested that because disputes are social constructs 'in order for disputes to emerge and remedial action to be taken, an unperceived injurious experience (unPIE) must be transformed into a perceived injurious experience (PIE)'.[4] The transformation, as the three authors suggest, goes through three stages: the naming of the injurious experience, the blaming of the author of the injury, and a claiming against that person or persons that is rejected. However, the transformation is not straightforward because there are personal and social factors that contribute to the recognition and consciousness of wrong and to any subsequent request for redress. For instance, family dynamics and roles, or the aim of preserving harmony within the family can determine whether an unperceived injurious experience is transformed into a perceived injurious experience and might limit individuals within the family from asking for redress.

The second clarification concerns the nature and characteristics of *family disputes*. In this chapter, we draw upon a broad understanding of family and family members. Consequently, our understanding of family disputes goes beyond a definition of family disputes concerning divorce/dissolution, distribution of finances following divorce and dissolution, and arrangements regarding children. Family disputes can concern intergenerational disputes; different decisions about family life and family members; inheritance disputes; disagreements about pets, family celebrations, whether and how to have children, how to address sexual orientation and gender identity; different perceptions and acceptance that each parent has about their child's special needs; and so on.[5] Sometimes the terms *dispute* and *conflict* are used interchangeably, but we should be aware of the differences. As described by Menkel-Meadow, 'While "disputes" may be about legal cases, conflicts are more broadly and deeply about human relations and transactions.'[6] This difference is important for our purposes in two regards. First, as we will see later in the chapter, legal aid for family mediation is only available when there is a family dispute legally defined as such. Secondly, in family settings legal disputes and other personal conflicts are often intertwined. As family disputes are shaped by the intersection of legal issues, emotions, feelings, relationships, and

---

[3] Palmer and Roberts, *Dispute Processes* (n1) 74.

[4] WLF Felstiner, RL Abel, and A Sarat, 'The Emergence and Transformation of Disputes: Naming, Blaming, Claiming ...' (1980–81) 15(3–4) Law & Society Review 631. See also L Mather and B Yngvesson, 'Language, Audience, and the Transformation of Disputes' (1980–81) 15(3–4) Law & Society Review 775.

[5] For an account of a mediator on this see A Sims, 'Exploring the Scope of Family Mediation in England and Wales' in M Roberts and MF Moscati (eds), *Family Mediation: Contemporary Issues* (Bloomsbury Professional 2020).

[6] C Menkel-Meadow, 'From Legal Disputes to Conflict Resolution and Human Problem Solving: Legal Dispute Resolution in a Multidisciplinary Context' (2004) 54(1) Journal of Legal Education 7.

personal experiences, they can be characterised as having a polycentric nature, often described as involving 'polycentric problems' that need to be addressed/resolved in different ways.[7] Fuller and Winston explain that polycentric disputes present a variety of parties, and multiple issues, and create multiple consequences that in turn might affect and influence parties other than those directly involved in the resolution process. We could argue here that diversity contributes to this polycentrism, which requires attention when choosing whether and how to deal with a dispute, and during the resolution.

Finally, although Family Procedure Rules adopt the term non-court dispute resolution and this terminology is reflected in the sections of this chapter that analyse the law, nevertheless this chapter encourages students to use the terms *alternative*, *appropriate*, *accessible dispute resolution*, or simply *dispute resolution processes*. Even if the aim of law is to divert disputants from court, the terminological choice of *non-court dispute resolution* paradoxically emphasises the centrality of courts, whereas *alternative*, *appropriate* and accessible call for attention on the parties, their needs and their characteristics – attention that is necessary to match their dispute with the process. As we shall see in our analysis, identifying and acknowledging the several factors that contribute to create and transform a family dispute helps in choosing the appropriate dispute resolution process, which might or might not be mediation.

Summary

To discuss fully whether and how family mediation and other dispute resolution processes outside the courtroom can enhance access to justice for family members in disputes it is important to position this more broadly within dispute resolution discourse, extend current understanding of family disputes, and be mindful of the importance of social context and personal characteristics on the creation of the dispute and its resolution.

Relevant law

The growing governmental and professional interest in family mediation and alternative dispute resolution has been gradual and linked to broader conversations and reforms concerning justice systems.[8] Although informal resolutions of

---

[7]   L Fuller and KI Winston, 'The Forms and Limits of Adjudication' (1978) 92 Harvard Law Review 353.

[8]   The professional interest in family mediation has encouraged conversations among mediators regarding the development of a regulatory framework and policies aimed at ensuring quality and ethics. For an overview see L Saunders, 'Development of Regulatory Framework for the Practice of Mediation in the UK' in Roberts and Moscati (eds), (n5). For current updates see at the website of the Family Mediation Council: https://www.familymediationcouncil.org.uk/, accessed 11 June 2025.

family disputes have characterised all societies and cultures, in the UK the professionalisation and institutionalisation of family mediation and other dispute resolution processes alternative to courts should be positioned within the broader Alternative Dispute Resolution (ADR) movement at the end of the 1970s that characterised civil justice systems in the US and in the UK.[9] Thus, legal developments concerning family mediation first and alternative dispute resolution processes should be understood as one of the several governmental steps towards diversion from courts and institutionalisation of out-of-court dispute resolution mechanisms aiming to overcome the dysfunction of the justice system.[10] This clarification is important for the critical conversation later on as it raises questions concerning access to justice, mediation's suitability, and the freedom of disputants to choose the most appropriate process for their dispute.[11]

Family mediation in the UK can be seen to have developed through four phases, each characterised by the different professions involved and by the distinct focus of interventions.[12] Marian Roberts describes the first phase, beginning in the early 1980s, as led by 'the welfare professionals', characterised by a focus on disputes concerning the welfare of children. This phase was followed by the 'family therapists' phase between the end of the 1980s and beginning of the 1990s, during which an intense debate about whether and how family therapy could be applied to family mediation started. The third phase, in the late 1990s, saw lawyers – both solicitors and barristers – embracing mediation in their practice. The final phase is the current family justice system (FJS) approach: 'Several recent developments in the family justice system confirm a growing trend to deny mediation its distinctive dispute resolution status as a genuine alternative to litigation and formal judicial determination and towards mediation becoming a form of legal process rather than an alternative to legal process, damaging to both judicial authority and party control.'[13] Further, Hunter and Barlow have

---

[9]   For an overview of ADR movement see Palmer and Roberts, *Dispute Processes* (n1). In the UK the legal developments towards embracing ADR started with changes to the Civil Procedures Rules in 1998 following Lord Woolf's reports on 'Access to Justice'. These were mirrored in European law with, among others, the Council of Europe's Recommendation No R (98)1 on family mediation, in the 'Directive 2008/52/EC of the European Parliament and of the Council of 21 May 2008 on Certain Aspects of Mediation in Civil and Commercial Matters' and European Parliament resolution of 25 October 2011 on alternative dispute resolution in civil, commercial, and family matters.

[10] For a comprehensive analysis of the debate concerning institutionalisation of ADR see Palmer and Roberts, chapter 13, 'Institutionalisation of ADR' in Palmer and Roberts, *Dispute Processes* (n1) and M Palmer, 'Formalisation of Alternative Dispute Resolution Processes: Some Socio-Legal Thoughts' in J Zekoll, M Balz, and I Amelung (eds), *Dispute Resolution: Alternatives to Formalisation – Formalisation of Alternatives?* (Brill 2014).

[11] See also S Roberts, 'Mediation in Family Disputes' (1983) 46 Modern Law Review 337.

[12] M Roberts, 'View from the Coal Face: Interdisciplinary Influences on Family Mediation in the United Kingdom' (2014) 9 Journal of Comparative Law 108.

[13] Ibid, 117.

pointed out that we are now in a post-justice world 'one in which access to justice is a commodity which must be paid for like any other'.[14] As we will see later, this is a consideration that sadly mirrors how mediation has been co-opted by the state and the current discrepancy between the encouragement of family disputants to choose processes other than litigation and the limited accessibility of some of them.

Proposals made for the Family Law Act 1996 created some opportunities for mediation to take place. In particular, parties could be encouraged to attempt mediation by the court after the period of reflection and consideration,[15] following the compulsory information meeting,[16] after the court had received a statement from the parties,[17] or when the parties were eligible for legal aid.[18] The legacy of the Family Law Act saw provision of legal aid for mediation included in the revised Legal Aid Act 1988, and reforms concerning the mediation assessment and information meeting. Other statutory recognition of mediation can be found in the Children and Families Act 2014 and Family Procedure Rules 2010 and subsequent changes that we will discuss later.

Following the COVID-19 pandemic, in 2021 the government launched the *Family Mediation Voucher Scheme*,[19] providing £500 towards mediation. Although the voucher has been welcomed by mediators,[20] there are three practical shortcomings that limit accessibility for family disputants. The first limit is that the voucher might not cover all costs of the mediation process and does not cover the costs for the mediation, information, and assessment meeting (MIAM). Thus, families will still carry the burden of additional costs if the resolution of their disputes requires more time. The second limitation of the voucher is that it applies only to legal disputes regarding children or family financial matters linked to child disputes.[21] Thus, family disputants involved in other types of family disputes cannot benefit from it. Finally, the initiative is time-limited.[22]

---

[14]   R Hunter and A Barlow, 'Reconstruction of Family Mediation in a Post-Justice World' in Roberts and Moscati (eds), (n5) 11.

[15]   Family Law Act 1996, s 7.

[16]   Parties in a marital breakdown were required to attend an information meeting aimed at giving information to the parties about marital breakdown and its consequences, counselling, legal advice, and mediation. During the meeting, the mediator would explain to applicants and respondents how mediation could assist them and assess whether they were suitable for mediation and eligible for public funding.

[17]   Family Law Act 1996, s 13.

[18]   Ibid, s 29.

[19]   https://www.gov.uk/guidance/family-mediation-voucher-scheme, accessed 11 June 2025.

[20]   Ministry of Justice, 'Family Mediation Voucher Scheme Analysis' (2023) https://assets.pub lishing.service.gov.uk/media/6419cd288fa8f547c7ffd692/family-mediation-voucher-scheme-analysis.pdf, accessed 8 October 2024; A Sixsmith, 'Mediators' Perspectives on the Family Mediation Voucher Scheme' (2023) 35(1) Child and Family Law Quarterly 9.

[21]   https://www.familymediationcouncil.org.uk/mediation-vouchers/, accessed 8 October 2024.

[22]   At the time of writing, the voucher has been extended until March 2026.

MIAM

The Family Law Act 1996 contributed to raising awareness about mediation and screening for the suitability of disputes for mediation. As a result, under the Children and Families Act 2014 the MIAM was made compulsory for any person submitting an application on a family matter to the Family Court. Section 10(1) requires a party, '[b]efore making a relevant family application ... [to] attend a family mediation information and assessment meeting'. Also, it can be ordered under Sections 11A and 11C of the Children Act 1989. There are circumstances, however, in which family disputants are exempted from attending MIAM. Family Procedure Rule 3.8(1) and the Practice Direction set out that the MIAM requirement does not apply where there is domestic abuse, child protection concerns, previous MIAM attendance, or other dispute resolution, attendance, bankruptcy, or difficulties in locating an authorised family mediator.[23] It is important to clarify that MIAM is not mediation; it is a meeting that occurs before mediation; it can take place in person or online.[24] According to Practice Direction 3A 'Prospective respondents are expected to attend a MIAM, either with the prospective applicant or separately. A prospective respondent may choose to attend a MIAM separately, but this should usually be with the same authorised family mediator.' Its general aims are to assess the safety and suitability of mediation and give information. The changes to the Family Procedure Rules that came into force in 2024 appear to have expanded the scope of MIAM.[25] Mediators must inform parties of the variety of non-court dispute resolution processes available and explain the potential benefits of their use; they may

---

[23] For details on the exemptions see https://www.justice.gov.uk/courts/procedure-rules/family/practice_directions/pd_part_03a#para17, accessed 11 June 2025.

[24] In exceptional circumstances, it can also take place on telephone.

[25] According to the Family Procedure Rules, Chapter III, para 3.9, during MIAM the authorised family mediator must:
  (a) provide information about the principles, process and different models of mediation, and information about other methods of non-court dispute resolution;
  (b) consider and explain the potential benefits of mediation and other methods of non-court dispute resolution as a means of resolving the dispute;
  (c) assess whether there has been, or is a risk of, domestic abuse; and
  (d) assess whether there has been, or is a risk of, harm by a prospective party to a child that would be a subject of the application;
  (e) indicate to those attending the MIAM which form, or forms, of non-court dispute resolution may be most suitable as a means of resolving the dispute, and why; and
  (f) where sub-paragraph (e) applies, provide information to those attending the MIAM about how to proceed with the form, or forms, of non-court dispute resolution in question.
  Further explanation about MIAM can be found in Practice Direction 3A, para 3, according to which 'A MIAM is a short meeting that provides information about mediation and other methods of non-court dispute resolution, as options for resolving disputes. A MIAM is conducted by a trained mediator who will consider and explain the potential benefits of different methods of non-court dispute resolution. A MIAM should be held within 15 business days of contacting the mediator.'

indicate their view on the suitability of the different non-dispute resolution processes; and finally, they should provide information and guidance on how to engage with these processes.

We now need to reflect on how these changes play out in practice and what issues might arise. A first issue that arises is about the breadth of the mediatory intervention. The new rules, by requiring the mediator to 'indicate [...] which form, or forms, of non-court dispute resolution may be most suitable as a means of resolving the dispute, and why' leave much to mediators' discretion to and raise questions on whether and how information on the different processes will be delivered neutrally in a way that leaves parties free to make their choice.[26]

The Rules also seem to assume an in-depth knowledge on the part of the mediator about the several dispute resolution processes that can be adopted and do not clarify the time frames for the delivery of information for each process. Similarly, although, the standards and policy set by independent professional organisations like the Family Mediation Council emphasise the importance of thorough suitability scrutiny during the MIAM, the Rules do not refer to the disadvantages of the various non-court dispute resolution options – the focus is fully on the benefits of the processes. Thus, the quality and comprehensiveness of information are left to the discretion of each individual mediator. This brings the risk of unequal access to knowledge for disputants, hampering fully informed choices on whether and how to resolve their disputes.

Non-court dispute resolution

For those parties who, after the MIAM, decide to continue to pursue a resolution via courts, repeated opportunities to revert to mediation and other non-court dispute resolution processes can be found throughout the litigation journey.[27] Non-court dispute resolution is a general term used in the Family Procedure Rules and Practice Directions that includes a variety of resolution processes performed outside the courtroom. Practice Direction 3A, para 9, lists mediation, arbitration,[28] evaluation by a neutral third party,[29] and collaborative law as non-court dispute resolution processes.[30] However, other types of dispute resolution processes could be used by the parties.

---

[26] Family Procedure Rules, Chapter III, para 3.9 (e)

[27] For example, in disputes concerning children, during the First Hearing Dispute Resolution Appointment, the parties, a Cafcass officer, and the judge would attend; this meeting aims at discussing a settlement.

[28] Arbitration is a form of dispute resolution process during which a third, neutral party – the arbitrator – decides the outcome of the dispute.

[29] Early neutral evaluation is a non-binding process during which the parties in a dispute have their dispute considered by a group of experts that provide a preliminary assessment of it.

[30] Collaborative law is a process during which the parties in a dispute meet, accompanied by their lawyers. The parties negotiate while the lawyers are there to offer advice if needed.

Courts, following the changes to the procedural rules in 2024, play a proactive role in encouraging parties to divert from litigation at every stage of proceedings if the judge determines suitability for the case. For example, according to the Family Procedure Rules Part 3, Chapter II, courts have a duty to consider non-court dispute resolution, encourage parties to obtain information and advice on this or undertake non-court dispute resolution,[31] and cost sanctions are provided for non-participation in these processes during financial and property cases.

To sum up, the procedural rules are not unproblematic, and they do not take into account the several hybrid processes that can be used by parties and their accessibility. Further, the Rules seem to be shaped to fit a traditional family that is binary, wealthy, healthy, and with family disagreements limited to distribution of finance upon divorce/dissolution and children. Another shortcoming is that many outcomes reached through alternative dispute resolution are not legally binding. Further questions arise on whether judges and magistrates who deal with family law cases possess the necessary technical knowledge and expertise to consider and direct the parties towards alternative dispute resolution processes. We also question the overall rhetoric of pathologising and anxiety-bringing conceptualisation of family disputes and their resolution that has been adopted as leitmotif of the legal reforms through the years. For instance, Lord Chancellor and Justice Secretary Alex Chalk KC, referring to the voucher scheme, said:

> Separation can be incredibly painful, but we know it is made more traumatic with toxic and protracted courtroom battles, which can cause lasting damage to children. This is why we're determined to take the temperature down. We've already delivered on no-fault divorces, and it's really positive to see the success of our voucher scheme. I hope more will feel able to take up this offer.[32]

However, disputes are tools of knowledge production; disputes present opportunities for families to learn from their experiences. Given the nature of family relations, it can also be said that during the resolution of family disputes parties may transition to new ways of performing their roles within the family and thereby the resolution can be transformative for the relationships between the parties and for the parties themselves. Although sometimes the legal dispute is resolved but the broader family conflict remains, the resolution ends the dispute and at the same time prepares parties to heal. A pathologised construction of disputes which somehow urges a quick resolution that might not fully resolve

---

31 For case law reiterating the importance of mediation and non-court dispute resolution see *Re X (Financial Remedy: Non-Court Dispute Resolution)* [2024] EWHC 538 (Fam); *K v K (Fact-Finding Hearings in Private Family Proceedings)* [2022] EWCA Civ 468.

32 https://www.gov.uk/government/news/thousands-of-families-spared-from-damaging-courtroom-conflict, accessed 11 June 2025.

disputes or might bring unfair outcomes prevents this process and its potential positive outcomes.

The procedural rules that encourage parties to divert the resolution of their disputes outside the courtroom pose several questions concerning suitability, accessibility, and availability of the different processes, and more generally questions of fairness. For example, some of the processes are expensive and therefore their availability is limited by the financial circumstances of the parties. Thus, the family justice system appears as a two-tier system, with different degrees of accessibility for future family disputants, whereas, as this chapter shows further, process pluralism, where a variety of processes are all equally available, is a condition of access to justice.

LASPO

Another legal development that concerns the resolution of family disputes is the Legal Aid, Sentencing and Punishment of Offenders Act 2012 (hereafter LASPO). As Rachael Blakey (Chapter 9) in this volume offers a detailed analysis of LASPO and its impact, here it suffices to make two critical observations. First, this Act has withdrawn legal aid for private family disputes, with some exceptions, such as where there is evidence of domestic abuse, while simultaneously allowing it for mediation. However, legal aid for mediation is available only if there is a family dispute as defined in LASPO and 'capable of resolution through family proceedings'.[33] Where 'there is no family dispute involving legal issues and the role of the mediation is simply to improve communication and the relationship between the parties, then this will not fall within the scope of legal aid'.[34] Thus, LASPO lends itself to somehow reducing the scope of mediatory intervention. Secondly, the other dispute processes are not covered by legal aid. Thus, family disputants without sufficient financial resources to pay for legal representation and who do not have access to legal aid are left with just two options – attend mediation or become litigants in person.

Summary

Since 1996, several statutes concerning family law have aimed at encouraging recourse to family mediation and other processes outside courtroom. These include the Family Law Act 1996, Children and Adoption Act 2006, LASPO, and the Children and Families Act 2014.

Procedurally, the Family Procedure Rules and Practice Directions set the rules concerning MIAM and recourse to non-court dispute resolution. Although there are some exceptions, it is generally mandatory to attend MIAM. Before starting

---

[33] See LASPO, sch 1, part 1, para 14.
[34] Legal Aid Agency, 'Family Mediation Guidance Manual' (2024) https://www.gov.uk/guidance/legal-aid-family-mediation, accessed 11 June 2025.

court proceedings, parties must submit a statement which explains their reasons for not attempting resolution through processes other than litigation.

Critical discussion

This section considers how to choose a dispute resolution process that is suitable for family disputants with intersecting traits and that aims at fairness and equity of outcomes. We will begin by discussing family diversity before moving on to consider access to justice, and we will reflect on how to choose the most appropriate process for resolving family disputes.

Diverse families and disputes

Families are diverse in their structures, size, roles played by the members, relations, and dynamics. Families have different functions and relations within them are created by genetic, biological, social, and emotional ties – there is the legal family, the chosen family, and the perceived family, and they (unfortunately) do not always correspond. For our purposes, I summarise here what I have argued elsewhere:

> Diversity permeates how families are created, their structures and the relations within them. Similarly, diversity involves the roles that family members play within the family unit. There is also the diversity brought by the various social identities of the family members who are in dispute, and those identities in turn intersect with the family members' identity as disputants [...] The social identities of the parties are made up of characteristics that include those protected by the Equality Act 2010 and more [...] [T]he diversity of the parties encompasses their role within the family unit; whether they have parental responsibility; their past experiences; their knowledge about the dispute; their financial situation; how they deal with emotions; their ability to articulate their ideas; the impact that, for instance, long Covid might have on their cognitive functions; changes in hormone levels; and knowledge of technology during online mediation.[35]

Thus, in our analysis we should be mindful of the combination of the heterogeneity of the family group with the intersecting identities of the family members that are in dispute. So, we are questioning: in what ways does diversity shape disputes and their resolution? After addressing this question, we can then move on to reflect on how best to choose the appropriate dispute resolution process.

---

[35] MF Moscati, 'Diversity, Equality and Inclusion in Mediation for Family Relations' (2023) 5(1) Amicus Curiae 126.

Generally speaking, diversity itself can give rise to a dispute; it can determine whether and how a dispute is resolved; it can hinder or enhance the resolution process; it can affect the outcome of the resolution and future implementation. For example, as a source of dispute *being different* can be a trigger; parents can disagree on how to address their children's neurodiversity or gender identity; partners can have disputes over their different religious beliefs; if the relationship involves three or four partners, they can have a dispute on how to manage their daily life. Also, decisions on whether and how to pursue the claim depend on diversity. For example, limited knowledge about protected rights can hinder the perception of the wrong and therefore the pursuit of the claim. Likewise, the parties in dispute might shape their choice on whether and how to pursue their claim depending on the intensity of family bonds, intergenerational hierarchy, gender roles, and/or financial circumstances.

During the resolution of disputes, diversity can play a significant role and, if not addressed, it can exacerbate power imbalances between the parties. All relations between family members bring power dynamics and imbalances; some sources are evident while others are hidden; some sources are real, and others are just perceived. Similarly, diversity can exacerbate power imbalances when these rely, for example, on self-confidence about personal identity, emotions, support that each of the disputants receives from other relatives, age and roles within the family, and/or legal recognition of the relationship or parenting role.

In addition, during the negotiation, mediation, or collaborative law approaches, parties interact and communicate with each other, although in some cases lawyers are in the room with them. Diversity frames and casts communication. Difference in knowledge, language skills, emotions, internalised phobia about gender, culture, age, ability, and hearing or visual ability/impairment determine how interactions between the parties take place and how their negotiation strategies are planned. For instance, disputants suffering with depression might find it stressful to engage during the negotiation, or those with chronic fatigue or brain fog might find it difficult to stay focused or to remember details of the dispute or to convey their ideas. Also, cultural constructions of gender roles and family relations, or different attitudes about divorce and/or reproduction can hinder and/or enhance participation during the resolution process.[36]

Other ways in which diversity manifests itself during the resolution of disputes relate to the number of parties involved and the nature of the relationship. For example, some families are based on the intimate relationship of three or more adults. Other disputes, although legally characterised as family disputes, involve parties that never considered themselves to be 'family' or even within a relationship – for example two adults who conceived a child together but have had no personal relationship. However, with some exceptions, most dispute resolution providers, governing bodies, and official institutions, in their

---

[36]   S Shah-Kazemi, 'Cross-Cultural Mediation: A Critical View of the Dynamics of Culture in Family Disputes' (2000) 14 International Journal of Law, Policy and the Family 302.

information to the public, describe both family disputes and family dispute resolution in narrow terms. In this representation, family disputes are limited to adult relationship break-ups and their consequences for children and financial redistribution involving only two disputants. As we will see in the next section, being mindful of diversity is important for access to justice.

Access to justice

The resolution of family disputes and the current processes raise questions about access to justice for those with intersecting character traits. Although a detailed analysis of what the broader concept of 'justice' means and how it can be achieved is out of the scope of this chapter, given the porous nature of the relationship between the FJS and mediation (and now more broadly non-court dispute resolution) it cannot be argued that 'justice' can be gained necessarily through one process or another one. We argue that 'justice' can be achieved only if the processes are all equally available and accessible for each of the family disputants. Also, the invitation here is to 'expand our imaginations of justice to include the work of repair and healing',[37] combined with freedom of choice among a variety of equally available interventions and processual justice.

In this chapter, access to justice is not conceptualised as simply access to courts, other dispute resolution processes, or legal representation. Rather, led by diversity, inclusion, and equity, this chapter embraces a broader and dynamic approach to access to justice that pays attention to the whole resolution journey from the choice on whether and how to resolve the dispute, to its end, and attends to the personal and social barriers that diverse family disputants face. Together with common barriers like limited legal knowledge, court delays, location and structure of courts, high costs of litigation and other processes (arbitration for example), a limited number of interpreters, difficulties in accessing files, and a shortage of staff, diverse family members face unique barriers to access to justice. A main barrier depends simply on being someone who does *not conform to the norm* – for example being a young parent, or a man who has given birth, or a child with special educational needs. Some barriers are rooted within family relations; others exist because of stigma and prejudices about diversity.[38] For example, women may face barriers arising from the intersection of their gender, their role in the family, or limits on their financial capacity. Or, for instance, transgender and non-binary people are subjected to barriers entrenched in exclusionary legislation, systemic marginalisation, and abuse at home because of their gender identity. Also, family bonds can represent a barrier that mitigates what parties agree on. Other barriers are created by the absence of a comprehensive legal framework on family relations and their consequences, or by the discriminatory uncertainty created by the law.

---

[37]   R Benjamin, *Imagination: A Manifesto* (Norton & Company 2024).

[38]   On stigma, I strongly recommend E Goffman, *Stigma: Notes on the Management of Spoiled Identity* (Penguin Books 1963).

With regards to the resolutions, my approach builds on the meaning of access to justice developed by Mauro Cappelletti and Bryan Garth, according to whom access to justice is 'the system by which people may vindicate their rights and/ or resolve their disputes under the general auspices of the state. First, the system must be equally accessible to all, and second, it must lead to results that are individually and socially just.'[39] Together with freedom of choice among a plurality of equally available dispute resolution processes, access to justice aims at outcomes that enhance equity, fairness, and also, we argue here, the well-being of the parties. During the resolution process, access to justice requires attention to the perceptions, ideas, emotions, and freedom of expression of all those in disputes and those who, although not in dispute, will be influenced by the resolution (imagine, for example, a polyamorous family in which only two of the partners are in dispute. In this case, access to justice will potentially require all the other partners to be involved).[40] Thus access to justice encompasses procedural and substantial justice, but also a subjective, personal, and embodied justice.

To enhance access to justice during the resolution of disputes, then, the process should match the needs of the parties. To explore this, the next section will focus on mediation, given the historical centrality that it has gained from institutional reforms, and will question its suitability for diverse families.

Mediation

Mediation is a process used to resolve disputes in which a third impartial, non-aligned party – the mediator – facilitates the negotiation between the parties in dispute. The principles governing mediation are respect, impartiality, confidentiality, party control, and voluntariness. It is important to look at mediation as a negotiation with a third party. This means that the parties in dispute retain control of the resolution of their dispute and the mediator's role is to facilitate their communication during the stages of negotiation. As suggested by Philip Gulliver, the key characteristic of negotiation is the exchange of information and learning; the exchange of information helps the parties to move towards the settlement.[41] If the parties find it difficult to communicate and therefore to negotiate by themselves, the mediator is there to facilitate this. But it must be made clear that the mediator does not decide the outcome of the mediation.[42] Instead, as Marian Roberts has suggested, 'the mediator's

---

[39]   M Cappelletti and B Garth, 'Access to Justice: The Newest Wave in the Worldwide Movement to Make Rights Effective' (1978) 27 Buffalo Law Review 181, 182. For overview of the developments of the concept of access to justice see M Galanter, 'Access to Justice in a World of Expanding Social Capability' (2010) 37 Fordham Urban Law Journal 115.

[40]   Moscati (n35).

[41]   PH Gulliver, *Disputes and Negotiations: A Cross-Cultural Perspective* (Academic Press 1979).

[42]   This marks a significant difference between mediation and other types of third-party interventions like litigation and arbitration where the judge or arbitrator have the power to decide the outcome of the dispute.

role is auxiliary to that of the parties. The mediator is there, unobtrusively, to clarify and focus on the parties' own negotiations and to assist *them* in finding areas of agreement. This requires a skilled exercise, neither passive nor directive, of creativity and control.'[43] There are, however, some variations in mediation practice according to type of disputes to be resolved, the degree of intervention of the mediator, the existence of regulation, and, more broadly, cultural traditions about the role.[44]

Mediation offers several advantages to family disputants, including being cheaper and quicker than litigation and, more importantly, protecting long-term relationships and giving parties the opportunity to creatively tailor the outcome of the dispute. It is also sensible to think that as mediation involves the parties more directly, it can create a space where parties can address the legal dispute and the broader family conflict and deal with their emotions. Mediation offers also a space to those who, although not in dispute, will be impacted by the outcome of the resolution. In addition, the confidentiality of mediation protects parties who, because of their diverse personal characteristics, cannot disclose some aspects of their identity.

However, an assumption that mediation can be suitable for all types of dispute or disputants is incorrect. Similarly, we should be realistic about the aims and limits of mediation. Although mediation is often mooted as an alternative to the FJS and considered appropriate for every dispute, there are instances in which mediation might not be appropriate to accommodate disputes involving diverse families. Mediation can work if parties are capable of negotiating and the mediator facilitates the communication. For our purposes, this task can be effectively accomplished if the mediator has dealt with their own bias and prejudices concerning diversity, and if diversity is acknowledged and addressed positively. If this attention to diversity is lacking, then power imbalances based on family relations or intersecting identity traits can be reinforced.

The risk of overlooking diversity lies also in the narrative used by the government since the 1980s to justify reforms on mediation that has emphasised how mediation enhances party autonomy and amicable solutions. In reality, these arguments fail to note that, within family units, the autonomy of their members is often limited by family dynamics and values and by different degrees of acceptance or rejection of diversity. Similarly, while the quest for amicable solutions is commendable, it highlights the principle of protecting harmony within social groups and avoiding conflict. However, this approach risks overlooking the individual needs of the parties involved. In addition, as suggested earlier, following the reforms to Family Procedure Rules and the introduction of LASPO, the focus of legally aided mediation intervention is on legal disputes.

---

[43] M Roberts, *Mediation in Family Disputes. Principles of Practice* (4th edn, Ashgate Publishing 2014).
[44] Palmer and Roberts (n1)

But disputes in diverse families can include, for example, whether and/or how to have child, how to manage polyamorous relationships, how to address gender-affirming journeys,[45] how to address children's special needs, and so on. Thus, although mediation is potentially an appropriate forum for diverse families, if their disputes do not fall within the scope of legal aid, mediation might not be an option for those with (diverse) financial constraints.

Similarly, within mediation practice and training, although knowledge of diversity is on the agenda of mediation providers and Continuing Professional Development courses, the way in which foundational family mediation training is developed rarely considers diversity in all its aspects and their intersections. Family mediation training mainly focuses on financial distribution and child arrangements following separation and divorce of opposite-sex couples.[46] While this may represent a large number of disputes, it brings with it the risk of not raising awareness among future family mediators about the impact of intersecting diverse characteristics and preparing them to address the specific needs of diverse families. The principle of respect governing mediation requires us to pay attention to the characteristics of each family disputant and their broader family network, to decide whether mediation is suitable and, if so, whether mediation interventions can be adapted in accordance with family diversity. For example, it is now generally agreed that children should be informed and offered the opportunity to express their views during the mediation process.[47] However, the debate and the practice concerning the participation of children during mediation do not seem to take account of children's varied upbringings and family arrangements and that childhood is culturally constructed.[48] So, what happens if the child has parents who assume that because of their age they are not capable? Or if the child has been raised by five parents and only two are in dispute, who needs to agree for the child to meet the mediator? And if the child is visually impaired or deaf, would they be given the chance to meet the mediator and would their needs be met?

These potential scenarios invite critical reflections on whether routinely institutionalising family mediation by modelling it like court proceedings with predefined procedures would be suitable to meet the needs of family disputants with intersecting traits.

---

45   MF Moscati, 'Gender Identity and Family Mediation: Reflections on Trans★ and Non-binary Partners in Family Mediation' (February 2022) Family Law 242.

46   Also the timing dedicated to the resolution seems to be routinely limited to a set number of meetings.

47   See M Roberts, 'Children in Family Mediation: A Rights Approach or the Right Approach? (2024) 5(2) Amicus Curiae 256;

48   MF Moscati, 'We Have Method But Still There Is So Much to Do: Mediation for Gender and Sexually Diverse Relationships' in Roberts and Moscati (eds), (n5).

Fitting the forum to the fuss

The expression 'fitting the forum to the fuss' was coined by Sander and Goldberg to refer to the search for the most appropriate resolution process for a particular dispute.[49] Several different factors, including the characteristics of the case and the goals and the characteristics of the parties, should be taken into account in choosing the most appropriate process. Matching cases and dispute resolution processes involves additionally matching the communication means (in person or online) for the resolution. To achieve this goal, a premise is the availability – financial and logistic – of a plurality of dispute resolution processes. The resolution of family disputes requires time, space, and imagination because, together with legal issues, relationships, emotions, feelings, and personal histories are at stake.

We now turn to the question of how best to understand the suitability of each process in relation to diversity. Although each resolution process presents unique characteristics and research shows that the resolution of family disputes follows different paths, here we aim to identify key questions that help determine when each option is most suitable. Sander and Goldberg identified some factors that should be considered when choosing the right process. These factors include the goals of the parties, their relationship, and the type of dispute.[50] Building upon those factors and considering diversity we can suggest three sets of questions focusing on parties, dispute, and process. In doing that, we should also be mindful of the broader social context and the impact of systemic barriers.

The questions include

- Parties: Who are the parties? How many are they? Are they acquainted with technology? Do they require specific logistic arrangements? Do they self-define as disabled? Can they pay? How do they define their relationship? Is their relationship legally regulated? Are the parties from different countries? What is their main language? What type of information do they need to make a well-informed choice? Are they aware of the full grievance? Which parties should be involved – only those in disputes or also those that will be affected by the decision (think about inheritance disputes)? What do they want to achieve? Are they interested in nonmonetised outcomes (including just looking for an apology)? Are the parties willing to involve lawyers? Are the parties ready and keen to negotiate?
- Dispute: What is the dispute about? When did it start? Are there other sources of dispute that the parties are not aware of? Is it private or public family law? Is domestic abuse involved? What are the non-legal issues that increase family conflict? Does the dispute require other types of interventions to deal with broader family conflict before resolving the legal dispute? Do the parties need

---

[49]   FEA Sander and SB Goldberg, 'Fitting the Forum to the Fuss: A User-Friendly Guide to Selecting an ADR Procedure' (1994) 10(1) Negotiation Journal 49.

[50]   Sander and Goldberg (n47).

to be signposted to services like counselling, family therapy, debt advice, parenting courses, and so on?

- Process: Is the resolution online? If so, how does one ensure that all parties have same access to technology? Is the mediator/arbitrator/lawyer knowledgeable about all processes and about diversity? Is the process covered by legal aid? Is the outcome legally binding? If it isn't, what will the parties need to do and will they face additional costs? Does the process allow children to express their voice?

Although each dispute is different and requires ad hoc scrutiny, some broad conclusions can be drawn here. If the parties are not keen to negotiate, the dispute is technical, and the parties can pay, then lawyer negotiation, arbitration or litigation might be suitable. But if the parties are ready to listen to each other, are more than two in number, need to vent their emotions and want to improve their relationship in the long term too, or they need to protect their identity somehow, and there are children willing to meet the mediator, then mediation is preferred, or collaborative law if the parties can pay. If domestic abuse is involved, then litigation is the route to follow and legal aid is available.

Meeting the needs of diversity during the process

Once disputants choose among a variety of processes, mediators, lawyers, arbitrators, and judges should accommodate diversity during resolution by providing guidance and proceeding with an intersectional approach. Kimberle Crenshaw's seminal work on 'intersectionality' described this as 'a metaphor for understanding the ways that multiple forms of inequality or disadvantage sometimes compound themselves and create obstacles that often are not understood among conventional ways of thinking'.[51] These intersecting forms of oppression and the several social identities that family disputants bring with them should be acknowledged and addressed during every stage of each chosen dispute resolution process. As good practice towards the inclusion of intersectionality during mediation, the 'Diversity and Inclusive Practice in Mediation: Policy and Guidelines' of the College of Mediators can be mentioned here:

> Diversity is intersectional; multiple dimensions of diversity will overlap and influence, to different extents, the life of the parties involved in mediation. The intersection of multiple characteristics will influence how parties communicate, behave and contribute to the mediation

---

[51] K Crenshaw, 'Demarginalizing the Intersection of Race and Sex: A Black Feminist Critique of Antidiscrimination Doctrine, Feminist Theory and Antiracist Politics' (1989) University of Chicago Legal Forum 139.

process. To the extent possible, mediators should pay attention and consider the different and overlapping aspects of diversity.[52]

Put into practice, addressing intersectionality should be a priority for the legislator, policy makers, and practitioners. This would involve a change to the current approach to family dispute resolution as embraced in the Family Procedure Rules, namely adding specific reference to intersectionality and eliminating the duty for courts to consider non–court dispute resolution processes and costs for not attempting them. As for mediation and the other dispute resolution processes, attention to intersectionality would require the inclusion of specific policy that address family diversity. Meeting the needs of diverse families should include training and awareness campaigns.

Professionals who handle family disputes should be prepared for diversity. Acknowledging their own possible bias and prejudices about diversity is necessary and can be reflected in professional training for mediators, arbitrators, lawyers, and judges with the inclusion of theories on race, gender, disability, class, and intersectionality. Practical efforts to shape processes according to needs of the family disputants include using gender-neutral language, dedicating more time to MIAM and to the other stages of the resolution, and decorating the rooms where the resolution takes place with pictures and books that celebrate diversity. Similarly, awareness campaigns on family dispute resolution should be created to address and represent diverse families on all informative material concerning family dispute resolution.

Putting the theory into practice

To offer a practical dimension to our analysis, let's look at Sally and their family:

Sally identifies as mixed-raced and non-binary and prefers the pronouns they/them. They are 14 years old and live in London; they attend a secondary school, and their biological parents have divorced and now both have other partners. Sally has one brother, Matt, who is 16 years old and is a wheelchair user, and two half-sisters, Amber and Rose, that their parents had with their new partners. They all live in the same building but in different flats and share a garden. Sally's mother is the owner of the flats and very generously lets Sally's father and his partner live there. Sally's family is diverse. Their relationships were fine until two events: Sally's father lost his job and Sally's mother had a terrible argument with her new partner regarding Amber's special educational needs. They cannot agree on what type of support Amber needs. Sally's father became depressed and began spending his days on the couch, which his partner was extremely irritated by; a week ago she left him, taking Rose with her. She is now asking Sally's father to send her money for Rose's maintenance, but he says that he cannot pay. Things in both homes escalated to

---

[52] The full policy can be downloaded at https://docs.google.com/document/d/1PVTlJmbPF 8PwTOedgTwo49VyJmjjzZCs/edit, accessed 11 June 2025. The author of this chapter has contributed to writing the policy and is the author of the section on intersectionality.

the point that nobody talked to each other and Sally was caught in the middle. Sally's mother comes to you seeking advice on what to do.

In order to ascertain how the disputes can be resolved, we should try to identify the appropriate dispute resolution process according to the needs of the parties. A first step would be to address the questions: what is this dispute about? What are the broader family conflicts that they are facing? The latter question might require consideration on whether different types of intervention (including counselling, family therapy) are needed here. Then we need to understand who the parties are and how they are involved in the dispute resolution – this might be only Sally's mother and her partner, or Sally's father and his partner, or alternatively other members of the family. The following step would be to consider how children can be involved in the mediation and, if so, ascertaining who needs to consent – only the biological parents or the new step-parents too? Further, if they do not have access to legal aid but cannot afford lawyers, and do not want to mediate but would like to attempt arbitration, who will pay? Finally, if the parties decide to attempt resolution, what can mediators, arbitrators, lawyers, or judges do to develop an inclusive process for all those involved?

Summary

Current family dispute-resolution legal framework and processes do not reflect the current heterogeneity of family forms, dynamics, and relationships, nor offer adequate space to the intersecting identities of family disputants. Thus, to enhance access to justice, changes are required to mediation and other dispute resolution practices and to family procedure rules. These changes should aim at shaping dispute resolution theory and practice to better take into account diversity in families and should be guided by intersectionality.

Conclusion

This chapter has provided an overview of how family diversity influences disputes and their resolution. In addition, the chapter has discussed the advantages and disadvantages of mediation, the recent reforms to family procedural rules, and concerns that arise when looking at so-called non-court dispute resolution on the one hand, and the lack of attention to diverse families on the other. The chapter has shown that without a focus on the individuals that form a family and their intersecting identities, resolutions of family disputes risk being routinely formalised without considering the specific needs of each disputant and their family.

The implications of this analysis are that policy makers, mediators, arbitrators, judges, magistrates, and lawyers should take concrete, practical steps to meet the needs of diverse families and of family members with intersecting traits. Efforts should be made to allow more time, more resources, and more freedom. A first significant step, without doubt, would be to reinstate legal aid and to broaden the legal definition of family disputes that are covered by legal aid. To achieve access to justice in a way that celebrates diversity and enhances equality, this chapter has suggested that disputants should be free to choose from a plurality of equally accessible processes and then, once in progress, mediators, lawyers, arbitrators, and judges should accommodate diversity within the process. Increased knowledge and awareness among professionals and disputants will enable 'fitting the forum to the fuss'. Simply put, it is the process that should reflect the families and not vice versa.

Overall, the chapter aimed at encouraging students to avoid assumptions about disputes, disputants, and dispute resolution processes. We should not assume that disputes are necessarily bad; that disputants are all the same; that one dispute resolution process can be the right fit for all types of disputes and disputants. More importantly, the chapter strongly reminds students that diversity is a resource and that family disputants are human beings, who must be listened to, seen, celebrated, and respected for who they are when they resolve their family disputes.

Further questions to consider

1. Discussion

- In what ways can diversity be accommodated during family mediation?
- How would you define 'justice' and 'access to justice' in the context of family dispute resolution?
- In what ways can power imbalances influence family mediation?
- Look at the book for children *Rainbow after the Storm: Mylo and His Dads Go To the Mediator*,[53] choose one of the families represented in the book, and reflect on what potential disputes might arise, what the appropriate process would be, how to ensure access to justice, and what potential power imbalances might arise.
- Think about a family dispute you have been involved and then reflect on the following:
- Who were the parties involved?
- What was the dispute about?
- How did you resolve it? Or if you decided not to resolve it, can you explain why?

2. Role play

Taken from fieldwork and readapted for this chapter.

Instructions: Divide into groups of three, read the scenario, and analyse it by identifying the parties in the disputes and those who will be influenced by the

---

53   See https://www.sussex.ac.uk/webteam/gateway/file.php?name=moscati-children-families-mediation.pdf&site=447, accessed 11 June 2025.

output of the resolution, the source of disputes, the interests and needs of each party, and the sources of power imbalance. Assign your roles and start acting. After the role play, reflect on your performance as negotiators and/or mediators.

Scenario: Elva and Maria were in a relationship and their friend Michael agreed to donate his sperm to Elva and father a child. Through this agreement, Evan was born 12 years ago. Michael was with Robert at the time of the birth. All four parents (biological parents and the partners of the biological parents) participated in Evan's life.

Two years ago, Elva and Maria separated and through mediation they agreed for Maria to meet Evan every week on Thursdays and alternate weekends. Elva started a new relationship with Joanna and they moved to another city, taking Evan with them, and had another child together, a daughter (with the assistance of an unknown sperm donor). Despite the mediated agreement, Elva limits contact between Evan and Maria. Maria has threatened Elva with court action.

Last year, the friendly relationship between Elva and Michael also deteriorated and court proceedings started because Michael had no access to Evan. The court issued a child arrangements order for Michael so that he could continue to see Evan. Elva refused to comply with the court order in favour of Michael.

Elva asked Maria and Michael to attempt mediation to resolve the issue of child arrangements for Evan.

Further materials

Reading

Allport L, 'Mediation and Cultural Change' (2023) 4(2) Amicus Curiae 367
Hampshire, S, *Justice Is Conflict*. (Princeton University Press, 2000).
Golombok S, *Modern Families* (CUP 2015).

Films
• *I Am Sam* (2021)
• *Marriage Story* (2019)
• *The War with Grandpa* (2020)
• *Wedding Crashers* (2005)

Ballets/dance about disputes and families
• *Romeo and Juliet*
• *Akram Khan's Giselle*
• *Carmen*
• *Don Quixote*
• *Swan Lake*

9

Accessing Family Justice without Lawyers

Rachael Blakey

Introduction

When we think about the meaning of 'family justice', we are often drawn to the images of litigation that we see in the media. The imposing and looming courtroom. A formidable judge wearing a bench wig and slamming down their gavel (even though gavels are not even used in England and Wales). Impassioned barristers fighting on either side for their client's best interests. And then, two parties anxiously waiting to hear the outcome of their dispute.

The reality for most separating families is very different. Most parties do not initiate court proceedings or seek a legally binding consent order for their private family law arrangements.[1] For many of these cases, family law principles are applied incorrectly or not even applied at all. For those who do attend court, they are often met with a much more informal setting. Judges and practitioners rarely wear robes (though in 2024 a London family court announced a judicial robing pilot as a result of inappropriate and violent behaviour by its users).[2] Crucially, very few private family law proceedings now involve legal support and representation on both sides. One decade after significant cuts to legal aid in 2013,

---

[1] A Saied-Tessier, 'What Do We Know about Adults in Private Family Proceedings?' Nuffield Foundation (2023) 4 https://www.nuffieldfjo.org.uk/wp-content/uploads/2023/09/Private_ Law_spotlight.pdf, accessed 12 June 2025; E Hitchings and others, 'Fair Shares? Sorting Out Money and Property on Divorce: Report' Nuffield Foundation (2023) 20 https://www.nuf fieldfoundation.org/wp-content/uploads/2021/03/Fair-Shares-Executive-summary_web.pdf, accessed 12 June 2025.

[2] Courts and Tribunals Judiciary, 'Robing Pilot Begins at Central Family Court' (15 April 2024) www.judiciary.uk/robing-pilot-begins-at-central-family-court, accessed 1 August 2024.

both parties have a lawyer in under a fifth of private family law proceedings.[3] Families no longer watch their case play out, but are instead actively involved in its resolution. The lack of legal representation and support in the contemporary landscape comes with endless difficulties, particularly where the majority of family law disputants possess some level of vulnerability. This phenomenon raises questions about the quality of justice being provided and whether the English and Welsh family law system can adapt to the challenges faced by families today.

This chapter considers the contemporary family justice system (FJS) without the widespread use of lawyers, uncovering the challenges for the everyday families who are accessing this system. It shows how access to justice is inaccessible and irrelevant for many families due to a lack of funding and affordable legal support. While this chapter does not concern the specific application/development of legal rules and precedent, it reveals a significant access-to-justice crisis in the English and Welsh family law system. This backdrop drastically shapes the operation of family justice for the many issues considered in this textbook.

The chapter begins by considering the policy on legal aid, a scheme which historically enabled people access to legal support through a lawyer. It then considers the impact of reforms to legal aid brought about by the Legal Aid, Sentencing and Punishment of Offenders Act 2012 (LASPO), with a particular reference to the declining availability of legal support. The chapter then considers the consequences of this development for those without legal representation, known as litigants in person (LiPs). The final section considers some changes to legal practice in light of the post-LASPO landscape, including the widening of work for lawyers, as well as the emergence of McKenzie Friends and other non-lawyer services.

Summary of relevant policy on legal aid

Before the 1950s, some funding was available for legal representation and support via the 'poor person's procedure'. The procedure was first introduced in 1914 through the rules of court,[4] though it was primarily provided 'on a philanthropic ad hoc basis'.[5] The majority of individuals accessing the poor person's procedure sought support for family matters, with roughly 90 per cent of cases heard under the scheme concerning divorce.[6] The high proportion of family cases was

---

[3] Ministry of Justice, 'Family Court Tables: January to March 2025' (26 June 2025) table 10 www.gov.uk/government/statistics/family-court-statistics-quarterly-january-to-march-2025, accessed 7 July 2025.

[4] RI Morgan, 'The Introduction of Civil Legal Aid in England and Wales, 1914–1949' (1994) 5(1) Twentieth Century British History 38, 39.

[5] KL Richardson and AK Speed, 'Restrictions on Legal Aid in Family Law Cases in England and Wales: Creating a Necessary Barrier to Public Funding or Simply Increasing the Burden on the Family Courts?' (2019) 41(2) Journal of Social Welfare and Family Law 135, 136.

[6] Morgan (n4) 44.

partially caused by the complex divorce law at the time, which required applicants to demonstrate that their spouse had committed a 'matrimonial offence' on the grounds of adultery.[7] Despite the inaccessibility of the divorce process for many families, the late 1940s saw more couples separating due to the additional pressures of wartime life.[8] As divorce and relationship breakdown increased throughout the early 20th century, the poor person's procedure became unsustainable.

In 1944, the Rushcliffe Committee was established to advise parliament on legal welfare. One year later, the group proposed legislation 'to provide legal advice for those of slender means and resources, so that no one would be financially unable to prosecute a just and reasonable claim or defend a legal right'.[9] The contemporary legal aid system was subsequently introduced through the Legal Aid and Advice Act 1949. Described as 'the fourth pillar of the welfare state', the purpose of the scheme was to provide funding for legal representation and support for the majority of individuals involved in a legal dispute.[10] Of the population in England and Wales, 70 to 80 per cent were originally eligible for legal aid, though many recipients were required to make some kind of financial contribution to their dispute.[11]

The legal aid system came under significant pressure after the divorce law was reformed in the mid to late 20th century. From 1971, the element of matrimonial offence was replaced with a sole ground of irretrievable breakdown, established by one of five facts.[12] Combined with the rising acceptance of family breakdown within society, the number of divorces soared. In the year after the reforms, the number of divorces in England and Wales increased 60 percentage points, from 74,437 to 119,025.[13] This figure continued to increase, reaching a peak of 165,018 in 1993.

While the legal aid system was regarded as a huge success of the post-Second World War welfare state, Hynes argues that the 'golden period' of funding came to an end in the late 1980s.[14] The constant rise in divorces created what the Law Commission described as a 'rapid escalation in legal aid expenditure'.[15] The legal

---

[7] The Matrimonial Causes Act (MCA) 1857.

[8] T Goriely, 'Rushcliffe Fifty Years On: The Changing Role of Civil Legal Aid within the Welfare State' (1994) 21(4) Journal of Law and Society 545, 550.

[9] Lord Chancellor, *Summary of the Proposed New Service* (Cmnd 7563, 1948) para 4.

[10] Richardson and Speed (n5) 137.

[11] H Sommerlad, 'Some Reflections on the Relationship between Access to Justice and the Reform of Legal Aid' (2004) 31(3) Journal of Law & Society 345, 354.

[12] The five facts were: unreasonable behaviour, adultery, desertion, two years' separation with the respondent's consent, or five years' separation without the respondent's consent. See Divorce Reform Act 1961 and MCA 1973.

[13] Office for National Statistics (ONS), 'Divorces in England and Wales' (22 February 2024) www.ons.gov.uk/peoplepopulationandcommunity/birthsdeathsandmarriages/divorce/datasets/divorcesinenglandandwales, accessed 1 August 2024.

[14] S Hynes, *Austerity Justice* (Legal Action Group 2012) 26–8.

[15] Law Commission, '*Facing the Future: A Discussion Paper on the Ground for Divorce*' (Law Com No 170, 1988) para 2.6.

aid scheme was first cut in 1986 and later reduced in the 1990s.[16] The amount of financial contributions expected of legal aid recipients also increased during this period. As a result of the reforms, the proportion of households in England and Wales eligible for civil legal aid had dropped to 53 per cent by 1992.[17]

The most significant reform to legal aid – and thus the funding of legal support through lawyers – came under LASPO. Following the 2007–08 financial crisis and subsequent recession, the newly elected Conservative-Liberal Democrat Coalition announced plans to reduce the Ministry of Justice budget by 23 per cent.[18] One month later, the Ministry of Justice published 'Proposals for the Reform of Legal Aid in England and Wales'.[19] The proposed reforms were wide-ranging and impacted the operation of legal aid in a number of areas, including employment law, welfare, and housing. Despite the majority of the 5,000 responses to the consultation being against the reforms, the Ministry of Justice went ahead with the proposals.[20] They cited four key objectives of the forthcoming legislation:

it remains our view that the legal aid scheme needs fundamental reform to:

- discourage unnecessary and adversarial litigation at public expense;
- target legal aid to those who need it most;
- make significant savings in the cost of the scheme; and
- deliver better overall value for money for the taxpayer.[21]

LASPO was implemented on 1 April 2013. Importantly for this textbook, the legislation removed legal aid for the majority of private family law matters in court.[22] This means that most separating couples could not (and still cannot) receive legal aid if they wanted to attend court for a dispute regarding their child arrangements or financial matters. There are two exceptions to this rule (critiqued in the next section), namely where an individual has been a victim of domestic abuse or obtains exceptional case funding. Applicants to either exception will only receive legal aid in court if they satisfy a standardised means test: as of August 2025, recipients must receive under £2,657 in gross monthly income (this increases by £222 if a recipient has a fifth child, and also for each child thereafter), have a disposable income under £733 per month, and own capital under £8,000.[23]

---

[16] Goriely (n8) 556–7.

[17] Hynes (n14) 29.

[18] HM Treasury, *Spending Review 2010* (Cm 7942, 2010) para 2.68.

[19] Ministry of Justice, *Proposals for the Reform of Legal Aid in England and Wales* (Cm 7967, 2010).

[20] Ministry of Justice, *Reform of Legal Aid in England and Wales: The Government Response* (Cm 8072, 2011) paras 5–6.

[21] Ibid, para 10.

[22] Public family law matters, such as care orders and supervision orders, remain eligible for legal aid in court. See LASPO, sch 1, part 1, para 1.

[23] Gov.UK, 'Civil Legal Aid: Means Testing' (27 June 2025) www.gov.uk/guidance/civil-legal-aid-means-testing, accessed 7 July 2025.

If neither exception can be claimed, a party to a private family matter can only receive legal aid through family mediation.[24] Concerns have thus arisen as to whether those with limited funds can even access family justice after LASPO.

Critiquing LASPO: a focus on 'need'

LASPO was not a one-off event, but rather an accumulation of decades of policy and reform that sought to reduce state responsibility for family law matters. The government proposed a similar reform back in 1995, arguing that the legal aid scheme 'should ensure that those who have the greatest need receive help and that the help should encourage the resolution of their problems in the most effective way'.[25] Nonetheless, LASPO undeniably had the largest impact on the legal aid system, premised on the idea that funding should only be provided 'to those who need it most, for the most serious cases in which legal advice or representation is justified'.[26] The days of providing funded legal support to the majority were clearly over.

Private family matters in particular were not seen to need financial support. The consultation document for LASPO reads:

> While we understand that those going through relationship breakdown may be dealing with a difficult situation, both emotionally and often practically too, we do not consider that this means that the parents bringing these cases are always likely to be particularly vulnerable (compared with detained mental health patients, or elderly care home residents, for example), or that their emotional involvement in the case will necessarily mean that they are unable to present it themselves. There is no reason to believe that such cases will be routinely legally complex.[27]

The Ministry of Justice trivialises private family matters in a number of ways.[28] To provide one example, the consultation document makes a sharp contrast between those involved in relationship breakdown and mental health patients or elderly care home residents. These extreme examples of vulnerability are used to downplay the poor levels of physical and mental health often experienced by people involved in these disputes. In a 2019 Legal Needs survey by YouGov, it was discovered that 47 per cent of people with family issues sought medical

---

24   LASPO, sch 1, part 1, para 14.

25   Lord Chancellor's Department, *Looking to the Future: Mediation and the Ground for Divorce* (Cm 2799, 1995) para 1.11.

26   Ministry of Justice (n19) para 1.2.

27   Ibid, para 4.207.

28   R Blakey, *Rethinking Family Mediation: The Role of the Family Mediator in Contemporary Times* (Bristol University Press 2025), 46–52.

help, the highest proportion among all legal issues.[29] Those with a family-related issue were also most likely to report stress (67 per cent), being harassed (25 per cent), or having to move home (26 per cent) because of the dispute. These findings are corroborated by an analysis of all private family law proceedings in Wales, with 41.7 per cent of women and 31.2 per cent of men visiting a GP or hospital concerning mental health in the year before proceedings commenced.[30] By comparison, the Ministry of Justice does not refer to any statistics on the health of those involved in private family cases. Furthermore, the Ministry of Justice overlooks the 'clear link between deprivation and private law cases' in both England and Wales.[31] This is despite research by Cusworth and others, which now shows that while relationship breakdown impacts families from all socio-economic backgrounds, the majority of private family law applications are made in the most deprived areas of the two countries. There is, therefore, a lot of evidence to suggest that family matters are very complex and stressful for the parties involved.

The impact of LASPO on vulnerable families

Unsurprisingly, the LASPO reforms had a profound impact on certain populations. Yet the government foresaw this outcome when LASPO was first proposed. In a 2010 Equality Impact Assessment, the Ministry of Justice admitted that civil legal aid (including legal aid for family law problems) was more likely to be used by women and ethnic minorities, as well as those with disabilities.[32] They concluded that the LASPO reforms would have 'a disproportionate impact' on these populations as a result. Nonetheless, the LASPO Bill continued to progress through parliament with little to no modifications. A review of LASPO six years after its implementation cited evidence from various stakeholders that confirmed this hypothesis: the legislation disproportionately impacted children, people with disabilities, ethnic minorities, and women.[33]

A particular issue with the Ministry of Justice's focus on need is their incredibly narrow construction of the concept. More specifically, those in need of legal aid

---

[29]   YouGov, 'Legal needs of Individuals in England and Wales: Technical Report 2019/20' (YouGov, 27 January 2020) <www.lawsociety.org.uk/topics/research/legal-needs-of-indi viduals-in-england-and-wales-report> accessed 1 August 2024 16–17.

[30]   L Cusworth and others, *Uncovering Private Family Law: Adult Characteristics and Vulnerabilities (Wales)* (Nuffield Family Justice Observatory 2021) 20.

[31]   L Cusworth and others, *Uncovering Private Family Law: Who's Coming to Court in England?* (Nuffield Family Justice Observatory 2021) 28; L Cusworth and others, *Uncovering Private Family Law: Who's Coming to Court in Wales?* (Nuffield Family Justice Observatory 2020) 23–4.

[32]   Ministry of Justice, 'Legal Aid Reform: Cumulative Impact Equalities Impact Assessment (EIA)' (2010) para 1.101 https://web.archive.org/web/20111113053154/http://www.just ice.gov.uk/consultations/legal-aid-reform.htm#equality, accessed 1 August 2024.

[33]   Ministry of Justice, *Post-Implementation Review of Part 1 of the Legal Aid, Sentencing and Punishment of Offenders Act 2012 (LASPO)* (CP 37, 2019) paras 180–94.

(and thus legal representation) are considered to be 'vulnerable'.[34] This association has been heavily criticised by two scholars: Kaganas and Diduck. Kaganas argues that the conflation between need and vulnerability means that those receiving legal aid are viewed as incapable of resolving their dispute themselves.[35] It is only because of this supposed incompetency that government-funded support becomes warranted. Yet this approach creates a harsh distinction between the recipients of legal aid and those privately paying for their dispute, as well as the taxpayers who fund the legal system. Diduck similarly argues that labelling someone as 'vulnerable' implies they are not to blame for their position.[36] By comparison, the Ministry of Justice considered all other litigants to be 'autonomous'. Diduck submits that the Ministry of Justice strategically picked these words to justify the removal of legal aid: if a party is autonomous, they are responsible for the resolution of, and thus the funding for, their family dispute. Consequently, the Ministry of Justice made 'vulnerable' a closed-list category that only included those found to be in need. The remaining families had the autonomy to resolve their dispute however they liked, so long as they footed the bill. Yet if a party is unable to afford legal services or support themselves, they may never obtain anything close to justice for their dispute. Thus, a significant access-to-justice crisis comes to light.

The LASPO exceptions

LASPO removed legal aid for private family law proceedings, but introduced two exceptions where funding could still be accessed. Nonetheless, these exceptions are so narrowly construed that many vulnerable individuals are still unable to obtain legal aid.

First, an individual can receive legal aid in court if they were a victim of domestic abuse or if there had been (or is a risk of) child abuse. Originally, the rules around the evidence required for this funding were set out in a 2012 legislative regulation.[37] The regulation listed the types of acceptable supporting evidence of such abuse, including an unspent conviction for a domestic violence offence or a non-molestation order. However, the forms of evidence covered in this list were based on an assumption that someone would report their abuse to a 'police or other official body'.[38] In reality, very few victims seek such support.

---

34   Ministry of Justice (n19) para 4.12.
35   F Kaganas, 'Justifying the LASPO Act: Authenticity, Necessity, Suitability, Responsibility and Autonomy' (2017) 39(2) Journal of Social Welfare and Family Law 168, 176.
36   A Diduck, 'Autonomy and Family Justice' (2016) 28(2) Child and Family Law Quarterly 133, 144–6.
37   The Civil Legal Aid (Procedure) Regulations 2012, reg 33.
38   S Choudhry and J Herring, 'A Human Right to Legal Aid? The Implications of Changes to the Legal Aid Scheme for Victims of Domestic Abuse' (2017) 39(2) Journal of Social Welfare and Family Law 152, 161.

The regulation also required all supporting evidence to have occurred within 24 months prior to the legal aid application. Both factors drastically limited the number of successful applications for legal aid: one survey found that 37 per cent of female victims of abuse did not have the relevant evidence to obtain legal aid and 23 per cent would have been eligible for funding if there had been no time limit on the evidence used.[39] Following a legal challenge by Rights of Women, the Court of Appeal declared that the regulation frustrated the purposes of LASPO and was thus invalid.[40] From April 2016, the time limit for evidence was extended to 60 months.[41] Then, in January 2018, nearly five years after LASPO was enacted, the time limit was completely removed.[42] New forms of supporting evidence were also introduced, including evidence from a domestic violence support organisation or housing authority that they had supported the applicant.[43] These developments appear to have made the exception more accessible: from 2013–14 to 2016–17, the number of applications to the domestic violence and child abuse gateway rose from 6,397 to 10,625.[44] The number of successful applications in the same period increased from 4,191 to 8,313.[45] More recently, there were 12,376 applications in 2023–24 and 15,907 applications in 2024–25.[46] However, evidence suggests that the number of applications does not reflect the prevalence of domestic abuse and child abuse within family matters, with many victims still unable to provide the necessary evidence.[47]

Secondly, legal aid remains available under exceptional case funding where not providing financial support would breach a person's human rights.[48] Similar to the exception for domestic abuse, this funding was heavily underused when first introduced. In 2013–14, only 1,516 applications for exceptional case funding (including family matters) were received. A total of 4.6 per cent of these applications were approved.[49] The inaccessibility of the scheme was a significant factor behind these low numbers. At the time, very few lawyers

---

[39]   Rights of Women, 'Evidencing Domestic Violence: Nearly 3 Years On' (2016) 1 www.rights ofwomen.org.uk/wp-content/uploads/2023/12/Evidencing-domestic-violence-nearly-3-years-on.pdf, accessed 1 August 2024.

[40]   *R (Rights of Women) v Secretary of State for Justice* [2016] EWCA Civ 91, [2016] 1 WLR 2543.

[41]   The Civil Aid (Procedure) (Amendment) Regulations 2016, reg 2.

[42]   The Civil Legal Aid (Procedure) (Amendment) (No 2) Regulations 2017, reg 2.

[43]   Ministry of Justice, 'Changes to Domestic Violence Evidence Requirements Come into Effect' (8 January 2018) www.gov.uk/government/news/changes-to-domestic-violence-evide nce-requirements-come-into-effect, accessed 1 August 2024.

[44]   Ministry of Justice, 'Legal Aid Statistics England and Wales: Tables Jan to Mar 2025' (26 June 2025) table 6.8 www.gov.uk/government/statistics/legal-aid-statistics-quarterly-january-to-march-2025, accessed 7 July 2025.

[45]   Ibid, table 6.9.

[46]   Over two-fifths of applications from both years were granted funding. See ibid, table 6.9.

[47]   Ministry of Justice (n33) para 651.

[48]   LASPO, s 10.

[49]   Gov.UK, 'Legal Aid Data: Exceptional Case Funding' (26 June 2025) https://data.justice.gov.uk/legalaid/legal-aid-ecf, accessed 7 July 2025.

provided services for exceptional case funding because there was no additional funding to help parties make an application.[50] In 2014, the Court of Appeal declared that the guidance for exceptional case funding set too high a threshold for legal aid and subsequently contravened the European Convention of Human Rights.[51] After the Ministry of Justice introduced a new application process (including free legal advice) and further guidance in 2015, the number of cases receiving exceptional case funding increased.[52] In 2023–24, nearly three-quarters of 3,344 applications were granted.[53] A similar number of applications were received and granted in 2024–25. Even so, these figures are way below the Legal Aid Agency's prediction of 5,000–7,000 applications each year when LASPO was enacted.[54] There are serious concerns around the accessibility of the scheme, with the National Audit Office claiming that many individuals cannot find a provider who will support them in applying for exceptional case funding.[55]

Despite the exemptions put in place, it seems that many vulnerable individuals will be unable to access court without funding the dispute themselves. If someone is unable to afford legal advice or the court fees involved yet cannot claim an exemption, their dispute may even go unresolved. Access to justice for some of the most vulnerable in society is constrained as a result.

It is thus evident that the two exceptions to the removal of legal aid in court, designed to provide protection for vulnerable parties, have been underutilised by families. Amnesty International has criticised the argument that legal aid remains available for people through these exceptions, calling it 'fundamentally flawed'.[56] Altogether, there has been a massive reduction in the number of parties to private family proceedings accessing legal aid and, as a result, a lawyer. In the year before LASPO's implementation, 204,247 family cases with legal support and representation began under legal aid (Figure 9.1).[57] This figure fell by 78.9 percentage points the following year to 43,106 cases. The number of family cases receiving legal support through legal aid has continued to decline, reaching a low of 24,765 in 2022–23.

LASPO has, in effect, created a 'two-tier justice system'.[58] While the families who can afford legal support are largely able to access lawyers, those

---

50   National Audit Office, *Implementing Reforms to Civil Legal Aid* (HC 2014–15, 784) para 3.7.

51   *Gudanaviciene and Others v Director of Legal Aid Casework and Anor* [2014] EWCA Civ 1622, [2015] 1 WLR 2247.

52   National Audit Office, *Government's Management of Legal Aid* (HC 2023–24, 514) para 2.24.

53   Gov.UK (n49).

54   National Audit Office (n50) para 3.6.

55   National Audit Office (n52) para 2.24.

56   Amnesty International, 'Cuts that Hurt: The Impact of Legal Aid Cuts in England on Access to Justice (2016) 17 https://www.amnesty.org/en/documents/eur45/4936/2016/en/, accessed 12 June 2025.

57   Ministry of Justice (n44) table 5.1.

58   Amnesty International (n56) 3.

Figure 9.1: Number of legal help and controlled legal representation matters (family) started under legal aid

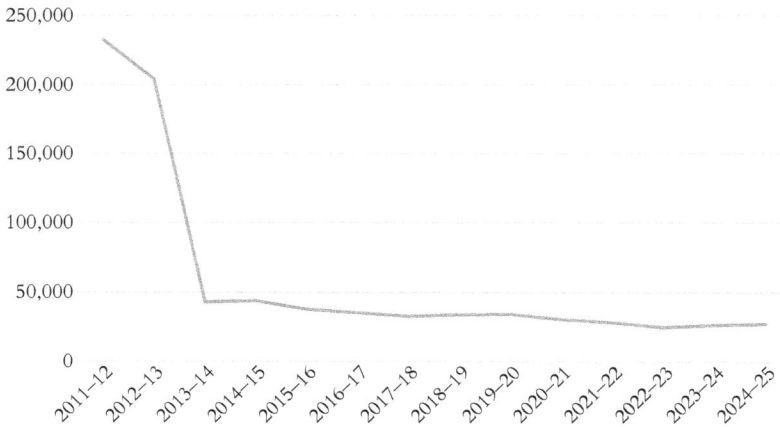

with limited funds – those who are often the most vulnerable – now have a very different experience of the FJS. Post-LASPO, funding is reserved for those said to fit the category of 'vulnerable'. Yet even if a disputant possesses the level of vulnerability necessitated under LASPO, namely being a victim of domestic abuse or requiring exceptional case funding, they will only receive legal aid if they satisfy a standardised means test. While these thresholds supposedly reserve legal aid for those with limited funds, the removal of legal aid for private family law proceedings means very few family law disputants are now able to receive government-funded support for their court proceedings. This problem demonstrates the inaccessibility of legal advice and support for many families (often due to costs), as well as a broader access-to-justice problem.

Summary

The Ministry of Justice claimed that the LASPO reforms would support those in need. It concluded that the majority of private family law matters were not concerning those in need or, in the organisation's words, 'vulnerable'. As a result, LASPO overlooked the many vulnerabilities of people involved in family breakdown, including poor mental health and low socio-economic status. Academic commentary has criticised the reforms for adopting a narrow meaning of 'vulnerability', with even the exemptions to LASPO rules failing to provide a safety net for the most vulnerable families. Unsurprisingly, this has led to a massive decline in the number of family cases receiving legal support or representation through legal aid.

The challenges of attending court without legal representation

Access to justice is heavily founded on the idea that both parties are effectively able to enforce their rights and obligations through the law. Even if family law is substantively just (meaning the law and its norms are fair), access to justice cannot be achieved unless its disputants can also access a procedurally just system. Unsurprisingly, access to the court system is largely regarded as a prerequisite to ensuring that justice has been achieved. Access to court is, in the words of Lady Hale, 'one of the most precious' constitutional rights in England and Wales.[59] This is because unless the parties can access court, there is a risk that the law has been incorrectly applied, if at all.

Yet it is not simply access to the courts that ensures family justice. If two parties are in disagreement with one another about their finances or child arrangements, they may apply to court to have their case decided by a judge. Under this system, there will be two opposing sides: an applicant and a respondent. Access to justice cannot be said to be achieved through this system alone. Rather, family justice is secured through access to legal support and representation – in other words, through access to a lawyer.

This process is described as the 'full representation model'.[60] Both parties to a private family matter have legal representation, meaning the lawyers become the 'actors' in a play. The parties are the audience, watching but not engaging in the performance. In many instances, this is their first and only interaction with the courtroom. By comparison, the judge acts as a 'director', giving some direction to the lawyers and deciding the play's outcome by making a legally binding decision. Trinder and others subsequently describe fully represented hearings as 'highly patterned and predictable in format'. The play is well rehearsed, with the lawyers performing their roles an endless number of times. They know what the judge wants to hear, what information is relevant to the legal aspects of the dispute, and, ultimately, how to make the best case for their client. Many of the issues raised in one case have been discussed in the numerous plays that came before it, giving the lawyers and the judge a strong ability to predict the case's progression and outcome. Combined, these elements ensure a streamlined and justiciable forum for the resolution of private family matters.

The dominance of litigants in person after LASPO

It is worth clarifying that the full representation model has never been the perfect depiction of *all* private family law matters. In fact, there have always been

---

[59] B Hale, 'Equal Access to Justice in the Big Society' Sir Henry Hodge Memorial Lecture (27 June 2011) 7 https://supremecourt.uk/speeches/lady-hale-at-sir-henry-hodge-memorial-lecture-2011, accessed 7 July 2025.

[60] L Trinder and others, *Litigants in Person in Private Family Law Cases* (Ministry of Justice 2014) 53.

instances where families do not go to court to resolve their dispute, or go to court but with very little (or any) legal assistance. Several years before LASPO, a study from 2005 found that many parties in civil and family law proceedings lacked legal representation because they were ineligible for legal aid and could not afford a lawyer themselves.[61] Out of 1,334 family law cases (including adoption orders and ancillary relief), 48 per cent involved at least one party without a lawyer.[62] Additional evidence showed that those without legal support could 'experience a number of problems', which, in turn, impacted the court process.[63]

LASPO massively increased the number of people attending court without legal representation, known as LiPs. The previous section acknowledged that the number of parties receiving legal support through legal aid for their family matter immediately declined after LASPO was implemented. The same issue occurred in the privately funded sphere which, as a result of the 2013 reforms, now included those once eligible for legal aid but no longer able to access the provision for private family proceedings. Data published every three months by the Ministry of Justice shows that in the financial quarter before LASPO's implementation, over two-fifths of private family law cases involved the full representation model.[64] The cases where neither side had legal representation (meaning both parties were LiPs) made up a small minority of roughly 13.6 per cent. Yet just one year later, the proportion of private family law cases involving the full representation model dropped to under a quarter, with two LiPs being present in 28.1 per cent. Yearly figures show that the number of cases involving two LiPs has increased from 11.6 per cent in 2011 to 38.6 per cent in 2024 (Figure 9.2). LiPs now dominate the family court system: in 2024, at least one LiP was present in four-fifths of all private family proceedings.

The prevalence of LiPs (and the failure of the FJS to respond to them) poses a particular problem for the courts. Take the scenario of a family going to court to resolve their financial or child arrangements. However, this time the parties cannot access legal support. There are no paid 'actors' available to perform the play. In comparison to a lawyer, a LiP will have little to no legal training. They will not have rehearsed their role and will be required to navigate the court process with limited assistance. Even if a LiP has questions about the process or their case, they will have no one there to support them. Unfortunately, it is doubtful that LiPs have the same access to justice as someone with legal representation throughout their dispute.

---

61   R Moorhead and M Sefton, 'Litigants in Person: Unrepresented Litigants in First Instance Proceedings' DCA, Research Series 2/05 (2005) 16 https://orca.cardiff.ac.uk/id/eprint/2956/1/1221.pdf, accessed 12 June 2025.

62   Ibid, 23.

63   K Williams, 'Litigants in Person: A Literature Review' Ministry of Justice, Research Summary 2/11 (2011) 5 https://assets.publishing.service.gov.uk/media/5a7c451b40f0b62dffde0f83/litigants-in-person-literature-review.pdf, accessed 12 June 2025.

64   Ministry of Justice (n3) table 10.

Figure 9.2: Percentage of private family law cases with legal representation

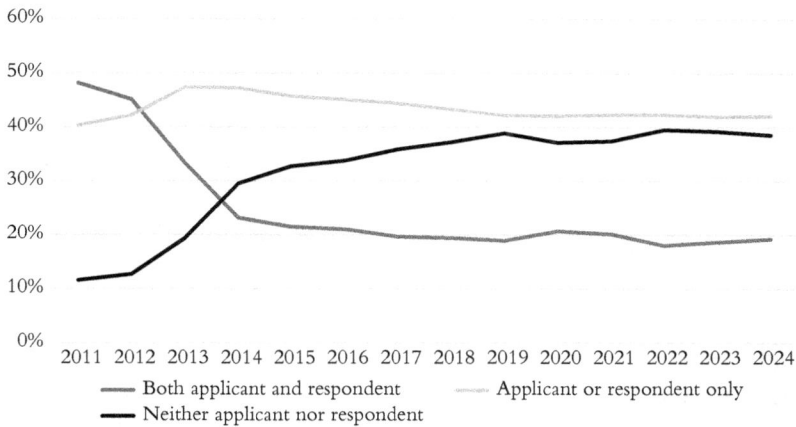

A particular injustice comes to light when a case involves only one LiP. While one side is represented by a lawyer who has performed this play time and time again, the LiP will have little to no time to even rehearse their lines. This reality has been noted by judges, with Judge Tolson commenting:

> I wish immediately to express my professional sympathy for the judge and indeed any judge in this not uncommon situation where one party is represented by a strong legal team and the other is a litigant in person. The requirement for the court to achieve a fair process by assisting the litigant in person almost inevitably draws the judge into the role of inquisitor, albeit on behalf of the litigant. It is a difficult line to tread ...[65]

Trinder and others find that hearings involving one or two LiPs are 'less standardised'.[66] These hearings vary in how tasks are performed and by whom. In some instances, a judge may provide more assistance to the LiP. Yet in others, they may continue to take on the role of the director and rarely intervene in proceedings. Similar findings are identified by Mant after LASPO, who concludes that many LiPs struggle to understand their hearings or even the legal norms involved.[67] While several years have passed since LASPO came into force, Mant argues that very few accommodations have been made for LiPs' various and complex needs.

---

[65] *Crowther v Crowther* [2017] EWCA Civ 2698, [2017] 2 WLUK 845 [12].

[66] Trinder and others (n60) 77.

[67] J Mant, *Litigants in Person and the Family Justice System* (Hart Publishing 2022) 68.

How vulnerable are litigants in person?

Building on the previous section of this chapter, LiPs are a particularly vulnerable population. Before LASPO, LiPs tended to have lower incomes than those with legal representation, inhabiting 'a socio-economic space between represented litigants who were privately funded and those who were legally aided'.[68] After LASPO, LiPs now include those who have very little money or savings but are unable to obtain legal aid as funding has been removed for private family law proceedings and they cannot claim an exemption. Mant comments that LASPO has created 'a whole new category of LiPs', specifically those 'on the lowest incomes and with the fewest resources'.[69] LiPs are likely to exhibit other vulnerabilities beyond socio-economic status, with around half of the LiPs studied by Trinder and others found to have at least one indicator of vulnerability.[70] These indicators included substance abuse, low literacy levels, language difficulties, and extreme anxiety. The largest indicator of vulnerability found within Trinder and others' sample of LiPs was exposure to domestic abuse.[71] Where a LiP was a victim of abuse, it was not uncommon for them to be coerced into an outcome that most likely would have been prevented had they acquired legal representation.

Similar to court proceedings without the full representation model, the vulnerabilities of LiPs are not standardised: one LiP may have a physical disability, whereas another may have a history of imprisonment. The impact of these vulnerabilities on a case also differs. It is thus clear that accommodating the various needs of LiPs requires a comprehensive, wide-ranging, and responsive approach. Without this kind of response, many LiPs will be unable to access any form of family justice.

Legal aid for private family proceedings is only available to victims of domestic abuse, not perpetrators. This legislative oversight means that many perpetrators of abuse are LiPs who represent themselves in court. This situation was particularly dangerous in the past when vulnerable women were cross-examined by their abusers in fact-finding hearings. Evidence from one study showed that judges took inconsistent approaches to this problem: some judges saw cross-examination as the 'right' of the alleged perpetrator, whereas others stopped this provision altogether after multiple LiPs had acted inappropriately.[72] The cross-examination of victims by their perpetrators in the family and civil courts has since been prohibited under the Domestic Abuse Act (DAA) 2021.[73] Even so, there may remain instances where a LiP who was – and often still is – a perpetrator of abuse

---

68   Trinder and others (n60) 12.
69   Mant (n67) 3.
70   Trinder and others (n60) 27.
71   Ibid, 27, 76.
72   NE Corbett and A Summerfield, *Alleged Perpetrators of Abuse as Litigants in Person in Private Family Law: The Cross-Examination of Vulnerable and Intimidated Witnesses* (Ministry of Justice 2017) 15–16.
73   DAA 2021, s 65.

inappropriately acts in court and even sabotages proceedings. Furthermore, as mentioned in the previous section of this chapter, many victims of abuse are unable to obtain legal aid due to the types of evidence required. Unfortunately, adults involved in private family law proceedings are more likely than the general population to have been exposed to domestic abuse.[74] Rights of Women summarise the injustices regularly seen in these cases: 'These women face not only the inequity of navigating the family justice system without specialist legal support, leading to unfair and unsafe outcomes, but also a continuing risk of further devastating and potentially fatal violence.'[75]

The lack of research on families' needs

A decade after LASPO was first implemented, the Ministry of Justice is starting to consider how to make legal advice more accessible and affordable for families. From 2020 to 2022, the Legal Support for Litigants in Person Grant funded 11 projects across England and Wales designed to assist LiPs. The support provided could relate to generalist advice, casework, pre-court support, or legal representation.[76] Nearly a quarter of advice and support provided under the grant concerned family matters.[77] There was some indication that the projects had provided support to vulnerable populations, with 65 per cent of family law clients identifying as female and 36 per cent having a known physical or mental disability.[78] A report on the grant concluded that the advice provided through the projects regularly reduced stress and anxiety among clients and enabled them to take steps to resolve their disputes.[79] While these findings are evidence of a wider FJS that *can* respond to the needs of its litigants, it is unclear how many of these services remain available across England and Wales. The National Audit Office acknowledges a similar problem, stating that there is no real data on 'whether those who are entitled to legal aid are able to access it'.[80]

The vulnerabilities of family law disputants, including LiPs, remain an understudied area of contemporary family law. The challenges covered in this section only provide a snapshot of problems faced by vulnerable litigants in the post-LASPO landscape, as demonstrated in other chapters of this textbook. Chapter 4 of this book showed that many financial arrangements are made outside of court. Chapter 8 considered the various problems with the rising use and promotion of family mediation. Chapter 10 explains how families resolve

---

[74]   Cusworth and others (n30) 31.

[75]   Rights of Women (n39) 9.

[76]   Ministry of Justice, 'Legal Support for Litigants in Person Grant (LSLIP): Final Report' (2023) 16 https://assets.publishing.service.gov.uk/media/6555e61a544aea0019fb2e25/MOJ_Legal_support_for_Litigants_in_Person_Grant.pdf, accessed 12 June 2025.

[77]   Ibid, 32.

[78]   Ibid, 55.

[79]   Ibid, 99.

[80]   National Audit Office (n52) para 9.

their disputes through religious dispute resolution forums. Beyond this edited collection, statistics suggest that only around 10 per cent of separating families use courts for their child arrangements.[81] We also know very little about the profile of disputants beyond parents, as Cusworth and others recognise:

> The current programme of family justice reform focuses almost entirely on the experiences and needs of parents. This research suggests that there is a need to look more broadly at the characteristics, circumstances and needs of families involved in non-standard applications in order to better meet needs.[82]

If anything is clear, it is that we know very little about how far justice is being achieved for today's families. It is hoped that the 2020s and 2030s will see increased interest in uncovering the characteristics of family law disputants: without this, the real impact of the LASPO reforms remains obscured.

Summary

The court system is heavily premised on the 'full representation model' whereby both parties are represented by their own lawyer. However, the number of LiPs has sharply risen after the LASPO reforms. The general population of LiPs struggle in the court process, both in relation to representing themselves in proceedings and preparing bundles. There is a particular concern that many LiPs exhibit vulnerabilities, including exposure to domestic abuse or language difficulties. Despite some attempts by the Ministry of Justice to provide additional support to LiPs, the state of family justice after LASPO remains anything but unclear. The need for further research and discussion is, thus, very apparent.

Improving access to justice in the contemporary family law system

Much of the discussion around the family law system recognises that access to justice has been diminished by LASPO. Eekelaar writes: 'It is probably too melodramatic to announce the death of family justice in England and Wales. But there is evidence that at least some policy-makers have a diminished concept of what constitutes justice in regard to family matters.'[83]

---

[81]   R Hunter, 'Family Justice Council Briefing Paper: Statistics on Private Law Applications' (2022) para 5 https://committees.parliament.uk/writtenevidence/110556/pdf, accessed 1 August 2024.

[82]   L Cusworth and others, *Uncovering Private Family Law: Exploring Applications that Involve Non-parents ('the Other 10%')* (Nuffield Family Justice Observatory 2023) 44.

[83]   J Eekelaar, ' "Not of the Highest Importance": Family Justice under Threat' (2011) 33(4) Journal of Social Welfare and Family Law 311, 311.

In a similar vein, Kaganas argues that LASPO was not intended 'to extend access to justice', as suggested by the Ministry of Justice, but 'to solve the problem of too much access'.[84] More recently, the Family Solutions Group, formed in 2020 to make recommendations on how to improve the experiences of separating families, recognised that the FJS 'is in crisis'.[85] This situation has arisen not only because of the increasing number of LiPs in court, but also a growing backlog of family law proceedings which have generated significant delays. In 2024, it took 42.0 weeks on average for a private family law case to reach a final order (meaning the case was resolved by the court) – an increase of two to three months compared to 2012.[86] Other problems include the increasing number of legal services providers leaving the legal aid sector,[87] as well as the small (but highly vulnerable) number of family law litigants going into debt in order to pay for legal support.[88] It is no surprise that the Family Solutions Group conclude that the FJS is 'broken and in need of radical reform'.[89]

A clear solution to the current access-to-justice crisis is to repeal LASPO. If funding for private family matters in court was restored, more families would be able to navigate the process with appropriate and recurring legal support. If fewer cases involved LiPs, more cases would be streamlined, potentially decreasing the time it takes to obtain a final order and reducing the backlog of disputes within court.

However, it is unlikely that any government in the next few decades would reinstate the previous rules on legal aid. LASPO has been in force for over a decade and, despite numerous papers and projects demonstrating the negative effect of the reforms on the FJS, very few of its provisions have been removed or changed. While the exceptions to legal aid for domestic abuse victims and exceptional case funding have since been widened, this chapter has shown how these schemes remain underused by even the most vulnerable disputants.

This is not to say that the downfall of the FJS is inevitable. Rather, the 2020s and beyond are a crucial period in which meaningful change can be implemented to resolve the issues around access to justice that have always existed. Mant, who considers the ways to centre LiPs in the discussions on family justice, makes the same claim: '*LASPO is by no means the end of the story of legal aid reform. Instead, it marks a key milestone at which many are finally recognising the extent of the damage that has been done and starting to ask questions about what might come next.*'[90]

---

84 Kaganas (n35) 184.
85 Family Solutions Group, '"What about Me?" Reframing Support for Families following Parental Separation' (2020) para 12 https://www.familysolutionsgroup.co.uk/wp-content/uploads/2021/10/FamilySolutionsGroupReport_WhatAboutMe_12November2020-2.pdf-final-2.pdf, accessed 12 June 2025.
86 Ministry of Justice (n3) table 9.
87 C Denvir and others, *Facing the Future of Legal Aid* (Bloomsbury Publishing 2023).
88 J Organ and J Sigafoos, *The Impact of LASPO on Routes to Justice* (Equality and Human Rights Commission 2018) 21.
89 Family Solutions Group (n85) para 12.
90 Mant (n67) 8.

The solution to fixing the post-LASPO landscape is complex and nuanced. It involves increased collaboration between local, regional, and national organisations. The Legal Support for Litigants in Person Grant is an example of such an approach that aims 'to holistically support clients through their journeys'.[91] Improving access to justice also involves improving the quality of outcomes provided through non-court procedures, such as mediation. In 2024, proposals to make family mediation mandatory for most private family matters were postponed, with the Ministry of Justice saying that more work must be done to improve the process for victims of domestic abuse.[92] Furthermore, effective reform involves understanding family disputes as not inherently legal, where appropriate. The Family Solutions Group argue that child arrangement cases should be seen as 'parenting disagreements', not legal matters, as this approach would better centre the needs of the parties and the child(ren) involved.[93] These are just a handful of small and incremental changes that, combined, could improve the operation of the contemporary FJS.

How are lawyers adapting to LASPO?

One area where changes have already been implemented is in the provision of accessible and affordable legal support. Since LASPO, lawyers have modified their practices. New forms of legal services, including the use of online information, have also emerged. This section considers some of the ways that legal services providers have begun to adapt to the changing family law landscape.

Starting with lawyers, many solicitors and paralegals have adjusted their services to cater to families' needs. In particular, there has been an increase in the availability of unbundled services. An unbundled service is where a legal practitioner provides assistance or support in relation to a small number of tasks. For those who cannot afford legal support through their dispute, unbundling provides an affordable and efficient way to obtain some form of guidance. Unbundled services have been around for some time: in Trinder and others' study of LiPs in private law proceedings before LASPO, they found that a number of LiPs received unbundled support from solicitors.[94] Evidence suggests that law firms are shifting towards more unbundled services after LASPO, with very few organisations providing any legal aid work at all.[95] This work can include ad hoc advice, as well as one-off support to fill in relevant documentation. Yet unbundling does not provide a comprehensive solution for *all* family law disputants, particularly those with vulnerabilities. This is because the legal support

---

91 Ministry of Justice (n76) 99.
92 Ministry of Justice, 'Supporting Earlier Resolution of Private Family Law Arrangements: Government Response' (2024) 19 www.gov.uk/government/consultations/supporting-earlier-resolution-of-private-family-law-arrangements, accessed 1 August 2024.
93 Family Solutions Group (n85) para 193.
94 Trinder and others (n60) 116–17.
95 S Wong and R Cain, 'The Impact of Cuts in Legal Aid Funding of Private Family Law Cases' (2019) 41(1) Journal of Social Welfare and Family Law 3, 6.

available through unbundling is 'piecemeal'.[96] The disputant is thus largely responsible for applying any support, such as advice, to their dispute.[97] This task is likely to be incredibly difficult for vulnerable disputants, such as those with poor language skills or anxiety. In many instances, these intersectional character traits will make family justice even more inaccessible. If a person has a limited understanding of English, coupled with poor levels of mental health following relationship breakdown, they will struggle to speak to a lawyer or any advisor. The push for the private resolution of disputes, including the private seeking of legal help, will further the access-to-justice crisis if the professionals within the family law system do little to adapt their practices to vulnerable populations.

New forms of legal advice have also begun to develop in recent years. The Divorce, Dissolution and Separation Act 2020, enacted in April 2022, removed the requirement for divorcing couples (or civil partners seeking dissolution) to demonstrate one of five facts to establish irretrievable breakdown. Instead, the divorce system in England and Wales became solely based on no-fault divorce. The legislation also allowed couples and civil partnerships to jointly apply for a divorce or dissolution for the first time. This change prompted various law firms to introduce a 'one-lawyer-two-clients' model of advice. Sir McFarlane, the President of the Family Division, provides a useful description of the model:

> as a result of the amendments made by the Divorce, Dissolution and Separation Act 2020, which allowed couples to make a joint application to end their formal relationship by divorce or partnership dissolution, there is now a market for legal advice to be given on the 'one lawyer, two clients' (or 'one couple, one lawyer') mode. The Divorce Surgery, an early entrant into this field, is an arms length agency run by two members of the Family Bar. For a fixed fee, which varies depending upon the type and complexity of the issues, the Surgery will appoint a barrister to meet with the two parties, absorb the relevant detail from each about their circumstances, and then deliver advice as to the likely outcome if the contested issues were to be litigated before a court. The model is applied to issues relating to both finance and children. Resolution, which is the umbrella organisation for Family Law Solicitors, has now launched its own one lawyer-one couple scheme ['Resolution Together'] meaning that this option should now be much more widely available throughout the country.[98]

Under a one-lawyer-two-clients model, a single lawyer advises and supports two parties in a dispute, notably divorcing or separating couples. This is an emerging

---

96   Ibid, 12.
97   M Maclean, 'The Changing Professional Landscape' (2014) 44(2) *Family Law* 177, 178.
98   A McFarlane, 'When Families Fall Apart, Do They Fall too Easily into Court? – or "Almost Anything but the Family Court"' (2022]) Family Law 1445, 1453.

form of legal support: its relative benefits have not yet been researched or even really discussed. The model may aid significantly in reducing the cost of legal support. However, it raises serious issues around whether a lawyer assisting two clients in the same case creates a serious conflict of interest. There is also a concern that the one-lawyer-two-clients model is a process, not that dissimilar to mediation, that will only be effective where the parties have relatively equal bargaining positions.[99] And so, it may be the unfortunate reality that many of the ways that lawyers have attempted to adapt to the post-LASPO landscape do not cater for the entire separating population, especially those with limited financial funds or a number of complex vulnerabilities.

Legal advice and support could possibly be provided through additional government funding. In 2021, the Ministry of Justice announced the Family Mediation Voucher Scheme.[100] This enabled families to claim up to £500 for the cost of family mediation. The scheme was available to all parties, regardless of their income and eligibility for legal aid. Statistics suggest that the Family Mediation Voucher Scheme has been hugely successful in encouraging mediation: nearly 13,500 families had used the voucher as of January 2023.[101] In a similar line of thinking, the Ministry of Justice announced an early legal advice pilot in early 2024.[102] While the specifics of the pilot have not been published as of August 2025, the Ministry of Justice claims that the pilot will consider 'the benefits of high-quality legal advice for families looking to resolve their issues through the courts'. Of course, the success of this advice will heavily depend on the level of funding provided.

The rise of non-lawyer services

Thinking beyond lawyers, there has been a rising number of non-lawyer legal service providers since the LASPO reforms. In particular, the withdrawal of lawyers and legal support from the legal aid sector has been partially filled by McKenzie Friends. A McKenzie Friend assists a LiP both in and outside court, but does not need to be legally qualified or a member of any regulatory body. They are not allowed to address the court and become an advocate, as this action requires the grant of a rights of audience which can only be performed by authorised legal practitioners.[103] However, the courts can grant someone a rights

---

[99] A Barlow and others, *Mapping Paths to Family Justice: Resolving Family Disputes in Neoliberal Times* (Palgrave 2017).

[100] A Sixsmith, 'Mediators' Perspectives on the Family Mediation Voucher Scheme' (2023) 35(1) Child and Family Law Quarterly 9.

[101] Ministry of Justice, *Supporting Earlier Resolution of Private Family Law Arrangements: A Consultation on Resolving Private Family Disputes Earlier through Family Mediation* (CP 824, 2023) 7.

[102] Ministry of Justice (n92) 15–16.

[103] Legal Services Act 2007, s 12(1)(a).

of audience in exceptional circumstances.[104] A McKenzie Friend also cannot act as the agent of the LiP, for example by signing documentation.[105]

McKenzie Friends have been used by litigants in England and Wales for many decades, if not centuries. The earliest date the court is known to acknowledge the right to assistance is 1831.[106] The term McKenzie Friend is specifically coined from *McKenzie v McKenzie*, a 1970 Court of Appeal decision which held that parties have a right to receive lay assistance in court if they lack legal representation.[107] Sachs clarified that the husband in the case was entitled to receive support so long as the person providing the assistance did not act as an advocate:

> That young man [the McKenzie Friend], however, had done nothing, so far as this court has been able to ascertain, other than sit quietly beside the husband and give him from time to time some quiet advice or prompting. In those circumstances, the husband was fully entitled to have that assistance, and the young man was fully entitled to give it.[108]

McKenzie Friends have been increasingly used in the 21st century. They were a 'common source of support' in Trinder and others' study of LiPs prior to LASPO.[109] The McKenzie Friends observed came from various backgrounds, including some volunteers from the Personal Support Unit (now called Support through Court) and Women's Aid. Trinder and others found that McKenzie Friends 'were largely silent in proceedings', instead providing emotional support to LiPs throughout their case.[110] Around the time of LASPO, evidence suggested that McKenzie Friends were extending their role and regularly seeking rights of audience.[111] The profile of McKenzie Friends had also changed: while McKenzie Friends were traditionally seen to provide unpaid support, more were now providing their services on a fee-charging basis.

There is noticeable concern among the judiciary, legal profession, and academic circles that McKenzie Friends could actually hinder access to justice. The potential problems are summarised by the Judicial Executive Board: 'The JEB remain deeply concerned about the proliferation of McKenzie Friends who in effect

---

[104] Ibid, s 13, sch 3.

[105] *Practice Guidance (McKenzie Friends: Civil and Family Courts)* [2010] 1 WR 1881 [4].

[106] KA Barry, 'McKenzie Friends and Litigants in Person: Widening Access to Justice or Foes in Disguise?' (2019) 31(1) Child and Family Law Quarterly 69, 69.

[107] [1971] P 33.

[108] Ibid, 41.

[109] Trinder and others (n60) 93.

[110] Ibid, 96.

[111] L Smith, E Hitchings, and M Sefton, 'A Study of Fee-Charging McKenzie Friends and their Work in Private Family Law Cases' Cardiff University (2017) 5 https://orca.cardiff.ac.uk/id/eprint/101919/1/A%20study%20of%20fee-charging%20McKenzie%20Friends.pdf, accessed 12 June 2025.

provide professional services for reward when they are unqualified, unregulated, uninsured and not subject to the same professional obligations and duties, both to their clients and the courts, as are professional lawyers.'[112]

A study on fee-charging McKenzie Friends in private family law cases identifies five (not mutually exclusive) types of McKenzie Friends: the business opportunist, the redirected specialist, the good Samaritan, the family justice crusader, and the rogue.[113] Smith, Hitchings, and Sefton express concern with the rogue, who 'unscrupulously exploits clients for personal gain or otherwise engages in wholly inappropriate conduct'.[114] There was very little evidence of this practice within the study, with most McKenzie Friends acting as business opportunists and redirected specialists. While the researchers behind the study conclude that the group provides an important form of support for those unable to access traditional legal support after LASPO, they also express caution around the opportunity for exploitative business practices without further regulation.[115] The practices of rogue McKenzie Friends could leave the most vulnerable in society even more open to exploitation: if this is the case, some McKenzie Friends may operate in a way that actually furthers the access-to-justice crisis. Despite calls to ban the profession, there is some consensus within the academic literature that the best way forward involves increased 'regulation, qualification and court supervision'.[116] This approach could encourage more accessible services in response to the LASPO reforms, while at the same time recognising that these providers must be held accountable and properly support the varying needs of their clientele.

Beyond McKenzie Friends, there are numerous online services that support LiPs (and even those who have legal assistance).[117] For instance, OurFamilyWizard is a popular co-parenting app, described on its website as 'a global co-parenting platform that empowers parents and caregivers with the tools they need to achieve healthy communication after divorce or separation'.[118] A subscription for the app can be purchased by families, as well as legal practitioners who can use the programme with their clients. For those seeking more tailored guidance,

---

[112] Lord Chief Justice of England and Wales, 'Reforming the Courts' Approach to McKenzie Friends: Consultation Response' (February 2019) 3 www.judiciary.uk/guidance-and-resources/consultation-reforming-the-courts-approach-to-mckenzie-friends, accessed 1 August 2024.

[113] Smith, Hitchings, and Sefton (n111) 17.

[114] Ibid, 21.

[115] Ibid, 81.

[116] Barry (n106) 78.

[117] L Smith and E Hitchings, 'Where the Wild Things Are: The Challenges and Opportunities of the Unregulated Legal Services Landscape in Family Law' (2023) 43 Legal Studies 658, 662.

[118] OurFamilyWizard, 'About Us | OurFamilyWizard' (2024) www.ourfamilywizard.co.uk/about, accessed 1 August 2024.

Amicable is 'an online legal service for divorcing and separating couples'.[119] It is a lawyer-free service that provides legal advice (including joint legal advice) on both child arrangements and financial matters. Amicable is said to provide a comprehensive approach to dispute resolution that is not solely focused on the legal elements of a case, but instead takes into account the relational aspects of family life and relationship breakdown. Some academic commentary has praised this approach. Smith and Hitchings, for example, argue that 'a relational approach to advice that is rooted in genuine conflict-resolution expertise might enhance the value of legal services'.[120] The service, and many others just like Amicable, thus raise fundamental questions about what family law practice should and could look like going forward.

The fact that this growing body of non-lawyer services is massively understudied (by both lecturers and their students) means very little is known about the quality of support provided. We do not know if these services are providing correct legal information. We do not know if they are supporting their client in a way that encourages the amicable but fair resolution of disputes. Crucially, we have little to no grasp on whether these services are accessible for the most vulnerable families and whether they enhance or hinder family justice.

Altogether, the various responses of legal (and non-legal) services to the post-LASPO climate are to be welcomed, albeit with apprehension. These are very recent developments in the history of the English and Welsh FJS, as well as the post-LASPO landscape. It will take many more years, and perhaps even decades, to understand the long-term impact of the 2013 LASPO reforms and the ways in which legal services have adjusted. Unfortunately, what remains clear is that many vulnerable individuals are unsupported throughout their private family disputes. More must be done to understand the use and accessibility of these services, as well as how different forms of legal advice and support can be adjusted to support vulnerable disputants.

Summary

It is very unlikely that the traditional legal aid system will be reintroduced. Therefore, it is important that academic debate, education, and policy consider pragmatic ways to respond to the post-LASPO landscape. A particular area of interest is the provision of accessible and affordable legal support. Innovative services have been provided by lawyers through unbundling and the 'one-lawyer-two-clients' model. Beyond lawyers, many LiPs use McKenzie Friends and online services or apps. A significant question for forthcoming discussion is how far these diversifying services can, first, accommodate the needs of vulnerable and at-risk families, and, secondly, support access to justice.

---

[119] Amicable, 'Amicable | Divorce, Separating and Cooperative Parenting' (2024) https://amicable.io/, accessed 1 August 2024.

[120] Smith and Hitchings (n117) 667.

Conclusion

The family justice landscape in the 2020s – and beyond – is drastically different to when the legal aid scheme was first introduced as a pillar of the welfare state. Self-represented litigants have always been a noticeable population in private family law matters, but are now the norm following the severe cuts to legal aid under LASPO. Even with exceptions put in place to ensure access to legal aid, representation, and thus justice in court, the Ministry of Justice has understood the concept of 'vulnerability' so narrowly that few people are eligible for this funding. From the needs of those with poor mental health to individuals with very limited financial resources, the various vulnerabilities of families involved in legal disputes are overlooked. Unfortunately, these vulnerabilities make the journey of being a LiP even more difficult. Nonetheless, there is some cause for optimism in the post-LASPO landscape, with a diverse group of legal and non-legal practices coming to the fore. A key question, then, is how these services can be adjusted to accommodate the complex and varied needs of families in today's family law system, ensuring access to justice in the process.

Further questions to consider

- How could the family court system be adapted to better suit the needs of LiPs?
- To what extent should the government fund the resolution of private family matters?
- How can we better understand the vulnerabilities of people with family disputes?
- Can legal services be adapted to suit the complex and varying needs of vulnerable litigants?

Further materials

Hynes S, *Austerity Justice* (Legal Action Group 2012)

Kaganas F, 'Justifying the LASPO Act: Authenticity, Necessity, Suitability, Responsibility and Autonomy' (2017) 39(2) Journal of Social Welfare and Family Law 168

Maclean M and Eekelaar J, *After the Act: Access to Family Justice After LASPO* (Hart Publishing 2019)

Saied-Tessier A, 'What Do We Know about Adults in Private Family Proceedings?' Nuffield Foundation (2023) https://www.nuffieldfjo.org.uk/wp-content/uploads/2023/09/Private_Law_spotlight.pdf, accessed 12 June 2025

YouGov, 'Legal Needs of Individuals in England and Wales: Technical Report 2019/20' (27 January 2020) www.lawsociety.org.uk/topics/research/legal-needs-of-individuals-in-england-and-wales-report, accessed 1 August 2024

10

Religious Communities and Family Dispute Resolution: The Sharia Councils Debate

Rehana Parveen

Introduction

The law frames and polices how parties enter into adult relationships, the status those relationships are given, and the consequences of breakdown. The impact of the law on family life is most visible when a relationship breaks down. The legal framework governing disputes for child living arrangements is overseen by the Children Act (CA) 1989,[1] while the legal framework exercised in the division of family wealth after formal relationship breakdown is contained within the Matrimonial Causes Act (MCA) 1973.[2] In both cases, as explored in Chapter 8, the law encourages parties to negotiate through the use of alternative dispute-resolution forums to reach a mutually agreed settlement. While the use of privatised spaces in family law, along with the tendency to equate settlements with the achievement of justice, has faced significant critique,[3] it is clear that alternative dispute-resolution forums are now part of the fabric of English family law. This may take the form of mediation, arbitration, some other form of collaborative practice, or negotiating via parties' legal advisers. The Family Procedure Rules require courts to encourage parties to undertake non-court dispute resolution (NCDR) where appropriate.[4] There are no clear parameters

---

[1]   CA 1989.

[2]   MCA 1973.

[3]   A Diduck, 'Autonomy and Family Justice' (2016) 28(2) Child and Family Law Quarterly 133.

[4]   Under Part 3.3 Family Law Procedure Rules the court must consider at every stage in proceedings whether NCDR is appropriate and under s 10(1) Children and Families Act 2014 parties are required to attend a mediation information assessment meeting in order to

defining appropriate alternative dispute-resolution forums, which opens up the space for more tailored forms of services, including faith-based forums.

If alternative dispute-resolution forums are to help parties reach agreements on relationship breakdown, they must not contravene the existing legal frameworks and must accommodate the needs of each party. They are not courts with the power to impose outcomes on the parties irrespective of their wishes. Instead, they work with the parties to reach a voluntary settlement. For religiously observant couples, negotiating the end of their relationship may include using a forum which takes account of their religious beliefs. For Muslim couples, one source of alternative dispute resolution are sharia councils. Our understanding of the work of sharia councils has developed over the past 20 years or so, with a body of academic research that has explored Muslim family practices within the UK.[5] Key questions explored include why they emerged; their relationship with state law; why they are predominantly accessed by Muslim women (rather than men); and how the spiritual, religious, and citizenship identities of minority Muslims communities coalesce in these alternative spaces.

English family law's framework of marriage and divorce does not always reflect the marriage and divorce practices of its minority communities.[6] As a result, Muslim communities have turned to internal religious authorities to obtain guidance on marriages and divorces, allowing them to negotiate relationship endings in ways that align with their religious, cultural, familial, and community values. This undoubtedly raises challenging questions about the relationship between Muslim family practices and state law, but perhaps more significantly, it also reveals the colonial legacies and Christian norms embedded within English

---

consider alternative non-court options to resolve disputes concerning children before pursuing court proceedings.

5   F Azzouz, 'Muslim Marriage and Divorce Practices in Britain: Avenues for Regulation' (PhD thesis, University of Bristol 2022); F Azzouz, 'Islamic ADR in Britain: Diversity, Hybridity, and Women's Experiences of Community Justice' (2023) 12(2) Oxford Journal of Law and Religion 199; SN Shah-Kazemi, 'Untying the Knot: Muslim Women, Divorce and the Shariah' Nuffield Foundation (2001) https://www.nuffieldfoundation.org/wp-cont ent/uploads/2020/01/Untying-the-Knot.pdf, accessed 12 June 2025; S Bano, *Muslim Women and Shariah Councils: Transcending the Boundaries of Community and Law* (Palgrave Macmillan 2012); JR Bowen, *On British Islam: Religion, Law and Everyday Practice in Shariah Councils* (Princeton University Press 2015); MM Keshavjee, *Islam, Sharia and Alternative Dispute Resolution* (Bloomsbury Publishing 2013); R Parveen, 'Do Sharia Councils Meet the Needs of Muslim Women?' in S Bano (ed), *Gender Justice in Family Law Disputes: Women, Mediation and Religious Arbitration* (Brandeis University Press 2017); I Uddin, 'Nikah-Only Marriages: Causes, Motivations and their Impact on Dispute Resolution and Islamic Divorce Proceedings in England and Wales' (2018) 7(3) Oxford Journal of Law and Religion 401; I Uddin, 'Islamic Family Law: Imams, Mosques, and Shari'a Councils in the UK' (2020) 8(1) Electronic Journal of Islamic and Middle Eastern Studies 25.

6   See generally, R Probert, R Akhtar, and S Blake, 'When Is a Wedding Not a Marriage? Exploring Non-legally Binding Ceremonies' Nuffield Foundation (2022) https://www.nuf fieldfoundation.org/wp-content/uploads/2020/11/When_is_a_wedding_not_a_marriage_A_ briefing_paper_for_the_Law_Commission-FINAL.pdf, accessed 12 June 2025.

family law. Though it is accepted that minority religious communities have been afforded *some* reforms to the law that would allow limited recognition of *some* of their practices, the law has nonetheless been very concerned to ensure that the dominance of English family law is maintained.[7] Despite accommodations, and the encouragement of alternative dispute resolution within the family justice system (FJS), anxieties permeate any discussions around sharia councils and policy considerations have focused on an underlying desire to minimise their impact, if not to completely ban them.

This chapter focuses on Muslim couples marrying and divorcing in England and Wales, examining how they engage with English marriage and divorce laws. It specifically explores the role of sharia councils, criticisms levelled against them, and some of the reform proposals made. This chapter should help law students to think about how family law and divorce processes are experienced by particular communities, in this case Muslim couples and Muslim communities, and the broader relationship between state law and Muslim family practices.

Contextual background

Before we begin to address the details of marriage and divorce laws it would be useful to set out some context on British Muslims and some relevant critique of the history of English family law. Both will be relevant to any discussion on Muslims and family practices. The overall population of England and Wales stands at a little under 60 million.[8] In the 2021 Census, 46.2 per cent of the overall population identified themselves as Christian, which means for the first time in UK Census history, less than half of the population are Christian. The second most common response to the 'religion' question was 'no religion' at 37.2 per cent, an increase of 12 per cent since the 2011 Census. Muslims make up the largest religious group after Christianity at 6.5 per cent, accounting for 3.9 million people in England and Wales. This is an increase of 1.6 per cent since the 2011 Census. Small changes were noted for other faith groups but nothing as significant as the decrease in Christianity or the increases in those of no faith.

The census data does not capture the extent of religious observance or the complex, pluralistic interactions between religious norms and state law. The heterogeneity within Muslim communities means individuals navigate diverse and often competing issues. For Muslim women in particular, some narratives on the work on sharia councils risk reinforcing essentialised and stereotypical notions of racialised women in need of 'saving'. Students of law should fully engage in

---

[7] See Chapter 2.

[8] Office for National Statistics, 'Census 2021' 59, 597, 300 https://www.ons.gov.uk/peoplepop ulationandcommunity/culturalidentity/religion/bulletins/religionenglandandwales/census2021, accessed 23 July 2025.

exploring how notions of agency, freedom of choice, and gender justice for Muslim women may not fit the dominant liberal interpretation of these ideas.[9]

In Chapter 2 of this volume, Naqvi explores the colonial legacies of English marriage laws, and this chapter reiterates the importance of noting the historical relationship between the state and the church. The influence of Christianity in shaping English laws of marriage and divorce has been profound. Not all forms of consensual adult relationships are equally recognised nor protected by the state and Naqvi illustrates the ways in which English laws of marriage have developed through coloniality to maintain hierarchies of marriage. For both marriage and divorce, in many respects the manner in which Muslim couples enter and exit intimate relationships is similar to their peers in wider society and should be understood within these broader contexts of the development of family life and family law. There are a multitude of ways in which couples may enter a relationship or end it, and the state imposes a legal framework that determines which of these relationships is legally recognised and afforded state protection. Just as state law and British society have not remained static, nor have Muslim communities or the religious teachings that they follow. Muslims continue to evolve as dynamic minority communities, though this evolution should not be framed of as some linear path to 'enlightenment'. Rather, it should be understood as Muslim communities in continuous re-negotiations with themselves and the state. They are not immune from the changing landscape of family law, which might include, for example, critical feminist methodologies exploring the 'Muslim female subject'. Feminist methodologies have provided an important conceptual set of tools for the critique of family law more broadly, with 'Islamic feminism' literature now also critiquing Muslim family law.[10] Scholars such as Bano situate the emergence and development of 'Muslim family law' in the UK as part of specific historical, social, and political conditions under which postcolonial migrations occurred. As Bano further points out, the process of 'reform' within Muslim communities is often fractured, contextual, and dependant on many variables, including state support and subsidy.[11]

A postcolonial legal theoretical lens offers a valuable yet underdeveloped framework for understanding the interactions between Muslim minorities and the state within the context of family law. Muslim communities in the UK often hail from geographical spaces that were once subject to British colonial rule. Indeed, scholars such as An-Naim have argued that 'Islamic Family Law' itself is a colonial fabrication.[12] Colonisation has left its impact on both the coloniser and the

---

[9]   L Abu-Lughod, *Do Muslim Women Need Saving?* (Harvard University Press 2013).

[10]   Z Mir-Hosseini, M Al-Sharmani, and J Rumminger (eds), *Men in Charge? Rethinking Authority in Muslim Legal Tradition* (Oneworld Publications 2015).

[11]   S Bano, 'Sharia Councils and Muslim Family Law: Analysing the Parity Governance Model, the Sharia Inquiry and the Role of the State/Law Relations' in S Bano (ed), *The Sharia Inquiry, Religious Practice and Muslim Family Law in Britain* (Routledge 2023).

[12]   AA An-Na'im, 'The Postcolonial Fallacy of "Islamic Family Law"' in S Choudhry and J Herring (eds), *The Cambridge Companion to the Comparative Family Law* (CUP 2019).

colonised. The academic scholarship on decolonisation and postcolonial thought has illustrated how colonisers presented themselves as civilised and superior, with universal behaviours, practices, and norms, and Christianity oftentimes provided for them the benchmark against which 'normality' was to be judged. The colonised on the other hand were perceived as uncivilised, savage, in need of educating, or at the very least in need of controlling due to their primitive natures.[13] These perceptions run deep and one can see their influence today. Within this, the 'individual European citizen is abstracted, homogenised, "degendered", and universalized'.[14] In contrast, Muslims are portrayed as 'non-universal, particular and different'.[15] These legacies of colonisation have an impact on the ways in which English law and English policy makers perceive themselves and the ways in which they regard Muslim communities and Muslim behaviours. Claims of universalism and neutrality often mask value-laden practices that are privileged as 'normal'.[16] As a consequence, there are underlying assumptions embedded in the discussions around the 'accommodation' of minority communities.

Summary

The landscape of faith and belief in England and Wales is undergoing significant transformation, with a decline in Christian identification together with a rise in those identifying as having no religious affiliation. Muslims in Britain represent a diverse and dynamic community, challenging uniform assumptions, yet their intimate relationships are often shaped by religious frameworks. Understanding how the state engages with Muslim family practices requires critical attention to the historical entanglement between the state and Christianity, as well as the enduring colonial legacies embedded within the legal system.

Marriage and cohabitation

Marriage has historically served as a foundational pillar of the legal framework governing family life in England and Wales. Despite the attempts of English policy makers, of academic scholarship, and of family rights activists to address

---

[13] M Mutua, 'Savages, Victims, and Saviours: The Metaphor of Human Rights' (2001) 42(1) Harvard International Law Journal 201.

[14] S Nahda, 'The Portrayal of Islamic Family Law in Europe' in R Heacock and E Conte, *Critical Research in the Social Sciences: A Transdisciplinary East–West Handbook* (Ibrahim Abu-Lughod Institute of International Studies Birzeit University and the Institute for Social Anthropology Austrian Academy Sciences 2011) 243.

[15] Ibid.

[16] R Parveen, 'A Study of Muslim Marriage (and Divorce) Practices in England and Wales: Making a Case for Reform' in S Mateusz and A Juzaszek (eds), *Relationships Rights and Legal Pluralism: The Inadequacy of Marriage Laws in Europe* (Routledge 2024).

the societal changes in British family life,[17] as far as the law is concerned, legal marriage remains uniquely protected. That is not to say that marriage law has not been reformed in any way, indeed it has undergone various evolutions in order to address differing religious and cultural norms including same-sex relationships, as explored by Hayward in Chapter 3 of this volume. These changes have not come about without considerable effort from rights campaigners, activists, and those willing to take legal action.[18] Societal changes indicate that the institution of marriage no longer holds the same significance for many in British society who choose to cohabit without undertaking any formal ceremony of marriage. This changing landscape is not reflected in the law and the failure to legally recognise cohabitation as akin to marriage has been the subject of sustained critique. While cohabitees *may* have some financial rights against one another in the event of a breakdown in the relationship or on the death of one party, those rights are nowhere near as robust nor as accessible as spousal rights.[19] The Labour Government of 2024 pledged to 'strengthen the rights and protections available to women in cohabiting couples', indicating that reform may be forthcoming.

The state's distinction between married couples and cohabitees becomes important for Muslim couples because, as we shall see, though a Muslim couple may declare themselves to be married, to the state they may be treated as cohabitees from a legal perspective. Muslim couples can occupy an odd space whereby they, their religion, families, and communities consider them married but the law treats them as cohabitees; consequently they are both 'married' and 'unmarried' at the same time depending on who is asking. Of course, if the Labour government did adopt measures that gave greater recognition to the financial rights of cohabitants, the distinction between declaring a couple to be married or not may not be as significant.

Muslim marriage and cohabitation

The Law Commission recently described British society as more diverse, multi-ethnic, multi religious, and multicultural,[20] with wedding ceremonies likely to reflect that diversity. Marriage as a mode and method for managing intimate adult relationships is central to family life in the Muslim faith. The existence of a marriage differentiates a legitimate and lawful sexual relationship from an illicit

---

17   For a recent discussion of ten main areas of family law that are, arguably, in need of reform to reflect a modern and diverse UK, see C Bendall and R Parveen, *Family Law Reform Now: Proposals and Critique* (Hart Publishing 2024). This collection provides analysis and debate concerning ten ideas for reform that are put forward by family law experts.

18   For example, *R (on the application of Steinfeld and Keidan) (Appellants) v Secretary of State for International Development (in Substitution for the Home Secretary and the Education Secretary) (Respondents)* [2018] UKSC 32.

19   R Akhtar, P Nash, and R Probert, *Cohabitation and Religious Marriage; Status, Similarities and Solutions* (Bristol University Press 2020).

20   Law Commission, *Celebrating Marriage: A New Weddings Law* (Law Com No 408, 2022).

or religiously unlawful one. A sexual relationship without a marriage would amount to a sin and Islamic jurisprudence is unequivocal as to the requirement of a marriage for the purposes of lawful sexual relations.[21] Marriage is a legal contract rather than a sacrament, referred to as a *nikah*. It is therefore capable of being terminated, though there are some differences between the ways in which men dissolve this union compared with women, which we will address in the section on divorce. For now, we can note that it is highly unlikely that religiously observant Muslim couples would openly cohabit without having undergone a valid religious marriage ceremony. And, in order to be religiously valid, there must be consent from the couple, the presence of witnesses or at least some publicity as to the marriage, a *mahr* gifted to the bride,[22] and, though disputed by some, many Muslims expect the presence of a *wali* to act as a 'guardian' for the bride.[23] All of these aspects of a Muslim wedding ceremony have been explored in literature and scholarship both historically by Muslim scholars and in contemporary academia.[24] The extensive documented discussions on each of the constitutive requirements for a valid Islamic marriage are beyond the scope of this chapter. What is important to note is that the fairly simple requirements for a valid Islamic marriage mean that Muslim marriages can take place anywhere and be relatively understated. It is customary practice for weddings to range from quite simple ceremonies within the home, or in a mosque, to more extravagant venues including hotels, stately homes, defined wedding venues, at restaurants, or outside in a garden or marquee, and so on.[25]

Recent debates concerning Muslim marriage practices within the English legal context have centred on the lack of legal recognition of Muslim religious-only marriage ceremonies. To understand why and how this has materialised, we

---

[21]   A Black, E Hossein, and N Hosen, *Modern Perspectives on Islamic Law* (Edward Elgar 2013).

[22]   This is usually a monetary gift that may be paid immediately at the time of the *nikah* or deferred to a later date as a debt owed by the husband to the wife. Often cultural norms will dictate whether this is nominal gift or a payment of more significant sums.

[23]   Black, Hossein, and Hosen (n21).

[24]   See, for example, D Friantoro and AA Susamto, 'The Determinants of the Value of Mahr in Muslim Societies: Evidence from the Indonesian Family Life Surveys' (2021) 22(2) Jurnal Ekonomi & Studi Pembangunan 323; R Mehdi and JS Nielsen (eds), *Embedding Mahr in the European Legal System* (DJOF Publishing 2011); EE Stiles, *Embedding Mahr in the European Legal System* (DJOF Publishing 2012).

[25]   In some reports it has been suggested that the value of the wedding industry as a whole amounts to around £14.7 billion annually, around half of which is accounted for by South Asian weddings (a significant proportion of which will include Muslim weddings). See HM Arshad, 'Cost of Living Crisis: Is it Affecting Big Fat British Asian Wedding Planning?' *Asian Sunday* (4 June 2022) https://www.asiansunday.co.uk/south-asian-brides-on-a-budget-is-the-uks-cost-of-living-crisis-causing-cuts-in-wedding-costs/, accessed 4 December 2024. Despite the relative simplicity of the requirements of a Muslim marriage, this does not mean that they are insignificant events in terms of their financial value to the economy or in terms of their religious value to Muslims.

need to have some understanding of the ways in which English law governs the validity of marriages.

English weddings law

English law recognises a marriage as valid if it has met the formality requirements of sections 25 or 49 of the Marriage Act 1949 (and its subsequent amendments). This statutory framework outlines specific requirements, including the provision of prior notice of the intended marriage, adhering to prescribed ceremonial rites, meeting stipulations regarding the venue, ensuring the use of specific wording during the ceremony, appointing authorised officiants, and fulfilling post-ceremony registration obligations. Leaving aside issues of capacity and age, English law imposes formality requirements that differ to Muslim marriage practices. Issues of diversity have been addressed by the legislation in a piecemeal, ad hoc fashion, resulting in an unnecessarily complex framework that produces contradictory outcomes when formality requirements are not met. For parties to enter a legally recognised marriage they must decide which route they will take (as addressed by Naqvi in Chapter 2). For legal recognition of their *nikah* ceremony, couples must either ensure that their religious marriage ceremony conforms with the requirements of the Marriage Act or undertake a separate valid civil ceremony. There is no simple method by which Muslim couples can acquire legal recognition for their *nikah* ceremonies without additional steps.

Muslim marriage ceremonies are not unique when it comes to non-recognition, and other groups such as Humanists have also protested non-recognition of their ceremonies. A 2022 study by Probert, Akhtar, and Blake investigated the range of non-legally binding ceremonies which occur in multiple different faith and non-faith communities in England ('Weddings Study').[26] The Weddings Study explored some of the ways in which the participants felt excluded by weddings law and highlighted some of the common barriers experienced by different groups. The restrictive requirements of English law leave couples with little room to negotiate how and where to marry, who may conduct the ceremony, and what words the parties may exchange as they marry.[27] It leaves almost no room for those of mixed faith backgrounds to combine differing aspects of their cultures and religions that they would like reflected in their ceremonies.

While it can be argued that English law has a legitimate interest in ensuring clarity that a marriage ceremony is indeed a marriage – and not, for example, an engagement, a blessing, or another form of celebration – the inconsistent outcomes in case law suggest that the law does not always provide the clarity it seeks to achieve. Case law shows that failure to comply with the formalities of English law has at times resulted in a marriage ceremony being recognised as

---

[26] Probert, Akhtar, and Blake (n6).

[27] R Sandberg, 'The Adult Intimate Relationship Bill' in Bendall and Parveen (eds), (n17).

valid, other times as void, and, for many Muslims, declared a non-marriage or a non-qualifying ceremony.[28] A non-marriage/non-qualifying ceremony means that the parties are effectively treated as cohabitants.

Why are so many Muslim couples entering into non-qualifying marriage ceremonies?

Exact figures on the prevalence of non-qualifying marriage ceremonies among Muslim couples are unavailable, largely due to the private and often undocumented nature of these practices. Various sources suggest figures somewhere between 25 per cent and 80 per cent of all Muslim marriages.[29] Thus, significant numbers of Muslim couples are treated by the state as cohabitants though they may refer to themselves as married having undergone a non-qualifying *nikah* ceremony. Whatever the exact figures are, the underlying reasons for entering non-qualifying ceremonies are important and there is no single motive.[30] It is at least as complex as asking the question why do so many British couples cohabit? Muslim couples are still getting married but just not in the way in which the law is requiring them to, either fully cognisant of their lack of legal recognition or otherwise and as a consequence of the current marriage law framework that is exclusionary.

Summary

Marriage has traditionally been central to English family law, yet an increasing number of British couples are choosing to cohabit rather than marry. Unlike legally married couples, cohabitants lack equal rights in areas such as inheritance and financial claims on relationship breakdown, often resulting in gendered disadvantages for women. In response, the Labour Party's 2024 Manifesto pledged to enhance protections for women in cohabiting relationships, potentially reducing the distinctions between married and unmarried couples.

For Muslims, a *nikah* ceremony – a religious marriage contract – can take place anywhere and typically involves a consenting couple, witnesses, a *mahr* payment,

---

28   R Probert, 'When Are We Married? Void, Non-Existent and Presumed Marriages' (2002) 22(3) Legal Studies 398; R Probert and S Salim, 'The Legal Treatment of Islamic Marriage Ceremonies' (2018) 7(3) Oxford Journal of Law and Religion 376.

29   In 2020, the Muslim Women's Network UK submitted written evidence to parliament in which it estimated 25 per cent of those who sought advice from them and provided them with information about their marriage status were in non-legally recognised marriages. The Register Our Marriage Campaign has cited figures as high as 80 per cent of all Muslim marriages as not legally recognised, whereas the 2017 Channel 4 documentary 'The Truth about Muslim Marriage' relied on the survey by True Vision Aire in which around 60 per cent of those surveyed were in a non-legally recognised marriage, with the vast majority aware that their marriages were not legally recognised.

30   SS Ali, J Jones, and A Shahid, 'To Register or Not to Register? Reflections on Muslim Marriage Practices in Britain' (2020) 10 Nordic Journal of Law and Social Research 41.

and sometimes a bride's guardian. Religiously observant Muslims are unlikely to cohabit without a *nikah*. However, a *nikah* that does not meet the requirements of English law is generally not recognised as a legal marriage, unless followed by a separate civil ceremony. If a legally binding ceremony does not occur, Muslim couples are treated as cohabitants under the law.

This raises questions about whether efforts should focus on encouraging Muslims to align their marriages with state requirements or whether the law itself is failing to accommodate Muslim couples. Furthermore, cases involving non-compliant ceremonies have led to inconsistent and confusing legal outcomes, highlighting the complexities within the current system.

Divorce in English law and Muslim practices

English divorce law has recently been overhauled by the Divorce, Dissolution and Separation Act 2020 (DDSA) which came into force on 6 April 2022. The law has been simplified to a 'no-fault' process whereby court oversight is largely dedicated to administratively processing divorce applications rather than interrogating whether a divorce should be granted. As long as parties have been married for at least one year, either party to a marriage, or both jointly, may commence proceedings for a divorce on the basis that the marriage has irretrievably broken down. The current civil divorce regime under the DDSA has substantially rectified many of the criticisms of the previous framework for divorce.[31] It has simplified the process for divorce as well as the language being used, with parties now referred to as claimant and respondent and court orders referred to as conditional and final orders granting divorce. There is an overall 26-week time frame from the start of proceedings to the granting of a final order (though this can be delayed by financial resolution) and these changes have coincided with digital divorce processes. The most significant and substantive change is the removal of fault as a basis for commencing divorce proceedings and it is enough for one party (or both) to state that the marriage has irretrievably broken down. The ability for the parties to make a joint application coupled with the removal of the respondent's ability to defend divorce proceedings is a seismic shift in the law on divorce, giving recognition in practical terms to the futility of forcing couples to remain legally married. Although historically divorce law has reflected Christian religious values, we have now arrived at a no-fault system.

The civil divorce framework is only available and necessary where there is a marriage legally recognised by the state, and the financial resolution provisions of the MCA 1973 are also dependant on a civil divorce taking place.[32] Where

---

[31]   L Trinder and others, 'Finding Fault? Divorce Law and Practice in England and Wales' Nuffield Foundation (2017) https://www.nuffieldfoundation.org/sites/default/files/files/Finding_Fault_full_report_v_FINAL.pdf, accessed 13 June 2025.

[32]   The orders for the redistribution of wealth, under the MCA 1973, may also be made where there is an annulment or judicial separation.

there is no recognised marriage, there is no civil divorce process available to the parties, placing the couple in the same legal position as cohabitants. Research and case law indicates that some affected couples only realise their marriage ceremony may not be legally recognised when they attempt to divorce or make some sort of financial claim. Research indicates that many Muslim couples who undergo non-legally binding ceremonies are fully aware that their marriages are not recognised in English law.[33] Even if they do not appreciate the full consequences of non-recognition there is an awareness that the marriage entered into will not be valid in law.[34] It is often a 'choice' on their part not to be bound by the requirements of civil law, whether in terms of marriage, divorce, or financial obligations, though the extent to which each party acts autonomously and purely in their own self-interest in making this 'choice' is debatable.[35] It may be the case that notwithstanding the lack of a legally recognised marriage, couples believe the state will provide them with greater financial protections than it actually does and this belief is one often held by cohabitees who assume they are protected by the 'common law marriage myth'.[36]

Muslim divorce practices

Muslim couples who have entered into a legally binding marriage must undergo the same civil divorce process outlined in the DDSA to terminate their marriage under civil law. However, in the same way that an Islamically valid marriage is important to Muslims couples, a religiously valid divorce is also likely to be important. This is where the role of sharia councils becomes significant, raising key questions: how do Muslims obtain an Islamic divorce? What role do sharia councils play in this process? And why have these councils been the focus of extensive criticism?

In most Muslim law states, divorce, along with marriage, has been incorporated into the state civil law, requiring parties to engage with court processes. In Muslim-minority legal contexts, particularly those of the 'Global North', Muslim

---

[33]   In 2016–17 True Vision Aire and Channel 4 commissioned a survey of 900 Muslim women in the UK in order to explore Muslim women's experiences of getting married and their understandings of the legal framework around marriage. A key finding from the survey was that 60 per cent of the women surveyed were in *nikah*-only marriages. Of that 60 per cent, 28 per cent were unaware that their *nikah* marriage was not recognised by the law. Conversely, this means that the overwhelming majority were at least cognisant as to the lack of legal recognition of their *nikah,* even if they may not have fully appreciated all of the consequences that this entails. See https://www.truevisiontv.com/films/the-truth-about-muslim-marriages, accessed 10 April 2025.

[34]   Probert, Akhtar, and Blake (n6).

[35]   S Kalra, 'Response to The Adult Intimate Relationships Bill' in Bendall and Parveen (eds), (n17).

[36]   A Barlow, 'Modern Marriage Myths: The Dichotomy between Expectations of Legal Rationality and Lived Law' in Akhtar, Nash, and Probert (eds), (n19).

couples in non-legally binding marriages need to find alternative ways to obtain religiously sanctioned divorces. This is where sharia councils play a pivotal role, explaining why they occur in Muslim-minority states.

In Islamic law, marriage is a contract which can be terminated by divorce using a religiously valid method. Prior to divorce, Muslim couples are encouraged to seek opportunities for mediation and potential reconciliation. Much of the regulation of divorce comes directly from verses in the Quran.[37] Muslim couples may mutually agree to end their relationship, a process that historically required no court involvement. However, in cases where mutual agreement is not reached, Islamic law provides distinct methods for divorce, with differences in the procedures and consequences depending on whether it is initiated by the husband or the wife. These differences undoubtedly reflect a power imbalance and have been the subject of much debate.[38]

In traditional Islamic jurisprudence, a husband can divorce his wife by pronouncing a *talaq* (a unilateral pronunciation of a divorce), without requiring the wife's consent. Once pronounced, the wife enters into *iddah* and the husband is required to pay any outstanding *mahr*.[39] The wife remains in *iddah* for three menstrual cycles or three months (if not menstruating), or, if the wife is pregnant, until the birth of the baby. During this time the husband is required to financially maintain the wife. Upon completion of the *iddah*, the parties are divorced. If they choose to reconcile in the future, a new *nikah* ceremony is needed, with all the same requirements as previously stated, including the consent of both parties.[40] In traditional Islamic jurisprudence husbands have been allowed to revoke the *talaq* during the *iddah* period. In most Muslim majority countries, the husband's ability to pronounce *talaq* and revoke that *talaq* have been subject to civil law restrictions that are often interpreted in a manner to reduce harm to women. As a result, both the pronouncement of the *talaq* and the ability to revoke it have been curtailed and subject to civil court processes. A lack of such religious court or binding religious authority in Muslim minority states like England and Wales means similar protections are not to be found here.

There are several ways in which a wife can initiate a divorce, though at first glance, none appear to be fully equivalent to the unilateral *talaq* available to the husband. These are *tawfid al-talaq*, *khul*, and *faskh*. The *tawfid al-talaq* is a significant mechanism for redressing gender imbalance and is where the husband delegates *talaq* to his wife. This arrangement, which can be agreed upon at the

---

[37] Black, Hossein, and Hosen (n21).

[38] See A Barlas, *Believing Women in Islam: Unreading Patriarchal Interpretations of the Qu'ran* (2nd edn, Saqi 2019) and A Kecia (ed), *Half of Faith: American Muslim Marriage and Divorce in the Twenty-First Century* (OpenBU 2021); though this latter collection is largely in the context of USA, the issues and navigations between civil law and Islamic family law practices that it addresses are relevant for Muslims living as minority communities within the Global North.

[39] *Iddah* is a 'waiting period' which arises in the event of a divorce or death of a husband.

[40] There is a limit on the number of times a divorced couple can marry – three times.

time of the *nikah* or later in the marriage, grants the wife parity with her husband in initiating divorce. Despite its significance, *tawfid al-talaq* remains underutilised in Muslim communities, both in minority contexts in the Global North and majority settings in the Global South.

Khul is the more prevalent approach to divorce for women, and this is where the wife initiates divorce on the basis that she will return her *mahr* or, if it has not yet been paid, will forgo it. There is debate as to whether the husband's consent is needed for this method of divorce and in many Muslim majority countries the requirement for the husband's consent has been removed, making this type of divorce more akin to a *talaq*.[41] Traditionally, this was not a method of divorce for which a wife necessarily required a judicial process.

Faskh is the third option for women and refers to a judicial dissolution. This is where the wife puts forward a legal ground for terminating the marriage and, while there is considerable variation on what those grounds may consist of, they are largely fault based. If the wife raises issues which have caused her some harm, a *faskh* divorce can be pronounced allowing her to retain her *mahr*. These are not the only methods of divorce discussed in Islamic jurisprudence, but they are most commonly used. There is an overlap between the *faskh* and civil divorce and we do now have Islamic jurists that accept a civil divorce, in which both parties have unequivocally consented, as a legitimate Islamic divorce.[42]

As mentioned, in Muslim law states, both parties to a divorce are generally required to approach a court as they tend to subsume the traditional Islamic methods of divorce for both men and women into their civil systems. A key point to appreciate from this is that the intervention of civil law has allowed judges to develop greater flexibility with dissolution and provide more flexible interpretations of Islamic jurisprudence that respond to contemporary issues.[43] For Muslims in the UK, while some religious scholars (and by extension, couples) accept that a civil divorce is sufficient to constitute a religiously sanctioned Islamic divorce, research indicates that this view is not universally held.[44] For those

---

[41] Pakistan is one example, where one of the most important developments in divorce law for women has been the removal of the need for the consent of a husband to a *khul* claim by the wife.

[42] Explained by Mufti Muhammad ibn Adam, Darul Iftaa in Institute of Islamic Jurisprudence https://daruliftaa.com/talaq-divorce/legal-civil-divorce-according-to-islamic-law/, accessed 4 December 2024.

[43] If we take, for example, Pakistan, legislation has been introduced requiring a husband to fulfil notice requirements to effect a *talaq*. But a failure to fulfil notice requirements does not automatically make the *talaq* ineffective, rather the court will consider the impact on the wife. For further discussion on this, see MZ Abbasi and SA Cheema, *Family Laws in Pakistan* (2nd edn, OUP 2024).

[44] For a similar discussion in the American context, see Z Ayubi, 'Negotiating Justice: American Muslim Women Navigating Islamic Divorce and Civil Law' in Kecia (n38). In her study, even the women who seemingly divorced exclusively according to civil law ensured the civil divorce also met the Islamic religious divorce requirements. It was not the case that these women ignored Islamic requirements.

Muslim couples in non-legally binding marriages, the only option for terminating their religious marriage is through a religious divorce. For Muslim men, this process is relatively straightforward through the unilateral *talaq*. However, for Muslim women, particularly those in non-legally binding marriages and where husbands refuse to consent to a divorce, the situation is more complex. In such cases, women are often left with little recourse other than to seek a religious authority capable of granting them a religious divorce. Sharia councils have been performing this role since the 1980s.

Sharia councils

Since the early 2000s, sharia councils have been the subject of a rich body of academic research and literature.[45] They have also attracted significant media attention, and been the focus of various campaigns by rights groups as well the subject of scrutiny by governmental enquiries. Their existence has been criticised on the grounds that they create a parallel legal system, potentially fostering an isolationist stance by Muslim communities, and are detrimental to the rights and well-being of Muslim women. Sharia councils have emerged since the 1980s and are a product of Muslim communities living in the Global North as religious minorities. They are often, though not always, affiliated to local mosques which uphold and propagate some of the religious and cultural norms of local Muslim communities. They typically engage local imams and religious scholars as decision makers, offering spaces for community members to seek guidance on questions related to Islamic faith while also serving as alternative dispute-resolution forums. Their primary dispute resolution function is the pronouncement of religious divorces, whether this is to confirm for parties that they are divorced or to adjudicate on a divorce application. The adjudications tend to occur on applications made by women. Despite the fact that most Muslim majority states have placed restrictions on men's ability to unilaterally pronounce a *talaq*, and require men to engage with a judicial process for a *talaq*, sharia councils have not engaged with these developments as they simply lack the power to do so in the absence of a Muslim religious hierarchy within England and Wales.

Sharia councils offer Muslim women an authoritative forum to seek a religious divorce, though they appear to adopt a more traditional and rigid approach to *talaq, khula*, and *faskh* than we see in Muslim majority states where civil law has redefined the parameters of each divorce pathway. Women are often compelled to use such forums for a religious divorce due to the absence of alternative religiously authoritative avenues. Existing research suggests that there is little appetite for sharia councils to declare themselves as 'courts' or grant judgments that may be enforced through civil court processes. Their legitimacy comes from

---

45   See n5.

Muslim (often female) users themselves who seek the decisions of a sharia council for a multitude of reasons.

Each sharia councils acts independently and there is no hierarchical structure or appeal process. There is nothing to prevent an individual from seeking the advice of multiple sharia councils and it is entirely possible for them to give contradictory opinions and for users to 'forum shop'.[46] Despite the independence of each sharia council, they seem to follow a generally similar process when a woman makes an application for a divorce. They begin by initially attempting to act as a mediation and reconciliation service to explore the possibility of reconciliation. Where that does not appear possible they will attempt to obtain the husband's consent to a *khul* and if that fails will then consider the pronouncement of a *faskh* divorce. These commonalities in the approaches of different sharia councils have been highlighted in different studies.[47] This slow process can mean that delays are built into the processes to the detriment of women wishing to be religiously divorced.

Having access to an authority capable of granting a religious divorce that fulfils Muslim women's spiritual needs holds immense significance for several reasons. It enables women to break free from the constraints of an unhappy marriage, providing them with determinations that are spiritually and socially accepted within their familial and communal contexts. Moreover, it allows them to enter new relationships that are both religiously valid and socially recognised as legitimate by their wider networks. A significantly under-researched dimension of this process is the spiritual equality, empowerment, and sense of comfort that such access offers Muslim women.

Criticisms of sharia councils

Sharia councils have faced criticisms for a variety of reasons. To begin, their very existence has been subject of debate. Critics argued that they establish a 'parallel' legal system, reflecting an isolationist approach to community relations among Muslims. Further, it is contended that their existence perpetuates gender inequality and disadvantages Muslim women. From this perspective, Muslim women are encouraged to seek resolutions through civil courts, with the assumption that such courts would produce more equitable outcomes for them. However, this ignores the reality that the cost of accessing the FJS can be very high, placing it out of reach for the majority and, where there is a non-legally binding marriage, it is not an option at all.

---

46 RC Akhtar, 'Plural Approaches to Faith-Based Dispute Resolution by Britain's Muslim Communities' (2019) 31(3) Child and Family Law Quarterly 189.

47 Shah-Kazemi (n5); T Walker, *Sharia Councils and Muslim Women in Britain: Rethinking the Role of Power and Authority* (Brill 2016); R Parveen, 'Religious-Only Marriages in the UK: Legal Positionings and Muslim Women's Experiences' (2017) 6(3) Sociology of Islam 1; RM Cusairi and Z Mahdi, 'Procedure of Issuing Religious Divorce and Resolving Matrimonial Disputes at Shari'ah Councils in the UK' (2018) 32(1) Arab Law Quarterly 1.

Bano's scholarship on sharia councils as models of dispute resolution has highlighted some fundamental conceptual questions around private community governance, legal liberalism and pluralism, and the management of migrant communities through a postcolonial understanding of relationships. Bano also juxtaposes Muslim religious identity with Western claims to secularisation and notions of democracy. These interactions are far more complex and nuanced than simply representing a potential 'parallel' legal system. This is particularly true in the context of family law, where additional attention to wider state policies encouraging the privatisation of family law dispute resolution is needed, facilitated by the removal of legal aid to access courts. A simplistic criticism of sharia councils acting 'outside' of state law as a parallel system fails to take account of the limitations of state law and the limitations of the outcomes achievable through court processes. Unlike marriage, English law itself does not directly provide Muslims with any opportunity to combine their religious divorce process with the civil one. The only provision in the civil divorce process which acknowledges the significance of a religious divorce is MCA 1973 s 10A, primarily intended for Jewish wives, which can be used to delay the final civil divorce order if a Jewish husband refuses to grant his wife a religious divorce (a 'get'). While this provision can be used by Muslim wives too, it is of little assistance as delaying or preventing civil divorce is rarely of any benefit to Muslim women who are pursuing a divorce. In any event Muslim women are not reliant on their husbands for a religious divorce in the same way that Jewish women are. Muslim women with access to a religious authority, such as a sharia council, can attain a religious divorce even if their husbands oppose it. Removing this option is counterproductive and harms their spiritual and practical needs. As it stands, the current civil divorce process largely ignores the religious needs of Muslim women or at best assumes the needs of all religious women to be the same. Where Muslims have accepted a civil divorce as fulfilling the requirements of an Islamic divorce, it has been due to intra-religious debates among Muslims and the religious rulings of Islamic scholars, rather than guidance from civil law policy makers.[48]

Another key theme of the criticisms levelled at sharia councils concerns their processes and the manner in which they provide their services. Given that the primary users of sharia councils for the purposes of divorce are women, a recurring criticism has been their inhospitality towards the multiple and diverse needs of their female service users and the unjustifiable deference that is shown towards husbands. This manifests in a number of ways such as the lack of appropriate safeguarding processes for women alleging domestic violence,

---

[48] https://islamqa.org/?p=7766, accessed 8 April 2025. This is an example of a question posed by a Muslim man about civil divorce and the response from the IslamQ&A website addresses the extent to which a civil divorce will be recognised as a religious divorce. This is an opinion provided by one scholar that demonstrates the intra-religious discussions on the interplay between civil and religious divorce.

the significant delays that take place while awaiting responses from unresponsive husbands, as well as the patriarchal and rigid interpretations of Islamic rules that benefit male power. For example, in considering a divorce by *khul*, it appears that sharia councils seem to unquestioningly accept that a *khul* needs the consent of the husband without engaging in any of the critical religious scholarship that challenges this assumption. In the section 'Proposals for reform' I will explore some of the suggested reforms in light of these criticisms.

Summary

English divorce law has recently undergone significant reform, transitioning to an administrative process though the court. For couples with a legally binding marriage, either party – or both jointly – can initiate divorce proceedings. It is no longer possible for one party to prevent the other from obtaining a divorce.

Muslims divorce practices are more complex. While many Muslims may accept a civil divorce as sufficient for religious purposes, others do not. A civil divorce is only available in cases where the marriage is legally recognised. Traditional Islamic jurisprudence differentiates the way in which Muslim men and women obtain a divorce, often privileging men in this regard. In Muslim majority countries, these methods of divorce have been integrated into civil legal systems, allowing for developments aimed at mitigating the unequal power dynamics between men and women in marital dissolutions.

In Muslims minority communities in the Global North, one of the ways religious divorces have been addressed is through the use of sharia councils. These councils have faced criticism from both within and outside Muslim communities. Despite this, they play a crucial role in providing Muslim women, in particular, access to a religiously sanctioned divorce.

Proposals for reform

Three proposed sets of reforms have been suggested that could significantly impact the functioning of sharia councils. I will briefly examine these here. The Law Commission's recommendations for reform of the law regulating weddings, the independent review into the application of sharia law in England and Wales ('the Review'), and the private members Bill of Baroness Cox, namely the Arbitration and Mediation Services (Equality) Bill ('the Bill'). While the Review and the Bill are primarily targeting sharia councils, some of their proposals have an impact on marriage laws too. These three sets of proposals are important as they each attempt to address some of the criticisms that are levelled at sharia councils and Muslim family practices within the context of the English legal framework. I argue that, of the three sets of proposals mentioned, the only one that adequately addresses the needs of Muslim couples is the package of reforms recommended by the Law Commission concerning marriage laws.

Before exploring each of these in greater detail, we must first consider some contextual matters that need to be addressed in more detail as we explore each of the sets of proposals. To begin, the current weddings laws (and now to a much lesser extent divorce laws) are historically embedded with Christian notions of marriage (see Chapter 2). This extends to notions of what a marriage entails, how one enters and exits from that union, and how these notions and practices are then settled into the legal framework as the 'normal' way to marry. The law may be presented as 'neutral' and universally applicable, while actually being value laden and discriminatory. For example, in the Weddings Study one participant stated 'white people are the norm ... and Christians are the norm, or not just the norm but the desirable or the best'.[49] A secular legal framework still makes value judgements about behaviours but cloaks them in language that is abstract and universalised. As a result, the onus is placed on minorities, such as Muslims, to unquestionably conform to the state's standards of 'normality' as embedded within its laws. If not to conform exactly, then it is assumed a similar alternative provision would be appropriate to meet the challenge of diversity.[50] Such alternatives provisions are addressed in an ad hoc manner without considering change more holistically.[51] In addition, the ad hoc approach fails to understand behaviours of minority communities within the context of wider societal developments (such as the challenges posed by increasing levels of cohabitation) and developments in law and policy (such as the drive towards privatisation of family law and the removal of legal aid in family proceedings). By not paying attention to this context, Muslims are perceived as uniquely problematic rather than as part of the messiness of family law and family life and further it is assumed that these wider contextual matters are not affecting British Muslim families in the same ways.

The Law Commission proposals

The Law Commission's proposals represent the clearest effort to create a set of family laws that not only address the interests of minority communities but also contextualise them within the broader trends of the majority, granting them equal legitimacy (Law Comm No 408, 2022). The Law Commission's narrow focus was on weddings; identifying the issues that pertain to respecting individual wishes, removing unnecessary regulation, and setting out a package of reform that would enable the state's interest to be protected while ensuring simplicity and fairness. The Law Commission recognised the diverse and changing landscape of marriage ceremonies, the complexity of the current legal framework, and its exclusionary consequences. It approached this topic by problematising *the law*

---

[49]   Probert, Akhtar, and Blake (n6).
[50]   Parveen (n16).
[51]   R Sandberg, 'A Fear of *Sharia*: Why the Independent Report Is a Wasted Opportunity' Law and Religion UK (2018) https://lawandreligionuk.com/2018/02/07/a-fear-of-sharia-why-the-independent-report-is-a-wasted-opportunity/, accessed 4 December 2024.

in failing to reflect the practices of significant proportions of British couples including Muslims, rather than problematising the behaviours and actions of those marginalised by the law.[52] It recommended an entirely new scheme to govern marriage ceremonies. Key aspects of this scheme include the removal of the requirement for a registered building in which a marriage ceremony must be conducted, thereby allowing parties much greater freedom as to the venue for the ceremony. It replaced this with a more effective use of the authorised officiant who conducts the ceremony and is responsible for registration. The scheme would still require preliminary steps to be undertaken in order to satisfy the state that parties are free to marry one another and that they both voluntarily consent to the marriage. Parties would be required to give notice of their intention to marry and, though the scheme differentiates between Anglican and other ceremonies in the giving of notice, generally the requirements are less complex than the current law. The scheme's most significant changes would permit parties to agree the form and ceremony between themselves and the officiant, provided it took place in a safe and dignified location. This means a *nikah* or any other religious ceremony could lead to a legally valid marriage. The officiant is central to the scheme in having the responsibility of ensuring parties freely express their consent to the marriage, ensuring other important legal requirements are met, and ensuring the relevant documentation is signed. Officiants would be authorised, categorised, and registered through local authorities. Under this regime more wedding ceremonies are likely to be captured by the law as valid and those that are not valid are more likely to fall into the void category rather than a non-qualifying ceremony. Consequently, the need for sharia councils may be reduced.

The Bill

Since 2012, Baroness Cox, a cross-bench peer, has repeatedly attempted to introduce her Private Members Bill to the House of Lords to address the existence of sharia councils and gender discrimination in arbitration, mediation, or quasi-court-type proceedings. On each occasion due to a lack of time and governmental support the Bill has failed to progress.[53]

The Bill seeks to tackle the perceived discriminatory practices of religious tribunals by emphasising equality obligations, assigning public sector duties to inform individuals of the 'need to obtain an officially recognised marriage in order to have legal protection', and providing courts with powers to set aside an agreed settlement if it considers one party's consent to lack genuineness. In addition, it created an offence of 'falsely claiming legal jurisdiction'. Although

---

[52]   Parveen (n16).

[53]   A Al-Astewani, 'Why Has Baroness Cox's Bill Failed to become Law?' Law and Religion UK (2016) https://lawandreligionuk.com/2016/04/04/why-has-baroness-coxs-bill-failed-to-bec ome-law/, accessed 4 December 2024.

the Bill itself does not explicitly mention sharia councils, there is little doubt that they are the primary target of the proposals. While the Bill may have received some popular support, there is very little in it that addresses the needs of Muslim women. Much of what the Bill proposes is already addressed in various existing pieces of legislation and under common law. The Bill fails to recognise the agency of Muslim women or their desire to approach family matters through a framework of religious laws. The Bill (and the Review) reflect a very narrow perception of Muslim women as needing to be saved by the state, from themselves, from their religion, from their communities, and specifically from the men of their communities. There is very little recognition of the diversity of Muslim women or even a desire to address the needs of Muslim women for whom faith forms an important prism through which they conduct their lives. Of course, this does not mean there are no valid criticisms of sharia councils or that Muslim women are not subjected to patriarchy; rather that the Bill does not give due recognition to understanding the significance of religion and spirituality in women's choices and the disempowering impact of the measures suggested. This will be addressed more fully later.

The Review

The recommendations of the Review are equally limited and, in some respects, worse than the Bill. In October 2015 the government commissioned an independent review to 'understand whether, and the extent to which, sharia law is being misused or applied in a way that is incompatible with the law within sharia councils'. This is a very vague and odd framing and the imprecise language makes it difficult to understand exactly which 'law' was being investigated and for what purpose. It also presupposes 'sharia law' is being misused or applied in an incompatible manner.

The subsequent bullet-pointed terms of reference attempted to expand on the overarching aim but they are indicative of a very problematic approach towards Muslim community practices and their status as minorities. The first aim was to consider the ways in which sharia may be being used to cause harm to communities and the last one to seek out examples of good practice that assured compliance and compatibility with 'UK law'. Leaving aside the misnomer of what is meant by the term 'UK law', to begin the terms of reference with a presumption of harm from sharia and end with the presumption that best practice is achieved through compliance or compatibility with UK law is symptomatic of a framing that is suspicious of Muslim practices, expecting them to be harmful. It presumes only those aspects of Muslim behaviour that are 'compliant' or 'compatible' with English law are indicators of best practices, and that only state law sets the standard for best practice; best practice cannot be achieved from the practices of minority diasporas themselves. This framing internalises a colonial notion of the ways in which minority religious and cultural norms ought to be accommodated within the supremacy of state law, unquestioned, prioritising 'Western' and European hegemony.[54] 'Accommodation' of Muslim family practices is at most viewed as the provision of alternatives that fit within the current legal framework without thinking about the appropriateness of that framework. The Review shares many of the same underlying assumptions about Muslim women's needs as the Bill, often portraying Muslim behaviour as uniquely problematic and isolated from the broader context of British society. The Review does not properly address the exclusionary and complex nature of the law nor the changing landscape of family life for Britons more generally. Its aim is to try and ensure Muslims comply with the current law, however unsuitable that law may be, and the approach of both the Bill and the Review is one of patronising containment.

The Review reluctantly concedes the impracticality of any attempts to ban sharia councils. Yet it does not really explore the spiritual significance of a religious divorce to Muslim women nor the potential harms to those women from curtailing access to a religious source that will grant them religious freedom through divorce. Its three main recommendations lack innovation or creativity. First, the Review recommended that the Marriage Act should be amended to require a civil marriage ceremony to be conducted before or at the same time as a religious ceremony. As part of this recommendation the Review sought to criminalise a celebrant or officiant to a *nikah* who failed to ensure that the marriage was also civilly registered. Secondly, it recommended awareness and education campaigns to educate and inform Muslim women, and, thirdly, regulation of sharia councils was seen as desirable and necessary. Both the Bill and the Review retreat to the safe space of placing the onus on Muslims to conform to a legal framework of marriage laws that is becoming progressively unsuitable for Britons more generally. The language of 'compatibility' and 'integration' continues to frame Muslim communities as homogenised guests who must be encouraged or even forced through criminalisation to follow 'our laws and customs' in order to fully participate in 'our societies'. While awareness and education campaigns are always important for informed choices, the evidence that we have demonstrates many Muslims are aware that their religious marriages are not legally valid. What may be more useful is to take the approach of the Law Commission and address ways in which the legal framework can meet the challenges of diversity through understanding the practices of different communities. Furthermore, we can question the law's insistence at protecting recognised marital unions when increasing numbers of adults are choosing to cohabit rather than marry.

Neither the Bill nor the Review explore the ways in which Muslim women may be supported in accessing religious authority nor of sharia councils in the UK being encouraged to engage with Muslim majority countries where family laws have continued to develop. Little thought is given to the importance of research and supporting intra-religious discussions concerning the ways in which

---

[54]   Parveen (n16).

civil law may be used by Muslim women in attaining a religious divorce. It is only the Law Commission that considered *the law* itself to be part of the problem.

Conclusion

There is no doubt that English marriage and divorce laws have a long, intertwined history with Christianity and the legacy of colonisation. While civil divorce law has recently undergone a significant shift away from its fault-based preconditions, the regulation of the marriage ceremony continues to reflect the country's Christian norms and heritage. Reforms have produced some benefits over the decades, but as the Law Commission research and recommendations suggest, more comprehensive change is needed. Muslim couples bring added layers of complexity, though there is nothing particularly unique about communities wishing to undertake marriage or divorce in ways that reflect their cultural, religious, and familial heritage. When it comes to the legal framework of marriage, this should be simpler and fairer to all members of the community.

Civil divorce law is now simpler but does not fully address Muslim women's need for religious divorce. The law and policy makers are wrestling with competing and at times contradictory positions when it comes to sharia councils, which do provide solutions despite their many shortcomings. On the one hand, the law is pursuing policies of privatisation by encouraging parties to enter into private mediation to resolve the consequences of the breakdown of their relationships. Coupled with the removal of legal aid, parties may have little choice but to attempt to navigate management of disputes concerning children or finances themselves, whether through mediation or as litigants in person in court proceedings. On the other hand, the state is very concerned by the existence of sharia councils which are providing a form of faith-based alternative dispute resolution. While parties are increasingly encouraged to negotiate in the 'shadow of the law' without the state seeking to be involved, conversely the state has been most vociferous regarding Muslim dispute-resolution practices. For British Muslims, there is much internal negotiation and discussion to be had. How should they interpret or reinterpret Islamic rules of marriage and divorce as a minority community within a civil law system? What are the ways in which civil law can be beneficial to Muslims, particularly in achieving spiritual, religious, and practical justice, especially for Muslim women? More broadly, how has colonisation and its enduring legacy influenced the ways in which former colonial powers now engage with communities whose heritage is as former colonial subjects? Additionally, how does the state approach its interactions with its minority religious communities, whose understandings of justice, equality, and accountability are shaped by different lived experiences? These are not matters to be solved through force, but rather deeper reflection, engagement, and an acknowledgment of the layered complexities of all family life.

Further questions to consider

- How should the law approach diversity of marriage and divorce practices?
- In what ways could English law of marriage recognise different types of marriages?
- Should parties to relationships similar to marriages (such as cohabitees) be granted the same rights and obligations as married couples? Why, or why not?
- Should the law do anything about sharia councils? If so, what?
- How could sharia councils in England and Wales engage with developments in Muslim family law in other parts of the world? How would this benefit Muslims living in the UK?
- Should the law use criminal penalties as a way of ensuring Muslims (or indeed any other minorities) comply with the requirements of English family law?
- What interests does the law protect by having marriage and divorce laws?
- Do Muslim women need special protections?

Further materials

Ali SS, 'Authority and Authenticity: Sharia Councils, Muslim Women's Rights, and the English Courts' (2013) 25 Child and Family Law Quarterly 113

Douglas G and others, 'Social Cohesion and Religious Law: Marriage, Divorce and Religious Courts' Cardiff Law School (2011) https://orca.cardiff.ac.uk/id/eprint/10788/1/Social%20Cohesion%20and%20Civil%20Law%20Full%20Report.pdf, accessed 13 June 2025

Malik M, 'Minority Legal Systems in the UK: Multiculturalism, Minorities and the Law' British Academy Policy Papers (2012) https://www.thebritishacademy.ac.uk/documents/289/Minority_Legal_Orders_report_WEB.pdf, accessed 13 June 2025

Norton JC and Ahmed F, 'Religious Tribunals, Religious Freedom and Concern for Vulnerable Women' (2012) 24 Child and Family Law Quarterly 4, 363

11

Participation of Children in Family Justice Processes

Connie Healy

Introduction

The place of the child within the family, and indeed their role within society has always been an emotive issue. Stone and Aries,[1] for example, propose the theory that 'childhood' did not exist in mediaeval times. Though not asserting that parents did not love and care for their children, in early law children were viewed more as a benefit to families, 'primarily as agents for the devolution of property within an organized family setting ... as furthering the interests of the family group as a whole and over time by maintaining and perhaps extending the family's land holding'.[2] Educating children, therefore, was useful as a means of possibly increasing their father's role within society but was not undertaken for the benefit of the particular child itself. The welfare of the child was inextricably linked with the welfare of the father. The father's right as guardian of his child would only be questioned if his actions were likely to have an adverse effect on the society in which he lived: 'The earliest measures for dealing with child neglect were activated solely by concerns about social cohesion rather than the implementation of the children's interests in their own right.'[3] There was some transition throughout the 15th and 16th centuries when children came to be recognised as a 'significant family member, to be nurtured and protected'.[4] These changes were first felt among the wealthier classes, who began to acknowledge the

---

[1] L Stone, *The Family, Sex and Marriage in England 1500–1800* (abridged edn, Penguin 1990); P Aries, *Centuries of Childhood* (Jonathan Cape 1962).

[2] J Eekelaar, 'The Emergence of Children's Rights' (1986) 6(2) Oxford Journal of Legal Studies 161, 163.

[3] Ibid, 168.

[4] RC Akhtar and C Nyamutata, *International Child Law* (4nd edn, Routledge 2020). 2

child's place within the family and their need for education, but such recognition was limited and not applicable across all class structures. It is perhaps then no wonder that deMause commented that '[t]he history of childhood is a nightmare from which we have only recently begun to awaken'.[5]

This chapter will examine such awakening, the extent to which it may have occurred with regard to children's participation in private family justice processes, and the frequent discrepancy between legal expectations and the reality in practice for children in private family law processes at a time of family transition.[6] The chapter highlights the barriers and difficulties that children encounter in exerting their right to be heard within family justice, whether in the court process or alternative means of dispute resolution such as negotiated settlement by lawyers, mediation, collaborative practice, or arbitration. Written from a children's rights perspective, it will encourage students to question whether adult stakeholders, parents, lawyers, mediators, and the judiciary are, perhaps inadvertently, causing or perpetuating this denial of rights and why this is so. In a modern era, where the concept of 'family' has evolved to encompass diverse forms, individuals enjoy greater autonomy in defining their identities, and children are leading debates into environmental and social issues, why do we persist in limiting children's participation in decisions concerning arrangements following the fracture of parental relationships?

An analysis of the trajectory of children's rights reveals a battle between the importance of upholding these rights and the desire to protect children. Strong opposition to the notion of children as autonomous rights holders comes principally from the supporters of the welfarist approach, arguing that children should be protected from adult concerns.[7] Questions arise such as: can participation lead children to feel anxious and have a conflicted sense of loyalty to their parents?[8] Is there a danger of children being manipulated by adults into promoting either parent's agenda? Conversely, what are the implications for a parent's due process rights if professionals unconsciously permit this to happen?[9]

---

[5] L deMause (ed), *The History of Childhood* (Souvenir Press 1976) 1–2.

[6] Private family law proceedings refer to private actions taken by individuals, for example, seeking a separation or divorce. Public family law proceedings occur, for example, when applications are made by the state to take children into the care of the state in specified cases where parents may be unable to care for them. In general, more support is in place for children and families within the public law system.

[7] M Guggenheim, *What's Wrong with Children's Rights* (Harvard University Press 2007).

[8] J Rawls, *A Theory of Justice* (OUP 1971) 462.

[9] N Taylor, 'What Do We Know about Involving Children and Young People in Family Law Decision Making? A Research Update' (2006) 20 Australian Journal of Family Law 154, 160; J Cashmore and P Parkinson, 'Children's Participation in Family Law Disputes: The Views of Children, Parents and Counsellors' (2009) 82 Family Matters 16; F Garwood, 'Children in Conciliation: The Experiment of Involving Children in Conciliation (1990) 28 Family and Conciliation Court Review 43, 49. See also R Emery, 'Children's Voices: Listening – and Deciding – is an Adult Responsibility' (2003) 45(3) Arizona Law Review 621.

Additional uncertainty arguably exists in determining what rights children are 'capable' of exercising and who should assist them in enforcing those rights. While parents, for the most part, may act in the 'best interests' of their children, can lawyers, mediators, and the judiciary continue to accept parents' partisan views without ensuring that the individuals most affected by these decisions – the children – are at least given the opportunity to voice their needs and concerns in navigating the significant changes imposed upon them?[10] Multiple studies conducted with children highlight their wish to be heard and have their opinions considered.[11] As noted by Morrison, 'children repeatedly tell researchers they need' a 'system of child advocacy that ensures independent advice, ongoing support and trusting relationships'.[12]

This chapter will begin by outlining the law underpinning children's rights and the extent to which children are heard. Next it will consider the impact of the particular dispute resolution process chosen by their parents on the voice of the child, namely: the adversarial court process or alternative methods of dispute resolution, negotiated settlement, arbitration, collaborative law, or mediation.[13] It will outline barriers to participation for children and, drawing on existing research, recommend steps that could be taken to reduce or remove those roadblocks. The chapter will conclude by acknowledging that children are resilient. The system needs to respect and foster that resilience by providing them, as an integral part of the changing family, with the information and support necessary to participate so that, as a matter of respect and upholding their rights, consideration is given to their views within family justice processes.

---

[10] C Healy, ' "Still My Parents' Child": Breaking through the Barriers of Determining Best Interests and the Voice of the Child Post-Separation and Divorce' (2021) 3 Child and Family Law Quarterly 237.

[11] The Family Solutions Group ((Subgroup of the Private Law Working Group), ' "What about Me?" (2020) https://www.judiciary.uk/wp-content/uploads/2020/11/FamilySolutionsGroupReport_WhatAboutMe_12November2020-2.pdf-final-2.pdf, accessed 13 June 2025; Healy (n10); C Healy, 'Resolution of Conflict in Family Law Matters: An Alternative and Child-Inclusive Approach' https://search.library.nuigalway.ie/primo-explore/fulldisplay?docid=353GAL_ARAN_DS10379%2F4415&context=L&vid=353GAL_VUJ&lang=en_US&search_scope=PRIMO_CENTRAL&adaptor=Local%20Search%20Engine&tab=local&query=any,contains,resolution%20of%20conflict&offset=0, accessed 29 April 2025; F Morrison, K Tisdall, and J Callaghan, 'Manipulation and Domestic Abuse in Contested Contact: Threats to Children's Participation' (2020) 58(2) Family Court Review 403.

[12] Morrison, Tisdall, and Callaghan (n11).

[13] Early neutral evaluation may also be considered. Here, an independent professional, often a barrister, will meet with the parties and actively assist them to reach settlement. Other hybrid models may also be used, for example, Med-Arb: mediation is attempted first and if unsuccessful, the matter will proceed to arbitration

Outline of the law on the child's right to participate

A central turning point in children's rights internationally was the adoption of the United Nations Convention on the Rights of the Child (UNCRC) in 1989. The UNCRC has been ratified by every county in the world except for the United States.[14] The Convention recognised children as rights holders. Its guiding principles centre around: non-discrimination (Art 2); the best interests of the child (Art 3); life, survival, and development (Art 6); and the voice of the child (Art 12). While acknowledging the importance of family as a fundamental unit in society,[15] it recognised the evolving capacity of the child in exercising these rights.[16] The Convention also imposes obligations on parents to uphold these rights and state parties to support parents and children in this endeavour.[17] The Committee on the Rights of the Child was established to provide guidance on the interpretation of the Convention and to report on states' adherence to its principles.

Determining children's 'best interests' (Art 3) has, however, been problematic. Framed as a standard that allowed for flexibility and consideration of the needs of each individual child, it has been criticised for being 'vastly indeterminate',[18] with this uncertainty leading to increased litigation and the potential for wide judicial discretion. While judicial discretion is important to allow full consideration of each child's particular circumstances, there can be a disconnect between the judge's world view and the specific socio-economic circumstances and intersectional background of the child before them, meaning that children from diverse or marginalised communities may not be heard or fully understood. Fuller argues that the '"best interests" standard is more aspirational in nature than a strict legal principle to guide custody decision-making'.[19] In an effort to address these concerns and provide some clarity, the Committee on the Rights of the Child published General Comment No 14,[20] describing the 'best interests' principle as a threefold concept encompassing:

---

14 UN Treaty Body Database, 'Ratification Status for the Convention on the Rights of the Child' https://treaties.un.org/Pages/ViewDetails.aspx?src=TREATY&mtdsg_no=IV-11&chapter=4&clang=_en, accessed 10 June 2024.

15 Preamble, UNCRC.

16 Article 5 of the UNCRC.

17 Article 18 of the UNCRC.

18 R Mnookin, 'Child Custody Adjudication: Judicial Functions in the Face of Indeterminacy' (1975) 39 Law and Contemporary Problems 226.

19 L Fuller, 'Human Interaction and the Law' (1969) 14 American Journal of Jurisprudence 1.

20 UNCRC, General Comment No 14 'On the Right of the Child to Have His or Her Best Interests Taken as a Primary Consideration' (2013) Art 3, para 1 https://www2.ohchr.org/english/bodies/crc/docs/gc/crc_c_gc_14_eng.pdf, accessed 13 June 2025.

(a) a substantive right to have their best interests taken into account;
(b) an interpretative principle outlining the importance of legal provisions being interpreted in a way which most effectively serves the 'best interests' of a child; and
(c) a rule of procedure to ensure that there is a framework in place to facilitate the assessment and determination of what is in the child's 'best interests'.

The Committee also clarified that justification of the decision must be provided and the extent to which the best interests of the child were considered outlined.[21] Specifically, in the context of this chapter, the Committee outlined the importance of participation for children in reaching any determination on what is in their best interests and the: 'complementary role' of participation under Article 12 in ensuring that the best interests of the child are accurately determined. The Commission went as far as saying that there 'can be no correct application of article 3 if the components of article 12 are not respected. Likewise, article 3 reinforces the functionality of article 12, facilitating the essential role of children in all decisions affecting their lives.'[22]

So, what does Article 12 provide and why is it considered one of the fundamental provisions of the Convention that underpins all others? Article 12 of the Convention provides that:

1. States Parties *shall assure* to the child who is capable of forming his or her own views the right to express those views freely in all matters affecting the child, the views of the child being given due weight in accordance with the age and maturity of the child.
2. For this purpose, the child shall in particular be provided the opportunity to be heard in any judicial and administrative proceedings affecting the child, either directly, or through a representative or an appropriate body, in a manner consistent with the procedural rules of national law.[23]

While the Convention has been, as noted earlier, widely ratified, its incorporation into domestic law has not been as promising. Legal systems are often slow to adapt and change. In 1998, almost ten years after the Convention came into force, Neale and Smart described the 'child of legal discourse' as:

primarily a dependent, who is defined within a developmental, welfarist and protectionist framework. Biologically, children are perceived in developmental terms as in the process of becoming and hence, their incompetence, irrationality and structural powerlessness are taken for granted. Legally they are minors ... in need of protection

---

[21] Ibid.
[22] UN Committee on the Rights of the Child, General Comment No 12 'The Right of the Child to be Heard' (UN Doc UNCRC/C/GC/12, 1 July 2009) para 74 https://www.refwo rld.org/legal/general/crc/2009/en/70207, accessed 13 June 2025.
[23] Ibid.

and, therefore, justifiably subordinate to adults ... The child of legal discourse is a somewhat generalised, theoretical child rather than a real, embodied, biographically unique and socially differentiated child.[24]

In 2010, the publication of the 'Guidelines of the Committee of Ministers of the Council of Europe on Child-Friendly Justice' in 2010, again highlighted the importance of upholding children's rights 'to participate in and to understand the proceedings'.[25] In attempting to break down the elements of participation and provide a working definition, the Voice of the Child Dispute Resolution Advisory Board, established by UK Ministry for Justice in 2015, defined child-inclusive practice as one which

> allows children and young people the opportunity to have a conversation (verbal, written, through play or storytelling) with professionals who are assisting their parents to make arrangements for the children's future. It enables consenting children and young people to share their experiences of parental/family separation and express their concerns and views, and for these to be sensitively considered with their parents so that their developmental needs and concerns can be better understood and taken into account within the dispute resolution process.[26]

Therefore, embodying the Child-Friendly Justice Guidelines, guidance from the Committee on the Rights of the Child, and attempts already noted at defining child-inclusive practice, the Lundy model of participation is widely recognised as providing a structured framework within which to ensure the children's rights are upheld. The model is based on four pillars:

- *Space*: providing the child with information, time, and space to consider and formulate their views;
- *Voice:* appropriate means to express those views and assistance to do so;

---

[24] B Neale and C Smart, 'Agents or Dependants? Struggling to Listen to Children in Family Law and Family Research' (1998) University of Leeds Centre for Research on Family, Kinship and Childhood Working Paper 3, 2 https://d1wqtxts1xzle7.cloudfront.net/30812 612/WP3_Neale_Smart-libre.pdf?1363387667=&response-content-disposition=inline%3B+ filename%3DAgents_or_Dependants_Struggling_to_Liste.pdf&Expires=1751967317&Signat ure=YpEy8-nljVnZMzTn~pDfeBJSFhlQMcuhBC0zmkJUF9298, accessed 13 June 2025.

[25] 'Guidelines of the Committee of Minsters of the Council of Europe on Child-Friendly Justice' (2010) https://rm.coe.int/16804b2cf3#:~:text=Justice%20should%20be%20children's%20fri end,them%20and%20be%20their%20friend, accessed 13 June 2025.

[26] UK Ministry of Justice, 'Voice of the Child: Dispute Resolution Advisory Group Report' (2015) https://assets.publishing.service.gov.uk/government/uploads/system/uploads/attachme nt_data/file/421005/voice-of-the-child-advisory-group-report.pdf, accessed 13 June 2025.

- *Audience*: that those views will be listened to and respected by decision makers; and
- *Influence*: feedback on the impact, if any of the views expressed on the final decision made, what weight was attributed to them, and clear explanations when final decisions made by parents or professionals differed from the stated wishes of those who chose to participate.[27]

Transcending national boundaries and the inadequacies in domestic legislation, the model provides a framework for professionals working within family justice processes and one which places the rights of the child front and centre. The following sections of this chapter will outline the key dispute resolution processes currently available to separating parents with a specific focus on child participation, namely, the adversarial court process or negotiated settlement, mediation, collaborative law (also known as collaborative practice or collaborative divorce), and arbitration, and assess how closely, if at all, they comply with the Lundy model of participation.

Summary

While relevant provisions under the Children Act (CA) 1989 will be outlined, as appropriate, in examining the options that are available for children to participate within the adversarial court process in England, Article 12 of the UNCRC, as outlined earlier, is considered the golden standard in ensuring a voice for children within the court process and through alternative methods of dispute resolution. Barriers at national level, including the lack of legislation directly incorporating the Convention in many jurisdictions, and arguably a paternalistic culture within the legal profession, has meant that progress on ensuring an effective, rights-based participation process for children within family justice processes has been quite limited.

Court process

Since April 2024, with the introduction of Practice Direction Update No 5 2024 ('Non-Court Dispute Resolution'),[28] there is now a requirement for all

---

[27] Professor L Lundy, 'Lundy Model of Child Participation' https://commission.europa.eu/sys tem/files/2022-12/lundy_model_of_participation_0.pdf, accessed 13 June 2025.

[28] Practice Direction Update No 5 2024 'Non-Court Dispute Resolution' https://www.just ice.gov.uk/documents/fpr-pd-update-no-5-of-2024.pdf, accessed 13 June 2025. Section 1a(1): 'The pre-application protocol annexed to this Practice Direction (Annex 2) outlines the steps parties should take before starting any court proceedings, including trying to resolve their dispute by non-court dispute resolution, where this is safe and appropriate. It also outlines sources of support and information available to parties. The court will expect parties to comply with the pre-application protocol.'

persons considering issuing court proceedings to attempt settlement through non-court-based methods of dispute resolution as a first step, unless there are any safety reasons, for example, allegations or evidence of domestic violence. These non-court dispute resolution methods include, but are not limited to mediation, explained in more detail later. Where such attempts at resolution have been unsuccessful, aggrieved parties, such as a parent who feels that they have been denied access to their children, may apply through the court process.

The CA 1989 is the key piece of legislation which governs applications relating to children in private family law proceedings. Section 1 of the Act provides that the welfare of the child is paramount and a checklist of factors to be considered can be found therein. Under section 1(3) regard must be given to the 'ascertainable wishes and feelings' of the child in light of their 'age and understanding'. A judge may, under section 7(1) of the 1989 Act, direct the Children and Family Court Advisory and Support Service (Cafcass) to produce a report on 'such matters relating to the welfare of the child as are required'. Cafcass is a body, sponsored by the Ministry of Justice, whose role is to represent the interests of children and young people.[29] Section 7 reports assist the court in determining, among other things, where the child shall reside and what, if any, contact they will have with a non-resident parent. These reports will also note any concerns that public bodies such as the child/children's school may have in relation to their attendance or care, and also issues that any healthcare workers or the police may be aware of. On occasion, if a judge has a particular concern in relation to any aspect of the child/children's upbringing, welfare, or care, or if any specific allegations have been made against either parent, such as allegations of abuse or mistreatment, the court can direct that these issues be addressed in the report. The family court advisers employed by Cafcass will speak to the children and it has therefore been argued that section 7 incorporates elements of Article 12 of the UNCRC by providing children with a voice in the proceedings. Indeed, research undertaken by Hargreaves shows that such reports are the 'most common marker of participation' for children whose parents' cases come before the court, although opportunities for children to engage with Cafcass in these types of situations can be limited to one-off, sometimes half-hour, conversations.[30] Nevertheless, children who were given the opportunity to engage through Cafcass, overwhelmingly described engagement with them as 'helpful'.[31]

---

[29] Cafcass was formed under the Parliament (Criminal Justice and Court Services Act) 2000. Section 12 of the Act provides that the services of Cafcass are available to public and private family law cases.

[30] C Hargreaves and others, 'Uncovering Private Family Law: How Often Do We Hear the Voice of the Child?' Nuffield Family Justice Observatory (2024) https://www.nuffieldfjo.org.uk/resource/uncoveringprivate-family-law-how-often-do-we-hear-the-voice of the child, accessed 13 June 2025.

[31] S Bailey, J Thoburn, and J Timms, 'Your Shout Too! Children's Views of the Arrangements Made and Services Provided when Courts Adjudicate in Private Law Disputes' (2011) 33(2) Journal of Social Welfare and Family Law 123.

Despite section 7 reports being the key documents relied upon by the courts in assessing a child's needs, research highlights that, in practice, almost half of children in private family law matters were not given any opportunity to contribute to these assessments.[32] This may be due to the procedures themselves. For example, the Child Arrangements Programme under Practice Direction 12B requires parents to attend a First Hearing Dispute Resolution Appointment (FHDRA) and prohibits direct consultation with children before the first dispute resolution meeting.[33] Where issues are resolved by parents during this first meeting, or otherwise settled privately, there is no statutory mechanism in place to mandate or ensure that the views of children of the relationship are sought.[34]

What happens if the children of the relationship are unhappy with the order made by the court? Section 10 of the CA 1989 also complies with the spirit of Article 12 of the UNCRC, which has been described as 'morally authoritative' in England and Wales,[35] in that it arguably provides a mechanism for children who are unhappy with orders made to seek a variation.[36] The process is, however, protracted. Permission has to be sought from a High Court judge before an application can be made and such order will only be made if, under section10(8), the court is satisfied that the child has sufficient understanding.[37] Measures like this, while 'ticking the box' of requirements by providing theoretical opportunities for children to voice concerns about decisions that affect them, are in reality almost impossible for children to action. The evidence suggests that children, in fact, frequently try to act as peace brokers between their parents or are often concerned with hurting or being seeming disloyal to one or other parent.[38] They are, therefore, unlikely to attempt to initiate such proceedings. Crucially, even if they wished to do so, there is a lack of suitable supports in place to allow them to access such processes, especially where children may be further disadvantaged by socio-economic constraints.

Appointment of a guardian ad litem

Where cases are more complex or specific concerns are raised, a child may be added as a party to proceedings. In these cases, a guardian ad litem (GAL) will be appointed to meet with the child. Their role is to hear the wishes and

---

[32] Hargreaves and others (n29).

[33] Practice Direction 12B – Child Arrangements Programme, para 13.6 https://www.justice.gov. uk/courts/procedure-rules/family/practice_directions/pd_part_12b, accessed 13 June 2025.

[34] A Cafcass officer 'will not initiate contact with the child prior to the FHDRA [First Hearing Dispute Resolution Appointment]' (PD12B, para 13.6).

[35] *A City Council v T, J and K* [2011, EWHC] Fam 1082.

[36] CA 1989, s 10.

[37] Section 10(8): 'Where the person applying for leave to make an application for a section 8 order is the child concerned, the court may only grant leave if it is satisfied that he has sufficient understanding to make the proposed application for the section 8 order.'

[38] Healy (n10).

views of the child and to advise the court as to what they consider in the child's best interests.[39] A GAL is typically more likely to be appointed for older children who, with the benefit of age and maturity, may freely express a wish to participate and be separately represented. In addition, the GAL may appoint a solicitor to represent the child in court. This model, often referred to as the 'tandem model', has been viewed as a 'Rolls-Royce model',[40] arguably providing the best opportunity for children to have their voices heard and their rights protected within the adversarial system. Children of a younger age may not have the capacity to seek the appointment of a GAL or a view may be taken by the courts that they are not of an age and maturity to express a view. Although this dismissal of the views of younger children often happens within the court process, it is contrary to the spirit of the UNCRC, which applies to all children regardless of their age.[41] Indeed, it has been specifically stated by the Committee on the Rights of the Child that age limits are not to be imposed.[42] Concerns, however, have been raised about the paternalistic nature of this model, with the danger that the child's own voice may get lost in an arguably protracted process, where solicitors are taking instructions from the GAL rather that from the child directly.[43] It would appear also from the statistics gathered by Cafcass that the number of cases where this 'tandem model' is actually provided for children is, when compared to the number of cases coming before the courts, quite low.[44]

The judicial interview

In disputes before the adversarial courts, another option is for the judge hearing the case to hold an interview with the children and seek their views directly. Guidelines were published by the Family Justice Council's Voice of the Child Committee in 2010 to assist members of the judiciary around this process.[45] These guidelines refer to the judge's *discretion* to consult the children having

---

[39]   16.4 of the Family Procedure Rules 2010.

[40]   *Mabon v Mabon & Ors* [2005] EWCA Civ 634.

[41]   General Comment No 12 of the UNCRC, para 21 'The Committee emphasizes that article 12 imposes no age limit on the right of the child to express her or his views, and discourages States parties from introducing age limits either in law or in practice which would restrict the child's right to be heard in all matters affecting her or him.'

[42]   Ibid.

[43]   A Parkes, *Children and International Human Rights Law: The Right of the Child to be Heard* (Routledge 2013) 107; G Douglas, 'Research into the Operation of Rule 9.5 of the Family Proceedings Rules 1991: Final Report to the Department for Constitutional Affairs' (2006) 190 https://citeseerx.ist.psu.edu/document?repid=rep1&type=pdf&doi=849ca3dd341a9f8ac 840d1b2bba0b4d075a6f9a4, accessed 13 June 2025.

[44]   Children and Family Court Advisory and Support Service, 'Annual Report and Accounts' (2022) https://www.familieslink.co.uk/download/jan07/familyprocrules_research.pdf, accessed 7 July 2025.

[45]   'Guidelines for Judges Meeting Children Who Are Subject to Family Proceedings Produced by the Family Justice Council and Approved by the President of the Family Division' (April

'considered representations from the parties'.[46] Again, as set out earlier, judges may not be best placed to understand the backgrounds and socio-economic status of litigants who come before them and may accept without question that parents will always act in the best interests of their child. Depending on the family circumstances, parents may be less well placed due to financial restraints, cultural issues, being affected by illness or addictions, or a lack of adequate support services to clearly advocate for their child's wishes. The potential for judges, therefore, to be influenced by parents or their lawyers arguably places another roadblock to participation. Additionally, judges have expressed concern that they may not be appropriately qualified to speak to children and to detect issues such as undue influence by parents or alienating behaviours. Some judges are reluctant to interview children because of concerns that it be too traumatic for the child. Parkinson argues that 'few children and young people have the confidence to speak to a judge who is making the decision that concerns them'.[47] The views expressed, however, by children when they have been given the opportunity to speak to a judge seem to contradict this:

> My miracle moment came when the judge agreed to meet with me. I thought WOW! This is it, my proper chance to tell my story.[48]
>
> I am 13 now. I do have moments where I dread it happening again, but if it did, I would ask to speak to the judge straight away. No hesitation.[49]

Children recognise the need for proper supports to be put in place to ensure that they are given information in advance on the nature and format of this interview and what is expected of them. They have highlighted the need to 'keep dialogue open' and to 'reassure' them 'if they feel uncomfortable at any time, that the meeting can be paused'.[50] Children, therefore, already have an innate understanding of the Lundy participation model, the need for information and the space to consider it, a voice and appropriate audience to hear their views, and the importance of the influence such voice may have. One of the key considerations during these interviews, therefore, is the extent to which the discussion between the judge and the child is confidential. The 'Guidelines

---

2010) https://www.judiciary.uk/wp-content/uploads/JCO/Documents/FJC/voc/Guidelin es_+Judges_seeing_+Children.pdf, accessed 13 June 2025.

[46] Ibid.

[47] L Parkinson and P Johnson, *Conversations with Young People in Family Mediation* (Bloomsbury 2024).

[48] D Reeves (ed), *In Our Shoes: Experiences of Children and Young People in the Family Justice System, Family Justice Young People's Board (FYYPB) and CAFCASS* (1st edn, Shared Press 2021) 17 https://www.cafcass.gov.uk/sites/default/files/2023-06/In-our-shoes-full-book-for-downl oad.pdf, accessed 13 June 2025.

[49] Ibid, 18.

[50] Ibid, 14.

for Judges' mentioned refers to the fact that judges cannot hold secrets and that everything will be relayed to the child's parents.[51] This can affect children's willingness to be forthright with a judge due to concerns around what they may perceive, or what they fear their parents may perceive, as taking sides or disloyalty. Despite the changes and turmoil often going on at this time, children strive to be 'fair', splitting time equally between parents, often at personal cost. Providing them with a safe space to express their views can help relieve some of the burden attached to trying to achieve this 'fairness',[52] but they also need to know the influence such views will have.

Other methods of hearing the voice of the child within the court process include children expressing their views to a psychologist or expert commissioned by the courts or parents. Again, concerns arise as to the extent to which views expressed by children may be accurately reflected in final reports or whether, perhaps, these views have been interpreted from the perspective of the adults preparing the report. The children involved are not given an opportunity to review the report to check whether the report writer has accurately understood and interpreted their views. This may be appropriate when the children are young, but older children who understand the process should have the opportunity to see how their views have been reflected in the final report. Children have also, on occasion, often as a result of the frustration they feel at not being heard, chosen to write directly to the judge.

Summary

Technically, while legislation is in place and some support provided through agencies like Cafcass, much of the framework provided to hear the views of children within the court process is not always accessible and can be cumbersome for children to navigate. Additionally, much weight is placed on the views of parents as to what they consider to be in the 'best interests' of their children without any consultation with the children themselves. The most striking statistic, however, is that 90 per cent of child arrangements are thought to be made outside of the court process.[53] This is coupled with the new requirements of Practice Direction Update No 5 2024 that all potential litigants must attempt resolution before issuing court proceedings.

Negotiated settlement

If parties fulfil the required statutory criteria for divorce and have themselves agreed upon the financial issues and arrangements for any children of the

---

[51]   See (n44).

[52]   Healy (n10).

[53]   R Hunter, 'Statistics on Private Law Applications' (2021) https://committees.parliament.uk/writtenevidence/110556/pdf, accessed 13 June 2025.

marriage, they may apply online or through the post for divorce by consent.[54] While this process provides for a mandatory reflection period (20 weeks), there are no requirements in relation to hearing the voice of the child. Similarly, in cases where proceedings are issued, but are settled through negotiation between the lawyers acting for the parties, no statutory obligations arise. Research indicates that a large percentage of cases are settled by lawyers in this way. This cohort of children are therefore potentially totally excluded from the process.[55] Acknowledging that if cases are settled amicably and quickly parents may be better placed to keep the needs of their children in mind, rather than being involved in prolonged litigation, children nonetheless value the opportunity to be consulted. The lack of opportunity to do so leads to a breach of children's rights under the UNCRC.[56] Research has also shown that lawyers tend to accept the 'partisan views' of parents as to what the parents think are in the best interests of the child. Children and young adults whose parents separated recognise a perception by parents that 'the children are fine'.[57] Children highlight, nevertheless, that there were varying reasons why their parents, though well intentioned, may not have fully understood the impact of the separation on them: the feeling of insecurity, absence of any or any unbiased information, and the overarching sense of fear of the unknown.[58] Many jurisdictions require court approval or oversight of negotiated agreements in family law matters before final orders are made. Where court hearing lists are long, there is no guarantee, however, the arrangements made by parents are given the thorough consideration that it is argued is fundamental to the court process,[59] or that children's rights are being upheld.

Arbitration

Arbitration is a process whereby disputants agree to submit their disputes to an individual, frequently an expert in the relevant subject area, and this decision will be final and binding on the parties. Initially used as a means of resolving international or commercial disputes where each of the parties had equal bargaining power, more recently it has been used in the resolution of family law disputes. Advantages of this form of dispute resolution are that it is quicker and, in some cases, may be less expensive and more convenient than going to court.

---

[54]   Matrimonial Causes Act (MCA) 1973 s 1(5).

[55]   Section 17 of the Children and Families Act 2014 removes the requirement previously in place under section 41 of the MCA 1973, that courts have to certify arrangements for children in divorce. Parents, once they agree terms, therefore have full autonomy.

[56]   'Final Report of the Voice of the Child Dispute Resolution Advisory Group' (2015) para 79 https://assets.publishing.service.gov.uk/media/5a7f96cced915d74e33f75c9/voice-of-the-child-advisory-group-report.pdf, accessed 13 June 2025.

[57]   Healy (n10).

[58]   Ibid.

[59]   O Fiss, 'Against Settlement' (1986) 93(6) Yale Law Journal 1073.

The case of *S v S (Financial Remedies: Arbitral Award)* paved the way for the use of arbitration in resolving the financial disputes post separation or divorce.[60] The President of the Family Division, Sir James Munby, held that: 'There is no conceptual difference between the parties making an agreement and agreeing to give an arbitrator the power to make the decision for them.'[61] More recently, a case brought before the Court of Appeal in England and Wales, *Haley v Haley*,[62] has provided additional clarification around the extent to which arbitrator's decisions can be considered 'final' in family law matters. The question arose as to whether such cases could or indeed should be governed by the provisions of the Arbitration Act 1996,[63] or whether decisions are to be adjudicated under the relevant provisions of the MCA 1973.[64] Seminal family cases, for example *White v White* and *Miller v Miller*,[65] have reiterated the importance of 'fairness', with the Supreme Court reiterating that

> the overriding criterion to be applied in ancillary relief proceedings is that of fairness and identify the three strands of need, compensation and sharing that are relevant to the question of what is fair.[66]

The court in *Haley* has clarified that family law cases, decided by an arbitrator, are likewise to be determined on the basis of 'fairness' and as such, if the decision can be considered 'wrong', it is open to either party to appeal under the MCA 1973. Opinions on this clarification are varied. Some view it as the death knell of family law arbitration in that there is no longer the desired finality normally associated with arbitration in general. Others view it as providing a measure of comfort that will possibly encourage more couples to choose arbitration for family law cases.[67]

There are two distinct Family Arbitration Schemes in place in England, one, as mentioned earlier focuses on the 'financial issues' arising following relationship fracture. A second set of rules is now in place on children's issues. While many of the fundamental provisions are the same, special rules have been put in place by the Institute of Family Law Arbitrators for any cases which are heard under section 1 of the CA 1989 and Practice Direction 12B (Child Arrangements Programme). The fifth edition of the 'Family Law Arbitration Children Scheme

---

[60] *S v S (Financial Remedies: Arbitral Award* [2014] EWHC 7 (Fam).
[61] Ibid, para 19.
[62] *Haley v Haley* [2020] EWCA Civ 1369.
[63] Arbitration Act 1996 https://www.legislation.gov.uk/ukpga/1996/23/contents, accessed 13 June 2025.
[64] MCA 1973.
[65] *White v White* [2001] 1 AC 596; *Miller v Miller* [2006] UKHL 24.
[66] *Haley v Haley* [2020] EWCA Civ 1369 [43].
[67] A Heenan, '*Haley v Haley*: Family Law Arbitration and the New Frontier of Private Ordering', (2021) 84(6) Modern Law Review 1385.

Arbitration Rules',[68] published in 2021, provides that where parties propose the appointment of 'an independent social worker' to ascertain the views of the children, the arbitrator may approve this appointment. If parents wish to instruct someone but cannot agree on whom that should be, the arbitrator has authority to decide. As one would expect, provisions are in place for safeguarding children. This includes the arbitrator having a duty to determine whether a case is not suitable for arbitration and to notify relevant authorities if they have any concerns.

In the recent case of *G v G*,[69] Mr Justice Peel reiterated that in any children's dispute resolved through arbitration the same requirements apply to ensure that the paramountcy principle is followed, noting, 'the court's overarching duty to consider whether the order is consistent with the best interests of the children remains the same'.[70] Interestingly, examining these guidelines, the arbitrator of their own motion may also decide to seek a report on the children's best interests and such 'appointment may be made irrespective of whether or not the parties agree',[71] which is akin to giving the arbitrator the rights of a judge and is positive from a children's rights perspective. Of note also in the guidelines is the provision that the arbitrator may not meet with the child at any stage of the proceedings.[72] This is contrary to the position of a judge in a court hearing. The recent report by Douglas has highlighted this as a matter which needs to be amended.[73] Of course, proper training for arbitrators would be essential if this is to occur.

Collaborative practice

Collaborative law is another more recent addition to the alternative dispute-resolution framework that occurs outside of the court process. This section outlines how the process began and what it aims to achieve. One would expect that a collaborative approach would by its very nature and ethos provide an inclusive and easily accessible method of hearing the voice of the child and,

---

[68] Under these rules, arbitrators have authority to deal with residence and contact orders, issues such as education, internal relocation hearings and external relocations, but only to countries that are part of the Hague Convention. Safeguarding questionnaires need to be completed in advance of any hearing and independent social workers may be engaged to hear the views of children. While it is hoped that representatives from Cafcass, if already involved with the family, can also be heard, this is not always possible due to ongoing staffing issues at Cafcass: https://www.judiciary.uk/wp-content/uploads/2018/07/pfd-practice-guidance-child ren-arbitration.pdf, accessed 13 June 2025.

[69] *G v G* [2022] EWFC 151 14.

[70] Ibid, para 14.

[71] 'Family Law Arbitration Children Scheme Arbitration Rules 2021' (5th edn, 11 January 2021) 8.2.4 https://ifla.org.uk/wp-content/uploads/01-Rules-CS-April-2020.pdf, accessed 10 June 2024.

[72] Ibid, reg 8.3.

[73] G Douglas, 'Improving Access to Justice for Separating Families: A Report by JUSTICE' (2022) 74, para 3.73 https://justice.org.uk/our-work/civil-justice-system/current-work-civil-justice-system/improving-access-to-justice-for-separating-families/, accessed 10 June 2024.

arguably, it can through a child specialist, specifically trained for this purpose. It has not, however, delivered on this promise due in large part to barriers which include, as with other processes, a lack of financial resources and supports but perhaps, moreover, a reluctance by parents, lawyers, and other professionals to see or attach value to hearing the voice of the child purely as it was enshrined, for the benefit of the child itself.

The process began in the US in the early 1990s, requiring each party to instruct a collaborative lawyer to resolve the issues between them through a series of scheduled four-way meetings.[74] If settlement cannot be reached within the process, a disqualification clause prevents the lawyer acting for any of the parties in court. Many see the disqualification provision as being the most important element of the process. Others see it as placing additional pressure on the parties to settle.[75] The collaborative model developed into collaborative practice or collaborative divorce, providing a framework for separating parties to engage additional experts to assist with the negotiation, such as a financial specialist. For the purposes of this chapter, this might include a trained child specialist who will meet with the children of the relationship and bring their views back to the parents in a non-confrontational manner, both parents hearing the views at the same time. This avoids time delays and additional acrimony associated with written reports in the adversarial system.[76] All experts work together for the benefit of the family as a whole.[77]

Research undertaken internationally has shown that, on average, 80 per cent of cases settle within the process.[78] Reasons given for choosing this process include a desire to resolve issues more amicably in the best interests of the children of the relationship.[79] Despite the framework for a holistic, interdisciplinary approach, unfortunately the extent to which child specialists are engaged in England and Wales is relatively low.[80] In contrast, research undertaken by the International

---

[74] S Webb, 'Collaborative Law: A Practitioner's Perspective on its History and Current Practice' (2008) 21 Journal of the American Academy of Matrimonial Lawyers 155, 160; S Webb and R Ousky, *The Collaborative Way to Divorce: The Revolutionary Method that Results in Less Stress, Lower Costs, and Happier Kids – Without Going to Court* (Penguin 2006).

[75] J Lande, 'The Promise and Perils of Collaborative Law' (2005–06) 12 Dispute Resolution Magazine 29.

[76] S Gamache, 'The Role of the Child Specialist' in N Cameron, *Collaborative Practice: Deepening the Dialogue* (Continuing Legal Education Society of British Columbia 2004).

[77] P Tesler and P Thompson, *Collaborative Divorce, The Revolutionary New Way to Reconstruct Your Family, Resolve Legal Issues, and Move On with Your Life* (HarperCollins 2007).

[78] J Macfarlane, 'The Emerging Phenomenon of Collaborative Family Law (CFL): A Qualitative Case Study' Department of Justice Canada (2005) https://www.justice.gc.ca/eng/rp-pr/fl-lf/famil/2005_1/index.html#a01, accessed 7 July 2025; International Academy of Collaborative Professionals www.collaborativepractice.com, accessed 17 June 2025; M Sefton, 'Collaborative Family Law: A Report for Resolution', Association of Family Lawyers in the UK; C Healy, *Collaborative Practice: An International Perspective* (Routledge 2017).

[79] Healy (n77) 82.

[80] A Barlow and others, 'Mapping Paths to Family Justice: A National Picture of Findings on Out of Court Family Dispute Resolution' (2013) 43 Family Law 306.

Academy of Collaborative Professionals in the US in 2010 noted that 68 per cent of cases engaged a child specialist as part of a team model and 24 per cent as part of a referral model.[81] This may be because it is a relatively new process in England, an underlying reluctance to engage with the arguably more difficult emotional issues, or, once again, the dichotomy between parents wish to protect children believing that they are acting in their best interests and the child's needs and rights to have a voice.

Mediation

Mediation, as discussed by the respective authors of Chapters 8, 9, and 10 in this volume, is an interests-based method of dispute resolution during which a neutral mediator actively assists the separating parties to reach a mutually acceptable agreement. Interests-based methods focus the separating parties on trying to reach a solution that meets their combined 'interests' rather than adopting the win/lose approach seen within the court system where parents may take a positional stance, refusing to consider anything but their own individual needs. Taking an interest-based approach aims to find a solution that works, as best as can be achieved, for both parties. Mediation is viewed as being particularly suitable for family law matters. Matters discussed during the mediation process remain confidential. In recent years, jurisdictions vary as to whether parties can be obligated to attend mediation. A recent decision of the Court of Appeal in England and Wales *Churchill v Merthyr Tydfil County Borough Council and Ors* paved the way for the possibility of mandatory mediation,[82] holding:

> The court can lawfully stay proceedings for, or order, the parties to engage in a non-court-based dispute resolution process provided that order made does not impair the very essence of the claimant's right to proceed to a judicial hearing and is proportionate to achieving the legitimate aim of settling the dispute fairly, quickly and at reasonable cost.[83]

The introduction of Practice Direction Update No 5 2024 in April,[84] as noted earlier, in response to the Churchill decision, will more than likely result in an increase in the number of persons seeking to resolve matters through mediation. The importance of mediation as a dispute resolution process in family law matters was acknowledged by the Committee on the Rights of the Child in 2009 and, correspondingly, the importance of children having an equal right to participation within the mediation process was affirmed: 'all legislation on separation and

---

[81] C Healy, 'The Child Specialist' (2012) 12(1) The Collaborative Review 22.
[82] [2023] EWCA Civ 1416.
[83] Ibid, 32.
[84] Practice Direction Update No 5 2024 (n27).

divorce has to include the right of the child to be heard by decision makers and in mediation processes'.[85] Parents and mediators take the view that where parents can agree the terms of the separation there is no need or benefit in involving their children in the process. They seem to 'implicitly share a view that children are not competent to understand the issues involved and participate in decision making, or that they should not be asked to take responsibility for decisions that are properly the responsibility of adults, and parents in particular'.[86]

One would expect, therefore, that, in upholding the rights of children to be heard within the mediation process as outlined and the argued advantages of such a process in providing a more 'family-friendly' approach to justice, mediators would be leading the way. Research undertaken internationally, has however shown that mediation largely remains child-focused at best, rather than child-inclusive.[87] In Australia, McIntosh compared outcomes from child-focused (indirect) and child-inclusive mediation for parents and their children. In the child-focused group, the mediator moved away from the traditional neutral role and actively advocated for the children in dialogue with the parents, seeking to educate the parents and provide therapeutic assistance to them to enable them to focus more on the children's needs. In the child-inclusive group, an independent qualified social services professional held a consultation with the child about their experiences of family separation 'in a supportive developmentally appropriate forum'.[88] The independent specialist then met with the mediator and the children's parents and reported back to the parents the issues which the children wanted to be brought to their attention. Sibling groups were seen together as well as having individual time. The research took place over one year. It was found that while both interventions led to less conflict and better resolution of conflict, where it did occur, '[a]greements reached by the child-inclusive group were significantly more durable and workable over the year, and these parents were half as likely to instigate new litigation over parenting matters in the year after

---

85 Committee on the Rights of the Child, General Comment No 12 'The Right of the Child to be Heard' (CRC/C/GC/12, 20 July 2009) 52 https://www.refworld.org/docid/4ae562 c52.html, accessed 17 June 2025.

86 AL James and others, 'The Voice of the Child in Family Mediation: Norway and England' (2010) 15 International Journal of Children's Rights 313, 314.

87 J McIntosh, Y Wells, and C Long, 'Child-Focused and Child-Inclusive Family Law Dispute Resolution: One-Year Findings from a Prospective Study of Outcomes' (2007) 13 Journal of Family Studies 8; J Goldson, 'Hello, I'm Voice, Let Me Talk: Child-Inclusive Mediation in Family Separation' Families Commission, Innovative Practice Report No 1/06 (December 2006) https://thefamilymatterscentre.co.nz/wp-content/uploads/2015/08/Hello_Im_A_Vo ice.pdf/, accessed 7 July 2025; A O'Kelly, 'How Do Children and Young People in Ireland Experience the Process of their Parents' Separation and Divorce and Subsequent Changed Family Life? Giving Recognition to Children's Experiences' (2017) https://aran.library.nuigal way.ie/handle/10379/6498, accessed 5 December 2023; A Barlow and J Ewing, *Children's Voices, Family Disputes and Child-Inclusive Mediation: The Right to Be Heard* (Bristol University Press 2024).

88 McIntosh, Wells, and Long (n86) 8.

mediation than the child-focused parents'.[89] After the child-inclusive process, children reported better relationships with their fathers, a reduction in parental conflict, and perceived their mothers to be more understanding. Of the adult participants who took part in the child-inclusive model, 'the majority named the feedback from their children as the greatest assistance in the resolution of their dispute' and, importantly, 'one-year post-intervention, no detrimental outcomes of child participation were reported by parents or children in any case in this sample. The vast majority of the children found the interview, although confined to a single session, helpful.'[90]

Similar research was conducted in New Zealand, however, in this study, the mediator meeting the parents also met separately with the children. The research findings were similar to the Australian study. On hearing their children express the need for co-operation between parents in arriving at decisions, parents had a heightened level of awareness of the impact of their decisions on their children's lives. Children, too, felt that this process gave them an opportunity to have a voice and that they were better able to cope with their parents' separation as a result of being given the opportunity to be heard. An important conclusion was the need for parents to refocus from claiming rights over their children to taking responsibility for them. This, Goldson found, 'led to the child being buffered from conflict, and enhanced that child's ability to develop greater resilience'.[91]

Research undertaken by O'Kelly in Ireland again supports these findings. A participant in O'Kelly's research commented that 'even though the change she desired did not occur, her involvement in the mediation process re-assured her that her concerns were taken seriously':

> I wanted to spend more time at my Mam's house. My Mam tried to sort it out, but I'd have to get up extra early for the school bus. It helped me though that I'd be listened to if I needed to change anything.[92]

Also:

> It was a lot better afterwards, I was clearer on what I thought, I don't think I realised what was bothering me until I said it out loud ... and I was able to talk to them [my parents] and it made it easier than just accepting things ... [the meeting] made Mam and Dad more conscious of how we were feeling and to include us ... I think it helped everyone ... [However, she continued,] just meeting someone once is not enough.[93]

---

89 Ibid, 12.
90 Ibid, 20.
91 Ibid, 15.
92 O'Kelly (n86).
93 O'Kelly (n86).

Despite these international research findings there is still a reluctance to engage with children, centred around the need to protect children and the view that parents know best.[94] Barlow and Ewing have identified practitioners as the first gatekeepers in keeping the voice of the child absent from the mediation process, citing a lack of confidence in the process or their ability to meet with children.[95] This research noted a clear difference in approach among mediators who had been sufficiently trained and who viewed the voice of the child as a right, in the way in which information was conveyed to parents. Taking a positive attitude which outlined the wider benefits for children's mental health and well-being and reducing conflict within family relationships, often caused by misinterpretation or misunderstanding, tended to encourage parents to engage.[96] It is argued, however, that financial resources in providing this training alone will not lead to change without an alteration in culture and attitude and a recognition of children as a central part of the family unit with, as noted previously, the right to express their own views and feelings.

Summary

Settling cases through less-hurried and potentially more inclusive processes outside the court system may seem to provide greater opportunities to consider the needs of the entire family. However, the evidence suggests the opposite to be true. As it stands, children have a better chance of having their voices heard within the courts rather than through out-of-court private dispute-resolution mechanisms. Equal attention should be focused on ensuring that children's voices are heard and respected within non-court-based methods of dispute resolution. This may, arguably, impact children from diverse families more if they are not in a financial position to litigate.

Evaluation of participation of children in family justice processes

Barlow and Ewing have previously commented on 'how easy it was for the focus on the child to be lost and for children's interests to recede into the background'.[97] They noted this to be the case 'across all dispute resolution practices within the family justice system'.[98] As it stands, and contrary to what one may have expected, more support and opportunities to be heard are available when separating parents resolve their disputes before the adversarial court system. Where a judge has oversight, they may order a report or provide an opportunity

---

[94] McIntosh, Wells, and Long (n86); Goldson (n86).
[95] Barlow and Ewing (n86) 54.
[96] Ibid, 40.
[97] Barlow and others (n79) 306.
[98] Ibid.

for children to meet directly. This, however, comes with the qualification as to the motivation behind reports commissioned or views sought within the court process. Routinely, these are to assist the court in decision making rather than to specifically ensure that the children are given a voice in accordance with their UNCRC rights. Research undertaken shows that any consultations that take place may be one-off and quite short, with little opportunity to provide feedback to the children when a decision is made. Children have expressed frustration with these measures, which focus on the court's needs, rather than their needs.[99] In dispute resolution processes, arguably presented as less adversarial and more 'family friendly', the research to date indicates that child-inclusive mediation is not prevalent and the development and uptake of collaborative law, in general, and the use of child specialists within the process, have been limited. The introduction of Practice Direction Update No 5 2024 in April means that many more cases will be referred into private alternative methods of dispute resolution.[100] Unless there is a corresponding acknowledgement of the rights of the child to participate in these processes, children will continue to be sidelined.

Conclusion

Lack of any or adequate training for professionals is one of the biggest stumbling blocks in ensuring that the voice of the child is heard within family justice processes. Much of this can be attributed to lack of financial resources being invested into the system, but also and perhaps more difficult to challenge, a paternalistic attitude among practitioners and a ready acceptance that parents know best what is in their children's interests. In many cases, this will be correct. It is not a case, however, of simply ensuring that this is ascertained, but is, more broadly, a matter of affording respect to children during a period of family transition. We can no longer ignore this by convincing ourselves that 'it doesn't concern them' or that they 'were fine'. It is important that the UNCRC is incorporated into domestic legislation and, whether within the courts or in alternative methods of dispute resolution, the default position is that children be afforded the opportunity to participate should they wish to do so.[101]

---

[99] Bailey, Thoburn, and Timms (n30) 136.

[100] Practice Direction Update No 5 2024 (n27).

[101] The most recent report on the UK's compliance with the standards set out in the Convention by the Committee on the Rights of the Child reiterated its previous recommendations that the UK needs to '[s]trengthen its efforts to fully incorporate the Convention into national legislation in England, Wales, Northern Ireland ...'. In Wales, steps have been taken steps to ensure that 'due regard' is given to the UNCRC under its Rights of Children and Young Persons (Wales) Measure 2011. While this is helpful, it falls short of full implementation of the Convention. On 16 July 2024, the United Nations Convention on the Rights of the Child (Incorporation) (Scotland) Act 2024 came into effect. Section 9 of the Act provides for the 'child's view on effectiveness of reliefs' in a manner which is suitable to the child. Under the Act, as per the UNCRC, children are to be presumed to have capacity. It is hoped that the Act will mean significant change for children in Scotland. In England, however, the CA 1989

Many studies have been undertaken with children since the inception of the Convention across numerous jurisdictions where, as noted by Morrison, Tisdall, and Callaghan, 'children repeatedly tell researchers they need' a 'system of child advocacy that ensures independent advice, ongoing support and trusting relationships'.[102] This, accompanied by specific, targeted education in children's rights for parents and professionals is required as a matter of urgency. The Lundy model for participation should apply in all dispute resolution processes and underpin training for lawyers, judges, arbitrators, and mediators. Proper information should be provided and appropriate and supportive mechanisms should be in place to help parents understand the importance of children's rights and to assist children in expressing their voice across all family justice processes. With the benefit of this training and understanding parents and professionals need to provide an audience for these views and a transparent process, to manage expectations and provide feedback to children as to the influence of those views. As noted in several studies, children are 'more resilient than adults think'.[103] They are vocal about many aspects of their lives and should be respected and valued for their contributions when participating in decisions about their future, particularly when adapting to change brought about by family transition.

Further questions to consider

- What practical steps can be taken to hear the voice of the child?
- What can a child do if decisions being made are not, in their view, in their best interests?
- Can society afford not to listen to children when we consider the long-term societal impact for young people?

Further materials

Barlow A and Ewing J, *Children's Voices, Family Disputes and Child-Inclusive Mediation: The Right to Be Heard* (Bristol University Press 2024)

Family Solutions Group (Subgroup of the Private Law Working Group), '"What about Me?" Reframing Support for Families following Parental Separation' (2020) FamilySolutionsGroupReport_WhatAboutMe_12November2020-2.pdf-final-2.pdf, accessed 17 June 2025

Healy C, *Collaborative Practice: An International Perspective* (Routledge 2017).

---

remains the main Act governing private family law matters for children where their parents are going through a separation or divorce. Section 1 of the Act provides that the 'welfare of the children is a paramount consideration' with a requirement under section 1(3) that the court has regard to the child's 'ascertainable wishes and feelings'. Such wishes and feelings are to be considered in light of the child's age and understanding.

102 Morrison, Tisdall, and Callaghan (n11) 413.
103 Barlow and Ewing (n86) 54; Healy (n10).

Ministry of Justice, 'Assessing Risk of Harm to Children and Parents in Private Law Children Cases: Final Report' (2022) https://consult.justice.gov.uk/digital-communications/assessing-harm-private-family-law-proceedings/results/assessing-risk-harm-children-parents-pl-childrens-cases-report.pdf, accessed 17 June 2025

Parkinson L and Johnson P, *Conversations with Young People in Family Mediation* (Bloomsbury 2024)

PART III

Domestic Abuse in Families

12

It Can Happen to Anyone, But Not Everyone Has the Same Experience: The Need for Better Legal Responses to Domestic Abuse in the Family Justice System

Mandy Burton

Introduction

This chapter will consider what happens in child arrangement cases where there are allegations of domestic abuse. When parents separate, many will agree the arrangements for who their children should live with and how much contact they should have with the non-resident parent and other family members. Some parents will litigate child arrangements in the family courts. These parents (or sometimes other family members) will need to frame their case under the Children Act (CA) 1989, which governs child arrangement cases, or as they are referred to, 'private law' proceedings. It is estimated that a large proportion of child arrangement/private law cases, two thirds or more, involve allegations of domestic abuse.[1] In these cases there are grave concerns about the ability of the family justice system (FJS) to recognise and respond appropriately to risk of harm posed by domestic abuse to children and the non-abusive protective parent. There are also concerns about the voices of children being ignored or minimised. The

---

[1] A Barnett, 'Domestic Abuse and Private Law Children Cases: A Literature Review' Ministry of Justice (2020) 20 https://assets.publishing.service.gov.uk/media/5ef3dd32d3bf7f7142efc034/domestic-abuse-private-law-children-cases-literature-review.pdf, accessed 17 June 2025.

issue of how allegations of domestic abuse are dealt with in child arrangement proceedings has been the subject of a public call for evidence in England and Wales in 2019. The Harm Panel received more than a thousand responses to that call, which it supplemented with other sources of evidence.[2] This chapter will begin by examining the legal framework for deciding child arrangements under the CA 1989, case law, and associated legal guidance. It will then look at the realities of how cases are decided and the issues that have been flagged by the Harm Panel and numerous academic studies.

As the title to this chapter suggests, domestic abuse is not confined to one particular group or community, it cuts across all social classes, racial, ethnic, and religious communities. It can take place in heterosexual or same-sex relationships and there is a growing literature on LGBT+ experiences of domestic abuse.[3] Domestic abuse does happen to men; however, research demonstrates that in terms of frequency and severity, women in heterosexual relationships suffer the most domestic abuse.[4] Coercive control, a form of abuse discussed in this chapter, has been characterised as a tool mainly used by men to dominate women.[5] Myhill and Kelly have critiqued the traditional approach of criminal law which fails to capture anything more than the most recent physical abuse and downgrades the significance of coercive control as a gendered form of abuse.[6] In this chapter, the focus will be on female victims or survivors of domestic abuse in heterosexual relationships and their children, particularly those from communities marginalised by race and ethnicity. How do women and children in general, and marginalised women and children in particular, experience the FJS in England and Wales? A discussion of the experiences of litigants navigating the FJS in England and Wales highlights how the barriers that all victims of domestic abuse encounter in accessing justice and protection can be magnified by intersections of other forms of oppression. Racism and classism, for example, impact on the way the legal system operates. It will be argued that the concept of intersectionality is useful in understanding the additional barriers to safety faced by victims of domestic abuse from marginalised communities.

---

[2] H Hunter, M Burton, and L Trinder, 'Assessing Risk of Harm to Children and Parents in Private Law Children Cases: Final Report' Ministry of Justice (2020) https://assets.publishing. service.gov.uk/media/5ef3dcade90e075c4e144bfd/assessing-risk-harm-children-parents-pl-childrens-cases-report_.pdf, accessed 17 June 2025.

[3] C Donovan and R Barnes, 'Making Sense of Discourses of Sameness and Difference in Agency Responses to Abusive LGB and/or T Relationships', (2019) 22(5–6) Sexualities 785; C Donovan and R Barnes, *Queering the Narratives of Domestic Violence and Abuse: Victims and/or Perpetrators* (Palgrave Macmillan 2020).

[4] RE Dobash and R Dobash, R (2004) 'Women's Violence to Men in Intimate Relationships: Working on a Puzzle' (2004) 44(3) British Journal of Criminology 324.

[5] E Stark, *Coercive Control: How Men Entrap Women in Personal Life* (OUP 2007).

[6] A Myhill and L Kelly, 'Counting with Understanding? What is at Stake in Debates on Researching Domestic Violence' (2021) 21(3) Criminology and Criminal Justice 280.

The legal framework

When the arrangements relating to children cannot be reached by agreement by parents, either party can apply to the court for a child arrangements order (CAO) under section 8 of the CA 1989. CAOs can specify who the child lives with and the type, frequency, and duration of contact with another parent or person with an interest, such as a grandparent. The courts have wide discretion to specify the degree and nature of the contact that is to take place; for example, they may order direct or indirect contact, or in some circumstances, no contact. There is a presumption of parental involvement in section 1(2A) CA 1989.[7] This presumption states that unless involving the parent in the child's life would be harmful to the child, then it is presumed that the welfare of the child is best served by parental involvement.

Under section 1(5) of the CA 1989, the court should only make an order when it considers that it is better for the child than making no order at all (the 'no order' principle). It is normally assumed that the child's best interests are served by the parties agreeing contact themselves (with or without the help of mediators), but as discussed later in this chapter, this may not always be necessary or advisable in cases where there is domestic abuse. In deciding whether to make a CAO the courts must consider the 'welfare checklist' in section 1(3) of the CA 1989. This list requires the court to have regard to a range of factors, including the physical, emotional, and educational needs of the child; the capacity of each parent or other relevant person to meet those needs; and any harm that the child has suffered or is at risk of suffering. Harm is broadly defined in section 31 of the CA 1989 and includes 'impairment of health or development', including 'impairment suffered from seeing or hearing ill-treatment of another'. Thus, where a child has suffered harm or is at risk of suffering harm as a result of domestic abuse, this should be taken into account. Indeed, the Domestic Abuse Act (DAA) 2021 makes clear that children are the direct victims of domestic abuse, irrespective of whether they are targeted by the abuser, and even if they do not directly witness domestic abuse.[8] Under the welfare checklist, the ascertainable wishes and feelings of the child should be considered when determining what CAO to make. These wishes and feelings do not take priority over other factors and have to be considered in the light of the child's age and understanding. In theory, the older the child is, the more influential their views are likely to be. The maturity of the child and their 'Gillick competence' will be relevant,[9] and children under ten may not be considered mature enough for their views to be given any weight.

---

[7]   As amended by the Children and Families Act 2014.

[8]   Under section 3 of the DAA 2021, the term 'victim' includes children who have seen, heard, or experienced domestic abuse.

[9]   *Gillick v West Norfolk and Wisbech AHA* [1985] UKHL 7.

Appellate case law

There is appellate case law relating to the making of CAOs where there are allegations of domestic abuse. In one of the earliest cases, *Re L and Others*,[10] the court said allegations of domestic abuse may be relevant to the child's welfare and influence the contact arrangements, depending on factors such as whether the perpetrator had acknowledged the impact of their behaviour and made genuine attempts to address it. The court held that it may be necessary for allegations of domestic abuse to be the subject to a 'fact-finding' hearing (FFH) to enable the court to determine which allegations are proven, which can then be used as a basis for an appropriate risk assessment. Under section 7 of the Children and Families Act 2014, the Children and Family Court Advisory and Support Service (Cafcass) – Cafcass Cymru in Wales – can be asked to produce a report containing a welfare and risk assessment, which can then be used by the court in their welfare determination.

Following *Re L*, the family courts were issued with guidance for dealing with cases where there are allegations of domestic abuse: Practice Direction 12J.[11] In line with *Re L*, Practice Direction 12J requires the court to consider the perpetrator's capacity to appreciate and address the effect of past abuse and also the motivation of the abusive parent in seeking contact. It is increasingly understood that, for some perpetrators of domestic abuse, one of the key motives for initiating child arrangement proceedings may be to perpetuate abuse of the primary carer, using litigation as a tool of coercive control. This is one of the reasons why section 91(14) of the CA 1989 allows for an order to be made by the courts which prevents a litigant making repeated applications for child arrangement orders without leave of the court.[12] Under Practice Direction 12J, domestic abuse allegations should be identified at the earliest opportunity and the court should give directions to enable findings of fact to be made in appropriate cases, taking into account whether such a FFH is 'necessary' and 'proportionate'. Where parties are alleging domestic abuse, they can be exempted from attending a mediation, information, and assessment meeting (MIAM), which has been mandatory since 2014 for parties prior to going to court for a CAO. Once an application for a CAO is made, safeguarding checks will be carried out by Cafcass/Cafcass Cymru. They will speak to the parents and check if social services or the police have been involved with the family. They will then produce a 'safeguarding report' for the court before the First Hearing Dispute Resolution Appointment. Typically, the safeguarding letter will state when Cafcass believes that an FFH is necessary. They may also recommend a full section 7 'welfare

---

[10]   *Re L, V, M and H (Contact; Domestic Violence)* [2000] 2 FLR 334.

[11]   https://www.justice.gov.uk/courts/procedure-rules/family/practice_directions/pd_part_12j, accessed 17 June 2025.

[12]   https://www.gov.uk/government/publications/domestic-abuse-bill-2020-factsheets/section-9114-barring-orders, accessed 17 June 2025.

report'/risk assessment, as discussed, but it is a matter for the discretion of the court as to whether to order one. At the final hearing, the court should only make an order for contact if it is satisfied that 'the physical and emotional safety of the child and the parent with whom the child is living can, as far as possible, be secured before, during, and after contact, and that the parent with whom the child is living will not be subjected to further domestic abuse'.[13]

The Practice Direction 12J guidance has been revised a number of times since it was first issued in 2008, and there have been important recent cases following on from the decision in *Re L and Others*. For example, in 2021 the Court of Appeal gave judgments in four co-joined appeals in *Re H-N and Others*.[14] The four cases illustrated the difficulties of identifying and evidencing domestic abuse as well as poor application of the guidance in Practice Direction 12J. In the first of the four co-joined cases, the mother was pressurised by the judge into agreeing to a consent order, having been told the allegations of domestic abuse were not going to affect the decision as to contact and being threatened with the child being removed from her care. In the second case, the judge refused to investigate whether alleged financial and emotional abuse had taken place. In the third, the judge treated domestic abuse as mutual, minimising threats to kill. In the fourth, the judge regarded abuse as a 'product of a dysfunctional relationship' and an allegation of rape as of 'limited' relevance. The trial judge criticised the mother for having a messy home, lacking childcare routines, and for her 'unpredictable and chaotic' lifestyle.[15]

Several of the trial judges in the appealed cases were dismissive of allegations of domestic abuse and/or hostile to a FFH being held. In the first case the judge was criticised for making 'unguarded' comments which pressured the mother to agree contact. In second case, the appellate court emphasised the need for a more modern understanding of domestic abuse that encompasses financial and emotional abuse. In a third case, the trial judge was criticised by the appellate court for his approach; in particular for saying that physical abuse (grabbing by the throat and putting a plastic bag over the mother's head') was 'minor' and attributable to 'relationship conflict'.[16] In the fourth case, the appellate court were critical of the trial judge for implying that the mother was playing the system by making allegations of domestic abuse to elicit sympathy and legal aid.

Looking at the four appeals in the round, the Court of Appeal found that the process for structuring domestic abuse allegations for FFHs (by using 'Scott schedules' to limit the number of allegations to be determined) was not conducive to establishing patterns of behaviour over time that are a feature of 'coercive control'. It did not provide a solution to the problem, albeit criticising the approach of focusing on separate incidents. For example, in relation to the third

---

13   Practice Direction 12J (n11).
14   *Re H-N and Others (Children) (Domestic Abuse: Finding of Fact Hearings)* [2021] EWCA Civ 448.
15   Ibid, para 204.
16   Ibid, para 1.

case, the appellate court was critical of the judge for failing to stand back and consider that the two incidents were close in time, with similar threats, establishing a 'pattern of behaviour'.[17] In relation to the fourth case, the Court of Appeal stated that the trial judge's remarks minimising the abuse were inappropriate and the police evidence that the father had slapped the mother while pregnant was not a trivial matter, nor was his surveillance of her through opening her private mail. The Court of Appeal observed that a person does not have to be 'blameless' to be the victim of domestic abuse and the judge in the fourth case was wrong to focus on the mother's lifestyle.[18]

In subsequent cases, such as *K v K*,[19] the appellate court has emphasised that not all allegations of domestic abuse require a FFH and it would be a 'misunderstanding' to interpret *Re H-N and Others* as suggesting that.[20] In the particular case, there were multiple allegations on the schedule, including coercive control and rape of the mother and pulling the hair and flicking the ear of one of the children. The appellate court said the allegations in relation to one child did not apply to all three and were not 'child abuse'. They criticised the fact findings in relation to coercive control and rape, stating in relation to the former that too much weight had been placed on messages sent in a single day, noting also that there were inconsistencies in the mother's testimony regarding dates, which undermined her credibility. The court said that even when there are 'serious' allegations of domestic abuse, a FFH may not meet the Practice Direction 12J criteria and is not an 'opportunity for the parties to air their grievances' or 'seek the court's validation of what went wrong in their relationship'.[21] The court encouraged attendance at the MIAM (noting that there needed to be careful scrutiny of claimed exemptions). It also endorsed making every effort to settle rather than have a contested hearing.

Summary

The CA 1989 sets out the legal criteria for the making of a CAO. The courts must apply the 'welfare checklist' in section 1(3), which includes a range of factors to be taken into account, including the child's wishes and feelings, though the latter are not determinative. If allegations of domestic abuse are made, these can be relevant to the welfare determination, and sometimes the court will need to have a FFH to assess their significance and potentially order a welfare report/risk assessment (Section 7 report). If there is a FFH, allegations of coercive control need to be assessed. Recent cases, such as *Re H-N*, encourage courts to look for patterns of behaviour and not just focus on isolated incidents of physical

---

17   Ibid, para 180.
18   Ibid, para 204.
19   *K v K* [2022] EWCA Civ 468.
20   Ibid, para 67.
21   Ibid, para 65.

abuse. However, the appellate courts are clear that FFH are not required in all cases where allegations of domestic abuse are made. There is encouragement to settle by mediation or at the door of the court, rather than proceed to a contested hearing.

Recognition of coercive control as a live issue for safety

Re H-N and Others was generally welcomed for promoting a more modern understanding of domestic abuse, including the need to identify coercive control, which manifests as a pattern of behaviour rather than isolated incidents and which can, although not always, include physical abuse.[22] In England and Wales, the route to recognition of coercive control has been a long and winding one.[23] Historically, the focus of legal remedies was for physical violence, albeit even in the 1970s when civil protection orders for domestic abuse first emerged, there was some acknowledgement that 'molestation' could include non-physical abuse.[24] Gradually, in a variety of different legal contexts, judges began to give more weight to non-physical abuse. Lady Hale, in a housing law case, interpreted domestic 'violence' to include threatening or intimidating behaviour or any abuse which may give rise to a risk of violence. She put emphasis on situations where one party is put 'in fear through the constant denial of freedom and money for essentials, through the denigration of her personality, such that she genuinely fears that he may take her children away from her however unrealistic that may appear to an objective outsider'.[25]

Finally, legislation began to incorporate definitions of 'coercive control'. For example, the Legal Aid, Sentencing and Punishment of Offenders Act (LASPO) 2012, which governs access to public funding for legal representation, referred to incidents and patterns of incidents of 'controlling, coercive or threatening behaviour, violence or abuse (whether psychological, physical, sexual, financial or emotional)'.[26] Various versions of Practice Direction 12J have also included definitions of domestic abuse which cover coercive control. The DAA 2021 was the last stage post on a journey to a more inclusive legal definition of domestic abuse. It lists physical or sexual abuse, violent or threatening behaviour, controlling or coercive behaviour, economic abuse, psychological and emotional abuse as types of domestic abuse.[27] Section 1(3) of the DAA says that abusive behaviour can include a single incident or a course of conduct. While the

---

[22] M Burton and V Bettinson, 'Domestic Abuse and Child Arrangement Proceedings: Identifying and Assessing the Risk of Harm, including Coercive and Controlling Behaviour' (2022) Child and Family Law Quarterly, 22(1) 3.

[23] M Burton, 'Defining Abuse' in *Domestic Abuse, Victims and the Law* (Routledge 2022) 1–18.

[24] Ibid.

[25] *Yemshaw v London Borough of Hounslow* [2011] UKSC 3.

[26] LASPO, s 1, para 12(9).

[27] DAA 2021, s 1.

definition is an improvement on some previous legal provisions which ignored coercive control, it has been argued, for example by Bishop, that it is problematic to list coercive control as one type of domestic abuse rather than a central component.[28] Wiener has also argued that the DAA definition represents a fundamental misunderstanding of coercive control; it is not one of a number of types of abuse but rather an overarching framework that brings meaning to all forms of domestic abuse.[29]

While it is arguably significant that child arrangement case law has begun to acknowledge coercive control as an issue that is relevant to the welfare determination, there are still examples of courts downplaying/minimising the significance of abuse. In *K v K*, highlighted previously, the court said that where coercive control is alleged, it is likely to be the 'primary matter requiring determination' and a 'live issue' for welfare of the children.[30] However, as mentioned, it then went on to criticise the fact-finding exercise by the trial judge, saying that the finding of rape was unsafe because there was unreliability in the mother's recall of dates and the doctor, to whom she said she had reported an incident of non-consensual sex while pregnant, gave evidence this was not the case. The decision was critiqued as disappointing and a backward step.[31] By focusing on minor inconsistencies in testimony, which are then seen to undermine the credibility of the complainant as a whole, the court showed little understanding that recall can be impacted by the trauma caused by abuse.[32] The court also, arguably, failed to tackle effectively the argument made by the father that the children were opposed to contact due to alienation by the mother.[33] It has been observed that allegations of parental alienation (PA) or alienating behaviours are used as counter allegations to domestic abuse as a strategy to silence survivors.[34]

---

[28]   C Bishop, 'Prevention and Protection: Will the Domestic Abuse Act Transform the Response to Domestic Abuse in England and Wales? (2021) 33 Child and Family Law Quarterly 163.

[29]   C Wiener, 'Defining Coercive Control: Problems and Possibilities' in M Burton and others (eds), *Research Handbook on Domestic Violence and Abuse* (Edward Elgar 2024).

[30]   *K v K* (n19), para 68.

[31]   J Birchall, *Two Years, Too Long* (Women's Aid 2022); Women's Aid, 'K v K: A Retreat from Progress' (2023) https://www.womensaid.org.uk/kvk-a-retreat-from-progress-in-the-family-courts, accessed 17 June 2025.

[32]   C Bishop and V Bettinson, 'Evidencing Domestic Violence, including Behaviour that Falls under the New Offence of "Controlling or Coercive Behaviour"' (2018) 22(1) International Journal of Evidence & Proof 3.

[33]   M Burton, 'Revisiting Fact-Finding in Child Arrangement Cases Where There Are Allegations of Domestic Abuse' (2022) 44(3) Journal of Social Welfare and Family Law 414.

[34]   J Birchall and S Choudhry, '"I Was Punished for Telling the Truth": How Allegations of Parental Alienation Are Used to Silence, Sideline and Disempower Survivors of Domestic Abuse in Family Law Proceedings' (2022) 6 Journal of Gender-Based Violence 115. A Barnett, 'Domestic Abuse, Parental Alienation and Family Court Proceedings' in Burton and others (n29).

Summary

The law has been slow to evolve to recognise the importance of coercive control. Even now some scholars are critical of recent legal definitions of domestic abuse, arguing they fail to recognise coercive control as the overarching framework of abuse rather than as. an example of it. Since *Re H-N and Others*, there have been some cases which suggest that the courts may still not fully understand coercive control and the impact that it may have on how a victim presents as a witness and the safety implications for child contact. In some cases, the courts may have failed to see how counter allegations of PA are used by abusers to try to silence survivors of domestic abuse.

The realities of day-to-day operation of the family courts

For many years there have been concerns about the way that the FJS responds to allegations of domestic abuse in private law/child arrangement cases. Academic studies have demonstrated that there have been substantial issues with the implementation of Practice Direction 12J. The headline findings of multiple research studies, considered in a literature review by Barnett, suggest that the safety of women and children experiencing domestic abuse is compromised by the courts and other professionals.[35] There have been specific studies, for example, of Cafcass officers, examining their role preparing safeguarding reports and how they downplay the significance of domestic abuse in pursuit of contact.[36] It has been argued that the FJS promotes an approach of 'contact at all costs'.[37]

There are well-documented challenges for parties in child arrangement cases, one of which is the lack of public funding for legal representation, which leaves parties in a position where they have to appear as litigants in person (LiPs) and face their abuser without an advocate.[38] Coy and others, for example, found that unrepresented women are under pressure to settle and those who do litigate may face abusive direct cross-examination.[39] The prospect of being

---

[35] Barnett (n1).

[36] G Macdonald, 'Domestic Violence and Private Law Proceedings: Promoting Child Welfare or Promoting Contact?' (2016) 22(7) Violence Against Women 832; G Macdonald, 'Hearing Children's Voices? Including Children's Perspectives on their Experiences of Domestic Violence in Welfare Reports Prepared for the English Courts in Private Law Family Proceedings' (2017) 65 Child Abuse and Neglect 1.

[37] A Barnett, 'Contact at All Costs? Domestic Violence and Children's Welfare' (2014) 26 Child and Family Law Quarterly 439.

[38] L Trinder and others, 'Litigants in Person in Private Family Law Cases' Ministry of Justice (2014) https://assets.publishing.service.gov.uk/media/5a7e2218ed915d74e33f0448/litigants-in-person-in-private-family-law-cases.pdf, accessed 17 June 2025.

[39] M Coy and others, 'Picking Up the Pieces: Domestic Violence and Child Contact' Rights of Women (2012) https://www.rightsofwomen.org.uk/wp-content/uploads/2023/12/picking_up_the_pieces_report-2012l.pdf, accessed 17 June 2025; M Coy and others (2015) ' "It's Like

directly cross-examined by their abuser has been addressed by provisions in the DAA 2021, which makes provision for lawyers to be appointed by the court to undertake that part of the case.[40] However, it does not mean that the stress and trauma of court proceedings are removed, only mitigated somewhat in one aspect, if the scheme for appointing a qualified legal representative works. Perhaps unsurprisingly, given the appellate case law discussed, research has highlighted the difficulty of uncovering coercive control in FFHs. Barnett, for example, has observed that the bar of 'acceptable' abuse seemed very high and the abuse had to be very severe to be considered relevant to the welfare determination.[41] Walsh, whose casefile study found domestic abuse in 72% of cases, noted a resistance to holding fact findings and questions whether there is a norm of safety in the family courts.[42]

It is clear then, that all victims of domestic abuse face substantial hurdles in getting domestic abuse to be taken seriously by the FJS and given appropriate weight in the making of CAOs. In 2019, the Ministry of Justice in England and Wales set up the Harm Panel to assess how the family courts were responding to allegations of domestic abuse and other risks of harm to children and parents in private law child-arrangement proceedings. The role of the Panel was to identify any systemic issues based, in part, on a public call for evidence which was answered by over 1,000 individuals and organisations. The evidence was analysed and cross-referenced with other sources and published as a report in mid-2020.[43] The Harm Panel concluded that there are 'deep-seated and systemic problems with how the family courts identify, assess and manage risk to children and adults' in child arrangement cases involving allegations of domestic abuse. The Panel identified four structural barriers to safe process and outcomes: resource constraints, the pro-contact culture and the minimisation of abuse, silo working, and adversarialism. The Panel said that these barriers result in the systemic minimisation of domestic abuse and ongoing harm from

---

Going through the Abuse Again": Domestic Violence and Women and Children's (Un)safety in Private Law Contact Proceedings' (2015) 37(1) Journal of Social Welfare and Family Law 53.

[40] DAA 2021, ss 65 and 66. Cross-examination is intended to be carried out by these court-appointed legal professionals, known as qualified legal representatives (QLRs) to ensure that justice is done fairly for both sides and reduce the risk of victims being retraumatised. However, the operation of the scheme has yet to be fully evaluated, with some concerns about lack of availability of QLRs because of the level of fees. Following calls from the DAC and others, since December 2023 travel and expenses can now be claimed by QLRs and this may have impacted positively on their availability in some courts.

[41] A Barnett, 'Like Gold Dust these Days: Domestic Violence Fact-Finding Hearings in Child Contact Cases' (2015) 23(1) Feminist Legal Studies 478; A Barnett, ' "Greater than the Mere Sum of its Parts": Coercive Control and the Question of Proof' (2017) 29 Child and Family Law Quarterly 379.

[42] K Walsh, 'The Gap between Facts and Norms: Contact, Harm and Futility' (2023) 35(1) Child and Family Law Quarterly 27.

[43] Hunter, Burton, and Trinder (n2).

court orders. It stated: 'the four factors identified all pull in the same direction, reinforcing each other in making abuse harder to address effectively'.[44]

Looking at each barrier in turn, starting with resource constraints, the Harm Panel found that the ability of the FJS to identify and address domestic abuse at all stages of the process was impacted by limited resources. Legal aid cuts, for example, have resulted in the significant increase in LiPs in family courts, and these unrepresented litigants are often ill-equipped to manage litigation where domestic abuse is in issue. The evidence submitted to the Harm Panel highlighted that disparity of resources is also a significant issue in cases where one party has legal representation and the other party does not. Unrepresented victims told the Panel that they sometimes faced well-resourced and legally represented respondents who used their financial position to exploit the unequal power dynamic and the financial abuse already underpinning the relationship. There was also a sense of unfairness among alleged perpetrators unable to access legal aid as, although they satisfied the means test for legal aid, they did not qualify on merits. The Panel found this inequality of arms operated in a way that undermined the perceived legitimacy of the court process and decisions. The Panel found that the resource constraints experienced by Cafcass and the courts also provide incentives to ignore or sideline domestic abuse allegations. For example, safeguarding requires Cafcass resources to do a detailed and careful risk assessment, FFHs require additional judicial time.[45]

On the second structural barrier, the pro-contact culture, the Harm Panel stated that this contributed to the minimisation of domestic abuse and disbelief of victims. The rebuttable presumption of parental involvement in the CA 1989 is 'rarely disapplied'.[46] Mothers told the Panel that they felt that the courts had given their abuser a 'legal weapon' to continue their abuse, ignoring their legitimate safety concerns and the wishes and feelings of the children. The Panel reported that mothers who object to contact are regarded are regarded as obstructive and labelled 'hostile'.[47] A range of stereotypes contributed to a perception that victims are not being believed or being blamed for abuse. For example, there is stereotype that a 'real' victim of domestic abuse would report to the police immediately and leave the abuser in order to protect the children. These stereotypes are inconsistent with research that shows that victims of domestic abuse may not report to any third party, least of all the police, and sometimes stay in an abusive relationship to try to protect the children from unsupervised contact.[48]

---

[44] Ibid, 40.

[45] Ibid, 41.

[46] Ibid, 88.

[47] Hunter, Burton, and Trinder (n2) 97 and chapter 5.

[48] S Holt, 'A Voice or a Choice? Children's Views on Participating in Decisions about Post-Separation Contact with Domestically Abusive Fathers' (2018) 40(4) Journal of Social Welfare and Family Law 459.

The third structural barrier to safer process and safer outcomes in child arrangement cases identified by the Harm Panel is silo working. The Panel found that the criminal justice system, the courts dealing with non-molestation orders, and the family courts often do not share information and may adopt conflicting approaches.[49] This finding is consistent with Hester's three planet model of how the justice system operates in domestic abuse cases: child protection, private family law, and criminal justice all operate with different objectives and ideologies.[50] In the criminal justice system, the non-abusive parent is treated as a potential 'victim', in child protection as a potential 'protector' of the child, and in private law as a potential 'obstructer' of contact. The Harm Panel found that even when the mother is being treated sympathetically in the criminal justice system, for example has bail conditions for protection or the police have arranged installation of emergency alarms, in the private law sphere she may be treated as a potential 'obstructer' of contact and a 'possible alienator'.[51] The contradictory approaches sometimes resulted in directly conflicting orders, for example prohibition on contact in bail conditions and orders for the mother to do contact handovers in the family court.

The fourth structural barrier identified by the Harm Panel is the adversarial court process where two opposing parties are pitted against each other, each trying to 'win' the case.[52] This process was found to be retraumatising for victims, posing a threat to their physical and psychological safety.[53] The family court infrastructure, including the ability to provide special measures such as separate waiting areas and screens in court, was often said to be inadequate. Victims and alleged perpetrators of domestic abuse often have to wait in the same area of the court building and in close proximity to each other. Screening in the courtroom or video link evidence did not appear to be routinely offered or used when the Panel was reporting. It appeared that such special measures were sometimes denied because judges thought it would convey the impression of prejudging the issue.[54] There was also reported reluctance to allow the help of McKenzie Friends, especially independent domestic abuse advocates (IDVAs), despite research suggesting these provide vital support for parties, especially unrepresented fathers.[55]

Since the Harm Panel reported, the Domestic Abuse Commissioner (DAC), whose role was put on a statutory footing by the DAA 2021, continues to receive

---

[49]   Hunter, Burton, and Trinder (n2) 44.
[50]   M Hester, 'The Three Planet Model: Towards an Understanding of Contradictions in Approaches to Women and Children's Safety in Contexts of Domestic Violence' (2011) 41 British Journal of Social Work 837.
[51]   Hunter, Burton, and Trinder (n2) 44.
[52]   Ibid, 45.
[53]   Ibid, ch 8.
[54]   Ibid, 118.
[55]   Barnett (n1) 82.

complaints about the way that domestic abuse allegations are dealt with in private law proceedings. Over a third of correspondence received by the DAC mentions family court proceedings, most often private law specifically.[56]

Alongside the four barriers to safe process and outcomes, the Panel also identified 'intersecting structural disadvantages' which arise where there are a combination of structural and systemic factors intersecting to influence an individual's experience of the FJS. The Panel observed 'How the four systemic barriers identified above operate in individual cases will not be the same for everyone … how the parties' experience of these barriers will be influenced by various forms of structural advantage or disadvantage.'[57] One of the three forms of structural disadvantage commonly raised submissions to the Harm Panel was being from a racialised background. It was clear to the Panel that women from a racially minoritised background experienced particular forms of disadvantage in child arrangement proceedings. The Panel referred to the evidence received, for example, from Southall Black Sisters, which attested to the 'vulnerabilities and sense of powerlessness experienced by BAME women who were victims of domestic abuse'[58] This issue of intersectional structural disadvantage will be explored more fully in the next section.

Summary

Where there are domestic abuse allegations, the safety of the processes and outcomes in child arrangement cases has long been a matter of concern, documented by numerous research studies. A government-appointed expert panel (the Harm Panel) reported in 2020 that there are four barriers to safety: resource constraints, a pro-contact culture and the minimisation of abuse, silo working, and adversarialism. These barriers intersect with other forms of structural disadvantage, such as race and ethnicity.

Women's experiences of domestic abuse and the family justice response

Many feminist scholars would argue that gender is a primary source of women's oppression, but as Crenshaw and others have argued, gender is not the whole story.[59] Not all women experience domestic abuse the same way or have the same

---

[56] https://domesticabusecommissioner.uk/wp-content/uploads/2023/07/DAC_Family-Court-Report-_2023_Digital.pdf 15, accessed 17 June 2025. The DAC continues to push for improvements in the family courts, piloting a review mechanism to identify and disseminate best practice.

[57] Ibid, 45.

[58] Ibid, 47.

[59] K Crenshaw, 'Mapping the Margins: Intersectionality, Identity Politics and Violence Against Women of Color' (1991) 43(6) Stanford Law Review 1241.

experiences of the legal system. The intersections of race, ethnicity, social class, and sexuality can affect whether safety can be obtained.[60] The experiences and support needs of victims from racially minoritised backgrounds were highlighted in Barnett's literature review for the Harm Panel.[61] Saunders and Barron, for example, noted many years ago that the experience of women from racially minoritised communities may have distinct features, such as intergenerational participation in abuse.[62] While IDVAs may be helpful to all victims navigating the court process, women from racially minoritised backgrounds may have additional specific support needs that only specialist 'by and for' services can effectively address.[63] In a study of the experiences of women from South Asian and African-Caribbean backgrounds, Thiara and Gill document how intersectional discrimination can place additional barriers to safety for women from racially minoritised backgrounds.[64] Thiara and Gill highlight the range of abuse experienced by the 45 women interviewed for their research on domestic abuse and child contact. They reported that women described regular and persistent verbal, mental, and physical abuse that escalated over time. For many women the control and isolation began at an early stage in their relationship. A quote from one of the South Asian women interviewed noted that the control was there from the outset and physical abuse started later as her partner's religious extremism developed and he wanted to control her in specific ways, for example by trying to enforce covering.[65] Thiara and Gill explain how women new to the country with language barriers might be particularly vulnerable to control because of higher levels of isolation. They observe: 'Knowing little about the outside world or about their options and not being able to speak English, such women were completely dependent on their partners and their families, something used by men as part of their strategy of abuse, with some habitually throwing women out or making threats to send them back to the country of origin.'[66] Women interviewed for this study spoke about being kept in the house and treated as 'domestic slaves' by the whole family. While a significant number of women in their study reported abuse from the extended family, Thiara and Gill noted that caution needed to be exercised in assuming it was a common experience for all racially minoritised women. Some of the women in their study reported that

---

[60] M Bograd, 'Strengthening Domestic Violence Theories: Intersections of Race, Class, Sexual Orientation and Gender' in N Sokoloff (ed), *Domestic Violence at the Margins: Readings on Race, Class, Gender and Culture* (Rutgers University Press 2005).

[61] Barnett (n1) s 6.4.

[62] H Saunders and J Barron, 'Failure to Protect: Domestic Violence and the Experiences of Abused Women and Children in the Family Courts' Women's Aid (2003).

[63] https://domesticabusecommissioner.uk/wp-content/uploads/2021/10/Safety-Before-Status-Report-2021.pdf, accessed 17 June 2025.

[64] R Thiara and A Gill, *Child Contact in the Context of Post-Separation Violence: Issues for Black and Minority Ethnic Women and Children* (NSPCC 2012).

[65] Ibid, 28.

[66] Ibid, 29.

they had positive support from families, including positive and practical support to separate.[67]

Thiara and Gill highlight the experiences of financial abuse of the 45 women in their study. Several African-Caribbean women interviewed for the study said that their partners were totally financial dependent on them and the women had run up debts and been unable to pay housing costs. Abuse was reported to worsen when financial support was withdrawn. Financial abuse is now a form of abuse that is more widely recognised and, as noted, is explicitly set out in the definition of abuse in the DAA 2021. Economic abuse is defined in section 1(4) of the DAA as any behaviour that has a substantial adverse effect on the victim's ability to acquire, use, or maintain money or other property, or to obtain goods and services. There is now a growing literature on this form of abuse.[68] Sharp-Jeffs, author of numerous studies examining financial/economic abuse, has written about how victims of domestic abuse from minority communities may be particularly vulnerable to economic abuse, especially when they have insecure immigration status.[69] In Thiara and Gill's study, South Asian women reported being made to sign papers they did not understand and losing their share of a house. Thiara and Gill observe: 'However, despite being financially dependent on women, some men prevented women from working in order to maintain their control over them.'[70] This reinforces the academic critique about coercive control being listed as a separate type of abuse in the DAA 2021 when often is part of the overarching framework of coercive control and it is conceptually flawed to see it as separate. Singh has written about the role of money in domestic abuse based on detailed conversations with migrant women from Indian and Irish/Celtic backgrounds living in Australia.[71] Her TED Talk on this, recommending further resources, provides a snapshot of some the stories in her book.[72]

Discussing women's responses to the abuse, Thiara and Gill note that the majority of the women in their study did seek professional help when separating but there was a reluctance to report domestic abuse. There are a range of reasons for under-reporting by racially minoritised women, which include notions of family honour and shame as well as personal shame. A particular issue for women from African-Caribbean backgrounds may be lower levels of trust of professionals due to other experiences of racism. Thiara and Gill observe:

---

[67]   Ibid, 32.
[68]   N Sharp, *'What's Yours Is Mine': The Different Forms of Economic Abuse and its Impact on Women and Children Experiencing Domestic Violence* (Refuge 2008); N Sharp-Jeffs, *Money Matters: Research into the Extent and Nature of Financial Abuse within Intimate Partner Relationships in the UK* (Refuge and the Cooperative Bank 2015).
[69]   N Sharp-Jeffs, *Understanding and Responding to Economic Abuse* (Emerald Publishing 2022).
[70]   Thiara and Gill (n64) 29–31.
[71]   S Singh, *Domestic Economic Abuse: The Violence of Money* (Routledge 2022).
[72]   https://www.ted.com/talks/supriya_singh_money_and_its_morality_from_use_to_abuse, accessed 17 June 2025.

> Protecting black men from criminal sanctions was a powerful factor for African-Caribbean women along with the pressure to have fathers in their children's lives. Honour and shame for some South Asian women from close-knit communities took a particular significance, with the prevention of family 'dishonour' a common pressure applied to make women keep quiet and comply.[73]

However, this under-reporting to professionals has been observed to be an additional barrier for racially minoritised women later in the court process when trying to establish their credibility and evidence abuse.[74]

The process of applying or responding to an application for a CAO involves, as described, a safeguarding interview by Cafcass/Cafcass Cymru. Thiara and Gill found that, while awareness of domestic abuse was increasing among these professionals at the time of their study, they were 'still grappling with their awareness of the intersection of ethnicity, culture and contact processes'[75]. The Harm Panel found that there are limitations on the ability of Cafcass/Cafcass Cymru to uncover domestic abuse in safeguarding interviews. Resource limitations mean that these interviews are often carried out over the telephone in half an hour or less. This is not conducive to establishing a connection which would facilitate the disclosure of abuse. In addition, Thiara and Gill observed that 'many South Asian and African-Caribbean women do not disclose full details of violence in the first statement due to pressures to keep quiet or as a result of distrust of professionals'. Cafcass professionals in their study reported undergoing 'huge learning curves' to know how to better ask the right questions and yet 'Many still struggled with the complex issues they encountered', including challenging cultural issues and cultural relativism.[76]

Almost a decade on from Thiara and Gill's study, the Harm Panel found that women from racially minoritised communities were still giving evidence about how they are pressured not to report domestic abuse because of expectations in the family or the wider community. Racially minoritised women in the focus group carried out by the Harm Panel talked about barriers to reporting abuse because of fear of bringing shame on the family or community:

> Participants also reported that victims could be under tremendous social and cultural pressure to reconcile and to agree contact. Women with uncertain immigration status were most at risk of this, as they might have to choose between staying in an abusive situation or risking deportation and the possible permanent loss of their children.[77]

---

73 Thiara and Gill (n64) 49.
74 Ibid, 34.
75 Ibid, 88.
76 Ibid.
77 Hunter, Burton, and Trinder (n2) 47.

There is little doubt that those with insecure immigration status and 'no recourse to public funds' face additional obstacles to safety, not least that they are unable to access refuges and safe accommodation.[78] Research shows that many are afraid of reporting to the police, fearing that information will be shared with immigration enforcement. Perpetrators use insecure immigration status as a tool of coercive control.[79] Alongside, participants giving evidence to the Harm Panel highlighted language difficulties for some victims from racially minoritised backgrounds navigating the family courts. Participants also reported feeling isolated and not appearing credible as witnesses, particularly when appearing against an alleged abuser from a White background. The Harm Panel received submissions which led it to report: 'Some participants felt that white ex-partners had benefited from racial privilege in courts; they felt acutely "othered" and belittled by the court and identified their experience as racism.'[80]

Racially minoritised victim survivors told the Harm Panel about the particular importance to them of having specialist support from IDVA services that were provided by and for their communities. In this way, any judicial resistance to IDVAs operates as an intersectional barrier to safe process and outcomes. One victim from a racially minoritised background told the Panel that she faced her well-resourced ex-partner without her own solicitor. Race, gender, and social class were all intersecting to put her in an especially vulnerable position. In situations like this, the Harm Panel observed, specialist provision can be a lifeline to effective participation and 'part of the jigsaw in finding ways to mitigate harm stemming from the process itself'.[81]

Summary

Women from racially minoritised backgrounds experience domestic abuse in all its forms, including coercive control, with all its elements. However, their ability to access legal protections is hampered by multiple other elements such as isolation, an element of coercive control, which may be increased by language barriers and involvement of wider family members in abuse, although this is not always present. Family and community pressures and experiences of racism may be factors in the under-reporting of domestic abuse to professionals. Professionals in child arrangement cases do not always fully understand the experiences of racially minoritised survivors or respond appropriately. Some survivors report racial discrimination in the FJS. The availability of specific 'by and for' support for racially minoritised survivors may mitigate some of the additional disadvantage, but victims with insecure immigration status are acutely vulnerable because of

---

78   DAC 2021 (n63).
79   Ibid.
80   Hunter, Burton, and Trinder (n2) 47.
81   Ibid, 121.

lack of access to funding for safe accommodation and fear related to deportation, manipulated by abusers.

Children's voices: ignored or minimised

The CA 1989, as discussed earlier, makes provision for children to be heard in private law cases and their wishes and feelings to be taken into account. However, despite children wanting to be heard, there are relatively few cases where the court hears from them directly.[82]

Why is it important for children to be heard, particularly so in cases where there are allegations of domestic abuse? As the Harm Panel observed:

> engaging with children directly provides a more accurate idea of what individual children might want. Research shows that children have widely varied feelings and views about their fathers and spending time with them in domestic abuse cases. The literature reveals that the priority for nearly all children, even those who do want a relationship with their fathers, is safety, for themselves, their mothers and the rest of their families.[83]

Thiara and Gill interviewed 19 children as part of their study of South Asian and African-Caribbean victims' experiences of child arrangement proceedings. They reported issues that impact on children as part of the process, such as the difficulty with Cafcass establishing children's wishes and feelings as part of the safeguarding and welfare assessments that may be undertaken. In the safeguarding process, Cafcass do not typically speak directly to the children, but for a welfare assessment under section 7 CA they will. Children may, however, find it difficult to talk about contact and they may feel under pressure to give expected responses. As with all victims of domestic abuse, it is important not to treat children's experiences of domestic abuse as the same. As Thiara and Gill state:

> Clearly, children are variously affected by domestic violence leading to differing feelings and attitudes towards contact. Some children were very angry at their fathers ... Other children who had not witnessed

---

82 Hargreaves and others, 'Uncovering Private Family Law: How Often Do We Hear the Voice of the Child?' Nuffield Family Justice Observatory (2024) https://www.nuffieldfjo.org.uk/wp-content/uploads/2024/02/Child_participation_08-02-24.pdf, accessed 18 June 2025. See also A Roe, 'Children's Experiences of Private Law Proceedings: Six Key Messages from Research' Nuffield Family Justice Observatory (2021) https://www.nuffieldfjo.org.uk/wp-content/uploads/2021/10/Childrens-experience-of-private-law-proceedings.pdf, accessed 18 June 2025; Family Solutions Group, 'What About Me? A Child's Right to Matter' (2023) www.familysolutionsgroup.co.uk/a-childs-right-to-matter-2/, accessed 18 June 2025.

83 Hunter, Burton, and Trinder (n2) 68.

domestic violence often expressed a wish to see their fathers or to return home, not understanding why they could not do so.[84]

These conflicted emotions around contact could arise from wider family influence. For example, Thiara and Gill found: 'Some South Asian children felt guilty about living away from their grandparents ... It was also evident from children's narratives that in some cases the grandparents put children under a great deal of emotional pressure ... Some grandparents paid children for each day they stayed with them.'[85] This quote comes in the light of wider comments from mothers about fathers also using gifts to try to pressurise or influence children. Children could be very confused; wanting to protect their mothers, but in some cases being manipulated by promises and expensive gifts.

Some children in Thiara and Gill's study were reported to be very distressed at contact visits, crying and resisting being taken. Some children reported neglect during contact visits; not being paid any attention or their basic care needs not being addressed. Some children witnessed abuse or were subject to abuse during contact. Children's behaviour was impacted before and after contact and some children experienced emotional and physical ill health as a result of contact.

The Harm Panel concluded that the variety of views and experiences of children experiencing domestic abuse made it 'essential that the courts understand the views of individual children and tailor arrangements to fit them individually'.[86] Not only is this good practice generally, it can guard against cultural assumptions. One participant from a Family Justice Young People's Board focus group 'noted that speaking to children directly about their experiences was important to correct unconscious bias in relation to culture and ethnicity, in their case assumptions about black men'.[87]

Aside from being consulted as part of the Cafcass Section 7 report if one is ordered, it is possible for a guardian to be appointed to represent a child under rule 16.4 of the Family Procedure Rules,[88] although this is rarely done. The Harm Panel found that some professionals wanted children to have a guardian in more cases, with one judge saying he would appoint them in every case if he could. Clearly there are resource issues with such an approach, but it is possible that separate legal representation for children, which comes with the appointment of a guardian, could result in more children having their voices heard. This may depend on how well trained the professionals are and how much time that they have to engage effectively with children.

---

[84] Thiara and Gill (n64) 69.

[85] Hunter, Burton, and Trinder (n2) 74–5.

[86] Ibid, 68.

[87] Ibid, 69.

[88] https://www.justice.gov.uk/courts/procedure-rules/family/parts/part_16, accessed 18 June 2025.

The Harm Panel found that children's voices are largely muted or unheard and this had a negative impact on children. They were 'left unable to understand why they were being made to spend time with someone who had abused them and/or their other parent'.[89]

Summary

Children's experiences of domestic abuse vary but they can feel very conflicted about contact. Post-separation abuse can negatively impact children and some children do not understand why they have to have contact, experiencing harm as a result. Abusers, and sometimes wider family members, may try to manipulate children's views as to contact. Despite processes being in place for establishing children's wishes and feelings, in general their voices are 'muted or unheard' in private law proceedings.

Conclusion

A modern understanding of domestic abuse is that it is much more pernicious than the legal system has historically appreciated. Coercive control was not criminalised in England and Wales until 2015, and as this chapter shows, the recognition of coercive control in the family courts is a process which has been developing over time and can be a case of one step forward and half a step back. There has been, until very recently, a focus on physical abuse and a failure to appreciate the significance of coercive control for adults and children experiencing domestic abuse. It can be difficult to evidence coercive control, to do so professionals need to understand better the barriers to reporting and the impact that it can have upon survivors. Traditional ways of 'finding facts' may not lend themselves well to establishing the extent and impact of abuse. If the FJS narrows its focus to violence, it will miss essential 'facts' it needs to make an appropriate risk assessment in child arrangement cases.

Domestic abuse is widespread in society but although it can happen to anyone (no matter their background), the experiences of women and children from minority backgrounds will differ in some respects. All victims of domestic abuse navigating the family courts have to contend with a system that is under-resourced and operates a pro-contract culture that minimises domestic abuse. However, women from South Asian families have spoken about their experiences of coercive control and isolation involving wider family members, about shame (personal and community) inhibiting help seeking. Women from African-Caribbean families have spoken about their experiences of financial abuse as part of coercive control, but also about racism (and fear of racist treatment of Black men in the criminal justice system) as a barrier to reporting. These barriers to safe

---

[89]   Ibid, 75.

process and outcomes in child arrangement cases are compounded by structural disadvantages associated with race and ethnicity. Children's wishes and feelings are generally not heard, yet as the Harm Panel noted, it is important that they are, and this may be a way of challenging cultural assumptions that can influence how cases are dealt with.

Further questions to consider

- If you could remove just one barrier to safe process and outcomes in child arrangement cases, what would it be and why?
- Why do you think that the legal system has tended to focus on physical abuse? Looking at the research, is that the 'worst' that can happen?
- Is it important that children's voices are heard in child arrangement cases where there is evidence of domestic abuse? If so, why? What is the best way to achieve this?

Further materials

Barnett A, *Domestic Abuse and Private Law Children Cases: A Literature Review* (Ministry of Justice 2020)

Burton M, *Domestic Abuse, Victims and the Law* (Routledge 2022)

Hunter H, Burton M, and Trinder L, *Assessing Risk of Harm to Children and Parents in Private Law Children Cases: Final Report* (Ministry of Justice 2020)

Singh S, 'Money and its Morality: From Use to Abuse' TED Talk (2021) https://www.ted.com/talks/supriya_singh_money_and_its_morality_from_use_to_abuse, accessed 17 June 2025

Thiara R and Gill A, *Child Contact in the Context of Post-Separation Violence: Issues for Black and Racially Minoritised Women and Children* (NSPCC 2012)

13

In the Shadow of Hostile Environments and Bordering Regimes: Understanding Migrant Women's Experiences of Domestic Abuse and Legal-Institutional Responses

Sundari Anitha

Introduction

Extensive evidence from worldwide surveys indicates the pervasive nature of violence against women and girls (VAWG).[1] While gender remains the most common predictor of domestic violence and abuse (DVA), not all women experience this abuse in the same way or are at similar levels of risk. Since 2015, the lens that has been utilised to understand DVA has expanded beyond a focus on the interpersonal, family, and community dynamics to incorporate the role of intersecting social relations of power based on gender, race, ethnicity, class, (dis)ability, sexuality, and citizenship in enhancing vulnerability for particular categories of women. The concept of intersectionality recognises that women's experiences of DVA are not universal nor shaped by gender alone.[2]

---

[1] World Health Organization (WHO), 'Global and Regional Estimates of Violence Against Women' (2013) https://iris.who.int/bitstream/handle/10665/85241/WHO_RHR_HRP_13.06_eng.pdf, accessed 18 June 2025; Fundamental Rights Agency, 'Violence against Women: An EU-Wide Survey' (2015) https://fra.europa.eu/sites/default/files/fra_uploads/fra-2014-vaw-survey-main-results-apr14_en.pdf, accessed 18 June 2025.

[2] K Crenshaw, 'Demarginalizing the Intersection of Race and Sex: A Black Feminist Critique of Antidiscrimination Doctrine, Feminist Theory, and Antiracist Politics' (1989) 14 University of Chicago Legal Forum 538.

Data suggests that barriers faced by racially minoritised victims of DVA in the UK may trap them within abusive relationships for longer.[3] For example, statistics from a ten-year overview of femicide between 2009 and 2018 shows that 19 per cent of the 1,419 femicide victims were born outside the UK.[4] Compared to the 13 per cent of the UK population who are born outside the UK, this indicates that migrant women are at higher risk of femicide. The over-representation of Black victims and suspects in adult family homicides is also supported by findings on adult family homicides.[5] Around a third of victims (30 per cent) and suspects (33 per cent) in adult family homicides were from a minoritised ethnic group. This is higher than minoritised ethnic group representation in the general population (14 per cent) and in intimate partner homicides (20 per cent of victims and 21 per cent of suspects). While disadvantages related to a history of migration will be an important factor in this enhanced risk, in the UK context the 'no recourse to public funds' (NRPF) status has also been documented as a contributory factor in some of these homicides.[6]

This increased risk of DVA for Black and minoritised women and girls cannot, however, simply be explained through a focus on individual circumstances (lack of awareness of services), personal factors (such as level of education or language proficiency), or family and community structures and socio-cultural norms (for example, notions of 'honour' and shame, son preference). Broader structural factors such as socio-economic disadvantages (for example, poverty, deskilling, and class dislocation upon migration), racism, the role of state policies, including service responses, immigration and welfare policies, funding regimes, and transnational legal regimes form a crucial 'conducive context' that can facilitate or sustain the violence that takes place in private spheres.[7] Structural barriers

---

3   SafeLives, 'Guidance for Multi-agency Forums: Cases Involving Victims Who Are Black, Asian and Racially Minoritised', undated https://safelives.org.uk/resources-library/guidance-for-multi-agency-forums-black-asian-racially-minoritised-clients/, accessed 7 October 2024.

4   HJ Long and others, 'UK Femicides 2009–18' Femicide Census (2020) https://www.femicid ecensus.org/wp-content/uploads/2022/02/010998-2020-Femicide-Report_V2.pdf, accessed 18 June 2025.

5   TTN Phan and others, 'Spotlight Briefing #1: Adult Family Homicides' Vulnerability Knowledge and Practice Programme (2021) https://www.vkpp.org.uk/assets/Files/AFH-Spotli ght-Briefing-Jan-2022-AC.pdf, accessed 18 June 2025.

6   A Jolly and A Gupta, 'Children and Families with No Recourse to Public Funds: Learning from Case Reviews' (2022) 38 Children & Society 16; BK Chantler, 'An Analysis of Minoritisation in Domestic Homicide Reviews in England and Wales' (2023) 43 Critical Social Policy 602.

7   L Kelly, 'A Conducive Context: Trafficking of Persons in Central Asia' in M Lee (ed), *Human Trafficking* (Willan Publishing 2007); SKB Vatnar, C Friestad, and S Bjørkly, 'Intimate Partner Homicide in Norway 1990–2012: Identifying Risk Factors through Structured Risk Assessment, Court Documents, and Interviews with Bereaved' (2017) 7 Psychology of Violence 395; A Kanyeredzi, *Race, Culture and Gender: Black Female Experiences of Violence and Abuse* (Palgrave Macmillan 2018).

such as immigration regulations, lack of access to housing and welfare benefits, and inadequate/discriminatory service responses towards migrant and/or racially minoritised women combine with interpersonal constraints such as the absence of social networks in the country of residence and a lack of proficiency in English to exacerbate the impact of DVA upon migrant women.[8]

The ways in which the experience of immigration and settlement shapes the nature and impact of the domestic abuse have been scrutinised in diverse contexts such as the US, Canada, Australia, and the UK.[9] There is a growing body of international feminist scholarship that has begun to examine the broader structural factors related to migration and immigration status as social relations of power that overlap with race or ethnicity but are distinct both conceptually and operationally.[10] Beyond the ways in which insecure immigration status may enhance the barriers to disclosure and exiting, and possible remedies to DVA, this scholarship draws attention to how precarity produces structural violence, which is then weaponised by perpetrators.[11]

---

[8]   R Alsop, 'Migration and Gender-Based Violence' in P Ali and M Rogers (eds), *Gender-Based Violence: A Comprehensive Guide* (Springer 2023).

[9]   NJ Sokoloff, 'Expanding the Intersectional Paradigm to Better Understand Domestic Violence in Immigrant Communities' (2008) 16 Critical Criminology 229; S Anitha, 'Neither Safety Nor Justice: UK Government Response to Domestic Violence against Immigrant Women' (2008) 30 Journal of Social Welfare and Family Law 189; S Anitha, 'No Recourse, No Support: State Policy and Practice towards South Asian Women Facing Domestic Violence in the UK' (2010) 40 British Journal of Social Work, 462; N Ghafournia, 'Battered at Home, Played Down in Policy: Migrant Women and Domestic Violence in Australia' (2011) 16 Aggression and Violent Behavior 207; M Abraham and E Tastsoglou 'Addressing Domestic Violence in Canada and the United States: The Uneasy Co-Habitation of Women and the State' (2016) 64 Current Sociology 568; P Okeke-Ihejirika and others, 'A Scoping Review on Intimate Partner Violence in Canada's Immigrant Communities' (2020) 21 Trauma Violence Abuse 788; M Segrave, 'Temporary Migration and Family Violence: How Perpetrators Weaponise Borders' (2021) 10 International Journal for Crime, Justice and Social Democracy 26.

[10] S Anitha, A Roy, and H Yalamarty, 'Gender, Migration, and Exclusionary Citizenship Regimes: Conceptualizing Transnational Abandonment of Wives as a Form of Violence against Women' (2018) 24 Violence Against Women 747; CJ McIlwaine, L Granada, and I Valenzuela-Oblitas, 'Right To Be Believed, Migrant Women Facing Violence Against Women and Girls (VAWG) in the "Hostile Immigration Environment" in London' Kings College London and Latin American Women's Rights Service (2019) https://kclpure.kcl. ac.uk/ws/portalfiles/portal/110500935/The_right_to_be_believed_Full_report_final.pdf, accessed 7 July 2025; Segrave (n9); Sokoloff (n9); S Vasil, ' "I Came Here, and it Got Worse Day By Day": Examining the Intersections between Migrant Precarity and Family Violence among Women with Insecure Migration Status in Australia' (2023) 30(10) Violence Against Women 2482.

[11] S Anitha, 'Legislating Gender Inequalities: The Nature and Patterns of Domestic Violence Experienced by South Asian Women with Insecure Immigration Status in the UK' (2011) 17 Violence Against Women, 1260; Segrave (n9).

In the UK, activists and researchers have continuously emphasised the disproportionate impact of violence and abuse on migrant women resulting from their intersectional location, which amplifies the ways in which abuse is experienced and the barriers to accessing support and justice.[12] Research documents how perpetrators weaponise their knowledge of the policy and service landscape, such as the hostile environment towards migrants, to limit the lives and possibilities of their victims.[13] Therefore, the nature of DVA experienced by Black and minoritised women, its impact on this group, and their responses to it can only be understood by examining how gender intersects with other social relations of power such as those based on ethnicity, race, (dis)ability, class, immigration status, and state policies.[14]

This chapter is underpinned by an understanding of DVA as gendered and as enacted and sustained within conducive contexts created by intersecting social relations of power at the levels of the family, community, and state. The following sections examine the following manifestations of DVA that disproportionately affect migrant and racially minoritised women in the UK – domestic abuse faced by women with NRPF and the problem of TMA. They draw upon research conducted on these two problems from a postcolonial feminist lens as well as on practitioners' briefings, submissions to government enquiries and select committees, annual reports, and surveys conducted by domestic abuse victims' support groups. Following a brief outline of the problem, the prevailing legal response to this problem within family law and legal-institutional responses in the associated domains of welfare and immigration policies will be outlined. This will entail a critical legal approach to the development and the workings of the law and its unequal impact.

---

[12] O Femi-Ajao, 'Intimate Partner Violence and Abuse against Nigerian Women Resident in England, UK: A Cross-Sectional Qualitative Study' (2018) BMC Women's Health 123; L Bates and others, 'Policy Evidence Summary 1: Migrant Women' University of Bristol (2018) https://researchinformation.bris.ac.uk/ws/portalfiles/portal/188884552/Policy_evidence_summary_1_Migrant_women.pdf, accessed 17 May 2024; McIlwaine, Granada, and Valenzuela-Oblitas (n10); Southall Black Sisters (SBS), 'Protection for All: The Domestic Abuse Bill and Migrant Women: Briefing Paper 2' (2019) https://southallblack sisters.org.uk/app/uploads/2023/05/da-bill-briefing-paper-2.pdf, accessed 18 June 2025; Safety4Sisters, 'Migrant Women's Rights to Safety: Pilot Project' (2016) https://www.safety4sisters.org/about-2#:~:text=In%202016%20we%20ran%20a,homeless%20or%20faced%20potential%20homelessness, accessed 18 June 2025; SBS and Latin American Women's Rights Service (LAWRS), 'Migrant Victims of Domestic Abuse Review Findings' (2020) https://lawrs.org.uk/wp-content/uploads/2020/12/SBS-and-LAWRS-joint-respo nse-to-the-Migrant-Victims-of-Domestic-Violence-Review-September-2020.pdf, accessed 17 May 2024.

[13] Anitha, Roy, and Yalamarty (n10).

[14] Crenshaw (n2).

Domestic abuse experienced by migrant women with no recourse to public funds

The problem

The British state has been slow to respond to manifestations of violence which are exacerbated and sustained by the intersection of gender, with social relations of power based on race, class, and immigration status/bordering policies. Though the term 'hostile environment' was introduced into British policy in 2012 by the then Conservative Home Secretary Theresa May, who stated, 'The aim is to create, here in Britain, a really hostile environment for illegal immigrants', these policies arguably have a much longer history.[15] Research indicates the differential gendered impact of immigration and welfare policies that are presumably designed to be gender-neutral.[16] This section outlines the adverse impact of one such policy on migrant victims of DVA. Women who migrated to the UK on the basis of their marriage to a UK resident were 'subject to immigration control', as defined in section 115 of the Immigration and Asylum Act 1999, and were granted dependent visas with the stipulation that they had 'no recourse to public funds' (NRPF). This NRPF stipulation means that they were not entitled to claim public funds (welfare benefits and housing assistance) unless an exception applied to them. Additionally, during the 1990s, marriage migrants had temporary or precarious immigration status in the UK during a probationary period of two years, during which their stay was dependent on their relationship with a settled partner. This probationary period was later extended to five years, whereby there is a provision for an extension after two and a half years and for settlement – the Indefinite Leave to Remain (ILR) – after five years.

Victims of DVA who were marriage migrants found that this probationary period exacerbated the gendered power imbalance within their relationship. Perpetrators of domestic abuse weaponise a victim's insecure immigration status to exert further power and control through threats to have them removed from the UK and separated from any children. The perpetrators of such physical, sexual, financial, and emotional DVA can often include the husband as well as the in-laws. The NRPF stipulation meant that migrant women in the probationary period were not entitled to financial assistance from the state, including most welfare benefits or social housing. This welfare state bordering has had a devastating impact on migrant women who are in an abusive relationship where they are wholly financially and otherwise dependent on their abusive spouse/

---

[15] A Gentleman, *The Windrush Betrayal: Exposing the Hostile Environment* (Guardian Faber 2019).

[16] W Menski, 'South Asian Women in Britain, Family Integrity and the Primary Purpose Rule' in R Barot, H Bradley, and S Fenton (eds), *Ethnicity, Gender and Social Change* (Palgrave Macmillan 1999); E Smith and M Marmo, 'Uncovering the "Virginity Testing" Controversy in the National Archives: The Intersectionality of Discrimination in British Immigration History' (2011) 23 Gender and History 147.

partner. This is one of the many ways in which the citizenship and residency regimes play a role in creating an imbalance between men and women who migrate, particularly as a family.

Before 2002, female marriage migrants to the UK who left their abusive husbands before they secured their ILR were routinely deported to their country of origin, often to face further abuse from their families for not 'making the marriage work'. Such deportation could be with their British children or could entail their separation from their children, who were detained by their husband in the UK. Because of the state immigration and welfare policies which denied them support, migrant women suffering domestic abuse faced the appalling 'choice' of staying in a violent relationship and risking their lives, or leaving to face destitution, deportation, and further exploitation that women who have no access to housing often face. One of the long-standing campaigns by South Asian feminist organisations from the mid-1990s was to highlight the impact of state immigration and welfare policies that effectively prevented migrant women from leaving abusive relationships for fear of being deported.[17]

The legal provisions

In 2002, in response to campaigning by South Asian feminist 'by and for'[18] organisations led by Southall Black Sisters (SBS), the Labour government passed the Domestic Violence Rule (DVR). These changes made it possible for a woman to apply for ILR in the UK before the end of the probationary period without her husband's support of her application if she could prove that her marriage had broken down because of domestic abuse (Appendix Victim of Domestic Abuse). However, she was required to provide evidence to prove that she was a victim of domestic violence.

Despite this, women with insecure immigration status were still subjected to the NRPF requirement, as this condition remained in place until their immigration status was regularised. This process could take several weeks. The first research on this problem entailed qualitative interviews with 30 South Asian women living in the North-West and Yorkshire regions of England who were seeking to or had left abusive relationships and were subject to the NRPF stipulation. This research – the first on this subject that documented the experiences of survivors – found that the introduction of the DVR had achieved little in relation to protecting

---

[17] P Joshi, 'Jumping through Hoops: Immigration and Domestic Violence' in R Gupta (ed), *Homebreakers to Jailbreakers: Southall Black Sisters* (Zed Press 2003).

[18] Specialist 'by and for' domestic violence services are uniquely run by staff who are from the communities they serve and their trustees are also from the relevant community. Their remit is to provide specialist support for women from these communities – hence the term 'by and for' services. This sets them apart from specialist VAWG organisations which may have projects catering to particular populations, but whose wider staff and governance structures might be dominated by White feminists.

migrant victims of domestic violence. One of the research participants recounted a life of domestic servitude and her lack of options:[19]

> Once here, I soon came to know that they only wanted a servant for their house ... I was busy the whole day doing housework and when my sister-in-law used to come to her house from work at five o'clock, she would ring her parents for me. So I always had to go her house, make food for her family, do some cleaning and come back to my home at night ... to make food for my in-laws' family. That was my routine ... My visa expired but (they) were not ready to apply for indefinite leave for me. His mother always used to say, 'Deport her!'

Women's precarious immigration status and fears associated with this precarity is exacerbated through techniques of coercive control, whereby their immigration documents are retained by abusive partners/in-laws and they are deliberately kept uninformed about their status, to keep them vulnerable and dependent – this is now recognised as immigration abuse. Immigration abuse is a form of DVA that is enabled and sustained by immigration legislation and welfare state bordering policy and practice, which refers to practices of controlling and managing access to social rights based on residence, migrancy, and/or citizenship in a given socio-political order.[20]

Another woman who fled her abusive partner with her baby found that she had nowhere to go:[21]

> My husband beat me up several times, especially when I gave birth to a baby girl. I never discussed my problems with anyone ... Not with my own family, because I was not allowed to take phone calls. When my in-laws turned against my baby – they refused to bring milk and nappies for her – then I decided to leave that house. I had no place to go to, no money for food and no friend or relative or any other person who knew me. I tried several refuges, but they would find out that I am on 'no recourse' and they refused to take me.

This was because spaces in women's refuges in the UK are funded through the housing benefits and refuges found themselves unable to accept women who did not have access to these benefits. Research documents how this rule left women destitute while they were expected to apply for ILR and often had the effect of locking women in abusive relationships since they could not access emergency housing or benefits. The NRPF requirement left the vast majority of women

---

[19]   Anitha, 'Neither Safety Nor Justice' (n9) 194.
[20]   S Bendixsen and L Näre, 'Welfare State Bordering as a Form of Mobility and Migration Control' (2024) 50 Journal of Ethnic and Migration Studies 2689.
[21]   Anitha, 'No Recourse, No Support' (n9) 470–1.

who were abused unable to utilise the DVR to escape an abusive relationship, as one woman recounted:[22]

> I have thought of leaving many times … I have tried to leave twice before … I don't know what is going to upset him – I cannot deal with his anger. He has become very violent and I worry about my safety. I am trying to find out what my options are if I leave …

Though access to housing and benefits are acknowledged by the government as essential prerequisites for all victims wishing to escape domestic abuse and are the very basis for the existence of domestic abuse refuges, state welfare bordering policies trapped migrant victims of DVA outside the scope of the protection afforded by domestic violence legislation and policies that were accessible to citizens.[23] This research documented how, beyond acting as a barrier to leaving abusive relationships, state immigration and welfare bordering policies were themselves part of the matrix of structural inequalities which enabled and sustained private violence, thereby creating conducive contexts for such violence and abuse.[24]

Between 2001 and 2003, SBS undertook a survey aimed at monitoring the impact of the domestic abuse concession/rule.[25] Out of over 100 agencies, mainly refuges, who responded, the majority stated that the NRPF requirement prevented women from reporting domestic abuse because they were unable to obtain welfare benefits and emergency local authority accommodation or access women's refuges. Their response showed that only a third of all women who had immigration problems were accommodated in refuges and that specialist 'by and for' refuges bore the brunt of accommodating women with NRPF. 'By and for' organisations tend to be small, independent domestic abuse services and seldom have large reserves, and this policy led to a severe drain on their resources.

In 2004–05 a Women's Aid survey found that there were 477 women with no recourse problems in refuges, and on a census day (2 November 2005), 177 women and their children with NRPF were provided with refuge-based services. Of these, 54 per cent were partially funded via social services, the remaining 81 women and children were supported by charitable donations. An additional 54 were turned away because refuge providers could not afford to support them.[26] A temporary source of funding, the '*Last Resort Fund*' was being utilised to

---

[22] Ibid, 471.

[23] Ibid.

[24] Kelly (n7); Anitha (n11).

[25] Select Committee on Home Affairs Written Evidence, 'Appendix 46: Memorandum Submitted by Southall Black Sisters' (2008) https://publications.parliament.uk/pa/cm200 708/cmselect/cmhaff/263/263we62.htm, accessed 24 July 2024.

[26] Ibid, citing E Williamson, 'Survey of Domestic Violence Services Findings Women's Aid Federation of England' (Women's Aid 2006).

support many of the women but was insufficient to meet the scale of the need. Since the demise of the *Last Resort Fund* in 2006, many refuges were unable to accommodate women with NRPF. For example, in 2006, London-based Ealing Women's Aid reported about a 50 per cent refusal rate (out of a total of 20 women) for women with NRPF.[27]

In earlier works, one woman's lived experience of trying to leave an abusive relationship in the face of a lack of institutional support from statutory services due to her NRPF status was documented:[28]

> I had no indefinite leave, so they first refused to help me. Then, after the birth of my baby, a social worker arranged a place in a B&B where I spent the whole day inside because it was near my in-laws' house, and they were all English men there. I had no money, nothing to eat for myself. She [the social worker] only provided milk and nappies for my baby. I spent two weeks without eating anything and she always used to say, 'Why don't you want to go to Pakistan?' I was so scared at what she said – I didn't want to go back.

Research also documented the impact of the NRPF requirement on children.[29] Many destitute survivors of DVA who were pregnant or with young children were being turned away by local authorities who refused to assist or interpreted their duty to protect children under the National Assistance Act 1948 or Children Act (CA) 1989 extremely narrowly. They would offer to take the children but not the mother into care or to pay for a flight back home to countries of origin, irrespective of the conditions or harm the women might face in that country, or they would threaten to take steps to ensure that custody of the child(ren) is awarded to abusive fathers. It was clear that standards of protection for children that were commonplace within the wider society were not being applied in cases where women had insecure immigration status.

Single women had scant chance of obtaining local authority assistance, even though many were vulnerable. Anitha documented the plight of single women faced in the absence of any support as they were forced to rely on relatives, friends, or even strangers who had offered them a place to stay.[30] Their dependency and lack of viable alternatives placed them at risk of exploitation and abuse:

---

[27] Select Committee (n25).

[28] Anitha (n11) 471.

[29] S Roy, 'No Recourse, No Duty to Care?' Imkaan (2008) https://static1.squarespace.com/static/5f7d9f4addc689717e6ea200/t/61e6a77f9b3bf9708d007261/1642506112688/2008+_+Imkaan+_+No+Recourse+-+No+Duty+to+Care.pdf, accessed 20 July 2024; Amnesty International and SBS, 'No Recourse – No Safety: The UK Government Failure to Protect Women from Violence' (Amnesty International 2008).

[30] Anitha 'No Recourse, No Support' (n9) 474.

My husband had me thrown out of the house ... I was scared as I didn't know about the laws in this country – I was not even registered with a doctor ... I stayed with an aunt but her husband tried to sexually abuse me. I fled from there and ended up with a friend. I've moved from place to place. I have no connection with my family now.

Pressure created by the Campaign to Abolish No Recourse to Public Funds resulted in the introduction of the Destitute Domestic Violence Concession (DDVC) in April 2012.[31] This provision enabled women on a spousal visa who were subject to NRPF the right to access benefits and social housing for a period of three months while they applied for expedited ILR to stay in the UK under the DVR.

Taking stock of the provisions and the way forward

These changes were a long-awaited response to the history of mobilisation by South Asian feminist groups that highlighted and challenged the differential gendered implications of what is often constructed as a gender-neutral policy of immigration control. Notwithstanding the gains made since the early 2000s, there remains a long way to go to ensure that immigration control does not serve to deny women their human rights. Several inadequacies remained in the provisions of the DDVC and the DVR.

The three-month limit on the DDVC while the application for ILR is being processed presents inadequate time to help women access immigration advice in the context of the shortage of specialist immigration advisers following legal aid cuts. The period also remains inadequate to enable them to access specialist services and obtain other advice and the holistic support that they need to address their often complex problems.

Some groups of migrant women experiencing domestic abuse continue to remain unprotected. These include women who entered or remained in the UK on other dependent visas such as student and work permit holders; women who had these visas in their own right, overstayed their visas, or were undocumented; and some categories of trafficked women and overseas domestic workers subject to abuse and exploitation. Research indicates that the safety net provided by these changes remains sparse.[32] Research highlights that women in these categories are reluctant to disclose violence and abuse for fear of the consequences, including the service responses they receive.[33] Given their inability

---

[31]   Amnesty International and SBS (n29).

[32]   RG Dudley, 'Domestic Abuse and Women with "No Recourse to Public Funds": The State's Role in Shaping and Reinforcing Coercive Control' (2017) 6 Families, Relationships and Societies 201.

[33]   Ibid; Bates and others (n12).

to pay rent or subsistence, victim-survivors with NRPF are frequently prevented from accessing women's refuges, unless refuges make exceptions, and so often face homelessness.[34] Not only are they unable to access social housing/housing benefit, but are also effectively unable to rent in the private sector because the Immigration Acts 2014 and 2016 prohibit renting to those 'unlawfully present' in the UK. While this deputisation of immigration control to ordinary citizens has profound implications for the relationship between citizens and the state, the surveillance and regulation of non-citizens particularly contributes to their social exclusion and marginality within everyday society.[35]

Services run by 'by and for' Black and minority ethnic women and children have long been the predominant sources of support for women with NRPF in a context where social service responses remain inconsistent at best and indifferent and negligent at worst.[36] Abused women with NRPF who fall outside the categories covered by the DVR and DDVC but have children should be able access support from children's social services under section 17 of the CA 1989, but in reality many are turned away if the mothers have NRPF. Social services instead offer to take children into care or place them with the perpetrator's family while offering to pay for women to return to the country of origin, ignoring the danger this represents for many women.[37] Indeed, the lack of a safety net has raised concern that women with NRPF are vulnerable to high rates of domestic and sexual abuse and sexual and economic exploitation.[38] Single women in such situations are faced with refusal from social services.

Barriers to accessing services enhances risk of DVA for some categories of racially minoritised and migrant women and their children.[39] For example, a domestic homicide review undertaken in February 2013 following the death of a migrant women from Bulgaria or Romania (referred in the review as an A2 migrant from the second wave of Accession countries to the European Economic Area) in Sheffield highlighted that systems were deficient in ensuring the victim had full access to the services she may have required:

---

[34] Findings from the first year of the No Women Turned Away project: Women's Aid, 'Nowhere to Turn' (2017) https://www.womensaid.org.uk/wp-content/uploads/2019/12/NWTA-2017.pdf, accessed 18 June 2025.

[35] M Griffiths and C Yeo, 'The UK's Hostile Environment: Deputising Immigration Control' (2021) 41 Critical Social Policy 521.

[36] S Anitha and A Gill, 'Domestic Violence during the Pandemic: "By and For" Frontline Practitioners' Mediation of Practice and Policies to Support Racially Minoritised Women' (2022) 29 Organisation 460.

[37] H Siddiqui, 'Ending the Stark Choice: Domestic Violence or Destitution in the UK' Open Democracy (2013) https://www.opendemocracy.net/en/shine-a-light/ending-stark-choice-domestic-violence-or-destitution-in-uk/, accessed 17 May 2024.

[38] H Siddiqui and M Patel, 'Safe and Sane' Southall Black Sisters (2010) http://www.southallblacksisters.org.uk/reports/safe-and-sane-report/, accessed 18 June 2025.

[39] SafeLives (n3); Jolly and Gupta (n6).

The Review has identified that after Adult D fled the home there were gaps in service responses, and finds that these were due not only to her status as an A2 migrant; and to the lack of knowledge and understanding of staff about her rights as an A2 migrant fleeing domestic violence; but most importantly, to deficits in the systems available to ensure she was provided with her rights in law and the resources for refuge, support and safety which would be provided to a UK national in similar circumstances.[40]

A snapshot survey found that between November 2012 and January 2013, 64 per cent (n = 154) of 242 women who approached services for support did not qualify for the DDVC and were without a safety net.[41] These findings were reiterated in other research.[42] The Women's Aid report showed that only 5.8 per cent of refuge vacancies in 2017–18 would even consider a woman who had NRPF and in some cases this was conditional on her having funding in place to cover her stay.[43] Problems in providing accommodation and/or assistance to those on non-spousal visas have been highlighted by many VAWG victim support organisations across the UK.

The Domestic Abuse Act 2021 presented a unique opportunity to redress these policy gaps. However, though three proposed amendments to the draft Domestic Abuse Bill to extend the eligibility for the DVR and the DDVC were successfully passed in the House of Lords, they were subsequently rejected by the government, thereby retaining the two-tier discriminatory system of support that exists for victims of domestic abuse in the UK.[44]

These UK government policies also contravene the 2011 Council of Europe Convention on Combating Violence against Women and Domestic Violence (hereinafter the Istanbul Convention or the Convention), which came into force on 1 August 2014. The Istanbul Convention, which created a binding legal framework for the ratifying states, aimed to protect women and girls from gender-based violence and frames domestic violence as a human rights issue by including

---

[40] NRPF Network, 'Domestic Abuse Bill Consultation' (NRPF Network 2018) 1.

[41] SBS, 'Campaign to Abolish No Recourse to Public Funds' (Home Office Concession for Destitute Victims of Domestic Violence and a Call to Save Lives of All Women and Children 2013) https://southallblacksisters.org.uk/news/campaign-to-abolish-no-recourse-to-public-funds-marks-international-day-for-the-elimination-of-violence-against-women-and-16-days-of-activism-2013/, accessed 18 June 2025.

[42] Bates and others (n12); SBS and LAWRS (n12) 7.

[43] S Davidge and L Magnusson, 'The Domestic Abuse Report 2019: The Annual Audit' Women's Aid (2019) https://www.womensaid.org.uk/wp-content/uploads/2019/12/The-Annual-Audit-2019.pdf, accessed 18 June 2025.

[44] K Dharni, 'The Struggle Continues: SBS Responds to the Government's Rejection of our Amendments to Protect Migrant Women' Southall Black Sisters (2021) https://southallblacksisters.org.uk/news/the-struggle-continues-sbs-responds-to-gov-rejection-of-amendments-to-protect-migrant-women/, accessed 18 June 2025.

a non-discrimination clause prohibiting discrimination based on migration or refugee status in relation to the implementation of the Convention.[45]

This clause states that victims of VAWG must be protected regardless of their migration or refugee status. In line with this principle, Article 59 (residence status) of the Convention is intended to provide an immigration relief to migrant women victims of abuse by carving out exceptions in the immigration control prerogatives of host states. This includes provisions for autonomous residence permit for victims of domestic violence where their residence status depends upon their spouse to enable victims to leave an abusive relationship.[46] Through this clause, the Istanbul Convention fosters a holistic approach to violence against women that addresses some of the structural underpinnings of VAWG which include disadvantages created by state policies, and thus extends state focus beyond criminal justice solutions to VAWG.[47] However, the UK government's Article 59 reservation when ratifying the Istanbul Convention in July 2022 means that migrant victims of VAWG in the UK do not have full protection. This undermines the principle of non-discrimination in Article 4.

In light of these exclusions, a report commissioned by the Domestic Abuse Commissioner for England and Wales who is the independent voice for victims and survivors of domestic abuse, lays out evidence-based estimates of the number of migrant survivors with NRPF in the UK in need of support as well as the cost of providing support and the benefits of doing so.[48] This report shows there are approximately 32,000 survivors with NRPF who could report the abuse to an authority each year if provided the ability to gain recourse to public funds, although in the first year it's not likely to be more than 7,000. It includes migrant survivors with insecure immigration status such as those on student visas, visitor's visas, work visas, or those who are undocumented. Police, NHS doctors, and local childcare services and housing are forced to pick up the pieces when the situation accelerates to an emergency and victims come in with injuries and complaints – this costs an estimated overall £16.2 million a year.[49] The gains

---

[45]   JA Ronagh McQuigg, *The Istanbul Convention, Domestic Violence and Human Rights* (Routledge 2017).

[46]   S De Vido, 'The Ratification of the Council of Europe Istanbul Convention by the EU: A Step Forward in the Protection of Women from Violence in the European Legal System' (2017) 9 European Journal of Legal Studies 69.

[47]   F Staiano, 'Protection beyond Victimization: The Significance of the Istanbul Convention for Migrant Women' in J Niemi, L Peroni, and V Stoyanova (eds), *International Law and Violence against Women: Europe and the Istanbul Convention* (Routledge 2020).

[48]   Domestic Abuse Commissioner, 'Safety before Status: The Solutions' (2022) https://domest icabusecommissioner.uk/wp-content/uploads/2022/12/Safety-before-status-The-Solutions. pdf, accessed 18 June 2025.

[49]   K Scanlon and others, 'Cost-Benefit Analysis of Extending Support to Domestic Abuse Victims with NRPF' LSE and Centre for Analysis of Social Exclusion (2022) https://www. lse.ac.uk/geography-and-environment/research/lse-london/documents/Reports/FINAL-REPORT-Dec-2022-COST-BENEFIT-ANALYSIS-OF-EXTENDING-SUPPORT-TO-DOMESTIC-ABUSE-VICTIMS-WITH-NRPF.pdf, accessed 24 July 2024.

from enabling all survivors to apply for DDVC (for public funds if destitute) and Domestic Violence Indefinite Leave to Remain (DVILR) (to seek ILR in the UK), including those with irregular migration status over a ten-year period, would exceed £2 billion.[50] The benefit-to-cost ratio for the first group of migrant survivors is one to four. For every £1 of cost, the gains to society are valued at £4 – these gains include physical and emotional harm prevented, homelessness and destitution prevented, employment and skills gained, including higher tax revenues, and gains to children.

Following campaigning by women's domestic violence services and criticism of the UK government's reservations to the Istanbul Convention, in February 2024, the UK government implemented changes to the Migrant Victims Domestic Abuse Concession (MVDAC), formerly known as the DDVC. The changes will result in the extension of the MVDAC to partners of worker and student visa holders with NRPF and entitle them to receive benefits and housing and limited leave to remain for three months. However, unlike those on spousal/partner visas, they will not be eligible to apply for settlement under the DVILR rule. This will create a cliff edge at the end of three months for these migrant victim-survivors and will prevent many victim-survivors from reporting abuse due to fear of deportation at the end of the three-month period.

There is an urgent need for the UK government to remove its reservation to Article 59 by extending a combined MVDAC–DVILR model for all victims of domestic violence with NRPF. UK government policy mirrors that of many countries in the Global North, where marriage migrants are granted dependent visas which tie their residence and entitlement to welfare benefits with their marital status by proscribing their entitlement to public funds. Many countries, including the Netherlands and Australia, have provisions within migration law and policy for victims of DVA who hold partner- or family-type visas that would allow them to access permanent residence in the country of destination. However, in many countries, these provisions are limited to certain categories of migrant women (eg those who entered the country on a spouse visa) and require a rigorous administrative process and have high evidential thresholds to prove domestic abuse, which make them difficult to access.[51] While the US has provisions that enable migrant women who are not on spouse visas to access support, Canada is one of the few countries which removed the conditional residence requirement for spouses in 2012 in order to redress the power imbalance that can sustain domestic abuse in transnational marriages. This is by far the most progressive policy response to enable all victims of domestic abuse to access the support they need; its very existence removes a key power imbalance that enables and sustains such violence and abuse.

---

50   Ibid, 11.
51   AB Jelinic, 'Australia's Family Violence Provisions in Migration Law: A Comparative Study' (2020) 21 Flinders Law Journal 259.

The UK government's NRPF policies and the wider 'hostile environment' seriously undermine protection and non-discrimination principles and heighten the vulnerability of migrant women to abuse. This state response makes the UK government complicit in the DVA of migrant women. Immigration controls seem to override the application of human rights principles which protect and support victims of domestic abuse and hold perpetrators to account.

Summary

Women's experience of DVA is shaped by the intersections of different social relations of power such as those based on gender, race/ethnicity, immigration status, class, and state policies. Not all women experience domestic abuse in the same way. For racially minoritised and women with insecure immigration status, the state bordering and welfare policies are a key part of the matrix of structural inequalities which enable and sustain private violence. 'By and for' domestic violence organisations have been at the forefront of highlighting and campaigning for an end to state policies which trap migrant women in abusive relationships. Despite progress through the provisions for particular categories of migrant women with NRPF, there remain significant gaps in the UK state's responses to this problem.

Transnational marriage abandonment as a form of domestic violence and abuse

The problem

Since the 2010s, activists and researchers began to document a growing form of violence and abuse perpetrated across national borders which has now come to be recognised as transnational marriage abandonment (TMA). Commonly accompanying and occurring in the context of DVA, TMA takes place in transnational marriages whereby the resident spouse – usually the husband – deliberately abandons his wife across national borders in order to deprive her of her financial, settlement, and other rights. Based on life history narratives of 57 women in India and interviews with 21 practitioners, this problem was documented in the first systematic research on this subject, which outlined three main contexts within which abandonment takes place in transnational marriages:[52]

1. A woman migrates upon marriage to join her husband in another country and is subjected to a period of neglect, abuse, and exploitation, following which she is thrown out of the marital home or, less commonly, leaves to

---

[52]   Anitha, Roy, and Yalamarty (n10).

escape the violence but is then prevented from returning to her husband's country on her spouse visa.

2. Following marriage migration and abuse, the woman is taken back to her country of origin either coercively or deceptively (for example, on the pretext of a holiday) and abandoned there while the husband returns and takes steps to prevent her from joining him.

3. Following transnational marriage, the husband returns to his country of residence with assurances to sponsor his wife's spouse visa without any intention to do so. The woman is left in her natal home or with her in-laws and is eventually thrown out or leaves because of domestic violence.

The following discussion focuses on the first two dimensions of the problem outlined, as the victims of DVA who are in the third category have never migrated following marriage, and hence commonly fall outside the purvey of family justice and criminal justice systems in their husbands' countries of settlement.

Related to the issue of NRPF, the abandonment of wives in their home countries by husbands who are UK residents has become a growing phenomenon, whereby a marriage migrant, within the probationary period of the dependent visa, is taken back deceptively to her country of origin and abandoned there with or without her children, while her husband returns to the country of residence and revokes her visa. Such abandonment commonly takes place within a context of other forms of violence, abuse, and exploitation. TMA has been reported in the context of Indian-, Pakistani-, and Bangladeshi-origin men in the UK as well as other countries with histories of migration and of transnational marriages. DVA enacted through border crossings and via the migration regime, including marriage abandonment, has been documented across various diasporic contexts in countries including the UK, the US, Canada, Denmark, and Australia.[53] Though the small body of existing scholarship on TMA has focused on South Asian women who have migrated to marry men in the Global North, different dimensions of this problem are beginning to be explored in relation to other diasporic communities as well as in relation to different origin countries of the victims/survivors. Existing research indicates that such abandonment is a

---

[53] N Merali, 'Experiences of South Asian Brides Entering Canada after Recent Changes to Family Sponsorship Policies' (2009) 15 Violence Against Women 321 http://dx.doi.org/10.1177/1077801208330435; SD Dasgupta and U Rudra, *Transnational Abandonment of South Asian Women: A New Face of Violence against Women* (Manavi 2011); A Stewart, 'Abuse, Danger, and Security in Transnational Marriages: Polity and Community in India and the United Kingdom' (2013) 19 Violence Against Women 1263; A Bajpai, 'Across the High Seas: Abuse, Desertion, and Violence in Transnational Marriages in India' (2013) 19 Violence Against Women 1246; A Liversage, 'Gendered Struggles over Residency Rights When Turkish Immigrant Marriages Break Up' (2013) 3 Oñati Socio-Legal Series 1070; Segrave (n9); Vasil (n10); S Bhandari, 'Experiences of Transnational Abandonment in the Lives of Abused South Asian Women in the United States' (2024) Journal of Family Violence, https://doi.org/10.1007/s10896-024-00683-2.

gendered problem; there is little evidence from research and case law of similar abandonment of male marriage migrants. TMA is embedded within a gendered pattern of violence and control within marriage that is exacerbated by the power asymmetries that operate in transnational contexts and are enabled by state bordering regimes.

Scholarship on TMA documents intense and severe manifestations of violence and abuse preceding abandonment. Research in the UK and India documents women's accounts of DVA following marriage migration, which commonly included being confined to the family home and a range of purposeful strategies to exert control over them and to prevent them from disclosing the abuse and seeking help, as recounted here:[54]

> My father had given me a mobile but they (in-laws) would hide the charger. My mother-in-law said, 'Once a girl is married she has to forget her parental family – who is going to pay the bill?' One day, when no one was at home, I saw my charger on the table. So, I tried to charge my mobile but found that they had removed the sim card. When my husband came home, and I asked him about it, he snatched the mobile, threw it forcefully on the floor and stomped on it, crushing it. (Manju, 31)

The impact of such coercion and control was exacerbated for marriage migrants who seldom had kinship networks in their husband's country and no knowledge of services or the law, and thereby faced extreme isolation. This scholarship on TMA also documents the extreme control surrounding women's domestic work, which includes conditions akin to domestic servitude: 'I used to do all the household chores, I was only given two rotis in the morning, two in the evening. I used to hide from them and eat a third roti.' (Anjali, 32)[55] Men weaponised women's precarity created by their insecure immigration status by threatening to send the women back to their home country, and often by threatening to keep the children.[56] In this case (documented in Anitha and others), Shiva's husband orchestrated her precarity, which she only discovered when she disclosed his abuse and sought help from a family friend:[57]

> His harassment escalated over the months. Eventually, I told him, 'You get me a ticket for India and give me back my passport which you have hidden somewhere.' He didn't want to hear such things from

---

[54] Anitha, Roy, and Yalamarty (n10) 12.

[55] S Anitha, 'Understanding Economic Abuse through an Intersectional Lens: Financial Abuse, Control and Exploitation of South Asian Women's Productive and Reproductive Labours' (2019) 25 Violence Against Women 1854, 1865.

[56] Anitha, Roy, and Yalamarty (n10).

[57] Ibid, 759.

me, so he started beating me in the presence of our landlord. I was very frightened. I later went to his friend for help but he told me, 'You can't go anywhere. You are staying here illegally, they (police) will put you in jail straightaway.' I learnt that he had not brought me there as his wife but as a visitor. The time limit for my stay was over, so I was in deep trouble … When he came home, he beat me badly that night. He threatened me, 'If I cut you into pieces and bury you, no one will know about it.' Over the next few months the beatings continued, got worse. I knew that I was staying there illegally, so I didn't know what to do. (Shiva, 29)

State immigration policies which seek to create a hostile environment towards migrants as well as the absence of effective transnational legal mechanisms create conducive contexts that exacerbate the power imbalance in transnational marriages. It was in the context of ongoing DVA that men who had citizenship or residence rights in the UK abandoned their migrant wives in their home countries.

The added vulnerabilities and dependence arising from their precarious status limited women's options in the face of violence and abuse. Perpetrators exploited the restrictive immigration policies and hostile environment towards migrants in their country of residence to treat their migrant wives as disposable women.

TMA commonly entails deception and/or coercion, as reported by one Indian woman who had migrated to the UK following marriage:

He often used to hit me. He would tell me that he had much better girls to choose from. After three years like this, we came to India for a holiday … After two to three days, he left me at my mother's place. We had return tickets – we were planning to go back together after two months. But he phoned me and said he was returning to the UK that very night and I should come back later. I was surprised, but I thought, he must have got some new project at work. We all went to the airport to see him off and he left. Later on, he suggested that I stay on to attend English classes so I could pass some exams that I was planning to take in the UK, so I extended my return ticket. It was only later that I realised that he was waiting for my visa to expire. As soon as the deadline passed, he called to say he was going to divorce me. (Hira, 32)

After stranding their wives abroad, men would cancel their visa and issue ex parte divorce proceedings in the UK. Women found it impossible to represent themselves in any divorce proceedings, to claim financial settlement, secure child support when abandoned with their children, or to participate in family court proceedings on child custody when separated from their children. Abandonment also prevented any criminal proceedings against the men for domestic abuse and deprived women of any settlement rights in the husband's country. The social impacts of abandonment were many – women were often blamed for the end of their marriages and for bringing dishonour to their families, and they reported a loss of relationships with extended family and friends, a detrimental impact on the social standing of their family, difficulty in securing employment, and the loss of good marriage prospects of younger sisters. For South Asian women, loss of dowry upon abandonment and having to return to their parental home placed women in a precarious position as a potential threat to the inheritance of their brothers and thus unwelcome returnees to the natal home.[58]

Lack of awareness about the laws in an alien country acted to the detriment of the abandoned women, as their husbands utilised the legal system of the foreign country to their own advantage. Within their home countries too, abandoned women tried for many years but often failed to obtain justice. Beyond the act of abandonment, men strategically choose between different legal jurisdictions to deprive their wives of their financial and settlement rights and child custody, and enact forms of control that can be categorised as transnational post-separation abuse. TMA entails deceptive and coercive behaviour to bring about the removal and immobilisation of the immigrant wife. The intention behind this purposeful action is to deprive her of her financial and settlement rights and to exercise coercive control over her. Based on its intention and impact, TMA needs to be conceptualised as a form of domestic abuse in and of itself.

For marriage migrants with insecure immigration status who are victims of DVA, the UK has policies in place (DDVC and DVILR) to enable them to gain residence rights in the UK and access welfare and housing benefits (see the section 'The legal provisions'). However, the biggest barrier was that these entitlements could only be claimed by those who were already within the UK, thus preventing victims of domestic abuse who had been abandoned abroad or who had fled to their home country in fear of their lives from accessing the provisions on the very basis of their victimisation. Immigration officers who were at the forefront of implementing the hostile environment policy prevented abandoned women's re-entry to claim their rights as victims of domestic abuse in the UK. Alongside this, even for the few who managed to make their way back to the UK, the lack of recognition of TMA as a form of domestic abuse often hindered them from meeting the evidential thresholds where they did not have proof of other forms of domestic abuse preceding their abandonment.

The legal provisions

The UK is one of the only countries in the world which has recently developed specific policy responses to this problem. TMA was recently recognised as a form of domestic abuse in the UK as a result of a coordinated campaign by academics and practitioners. Following research on TMA,[59] this author established a

---

58   Ibid, 20–1.
59   Anitha, Roy, and Yalamarty (n10).

working group with frontline domestic violence practitioners from SBS and lawyers working in the area of international family law to make recommendations to address this problem. They persuaded the President of the Family Division in England and Wales to recognise TMA as a form of domestic abuse in and of itself within the family justice system (FJS). In October 2017, a revised definition of domestic abuse incorporated 'dowry-related abuse and transnational marriage abandonment', whereby

> 'abandonment' refers to the practice whereby a husband, in England and Wales, deliberately abandons or 'strands' his foreign national wife abroad, usually without financial resources, in order to prevent her from asserting matrimonial and/or residence rights in England and Wales. It may involve children who are either abandoned with, or separated from, their mother.[60]

This change enabled abandoned women to access legal aid. However, victims who were stranded abroad found that immigration officers were unwilling to act on this change and routinely prevented women's re-entry to the UK to take part in family proceedings.

In 2022, a High Court case was brought against the Home Office by AM, a 31-year-old woman who was a Pakistani national married to a British citizen. She suffered severe financial, physical, emotional, and sexual abuse at the hands of her husband for years while in the UK on a spouse visa.[61] One day, her husband effectively forced her to travel to Pakistan along with their then two-year-old daughter. Once there he took her travel documents away and returned to the UK with their daughter, thus preventing her from accessing the protections available in the UK for migrant victims of DVA. In a landmark ruling on 14 October 2022, the High Court found that failure to make provision for victims of TMA was unlawfully discriminatory and a disproportionate interference with their Article 8 rights. This led to the creation of a new entry route to the UK for victims of TMA, which came into force on 31 January 2024.

These immigration rules – Appendix Victim of Domestic Abuse – enable victims of domestic abuse abandoned overseas to apply for an ILR visa to re-enter the UK. This entry route closes the justice gap for migrant victims of DVA and abuse who came to the UK on a spouse visa prior to their transnational abandonment and cannot apply for DDVC and DLR from outside the UK.

---

60   Practice Direction 12j: 'Child Arrangements & Contact Orders: Domestic Abuse and Harm' para 3 https://www.justice.gov.uk/courts/procedure-rules/family/practice_directions/pd_p art_12j, accessed 7 October 2024.

61   *AM v SSHD* [2022] EWHC 2591.

Taking stock and the way forward

These recent policy changes in the UK also point to the important role of academic research in enabling us to understand and address the problem of violence against women. It also redresses a gap that prevented migrant victims of DVA from participating in the proceedings of the FJS and initiating any criminal proceedings against the perpetrators.

There are some promising elements within these provisions that address the concerns of researchers and campaigners and acknowledge the particular constraints facing transnationally abandoned women. For example, the caseworker guidance notes that the standard of proof for applications made from outside the UK on the TMA route is lowered to 'reasonable degree of likelihood' in recognition of the fact that 'victims abandoned overseas are more likely to be in situations of vulnerability and face additional barriers to applying as compared to those in the UK who may be able to access support services'.[62]

However, the eligibility for ILR under these rules is similar to in-country applications for migrant victims of DVA with NRPF, which excludes those linked to non-settled persons, such as sponsored workers or students, which remains an area for concern. On a more positive note, this policy recognises that domestic abuse can originate from the partner or another family member, and that TMA is a form of domestic abuse in and of itself. It remains to be seen whether the implementation of this policy addresses the problem adequately, so this remains an area for future research.

Summary

TMA is a form of DVA that takes place across national borders and is enabled by state bordering policies and regimes. TMA entails deceptive and coercive behaviour to bring about the removal and immobilisation of the immigrant wife by abandoning her outside the UK with the intention of depriving her of her financial and settlement rights. Based on its intention and impact, TMA needs to be conceptualised as a form of domestic violence in and of itself. Through an alliance between academics and activists from 'by and for' domestic violence organisations, this form of domestic abuse has been recognised in the UK, the first country to name and respond to this problem. Provisions such as an entry route back to the UK for transnationally abandoned women represent a significant victory, but the implementation of this policy needs to be monitored.

---

62   UK Visas and Immigration, 'Victims of Domestic Violence: Caseworker Guidance' (2024) https://www.gov.uk/government/publications/victims-of-domestic-violence, accessed 24 July 2024.

Conclusion

Women with insecure immigration status and NRPF or those lacking immigration documentation find that immigration control takes precedence over their rights as victims of VAWG. Policies created with the aim of fostering a hostile environment towards migrants reinforces statutory and other support service responses that criminalise migrant victims of DVA who are framed outside of expected standards of best practice in supporting VAWG survivors. Consequently, migrant women are frequently left with little choice other than to either remain trapped in abusive contexts or face the threat of destitution, detention, and/or deportation, and remain forgotten and disposable, exposed to further economic and sexual exploitation. South Asian feminist activism in Britain has challenged both dominant gendered norms within South Asian diasporas which scaffold VAWG and challenged the British state to respond to this violence through protective and preventative mechanisms to protect racially minoritised and migrant victims of DVA.

The experience of victims of domestic abuse who have NRPF and TMA alerts us to the need to recognise how DVA is shaped by women's location at the intersection of different social relations of power such as gender, immigration status, class, race/ethnicity, and state policy/practice. We need to understand how these vectors of power not only shape the impact of the violence by creating barriers to accessing services but also the very nature and forms of the abuse. Perpetrators weaponise hostile policy and media environment towards migrants and power derived from their citizenship/residence in the Global North to exacerbate their control over victims, secure in the prospect of immunity and state complicity in this violence. State policy and transnational legal regimes thus become part of the matrix of control that sustains the domestic abuse within transnational marriages. An intersectional postcolonial lens can help us understand the specificities in migrant women's experience of abuse while avoiding cultural essentialism and locate these harms within the structural inequalities between nations as well as in hostile bordering regimes in the Global North which create gendered precarity.

Further questions to consider

- Critically reflect on this oft-repeated characterisation of domestic abuse: 'It can happen to anyone'.
- How does gender intersect with other social relations of power to shape migrant women's experience of domestic abuse and its impact?
- What changes are needed in policy and practice to better protect migrant victims of domestic abuse?

Further materials

Amnesty International and Southall Black Sisters (SBS), 'No Recourse – No Safety: The UK Government Failure to Protect Women from Violence' (Amnesty International and Southall Black Sisters 2008)

Anitha S, 'Understanding Transnational Marriage Abandonment' (SafeLives) https://soundcloud.com/domestic-abuse-podcast/dr-sundari-anitha-transnatio nal-marriage-abandonment, accessed 18 June 2025

Anitha S and Gill A, 'Domestic Violence during the Pandemic: "By and For" Frontline Practitioners' Mediation of Practice and Policies to Support Racially Minoritised Women' (2022) 29 Organisation 460

Anitha S, Roy A, and Yalamarty H, 'Gender, Migration, and Exclusionary Citizenship Regimes: Conceptualizing Transnational Abandonment of Wives as a Form of Violence against Women' (2018) 24 Violence against Women 747

Bates L and others, 'Policy Evidence Summary I: Migrant Women' University of Bristol (2018) https://researchinformation.bris.ac.uk/ws/portalfiles/portal/ 188884552/Policy_evidence_summary_1_Migrant_women.pdf, accessed 17 May 2024

BBC News, 'The Wives Abandoned by British Asian Men' (2016) https://www. youtube.com/watch?v=k6OmhfOgj_4, accessed 18 June 2025

Bhandari S, 'Experiences of Transnational Abandonment in the Lives of Abused South Asian Women in the United States' (2024) Journal of Family Violence https://doi.org/10.1007/s10896-024-00683-2.

Domestic Abuse Commissioner, 'Safety before Status: The Solutions' (2022) https://domesticabusecommissioner.uk/wp-content/uploads/2022/12/Saf ety-before-status-The-Solutions.pdf, accessed 18 June 2025

NRPF Network, 'Domestic Abuse Bill Consultation' (NRPF Network 2018).

Southall Black Sisters (SBS), 'Campaign to Abolish No Recourse to Public Funds' (Home Office Concession for Destitute Victims of Domestic Violence and a Call to Save Lives of All Women and Children 2013) https://southallblacksisters.org. uk/news/campaign-to-abolish-no-recourse-to-public-funds-marks-internatio nal-day-for-the-elimination-of-violence-against-women-and-16-days-of-activ ism-2013/, accessed 18 June 2025

UK Visas and Immigration, 'Victims of Domestic Violence: Caseworker Guidance' (2024) https://www.gov.uk/government/publications/victims-of- domestic-violence, accessed 24 July 2024

14

The Invisibilisation of Male Victims in the Family and Criminal Courts: Domestic Abuse, Honour-Based Abuse, and Parental Alienation

Mohammad Mazher Idriss, Elizabeth Bates, and Ben Hine

Introduction

This chapter explores the diverse experiences of male victims of domestic abuse, false allegations, parental alienation (PA), honour-based abuse (HBA), and forced marriages (FMs). It examines male victims' experiences of the civil and criminal justice systems, the family courts, and their interconnectedness. It begins with an exploration of the way in which domestic abuse continues and escalates post-separation for male victims. Despite the wealth of literature exploring female victimisation, male victimisation in domestic abuse studies has been largely omitted from the discourse until relatively recently. This exclusion does not provide the full picture of victimhood and how a significant minority of male victims become the target of abuse. One explanation for this might be that male victimisation is at odds with certain understandings of violence against women and girls (VAWG) – historically, domestic abuse studies have been viewed as a form of abuse perpetrated by men against women and so has been framed as a substantive 'women's issue' within the valuable body of work that has been produced. Activists and academics alike have therefore focused their attention almost exclusively on female victims. However, as an accepted field of study, it is essential that *all* victims are studied so that appropriate measures and services can be put into place. The lack of studies on male experiences limits scientific knowledge, capturing only the paradigmatic examples, while simultaneously limiting scientific knowledge and understanding of other groups and their experiences. As the area of study matures, the full range of victims must be considered to ensure appropriate approaches are implemented across the board. The way in which domestic abuse has been politically and theoretically constructed over the decades has contributed to the invisiblisation and marginalisation of male victim groups.

In this chapter, male experiences of 'post-separation abuse' are seen within the wider academic literature through false allegations, manipulation of the criminal and family court system, legal and administrative aggression, and in what Corbally describes as 'second wave' abuse .[1] It presents a range of ways in which female perpetrators have continued to manipulate, control, and abuse male victims through children, the legal system, and the use of other perpetrators (for example, new partners). The concept of PA is also explored, focusing on male experiences of parental alienating behaviours (PABs), including control of contact and campaigns of denigration, as well as the impact on mental health issues, including suicide ideation. Finally, this chapter also discusses the often forgotten and hidden group of male victims who experience HBA and FMs at the hands of other men and sometimes female perpetrators. Overall, the chapter explains the barriers faced by males, including being disbelieved, ridiculed, and discriminated against by state agencies and the legal system, including the family courts, and how these barriers can prevent males from coming forward and disclosing abuse, as well as preventing males from recognising their own victimisation and accessing justice. The chapter highlights the invisiblisation of male victims and the importance of recognising this marginalised group if we are to protect male victims and afford them access to justice.

Men's experiences of post-separation abuse

Given that various domestic abuse laws are outlined in other chapters of this volume, this chapter will not restate them.[2] Instead, it will proceed directly with a detailed analysis of the experiences of male victims. Post-separation abuse has been defined as 'the ongoing, wilful pattern of intimidation of a former intimate partner including legal abuse, economic abuse, threats and endangerment to children, isolation and discrediting and harassment and stalking'.[3] Our understanding of the ways in which domestic abuse can continue or change after the end of the relationship has originated from the literature exploring women's victimisation, which explore divorce and custody disputes, and from the stalking and harassment literature. We know from this that the period of time immediately post-separation is the most dangerous for women in terms of being

---

[1]   MA Corbally, 'Making Sense of the Unbelievable: A Biographical Narrative Study of Men's Stories of Female Abuse' (PhD thesis, University of Salford 2011).

[2]   See Chapters 12 and 13 in this volume.

[3]   KJ Spearman, JL Hardesty, and J Campbell, 'Post-Separation Abuse: A Concept Analysis' (2023) 79(4) Journal of Advanced Nursing 1225.

at risk of homicide,[4] that violence can often escalate,[5] and that coercion can be exerted through both family and criminal justice court systems.[6]

In reference to men's experiences, we have seen evidence of the prevalence of this behaviour through large-scale surveys; for example, figures from the 1999 Canadian General Social Survey revealed that of those who had identified they had been in a violent relationship, 40 per cent of women and 32 per cent of men reported some violence occurred after the end of the relationship.[7] Similarly, during the year ending March 2019, 0.6 per cent men (111,000) and 1.7 per cent of women (279,000) experienced stalking from a partner/ex-partner.[8] However, there have been fewer focused explorations of men's experiences of post-separation domestic abuse. One such was a small-scale interview study (n = 13) that revealed men experienced continued abuse from their ex-partners through threats of false allegations, manipulation of the parental relationship, and harassment and stalking behaviours.[9] In a larger scale follow-up study,[10] similar behaviours were seen in a larger sample (n = 130); the men's descriptions of the abuse they experienced before separating helped explain the ongoing abuse they faced after separation as part of their overall abusive relationships. This abuse was experienced through manipulation of children, legal, and administrative systems (eg through false allegations), and had significant impacts on their health and well-being, their relationships with their children, and their extended family.

False allegations and legal and administrative abuse

There are some specific behaviours seen in the two studies described that are mirrored in other research on men's experiences. To begin, the threat of, and use of, false allegations as a mechanism of coercive control. False allegations can be categorised into intentional and unintentional behaviours; the former comprising their use with the intent to deceive, and the latter where the accuser genuinely

---

[4] M Wilson and M Daly, 'Spousal Homicide Risk and Estrangement' (1993) 8 Violence and Victims 3.

[5] DA Brownridge, 'Violence against Women Post-Separation' (2006) 11(5) Aggression and Violent Behavior 514.

[6] AM Zeoli and others, 'Post-Separation Abuse of Women and their Children: Boundary-Setting and Family Court Utilization among Victimized Mothers' (2013) 28 Journal of Family Violence 547.

[7] T Hotton, 'Spousal Violence after Marital Separation' (2001) 21(7) Statistics Canada 2.

[8] Office for National Statistics, 'Domestic Abuse Victim Characteristics, England and Wales: Year Ending March 2020' (Census 2021), figure 1 https://www.ons.gov.uk/peoplepopulationandco mmunity/crimeandjustice/articles/domesticabusevictimcharacteristicsenglandandwales/year endingmarch2020, accessed 23 July 2025.

[9] EA Bates, '"I Am Still Afraid of Her": Men's Experiences of Post-Separation Abuse' (2019) 10(3) Partner Abuse 336.

[10] EA Bates and others, '"She Punched, Punched, and Scratched Me While I Was Holding My Children after We Broke Up": Men's Experience of Post-Separation Domestic Abuse' (2024) *Partner Abuse* DOI: 10.1891/PA-2023-0025.

believes this has happened but there is no evidence of behaviour by the so-called perpetrator. The majority of the literature base, and indeed this discussion here, refers to intentional false allegations.

One of the most significant challenges in this situation involves determining how to differentiate between allegations that are true and those that are false. There is a lack of reliable method to assess this, especially in the context of intimate partner conflicts where each party often holds their own perspective on events and there are rarely any witnesses to provide independent accounts.[11] Consequently, an understanding of current prevalence is nearly impossible. Some researchers posit that the rates of false allegations by women are in fact low and that it is instead a tool used by abusive men to gain control.[12] There is other evidence which suggests that the majority of those making false allegations are women against men.[13]

Despite the disagreement and controversy, there is evidence across the male victim literature of the presence of false allegations. Both the threats of, and use of, false allegations can be seen as a form of coercive control: they are used to manipulate and control the behaviour of the victim and can create a state of 'hypervigilance', a symptom in battered women syndrome.[14] This threat can leave men feeling like they are 'walking on eggshells' and unable to defend or protect themselves when they are being physically attacked. This can be seen in the following quote from Bates' study:

> I have never attacked her or fought back at all. I have tried to restrain her at times to prevent her from attacking me ... she would then show me bruises a couple of days later and tell me that she could report me to the police for assault and that they would believe her story.[15]

According to Dutton and Goodman's conceptualisation of coercion,[16] there is the communication of coercive threats, negative consequence for non-compliance,

---

[11] Y Mazeh and M Widrig, 'The Rate of False Allegations of Partner Violence' (2016) 31(8) Journal of Family Violence 1035.

[12] M Flood, 'Fact Sheet# 2: The Myth of Women's False Accusations of Domestic Violence and Rape and Misuse of Protection Orders' XY Online (28 May 2010) https://xyonline. net/content/fact-sheet-2-myth-womens-false-accusations-domestic-violence-and-rape-and-misuse-protection, accessed 10 December 2010; E Stark, 'Preparing for Expert Testimony in Domestic Violence Cases' in AR Roberts (ed), *Handbook of Domestic Violence Intervention Strategies (*Policies, Programs, and Legal Remedies 2002*).

[13] PN Rumney and KF McCartan, 'Purported False Allegations of Rape, Child Abuse and Non-Sexual Violence: Nature, Characteristics and Implications' (2017) 81(6) Journal of Criminal Law 497.

[14] LE Walker, *The Battered Woman* (Harper & Row 2017).

[15] EA Bates, '"Walking on Egg Shells": A Qualitative Examination of Men's Experiences of Intimate Partner Violence' *(2020)* 21(1) Psychology of Men & Masculinities 120.

[16] MA Dutton and LA Goodman, 'Coercion in Intimate Partner Violence: Toward a New Conceptualization' (2005) 52 Sex Roles 743.

and, importantly, the victim's appraisal of the likelihood that their abusive partner would enact the threat. False allegations are a particularly impactful form of abuse and Avieli found that both male and female participants in their study had experienced physical, emotional, and psychological abuse, yet they described the false allegations as a more 'staggering and invasive form of DV'.[17]

In the Bates and others' post-separation study, mentioned earlier,[18] male participants described the ways in which coercive control would be exerted through the threat of having false allegations made against them, for example:

> I moved into a separate part of the house, (large enough house to do that). We crossed on the stairs, and she stopped me and said, 'I wonder what the police will say if I fall down the stairs and hurt myself and tell them you assaulted me?'[19]

The fear of these threats being realised was also enough to make some men take protective action to ensure they had evidence or support of interactions with their ex-partners, for example one man said: 'I used to have to take a mate to changeovers to deter the false allegations.'[20]

The use of false allegations can be powerful in affecting custody disputes and Harman and others describe them as the 'silver bullet' because of the detrimental impact they can have on contact and access agreements.[21]

False allegations are one example of the ways in which an abuser can utilise the legal and administrative systems to exert control and continue to manipulate a victim's life. This has been described in the literature as legal and administrative aggression or abuse.[22] It is evident in the misuse of the criminal justice system as a mechanism of control, characterised by 'vexatious, unfounded' actions in the behaviour of female perpetrators.[23] There is a dearth of research exploring legal and administrative aggression, but existing research has collected evidence of this behaviour through men's accounts of their experiences of abuse. Hines and others found one of the most common reported acts of coercive control was the manipulation of services and legal systems, with 50.3 per cent of their sample of male victims reporting these systems were used in some way.[24] Similarly, Dim

---

[17] H Avieli, 'False Allegations of Domestic Violence: A Qualitative Analysis of Ex-Partners' Narratives' (2021) Journal of Family Violence 9.

[18] Bates and others (n10).

[19] Ibid.

[20] Ibid.

[21] JJ Harman, E Kruk, and DA Hines, 'Parental Alienating Behaviors: An Unacknowledged Form of Family Violence' (2018) 144(12) Psychological Bulletin 1284.

[22] E Tilbrook, A Allan, and G Dear, 'Intimate Partner Abuse of Men' Western Australia: Men's Advisory Network (2010) https://www.ecu.edu.au/__data/assets/pdf_file/0007/685276/10_Tilbrook_Final-Report.pdf, accessed 18 June 2025.

[23] Ibid.

[24] DA Hines, J Brown, and E Dunning, 'Characteristics of Callers to the Domestic Abuse Helpline for Men' (2007) 22 Journal of Family Violence 63.

and Lysova found in their interview study with male victims (n = 16) that themes related to the court process included the presence of legal and administrative abuse by female partners, including the use of false allegations, the manipulation of child custody processes, and the feeling of gender bias against men within the courtroom setting.[25] Ingram's focused exploration of men's experiences of legal and administrative aggression found that the proportion of threats being made were only slightly higher than the rate at which threats were carried out, indicating the high risk of threats being carried out.[26]

Another term used to describe this type of abuse, proposed by Corbally, is 'second wave abuse',[27] which is described as abuse initiated by the intimate partner/ex-partner but not enacted by them. Instead it can be perpetrated by a range of systems, services, other actors, new partners, and so on. Examples of this type of abuse have been further identified within the literature. Corbally found men reported second wave abuse perpetrated by police, solicitors, and psychologists, with social services and legal systems being utilised.[28] Walker and others found similar behaviours in accounts of male victims, including use of children for personal gain, making false allegations, and social and legal manipulation.[29] In Walker and others' study, the second wave abuse was also perpetrated by police and other legal professionals; people who failed to respond appropriately or adequately to men's reports, who expressed ridicule, doubt, or disbelief. Similarly, Lysova and others' study with men across four English-speaking countries found evidence of negative experiences with the criminal justice system and a perception of bias, including within the courts.[30] The authors described the 'gendered enterprise' of the criminal justice system that was reflected in their biased treatment around domestic abuse.[31]

Other examples seen within the literature include an exploration of those working directly with victims. For example, Hine and others interviewed four call handlers on a dedicated male victim helpline within the UK and they reported hearing many men share experiences of this type of abuse, biases within the

---

[25]   EE Dim and A Lysova, 'Male Victims' Experiences with and Perceptions of the Criminal Justice Response to Intimate Partner Abuse' (2022) 37 Journal of Interpersonal Violence 15.

[26]   MK Ingram, 'An Examination of the Male Experience of Legal Aggression as a Form of Intimate Partner Violence in Canada' (thesis, University of Lethbridge 2021).

[27]   Corbally (n1).

[28]   M Corbally, 'Accounting for Intimate Partner Violence: A Biographical Analysis of Narrative Strategies Used by Men Experiencing IPV from their Female Partners (2015) 30(17) Journal of Interpersonal Violence 3112.

[29]   A Walker and others, 'Male Victims of Female-Perpetrated Intimate Partner Violence, Help-Seeking, and Reporting Behaviors: A Qualitative Study' (2020) 21(2) Psychology of Men & Masculinities 213.

[30]   A Lysova and others, 'A Qualitative Study of the Male Victims' Experiences with the Criminal Justice Response to Intimate Partner Abuse in Four English-Speaking Countries' (2020) 47 Criminal Justice and Behavior 1264.

[31]   Ibid, 1273.

system, and perceptions of bias within the courts.[32] These findings are echoed in other literature exploring the treatment of male and female victims within the court system. Muller and others explored differences in granting restraining orders to male and female perpetrators across a random sample of 157 of such orders involving intimate partners, dating or married couples, with mostly low or moderate violence.[33] They found that judges were almost 13 times more likely to grant a restraining order to a female victim (against a male perpetrator) compared to a male victim (against a female perpetrator). Interestingly, they found no difference in the level of violence between men and women, so discrepancies in granting these restraining orders was not a response to risk or level of violence.

The existing gendered culture within domestic violence and abuse (DVA) services creates a forum for some partners to use legal and administrative systems as a further mechanism for control. As Hines and others assert:

> in addition, male victims have unique experiences in that their female abusers are able to use a system that is designed to aide female victims of domestic violence. Thus, some female perpetrators of IPV [intimate partner violence] manipulate their husbands because they know that the system is designed without the abused male's experiences in mind and that, more often than not, people will not believe or take seriously these men's victimisation.[34]

Despite the perception that the end of an abusive relationship will mean the end of the abuse, the literature details a multitude of ways in which the abuse can continue, change, and even escalate. While much of this abuse is perpetrated by the male victim's ex-female partners, it is often also enacted by third parties (eg legal systems, new partners, children) as second wave abuse. The ongoing nature of this abuse has significant ramifications for the physical and mental health of victim/survivors, which points to the need to raise awareness of this within current legal and administrative systems for male victims.

Summary

Domestic abuse is impactful for male and female victims, and there is significant overlap in behaviours and experiences for all victim groups. We have described

---

[32]   B Hine, EA Bates, and S Wallace, '"I Have Guys Call Me and Say 'I Can't Be the Victim of Domestic Abuse'": Exploring the Experiences of Telephone Support Providers for Male Victims of Domestic Violence and Abuse' (2022) 37(7–8) Journal of Interpersonal Violence https://journals.sagepub.com/doi/epub/10.1177/0886260520944551, accessed 23 July 2025.

[33]   HJ Muller, SL Desmarais, and JM Hamel, 'Do Judicial Responses to Restraining Order Requests Discriminate Against Male Victims of Domestic Violence?' (2009) 24 Journal of Family Violence 625.

[34]   Hines, Brown, and Dunning (n24) 71.

here the ways in which male victims of domestic abuse, perpetrated by women, experience abuse through the use of false allegations and legal and administrative aggression, which is often perpetrated post-separation.

Parental alienating behaviours and the family court

One of the ways that male victims experience post-separation abuse as fathers is through the enactment of PABs. Put simply, these are behaviours enacted by an (alienating) parent that attack and destabilise the relationship between the child and the other (targeted) parent and are described by Rowlands as 'activities that contribute to the child's rejection of the alienated parent'.[35] If successful, these activities can result in an outcome of PA:

> One type of contact refusal, when a child – typically whose parents are engaged in a high-conflict separation or divorce – allies strongly with one parent and resists and rejects contact and/or a relationship (i.e., contact refusal) with the other parent without legitimate justification. PA refers to the actions and attitudes manifested by the child. PA is brought on by the alienating behaviours of the parent with whom the child is aligned.[36]

As outlined in several recent reviews and texts,[37] research on PA and PABs has burgeoned, illuminating exactly what PABs look like and how they are enacted,[38] how PA differs from other forms of contact refusal,[39] how PA maps onto other frameworks of violence,[40] and the impact of PABs on parents,[41] and children.[42]

---

[35] GA Rowlands, 'Parental Alienation: A Measurement Tool' (2019) 60 Divorce & Remarriage 317.

[36] W Bernet, AJL Baker, and KL Adkins, 'Definitions and Terminology Regarding Child Alignments, Estrangement, and Alienation: A Survey of Custody Evaluators' (2022) 67 Journal of Forensic Sciences 279.

[37] JJ Harman and others, 'Developmental Psychology and the Scientific Status of Parental Alienation' (2022) 58(10) Developmental Psychology 1887; BA Hine, *Parental Alienation: A Contemporary Guide for Parents, Practitioners, and Policymakers* (Amazon 2023); BA Hine, 'Parental Alienation – What Do We Know, and What Do We (Urgently) Need to Know? A Narrative Review' (2024) 14(1) Partner Abuse 35.

[38] JJ Harman and M Matthewson, 'Parental Alienation: How is it Done' in D Lorandos and W Bernet (eds), *Parental Alienation: Science and Law* (Charles C Thomas 2020).

[39] D McCarten, *Parental Alienation: An Evidence-Based Approach* (Routledge 2022).

[40] Harman, Kruk, and Hines (n21) 1275.

[41] S Lee-Maturana, M Matthewson, and C Dwan, 'Ten Key Findings on Targeted Parents' Experience: Towards a Broader Definition of Parental Alienation' (2022) 43 Journal of Family Issues 2672.

[42] P Miralles, C Godoy, and MD Hidalgo, 'Long-Term Emotional Consequences of Parental Alienation Exposure in Children of Divorced Parents: A Systematic Review' (2023) 42 Current Psychology 12055.

Importantly, research has demonstrated that while there may be some gender differences in how PABs are enacted, both mothers and fathers are susceptible to PABs, particularly post-separation. Indeed, prevalence research from both the United States and Canada,[43] as well as the United Kingdom,[44] has shown that separated mothers and fathers report similarly high levels of PAB exposure. Moreover, these reports and other studies indicate that the effects of PABs are equally traumatic for mothers and fathers,[45] with both groups reporting severe issues with mental health, including suicide ideation.

Other work has demonstrated potentially gendered elements to PABs for fathers, including its impact and the use of systems to perpetrate this abuse. In relation to impact, some work has suggested that the link between PABs and suicide ideation in fathers may be stronger than in mothers. Indeed, there is already robust evidence of increased suicidality in men following divorce compared to women, with men around nine times more likely to engage in such ideation.[46] Scholars such as Sher have now started to theorise that PABs may be a critical factor in poor mental health outcomes for fathers.[47] Moreover, both quantitative and qualitative evidence from the large-scale 'Lost Dads' project in 2022 showed a high level of suicidality in fathers seeking help following separation (42 per cent) that coincided with abusive experiences including PABs.[48] Several specific examples of PABs and their impact were also provided by participants during interviews:

> She's trying to sabotage the image that they have of me, and the role that I can play. (AS24AI)

> But the reality is that for as long as my children, or me, or my ex-partner are alive, she's going to do her damnest to make life a living hell and to diminish, minimise, and destroy whatever relationship and contact I have with my children. I can't do anything about that. (DU10PA)

---

[43] JJ Harman, S Leder-Elder, and Z Biringen, 'Prevalence of Parental Alienation Drawn from a Representative Poll' (2016) 66 Children and Youth Services Review 62; JJ Harman, S Leder-Elder, and Z Biringen, 'Prevalence of Adults Who Are the Targets of Parental Alienating Behaviors and their Impact' (2019) 106 Children and Youth Services Review 104471.

[44] BA Hine and others, 'Examining the Prevalence of Childhood Parental Alienating Behaviours (PABs) in Separated Parents in the United Kingdom' (2025) Journal of Family Violence https://doi.org/10.1007/s10896-025-00910-4.

[45] Lee-Maturana, Matthewson, and Dwan (n41).

[46] R Evans, J Scourfield, and G Moore, 'Gender, Relationship Breakdown, and Suicide Risk: A Review of Research in Western Countries' (2016) 37 Journal of Family Issues 2239.

[47] L Sher, 'Parental Alienation and Suicide in Men' (2015) 27 Psychiatria Danubina 289.

[48] BA Hine and E Roy, 'Lost Dads: Examining the Experiences of Men Following Family Breakdown, Separation, and Divorce (FBSD)' University of West London (2023) https://www.uwl.ac.uk/media/9681/download, accessed 23 July 2025.

There was quite clearly evidence that my ex was badmouthing me to our children, that she'd been using contact arrangements – the lockdown and things – to try and prevent the children having contact with the father, to denigrate me in front of the children, to sow seeds of anxiety and fear in the children (Crabby Dad)

She accused me of stealing one of their piggy banks at one stage out of their house. And that was said in front of the children. She has said in front of the children that she doesn't want me to have any contact, which is abuse itself. (LO02BA)

But [son] said at contact me, […] "Mummy says that we are not to be alone with you in case something happens." Now that is abuse of children. (LO02BA)

Her mother had told her that I killed our dog. And if little one told me about mum's new boyfriend, I'd come round and kill their dog. […] It was all complete and utter rubbish designed to make her scared. (LO14AB)

She makes it very clear to my son. She tells him that it's not safe for him to be with me. (WI13FA)

The only information that will be passed to me is information she wants to tell me, which is usually virtually nothing. If I ask any questions, for example, medical things […] I've subsequently found out that my eldest has been put on to a Ritalin derivative medicine with no consultation, with no discussion. I find out this about three months after taking place second hand. (DU10PA)

If there's any sports or any things like that, I go there to support him, and you can see he can only give me a little quick wave or something unless she tells him to come over to me. Otherwise, he's, you can see he's not allowed to. And I don't want to push it because there's going to be repercussions for him. (ST03ST)

Fathers spoke about how this resulted in suicidal thoughts: 'There were a couple of times where I felt, not that I wanted to kill myself, but I felt so low that I didn't want life to continue' (SR23WO).

Crucially, in this same project, fathers also spoke about how many forms of post-separation abuse (see previous section 'False allegations and legal and administrative abuse') as well as PABs were perpetrated through the family court system as a form of 'state-sanctioned' abuse. Fathers spoke about how the courts were used as a threat, due to their perceived bias towards mothers:

> She also said, "If you don't like it, you can see me in court and I'll keep the kids until we've settled this." Despite knowing the fact that the court case would take at least a year. So basically, it was a gun to my head to say, "Accept this or you won't see your children." (EL12DU)

This was reflected in experiences of court orders being breached with impunity by mothers (and access to children thus restricted):

> I think I'm up to about six or seven occurrences where my ex-partner has now directly acted against the sheriff's court order [...] If you don't follow the sheriff's orders that's contempt of court, and, in theory, that's a pseudo-criminal offence. I know from speaking to other fathers it never gets prosecuted or pursued, so there's no penalty. (DU10PA)

Men also described how the court was a weapon for mothers to use against them: 'The court has handed her all the weapons. [...] The legal system has created utterly perverse incentives against being able to co-parent' (WI13FA). They further stated that the court process was the leading factor in their poor mental health:

> I'd like to think of myself as quite resilient. But I've never experienced something that has messed up my mental health than this whole process has done. The breakup was bad. Don't get me wrong. But what's actually messed up my mental health is going through this court system. (GR31TO)

This was mainly due to the limit this placed on their contact with children as a result of the mothers' litigation: 'I lost a year of my daughter's life from the court process simply because no one could tell the mum to get her act together' (KI09BE).

Other work supports the narrative that courts are 'weaponised' against victim fathers. For example, male victims, in a study by Bates and Hine, spoke about how systems were used against them and acted as vehicles for these behaviours, specifically by mothers making false allegations of DVA to the family courts and by breaching orders put in place with no repercussions.[49] In the second part of Bates and Hine's study,[50] the impact of these behaviours was explored, with fathers highlighting a significantly negative impact on their physical health, mental health, identity, and relationships. They also spoke of the grief they felt in 'losing a child that was still living' and the financial stresses that came from

---

49 EA Bates and BA Hine, '"I Was Told When I Could Hold, Talk with or Kiss Our Daughter": Exploring Fathers' Experiences of Parental Alienation within the Context of Intimate Partner Violence' (2023) 14(2) Partner Abuse 157.

50 BA Hine and EA Bates, '"There is No Part of My Life That Hasn't Been Destroyed": The Impact of Parental Alienation and Intimate Partner Violence on Fathers' (2023) 15(1) Partner Abuse 1.

fighting court cases. Indeed, many participants across these studies spoke about feeling that mothers purposefully engaged in (lengthy) court proceedings in order to enact financial abuse and to bankrupt them (as most female litigants in these cases had gained access to legal aid).

In the two studies cited, it was noted that fathers may be at higher risk of PABs as they constitute the majority of non-resident parents in the UK,[51] a phenomenon partly caused by uneven contact arrangements administered by family courts. Moreover, and evident in the testimony given, it was also argued that societal stereotypes which place lower value on fathers' involvement in children's lives lead to greater susceptibility of disrupted child contact (as well as fewer issues or protest arising from society and systems when this occurs). Indeed, these stereotypes appear to be reflected in how family courts deal with disputes between parents and may in fact end up facilitating abuse towards fathers.

A word of caution, however. The studies cited thus far are not systematic reviews of court documentation or judgments and therefore may not be reflective of many parents' experiences in the family court system. Indeed, it is important to acknowledge that several studies with similar methodologies have also raised contrary concerns about the minimisation of women's' and mothers' DVA experiences in family court, including when 'false' allegations of PABs are brought by fathers in order to 'counter' such claims.[52] Indeed, when studies have been conducted on mothers and fathers jointly,[53] both report equally traumatic, albeit gendered, experiences of family court that raise serious questions about its role. It is therefore important to recognise that father's experiences of DVA and PABs within family courts are part of the complex family justice landscape within the UK and that these affect the family unit as a whole. This is particularly evident in the challenges of addressing and enforcing judicial outcomes for criminal behaviours within a civil court, compounded by the lack of co-ordination between the two systems. Nonetheless, it is clear that men face significant difficulties within the family court system – not only in relation to PABs specifically but also more broadly as victims of DVA and, fundamentally, as fathers.

Summary

PABs refer to actions by one parent intended to damage the child's relationship with the other parent, which can result in PA. Family courts, while designed to act in the best interests of the child, may inadvertently contribute to these behaviours by failing to recognise or address alienation. Fathers, in particular,

---

[51]   Hine and Roy (n48).

[52]   J Birchall and S Choudhry, '"I Was Punished for Telling the Truth": How Allegations of Parental Alienation are Used to Silence, Sideline and Disempower Survivors of Domestic Abuse in Family Law Proceedings' (2022) 6(1) Journal of Gender-Based Violence 115.

[53]   M Bogotto, BA Hine, and EA Bates, 'The Impact of Family Court Involvement on Parents in the United Kingdom, and How They Cope' (2024) Partner Abuse (in preparation for submission).

can face systemic challenges in these cases, as courts may uphold decisions that favour maternal custody or dismiss signs of PA as normal post-separation conflict. However, it must be noted that the family courts' frequent failure to recognise and act on alienating behaviours is an issue for both fathers and mothers, and that this system frequently fuels post-separation abuse and enables long-term damage on both parents, and most importantly, children.

Male victims, honour-based abuse, and forced marriages

Research into HBA and FM has significantly increased since 2000, part of the crucial continuum of worldwide research into VAWG.[54] HBA research reveals the hidden and unreported nature of such harmful practices, as well as the poor responses to victims seeking intervention and support.[55] Such research has also played a crucial role in uncovering male violence against women, including so-called honour killings, where women are killed for allegedly violating cultural norms relating to their sexual autonomy and perceived to have 'tarnished' their family's reputation. However, a small number of studies are now beginning to draw attention to the experiences of male victims of HBA and FM, outside the general remit of domestic abuse, although current understanding in this area remains significantly limited.[56] There is scant research conducted on male victims of HBA and FM, how and why they are affected by patriarchal violence committed by other men, and even HBA committed upon male victims by female perpetrators. This is an important area of enquiry because the gender-specific experiences and needs of male victims have traditionally been neglected within the fields of law, criminology, sociology, and social policy, and it is important, within the scope and breadth of this book on diverse voices, to provide an analysis of male experiences and the typology of their abuse.

It is often assumed that HBA and FM solely involve male perpetrators who are coached within an everyday culture of patriarchy, inculcating traditional sex roles, misogyny, and the objectification of women. So-called honour killings fall within the definition of femicide as the misogynistic killing of women and represent a brutal end of the broad continuum of VAWG.[57] This is because 'honour' is said

---

54 AK Gill, C Strange, and K Roberts (eds), *Honour Killing and Violence: Theory, Policy and Practice* (Palgrave Macmillan 2014).

55 MM Idriss, 'Key Agent and Survivor Recommendations for Intervention in Honor-Based Violence in the UK' (2018), 42(4) International Journal of Comparative and Applied Criminal Justice 321.

56 MM Idriss (ed), *Men, Masculinities and Honour-Based Abuse* (Routledge 2020); MM Idriss, 'Abused by the Patriarchy: Male Victims, Masculinity, "Honor"-Based Abuse and Forced Marriages' (2021), 37(13–14) Journal of Interpersonal Violence NP11905.

57 MA Gryzb, 'An Explanation of Honour-Related Killings of Women in Europe through Bourdieu's Concept of Symbolic Violence and Masculine Domination' (2016) 64(7) Current Sociology 1036; A Sev'er and G Yurdakul, 'Culture of Honor, Culture of Change' (2001) 7(9) Violence Against Women 964.

to reside within the bodies of women as women are the supposed 'repositories' of honour.[58] A radical feminist framework explains that women are expected to guard their sexual honour for the rest of their lives, and that they must also protect the honour of the other women related to them. While honour relates to the chastity of women, it is considered far too important to be entrusted to women alone to safeguard. This is an overt demonstration of patriarchal violence, since it is centred upon controlling women's sexual and reproductive powers by claiming the female body as 'man's territory'.[59] Like other forms of VAWG, honour killings are nothing more than a conscious process of intimidation by which men keep women in a state of fear.[60] Sev'er and Yurdakul famously state that 'the patriarchal culture... [is] ... frightened by the emerging sexuality of young women and their (potential) challenge to male rules ... cutting down a few women in the prime of their youth is expected to deter other young women from expressing themselves in a sensual way'.[61] HBA and so-called honour killings therefore represent a powerful tool of control over women. In taking a diverse voices approach, the question arises as to how this relates to male victims?

Men may also experience HBA or FM if they challenge patriarchal ideology and traditional notions of masculinity. This can occur through the discovery of their sexual orientation, homosexuality, or perceived criminal, wayward, or Westernised behaviour (for example, drug dealing, robbery, burglary, car crime). Such experiences have historically been overlooked in academic research,[62] despite the potential for this behaviour to 'tarnish' the family reputation. The omission of men's victimisation in HBA and FM studies distorts the full picture of victimhood, overlooking the significant minority of male victims who are targets of abuse. One explanation for this might be that male victimisation is at odds with certain understandings of VAWG – historically, HBA and FM have been viewed as a form of abuse perpetrated *by* men *against women* and so this has been framed as a substantive 'women's issue' within the valuable body of VAWG research. Researchers have therefore focused their attention almost exclusively upon female victims. However, as an accepted field of study, it is essential that *all* victims are studied so that appropriate policies, measures, and services can be put into place – to exclude certain experiences from the discourse and analysis would be a betrayal to the academy, or worse yet, demonstrate the politicisation or ideological inclination to amplify the voices of some victims, but not others. The lack of studies on male victimisation limits scientific knowledge, capturing only the paradigmatic examples (and therefore creating stereotypes), while simultaneously limiting scientific knowledge and understanding of other groups, such as male

---

[58] Gill, Strange, and Roberts (n54).
[59] Sev'er and Yurdakul (n57) 964.
[60] S Brownmiller, *Against our Will: Men, Women and Rape* (Fawcett Columbine 1975).
[61] Sev'er and Yurdakul (n57) 986.
[62] Idriss, 'Abused' (n56).

victims.[63] As the area of HBA and FM studies matures, the full range of victims must be considered to ensure that appropriate approaches are implemented across the board. The way in which HBA and FM has been politically and theoretically constructed since 2000 has contributed to the invisiblisation and marginalisation of male victim groups. By portraying men solely as perpetrators, theoretical connections between patriarchy, male perpetrators, and masculinity have become so well established that any conceptualisation of men as 'victims' (or women as perpetrators) requires one to move outside the traditional boundaries of thinking, all within a climate that has been slow to acknowledge other paradigms.[64]

The (UK government's) Forced Marriage Unit (FMU, part of the Home Office), on 9 May 2024, detailed FM statistics for the year 2023.[65] That year, the FMU received 802 contacts related to a possible FM and/or possible female genital mutilation (FGM). The figure includes contact made to the FMU through its public helpline or email regarding new cases. It comprised 280 cases of FM where advice and support was provided, three cases of FGM, and 519 FM enquiries, which required signposting and general advice rather than specific or direct intervention. Thus, the FMU provided support and intervention specifically in 283 cases in 2023. The statistics represent only the cases that have been reported to the FMU and where the FMU has actively given advice or support. It does not include reporting and data collection for other statutory agencies or third-sector organisations. FM is a hidden crime and these figures do not reflect the full scale of this type of abuse. Of the 283 cases in which the FMU provided advice or support in 2023: 195 cases (69 per cent) involved female victims and 88 cases (31 per cent) involved male victims. Seventy cases (25 per cent) involved victims aged 17 and under; 95 cases (34 per cent) involved victims aged 18 to 25; 67 cases (24 per cent) involved victims with mental capacity concerns. These statistics should not be interpreted as reflective of prevalence, as they do not account for other (very few) organisations that support men, nor do they consider the broader under-reported and hidden nature of such crimes. The actual figures relating to male victims of FM are likely to be significantly under-reported in terms of prevalence (a point that is, of course, also true for women).

What is interesting is that the FMU data reveals that 31 per cent of its caseload in 2023 specifically concerned male victims and, in particular, young males. This sizeable minority highlights the presence of male victims in official figures, a trend that has been consistently reflected in FMU statistics for several years, with around one-fifth of the FMU's total workload typically involving male victims. Despite this prevalence, these victims have continued to be ignored and

---

63 Y Samad, 'Forced Marriage Among Men: An Unrecognized Problem' (2010) 30(2) Critical Social Policy 189.

64 Idriss, 'Abused' (n56).

65 FMU, 'Forced Marriage Unit Statistics 2023' (2024) https://www.gov.uk/government/statistics/forced-marriage-unit-statistics-2023/forced-marriage-unit-statistics-2023#sex-of-victims, accessed 10 December 2024.

overlooked in the wider literature since the early 2000s. What is of concern is that the FMU appears to be the only statutory organisation actively collecting and reporting data on male victims in addition to female victims. Most interested organisations focus almost exclusively on female victims of HBA and FM. This is concerning as it provides an incomplete and inaccurate picture of HBA and FM victimisation among male victims – where there is no data collection on male victims, it can lead to the erroneous impression that male victimisation in HBA and FM does not require a response. This lack of attention ultimately has an impact on recognition, disclosure, and the existence of service provision and policies on male victims, ultimately invisibilising such victims and erasing them from intervention and support. Furthermore, this may have an impact on the application of the law.

In 2023, 272 forced marriage protection orders (FMPOs) were issued by the family courts,[66] yet these figures do not include a gender breakdown. It is assumed that the vast majority of these orders will have related to women and girls. Much more work is needed to protect male victims and promote access to justice within the Forced Marriage (Civil Protection) Act 2007. The inaccurate representation of FM could undermine the effectiveness of reforms under sections 120–2 of the Anti-Social Behaviour, Crime and Policing Act 2014, which established FM as a specific criminal offence. These sections also made it a criminal offence to breach a FMPO. Without proper recognition of male victims, even by statutory organisations including the police and by society in general, these reforms may fail to adequately address the needs of all affected individuals, perpetuating a skewed understanding of FM that overlooks the experiences of men. This misrepresentation can impact the criminal justice system's response to crimes against male victims, potentially limiting their access to protection and justice under these legal frameworks.

The existing discourse on HBA and FM presents this abuse as a gendered issue or crime, yet 31 per cent of the FMU's caseload in 2023 involved male victims. This questions the premise upon which FM can be called a 'gendered' issue that only affects women and young girls. Similarly, in the year ending March 2023, there were 2,905 HBA-related offences recorded by the police in England and Wales between 2022 and 2023.[67] The government did not offer any breakdown of these statistics based on gender, though some national charities estimate that

---

66 Ministry of Justice, 'Justice in Numbers; Court Data; Family Court; Forced Marriage Protection' (2024) https://data.justice.gov.uk/courts/family-courts/courts-family-forced-marriage, accessed 10 December 2024.

67 Home Office, 'Statistics on So Called "Honour-Based" Abuse Offences, England and Wales, 2022–2023' (2023) https://www.gov.uk/government/statistics/so-called-honour-based-abuse-offences-2022-to-2023/statistics-on-so-called-honour-based-abuse-offences-england-and-wales-2022-to-2023, accessed 10 December 2024.

around 76 per cent of victims of HBA are female.[68] Based on these estimates, around 24 per cent of HBA victims are male. This is a sizeable minority which again questions whether HBA can continue to be viewed as a singular gendered issue. Is it now time to differentiate the experiences, by gender, of the different victims in this form of abuse?

There are several situations in which males may be victims of HBA or FM. For example, males may be viewed as 'dishonourable' if they refuse to participate in an arranged marriage, or they may be forced into marriage due to disabilities, with families believing this is the best way to provide them with long-term support.[69] Men may also be forced into marriage 'as an antidote for their gayness'.[70] Due to the stigma associated with being gay in South Asian communities, males may be forced to marry women and emotionally blackmailed into silence for the sake of the family's 'honour'.[71] There is, thus, a need for male victims to be conceptualised as a subset of the victims of patriarchy, where similar kinds of domination exist as make up the cornerstone of hegemonic masculinity and VAWG.[72] An illustration of this is the tragic death of Nazin Mahmood, who took his own life in 2014.[73] Nazin had been engaged to Matt Ogston and the couple had been in a relationship for 13 years, but two days after coming out to his parents, Nazin killed himself. Nazin had travelled to his family's home in Birmingham to celebrate Eid, and after being confronted about his sexuality for the first time, was told to see a psychiatrist to be 'cured'. After returning to his London home which he shared with Matt, Nazin took his own life. Both Nazin and Matt experienced emotional blackmail from Nazin's family because the family wanted the relationship to be kept a secret, warning that 'shame would be brought upon the family' if their relationship was to become known to the wider community. The case is illustrative of male experiences of hiding their sexuality from their families because of their religion and their culturally conservative families. The intersection between their GBTQ identities and other aspects of their cultural and religious identities, including traditional notions of (hyper-) masculinity within their communities, can make some males feel discriminated against and rejected. Feelings of shame and rejection and having his identity

---

[68] Reducing the Risk, ' "Honour" Based Abuse (HBA)' (2024) https://reducingtherisk. uk/honour-based-abuse-fgm/#:~:text=It's%20estimated%20that%20around%2076,and%20 sometimes%20the%20wider%20community, accessed 10 December 2024.

[69] R Clawson and R Fyson, 'Forced Marriage of People with Learning Disabilities: A Human Rights Issue' (2017) 32(6) Disability and Society 810.

[70] Samad (n63) 199–200.

[71] R Jaspal and A Siraj, 'Perceptions of "Coming Out" among British Muslim Gay Men' (2011) 2(3) Psychology and Sexuality 183; A Siraj, 'On Being Homosexual and Muslim: Conflicts and Challenges' in L Ouzgane (ed), *Islamic Masculinities* (Zed Books 2006).

[72] A Javaid, 'Feminism, Masculinity and Male Rape: Bringing Male Rape "Out of the Closet"' (2016) 25(3) Journal of Gender Studies 284.

[73] For further details, see https://www.nazandmattfoundation.org (accessed 18 June 2025) a UK-based charity in loving memory of Nazin Mahmood.

questioned by his own family may have contributed to Nazin taking his own life, demonstrating the psychological pressures and stresses GBTQ men may feel about their sexuality and 'coming out'.[74]

There is evidence within recent criminology and psychology research that past/current trauma can lead to males committing serious crimes,[75] and within the context of this chapter this may even be extended to South Asian males who are desperate to conceal their sexual identity. A particularly harrowing example of this is the case of Jasvir Ginday in 2014,[76] a homosexual man who entered a marriage with Varkha Rani to conceal his sexual orientation, and then murdered her when she found out and threatened to reveal his homosexuality to friends and family. Ginday was convicted of murder and sentenced to serve a minimum of 21 years in prison. In analysing Ginday's state of mind, the disciplines of criminology and psychology requires professionals and researchers to ascertain theoretical explanations as to *why* perpetrators commit their crimes and to make appropriate assessments based on any trauma they may have experienced. To be clear – there is no excuse or justification for his crime and this analysis is intended to uncover what led to it. In examining why Ginday chose to marry in order to conceal his sexuality rather than reveal it to his community, it is important to consider the role of South Asian hyper-masculine culture, which often opposes gay relationships. His secret life of homosexuality may have been too embarrassing and shameful for him to reveal, demonstrating the psychological pressures of a culture that did not look favourably upon him and rejected him. Ultimately, he committed the most heinous of crimes by murdering his wife, rather than have his sexuality revealed. From criminological and psychology perspectives, it reveals how far perpetrators are willing to go to protect their own and their family's 'honour' to avoid 'shame' and 'embarrassment'. This also raises an important point, as academic research often overlooks male-specific explanations for acts of criminality and violence. As Mackay and others state:

> Understanding the offence process of those who perpetrate IPV requires carefully listening to the stories and narratives of their own lives and offending behaviour. There has been some reluctance to do this for men who perpetrate IPV. Some researchers and practitioners have been quick to disregard men's 'reasons' for their committing

---

[74] See the various chapters on male victims, HBA, FMs, and sexuality in the edited collection, Idriss (ed), *Men* (n56), and specifically, the chapters drafted by experts in male psychology and victimisation: Drs Roxanne Khan and Michelle Lowe and Professor Rusi Jaspal.

[75] J Mackay, E Bowen, and K Walker, '"What's the Point in Talking About It, When I'm the One Being Punished for It?" Men as Both Perpetrator and Victim of Intimate Partner Violence' in EA Bates and JC Taylor (eds), *Domestic Violence against Men and Boys: Experiences of Male Victims of Intimate Partner Violence* (Taylor & Francis 2023).

[76] BBC News, 'Jasvir Ginday Jailed for Life for Murdering Wife to Hide His Sexuality' (2014) https://www.bbc.co.uk/news/uk-england-birmingham-26937466, accessed 10 December 2024.

offences as excuses, fearing that this takes responsibility from perpetrators and places it with victims, whereas research to understand female perpetrators has prioritised motive and taken them on face value ... Media portrayal of cases involving women perpetrating IPV tends to highlight them as somehow different or unique, and requiring more understanding of motivations. In addition, reviews demonstrate that there is more research exploring the motivations of women who perpetrate IPV than men. This suggests more of an acceptance and willingness to listen to women's explanations for this behaviour than men's.[77]

The extent to which Ginday (a perpetrator) was also a victim (of his conservative family's culture and religious views on homosexuality) should be debated, in terms of psychological and situational triggers and the development of problematic emotional systems within the family setting, all of which can contribute to difficulties in interpersonal relationships, unhealthy dynamics, coping skills, attachment bonds, and mental health issues. All of these could have exacerbated Ginday's problems.[78] To date, there appears to be no research on male perpetrators of HBA and their experiences of past victimisation in childhood, adolescence, and even into adulthood within the family home, let alone based on their sexuality and identity.[79] As Mackay and others state, 'Whilst these examples of ... IPV victimisation do not excuse or justify the IPV behaviours perpetrated by the men, they demonstrate how anger and resentment build up and are contributory factors, aiding our understanding of why men were violent towards their partners.'[80]

It is well documented that most so-called honour killings victims are female and this is a serious VAWG issue concerning male violence against women. However, men are also killed in the name of 'honour', even here in the UK. If men are the victims of HBA, the assumption is that they have 'tarnished' the reputation of a woman and so have been killed as an act of revenge for 'dishonouring' the girl's family. In the case of *R v Chomir Ali*,[81] a young Bangladeshi woman became pregnant by her Iranian boyfriend Arash Ghorbani-Zarin, much to the dismay of her family due to her strict Muslim upbringing. On the instructions of her father, her two brothers murdered Arash in his car on a street not far from the family home. The male victim was found sitting in his car and had been attacked with a knife. There were 46 different stab or slash wounds, including 13 stab wounds penetrating the chest. He had also been tied with a rope around his neck and the headrest of the seat. It was stated in court that the male victim had

---

[77] Mackay, Bowen, and Walker (n75) 212.
[78] Ibid, 213–16.
[79] Ibid, 213.
[80] Ibid, 219.
[81] *R v Chomir Ali* [2011] EWCA Crim 1101.

been unable to make any effort to defend himself. The reason for the killing was punishment for the male victim's relationship with the young woman. Similarly, in *R v Tabraz (Mohammed)*,[82] the male victim, Soheil Mumtaz, worked with the perpetrator's sister, Shaiha Zahid, in a factory in Luton. Zahid told a friend that the male victim had approached her saying that he found her attractive. Zahid told Mumtaz that she was going to tell her brother who would 'beat the hell out of him'. What followed was an unprovoked revenge attack upon Mumtaz for a perceived slight against the perpetrator's sister. The perpetrator felt that his family's standing in the community had been disrespected by Mumtaz and so he sought revenge. He was attacked with a claw hammer outside his home, with two significant blows to the head. Independent witnesses saw Mumtaz raise his arm in self-defence and he had no weapons with which to defend himself.

In both *Chomir Ali* and *Tabraz* both male victims were killed by male perpetrators for supposedly tarnishing the reputation of a girl within the family and both are examples of patriarchal male-on-male violence. However, are there examples of male victims being killed by female perpetrators in the context of so-called honour? One such possible case is that of TikTok influencer Mahek Bukhari and her mother, Ansreen Bukhari, who were both convicted in a case that involved an affair, blackmail, and ultimately murder.[83] However, this case has never been framed as a so-called honour killing of male victims by the mainstream press, media, or even by academic experts – one might be forgiven for thinking that this is primarily due to a lack of understanding. However, more troubling is the potential stereotype that men cannot be victims of honour killings perpetrated by women.

Mahek was a well-known influencer with over 100,000 followers and involved with promotions for commercial brands. She was often joined by her mother Ansreen. Ansreen had an on-and-off extramarital affair with Saqib Hussain for three years, after which she tried to end the relationship. Saqib was upset by this and pleaded with her to reconsider. When Ansreen rejected his plea, the situation escalated and Saqib threatened to send explicit material of them together to her husband. Ansreen confided in Mahek; however, instead of going directly to the police to report the blackmail, Mahek decided to take matters into her own hands. To help her mother, Mahek turned to a friend, plotting to lure Saqib to a meeting point by offering to hand over £3,000 (an amount that Saqib had complained that he spent on Ansreen over the years while they were lovers). They planned to meet at a Tesco car park in Leicester with a group of other accomplices and ambush Saqib. Saqib arrived at the car park in the early hours, with Hashim Ijazuddin, a friend who was totally innocent and who probably had no knowledge of the situation. On arriving at the car park, they slowed down and waited for a few seconds and quickly left. Their car was followed by two

---

82   *R v Tabraz (Mohammed)* [2020] EWCA Crim 1160.
83   G Torr, 'Mahek Bukhari: TikTok, Blackmail and Double Murder' BBC News (2023) https://www.bbc.co.uk/news/uk-england-leicestershire-66307221, accessed 4 July 2024.

cars and the trial heard that Mahek and Ansreen were passengers in one of the two vehicles. Saqib called 999 to report that he was being chased, saying that one of the cars was trying to ram him off the road and they were running through red lights. Their car crashed on the A46 and was found by a passing recovery driver, who saw a car on fire next to a tree. Police were able to identify all the perpetrators thanks to Saqib's 999 call, which allowed them to use automatic number plate recognition footage to track the two cars that had been following them. When police investigated, Mahek and Ansreen made up lies to explain their movements and denied any involvement. Later, they were arrested – Mahek, Ansreen, and six others were charged with murder. Mahek and Ansreen were found guilty of murder and sentenced to life in prison, with Mahek ordered to serve a minimum term of 31 years and 8 months, while Ansreen was given a minimum term of 26 years and nine months. The drivers of the two vehicles were also found guilty of murder, while three other defendants were each found guilty of two counts of manslaughter.

Was this a so-called honour killing case of a male victim (with a second male an additional victim)? Some may argue that this is not a traditional case of so-called honour and so should not be subsumed within this category as a 'typical' so-called honour killing case. This is because the case is one of premeditated murder, where the perpetrators wanted to 'get rid' of Saqib for his blackmail, and that 'honour' was not a motivation. Instead, the case was primarily about blackmail and extortion by Saqib (itself a potential criminal offence), which then escalated and got out of hand, resulting in Saqib's death. As the police detectives described in media reports, had Mahek and Ansreen contacted the police about Saqib's blackmail, none of the subsequent events and deaths would have unfolded. Furthermore, it could be argued that Saqib tried to 'dishonour' Ansreen and Mahek through his blackmail and by revealing the sex tapes to her husband. We cannot then claim that he is the victim of HBA due to acts initiated by him. The fact that it has not been labelled as a so-called honour killing case by the media or other academic commentators lends some credibility to this point.

However, there are compelling reasons why the murder of Saqib could be interpreted as HBA and a so-called honour killing, as the case seems to fit relevant academic definitions. The case itself relates to female sexuality, infidelity, and sex outside the bonds of marriage (in this case, Ansreen, a married woman and the mother of Mahek), contrary to 'honour' cultures. Saqib (blackmail, revenge porn) and Mahek and Ansreen (murder) all committed criminal offences within the series of events, and although these two crimes in no way compare to each other in gravity, it is arguable that 'honour' was a motivation for all three individuals. Saqib had tried to blackmail Ansreen and Mahek into giving him £3,000, knowing very well it would be a source of 'shame' and 'dishonour' if the sex tapes were revealed to Ansreen's husband, family, and the wider community. How embarrassing and shameful would it be for the reputation of Mahek and Ansreen if the tapes were revealed? Both were Muslim TikTok influencers and had a strong reputation and standing in their community. The damage to their reputation, business, commercial activities, and brand would be immense if the sex tapes had been revealed. Thus, the case relates to Mahek and Ansreen's social standing and monetary capital – qualities that also exist in traditional HBA and so-called honour killing cases. HBA cases can be very fluid and will vary based on their facts. Although one could argue that this situation had been instigated by Saqib, it transformed into the so-called honour killing of Saqib and his friend. Usually, in these types of cases, the woman committing the infidelity is normally the one at risk of being killed. However, in this case, any risk to Ansreen was minimal and it was Saqib who was eventually killed. For whose 'honour' was Saqib killed? Both Mahek and Ansreen wanted to protect their 'honour' by killing Saqib and attempting to make his death look like an accident, so that the tapes would not be revealed, that no blackmail money would be paid, and that their reputations ultimately would remain intact. The case is also at odds with patriarchal explanations of such violence – Saqib and Hashim died at the behest and conspiracy of Mahek and Ansreen, two female perpetrators. They wanted to protect their 'honour' for their own personal and financial reasons. If this interpretation is correct, the next logical question is why there has not been greater coverage or outrage over the killing of a male victim in the name of so-called honour in this case? Is it because there is a lack of understanding that men can be killed in the name of honour? Is it because the primary perpetrators in this case are women and the stereotype is that women do not kill men in the name of honour?

Summary

This section has demonstrated that males can be victims of HBA, FM, and, sometimes, so-called honour killings. In many instances, this may be because of their 'wayward' behaviour or criminality, differentiating their victimisation from female victims. However, there is a crossover between males and females when it comes to sexuality, sexual behaviour, and sexual autonomy, particularly when it has been discovered that a male has 'come out' as being gay. While males are more likely to be perpetrators against females and other males, as some of the literature and case studies in the section have shown, women can also be perpetrators in this area too. Overall, much more work needs to be undertaken to raise the profile of male victims to allow them to access support.

Conclusion: Stereotypes, men, and justice

This chapter has examined the experiences of male victims of domestic abuse across various domains of justice and forms of abuse. While these experiences are diverse, they are fundamentally shaped by a common issue – men are often not perceived, nor accepted, as valid victims. Numerous researchers have highlighted how stereotypes surrounding DVA, as well as broader societal constructs of masculinity, impede the recognition of men as victims.[84] The evidence demonstrates that this issue persists across different contexts, including HBA, FM, post-separation abuse, and PABs. Men's experiences in these contexts are routinely minimised, denied, and even exacerbated by the very systems designed to protect them. Consequently, while various studies have proposed specific actions and practical improvements, more fundamental changes to policy, societal beliefs, and expectations are necessary to meaningfully address the challenges faced by male victims. We call for policies that are genuinely gender-inclusive – both 'in name and spirit',[85] and that account for and respond equitably to *all victim groups*. Such an approach is essential to address the pervasive issue of domestic abuse, reducing its prevalence and improving access to justice within the family courts for male victims, whose voices are too often overlooked.

Further questions to consider

- Do you think male victims of domestic abuse, HBA, and FM receive appropriate societal and media attention?
- What more can be done in law and policy to improve support and intervention for male victims?
- What do you think about the Home Office (2022) position statement 'Supporting Male Victims', which they consider to be a part of the VAWG Strategy? For definitional purposes, do you think this is appropriate?
- What would 'working inclusively' in the criminal justice system look like?
- Do you think fathers are important in the lives of children?
- How hard do you think it is to identify if a parent is being rejected by the child and the reasons for this?

Further materials

Harman JJ and others, 'Developmental Psychology and the Scientific Status of Parental Alienation' (2022) 58(10) Developmental Psychology 1887 https://doi.org/10.1037/dev0001404, accessed 19 June 2025

Hine BA, 'Parental Alienation: What Do We Know, and What Do We (Urgently) Need to Know? A Narrative Review' (2024) 15(3) Partner Abuse https://doi.org/10.1891/PA-2023-0015, accessed 19 June 2025

Khan R, *The Psychology of Honor Abuse, Violence, and Killings* (Routledge 2025)

---

84   RW Connell, *Masculinities* (University of California Press 2005).

85   EA Bates and EM Douglas, 'Services for Domestic Violence Victims in the United Kingdom and United States: Where Are We Today?' (2020) 11(3) Partner Abuse 350.

Conclusion

Rajnaara C. Akhtar

Diverse Voices in Family Law examined how family justice is experienced by diverse individuals and families, highlighting the varying degrees to which the law accommodates differences among marginalised and minority groups. The notion of the family as a defined unit, easily regulated by a single legal framework, no longer holds true. Modern families are complex and multifaceted, formed in a myriad of ways, and the law often fails to respond adequately to these realities. Outdated legislation, limited access to the family justice system (FJS), and the deliberate design of informal spaces outside formal legal frameworks mean the law's impact is uneven and, for many, insufficient.

This volume navigated family law through three thematic parts: Marriage, Divorce, and Parenthood; Dispute Resolution in Family Law; and Domestic Abuse in Families. While each chapter had a distinct focus, a clear interconnectedness emerged, underscoring a shared discourse on marginalisation. Naqvi, in Chapter 2, examines the colonial entanglement of law and religion, revealing how marriage laws were historically crafted to enforce Anglican values. This historical foundation is juxtaposed in Hayward's Chapter 3, which discusses the rights of same-sex couples. Religious exemptions allow the Church of England and the Church in Wales to refuse to officiate same-sex ceremonies, while other religious organisations must actively opt in. Parveen's Chapter 10 further highlights the interplay of religion and law, focusing on how faith-based dispute resolution thrives within informal mediation spaces. This chapter specifically examines the experiences of Muslims navigating marriage and divorce in England and Wales, illustrating the challenges posed by the interaction of English legal frameworks with Muslim community practices.

The consequences of entering and exiting marriage are explored in depth. Gill, in Chapter 5, addresses the issue of forced marriages (FMs) and assesses the efficacy of legal interventions in protecting victims. Conversely, Hitchings, Bryson, and Douglas in Chapter 4 discuss the financial precarity that often follows the dissolution of voluntary marriages. They detail how everyday couples, particularly mothers, face significant economic penalties upon divorce, shedding light on the systemic vulnerabilities embedded within family law.

Children's voices are expected to be central to child law, as reflected in the foundational principles of the Children Act. However, in practice, children are often marginalised, their perspectives overshadowed by a system that prioritises parental concerns. Burton, in Chapter 12, highlights how children's voices are frequently ignored or minimised, particularly in cases where the focus is on maintaining contact with both parents – perhaps at a cost to the child's well-being where domestic abuse is present. Recent case law has begun to address this imbalance, emphasising the importance of considering the full range of abuses defined under the Domestic Abuse Act 2021. Similarly, Healy, in Chapter 11, critiques non-court dispute resolution (NCDR) processes for failing to uphold children's rights to be heard. Despite older children often expressing a desire to participate, the FJS routinely falls short in involving them meaningfully.

The rights of children are often closely tied to parental rights and the overriding protective duties of the state, which can relegate children's wishes. Pimm-Smith, in Chapter 7, examines the disparities faced by racially minoritised and asylum-seeking children in public child law. These children are disproportionately represented in the state care system, a troubling phenomenon that Pimm-Smith attributes in part to Eurocentric approaches that evaluate parenting through narrow, culturally specific lenses. Such biases risk overlooking the diversity of parenting practices across different social groups. Additionally, Sloan, in Chapter 6, explores how the rights of children born to same-sex couples are deeply intertwined with legal concepts of parenthood. The gender of the parents significantly influences the legal pathway to parenthood, particularly due to the law's entrenched notions of legal motherhood. For children of same-sex couples, genetic parenthood is often a lesser priority in law compared to the treatment of children born to opposite-sex parents.

Access to family justice spans a range of issues, from divorce and dissolution to protection from domestic abuse. Blakey, in Chapter 9, examines how cuts to legal aid have disproportionately affected vulnerable groups, including women, ethnic minorities, individuals with disabilities, and children. As predicted in the Ministry of Justice's 2010 Equality Impact Assessment and later confirmed in post-implementation reviews, these cuts exacerbate power imbalances within the legal process. Meanwhile, Moscati, in Chapter 8, challenges conventional approaches to family mediation. By disrupting traditional expectations of disputants, Moscati advocates for a reimagining of family disputes and access to justice, highlighting the inadequacies of mediation and other NCDR processes in accommodating diverse family structures and dynamics.

The issue of domestic abuse reveals significant disparities in how it is experienced by marginalised groups, both female and male victims. Anitha, in Chapter 13, examines the precarious position of highly vulnerable migrant women who face domestic abuse exacerbated by state-imposed immigration controls and visa restrictions. These systemic barriers often trap women in abusive relationships, limiting their ability to seek help or escape their circumstances. In contrast, Idriss, Bates, and Hine, in Chapter 14, explore the under-represented experiences of male victims of domestic abuse. Male victims often face unique challenges, including a reluctance to report abuse, limited access to support services, and minimal focus in academic and policy studies. As a result, their experiences remain largely unacknowledged and poorly addressed. Whether through family courts, FM, or so-called honour-based abuse, the ways in which male victims suffer differ significantly from those of female victims. This nuanced understanding of abuse highlights the need for tailored responses that consider the diverse ways in which domestic abuse manifests across different demographics.

In conclusion, this volume emphasises the need for a more nuanced and inclusive legal framework that reflects the realities of contemporary families, while critically interrogating the marginalisation perpetuated by existing legal structures.

Index

References to figures appear in *italic* type.

www.ingramcontent.com/pod-product-compliance
Lightning Source LLC
Chambersburg PA
CBHW051750200326
41597CB00025B/4499